W9-APH-945

The NOLO *News*—

Our free magazine devoted to everyday legal & consumer issues

To thank you for sending in the postage-paid feedback card in the back of this book, you'll receive a free two-year subscription to the **NOLO** *News*—our quarterly magazine of legal, small business and consumer information. With each issue you get updates on important legal changes that affect you, helpful articles on everyday law, answers to your legal questions in Auntie Nolo's advice column, a complete Nolo catalog and, of course, our famous lawyer jokes.

Legal information online—24 hours a day

Get instant access to the legal information you need 24 hours a day.

Visit a Nolo online self-help law center and you'll find:

- hundreds of helpful articles on a wide variety of topics
- selected chapters from Nolo books
- online seminars with our lawyer authors and other experts
- downloadable demos of Nolo software
- frequently asked questons about key legal issues
- our complete catalog and online ordering info
- our ever popular lawyer jokes and more.

Here's how to find us:

America Online Just use the Keyword **Nolo** or to get to our website from AOL use Keyword: **http://www.nolo.com**

On the **Internet** our World Wide Web address (URL) is: **http://www.nolo.com**

Prodigy/CompuServe Use the Web Browsers on CompuServe or Prodigy to access Nolo's Web site on the Internet using **http://www.nolo.com**

OUR SPECIAL UPGRADE OFFER
It's important to have the most current legal information. Because laws and legal procedures change often, we update our books regularly. To help keep you up-to-date we are extending this special upgrade offer. Cut out and mail the title portion of the cover of your old Nolo book and we'll give you 25% off the retail price of the NEW EDITION when you purchase directly from us. For details see the back of the book.

OUR NO-HASSLE GUARANTEE
We've created products we're proud of and think will serve you well. But if for any reason, anything you buy from Nolo Press does not meet your needs, we will refund your purchase price and pay for the cost of returning it to us by Priority Mail.
No ifs, ands or buts.

NOLO PRESS
25 YEARS
LAW FOR ALL

NATIONAL SECOND EDITION

TAX SAVVY

for

Small Business

YEAR-ROUND TAX ADVICE
FOR SMALL BUSINESS

by Attorney Frederick W. Daily

NOLO PRESS BERKELEY

Your Responsibility When Using a Self-Help Law Book

We've done our best to give you useful and accurate information in this book. But laws and procedures change frequently and are subject to differing interpretations. If you want legal advice backed by a guarantee, see a lawyer. If you use this book, it's your responsibility to make sure that the facts and general advice contained in it are applicable to your situation.

Keeping Up-to-Date

To keep its books up-to-date, Nolo Press issues new printings and new editions periodically. New printings reflect minor legal changes and technical corrections. New editions contain major legal changes, major text additions or major reorganizations. To find out if a later printing or edition of any Nolo book is available, call Nolo Press at 510-549-1976 or check the catalog in the *Nolo News,* our quarterly newspaper.

To stay current, follow the "Update" service in the *Nolo News.* You can get a free two-year subscription by sending us the registration card in the back of the book. In another effort to help you use Nolo's latest materials, we offer a 25% discount off the purchase of the new edition of your Nolo book when you turn in the cover of an earlier edition. (See the "Recycle Offer" in the back of the book.)

This book was last revised in: **FEBRUARY 1997.**

Second Edition	**FEBRUARY 1997**
Editors	RALPH WARNER
	MARY RANDOLPH
	ROBIN LEONARD
Illustrations	MARI STEIN
Cover Design	TONI IHARA
Book Design	JACKIE MANCUSO
Manuscript Preparation	STEPHANIE HAROLDE
Proofreading	KRISTIN BARENDSEN
Index	SAYRE VAN YOUNG
Printing	BERTELSMANN INDUSTRY SERVICES, INC.

Daily, Frederick W., 1942-
    Tax savvy for small business : year-round tax advice for small
business / by Frederick W. Daily. -- National 2nd ed.
      p. cm.
   ISBN 0-87337-372-3
   1. Small business--Taxation--Law and legislation--United States.
2. Tax planning--United States. I. Title.
KF6491.D35 1996
343.7305'268--dc21
                          96-39243
                          CIP

Copyright © 1995, 1996, 1997 by Frederick W. Daily. ALL RIGHTS RESERVED. Printed in the U.S.A.

No part of this publication may be reproduced, stored in a retrieval system, or transmitted in any form or by any means, electronic, mechanical, photocopying, recording or otherwise without the prior written permission of the publisher and the author.

Quantity Sales: For information on bulk purchases or corporate premium sales, please contact the Special Sales department. For academic sales or textbook adoptions, ask for Academic Sales. 800-955-4775, Nolo Press, Inc., 950 Parker St., Berkeley, CA, 94710.

Dedication

To my wife, Brenda, who has brought me everything that is good in life.

Acknowledgments

Trying to translate the tax code into plain English for the small business person was a challenge that all but overwhelmed me. Without the help of many others I could not have done it.

Nolo Press has some of the most caring (and careful) editors on the face of this earth. First and foremost in both categories is Mary Randolph. Other Nolo folks with a hand in the project were Jake Warner, Robin Leonard, Lisa Goldoftas and Steve Fishman. Stephanie Harolde, Ely Newman, Robert Wells and Susan Cornell made valuable contributions in copyediting, proofreading and production. Thank you one and all for putting up with me.

My peers in the tax community contributed immensely and without complaint. The most helpful in making sure the things you need to know were covered: Gerry Shaver, EA; Chris Kollaja, CPA; Dewey Watson, Tax Attorney (all in San Francisco); Lew Hurwitz, EA (Oakland), Steven Mullenniex, EA (Berkeley); Malcolm Roberts, CPA of Roberts Schultz & Co. in Berkeley; and my newly-minted associate and tax lawyer, Gino Bianchini.

Contents

Introduction

CHAPTER 4

Tax Benefits of Business Losses

CHAPTER 5

Tax Concerns of Employers

PART 2

THE FORM OF YOUR BUSINESS

CHAPTER 6

Sole Proprietorships

CHAPTER 7

C Corporations

CHAPTER 8

S Corporations

CHAPTER 9

Partnerships

CHAPTER 10

Limited Liability Companies

CHAPTER 11

Personal Service Corporations

PART 3
THINKING SMALL

CHAPTER 12

Family Businesses

CHAPTER 13

Microbusinesses and Home-Based Businesses

PART 4
FRINGE BENEFITS

CHAPTER 14

Fringe Benefits

CHAPTER 15

Retirement Plans

PART 5

BUYING OR SELLING A BUSINESS

CHAPTER 16

Buying a Business

CHAPTER 17

Selling a Business

CHAPTER 18

When You Can't Pay Your Taxes

CHAPTER 19

Audits

CHAPTER 20

Appealing IRS Audits

CHAPTER 21

Penalties and Interest

CHAPTER 22

Help Beyond the Book

Glossary

Appendix

IRS PUBLICATIONS LIST

FORMS CHECKLIST

Index

Introduction

If looking at the thousands of pages of tax code were a prerequisite to starting a business, no one would dare. Luckily, most of the tax code has little or no application to you, the small businessperson. The basics are right here in this book. And once you grasp the fundamentals, you can pick up the rest as you go along, with the help of a tax advisor or on your own. As the well-worn phrase goes, "It's not brain surgery."

Owning and operating a small business—full- or part-time—has been called the little guy's tax shelter. Business owners get tax benefits for any number of expenditures not allowed to "wage slaves." In effect, you are sharing expenses (as well as profits) with Uncle Sam. Here are some tax advantages open to folks going into business for themselves:

1. Personal expenses can become wholly or partially deductible: your home, car, computer, meals, education and entertainment.

2. Tax-advantaged pension and savings plans can shelter part of your business income, accumulate tax-deferred and provide for your retirement.

3. Family members can be put on the payroll and income can be shifted to children, reducing a family's taxes.

4. Travel and vacations can qualify as business expenses.

Sound interesting? With all of these possibilities, your business can earn less than if you were working for someone else, and you still can come out

ahead. All these and more ways to beat the tax man are covered in this book.

Of course, by going into business you might be trading an eight-hour-a-day job for a 24-hour one. But for many of us, it is worth it. Having your own business might prove disastrous, but it could be the most rewarding thing that ever happen to you—especially if you are doing something that you enjoy.

Our country has 15 to 20 million small businesses that the IRS knows about and probably more. Unhappily, U.S. Chamber of Commerce statistics show that a business has an 85% chance of closing its doors within its first five years. But the entrepreneurial spirit is strong, and many people who fail go back and try again and again. Four out of five of these brave souls are sole proprietors—one-man shows or mom 'n' pop operations. Ten million of these businesses provide jobs only for the owners and their families. The rest of the small businesses are either partnerships, limited liability companies or corporations.

No one likes paying taxes or dealing with the IRS, but operating a business without some tax awareness is like skydiving without a parachute—certain to end in calamity. Undoubtedly, many failures stem from ignoring the financial and tax side of the business. Like it or not, the government is always your business partner and must be reckoned with.

On the brighter side, tax knowledge has powerful profit potential. Knowing what the tax law has to offer can give you a far better bottom line than your competitors who don't bother to learn. For instance, there are a number of different ways to write off car expenses. Your choice can mean several thousand dollars more after-tax dollars in your pocket each year.

WHAT YOU'LL GET FROM READING THIS BOOK

1. An explanation of the tax benefits of each legal form of business—sole proprietorship, partnership, limited liability company or corporation.

2. Ways to minimize taxes for you and your business.

3. Information on what to do if the IRS ever challenges your business tax reporting or sends you a tax bill you don't agree with.

The Three Kinds of Business Taxes

In general, three types of federal taxes affect most small businesses:

- Income taxes (everyone who makes a profit owes these)

- Employee taxes (if your business has employees), and

- Self-employment taxes (Social Security and Medicare taxes)

Thousands of tax laws, regulations and court decisions deal with these three categories. We will look only at the relatively few of them most likely to affect you, and translate them into plain English. We don't have room to cover the various state and local taxes (such as sales taxes) you may be subject to, but will give you leads on where to get this information.

Do You Need a Tax Professional?

As good as we hope this book is, nothing takes the place of a personal tax advisor. Everyone's tax situation is unique, and tax laws change annually. However, the more you know, the better you can work with your tax professional (referred to as "tax pro" throughout this book)—and the less you will have to pay him or her. (See Chapter 22 for tips on finding and using a tax pro.)

How Tax Law Is Made and Administered—the Short Course

The following discussion may help put the world of business taxes into perspective. Think of it as a high school government lesson, only try to stay awake this time—it could be money in your pocket.

The Government. Visualize a three-branched tree. Congress, the federal Legislative branch of government, makes the tax law. The Executive branch, which includes the Treasury Department, administers the tax law. The Judicial branch comprises all the federal courts, which interpret the tax laws.

The power to tax incomes was granted by the 16th Amendment to the U.S. Constitution; the first Income Tax Act was passed in 1913. Contrary to what some nuts and con artists would like you to believe, income tax law and the IRS are legal and are not going to go away.

The tax law begins with the Internal Revenue Code. Congress revises it annually in some fashion, and last gave it a major overhaul in 1986. This was officially called the Tax Reform Act, but was known to tax pros as the "Accountants' and Tax Attorneys' Relief Act." The funny thing is that it started off being called the Tax Simplification Act. Even the merry pranksters in Washington didn't think they could put that one over on us, and changed the title somewhere along the line. The tax code is now up to 2,800 pages of exceedingly fine print.

The IRS. The Internal Revenue Service (IRS or whatever other name you want to use) is headed by the Commissioner of Internal Revenue, a Presidential appointee. The stated mission of the IRS is to "collect the proper amount of tax revenues at the least cost to the public, and in a manner that warrants the highest degree of public confidence in its integrity, efficiency and fairness." As to how well they carry out their mission, your opinion is as good as mine.

IRS tax administration policy is set in Washington, but it is doubtful you will ever deal directly with anyone in our nation's capital about a tax matter. The real work is done at various IRS regional and district offices. Tax return processing is done at one of eleven Service Centers. The arm of the IRS that reaches out and occasionally touches us likely extends from one of 63 (in the process of being downsized to 33) local IRS Districts and sub-offices. I'll bet one is near you—too close, probably, for comfort.

The Courts. The United States Tax Court is a special court formed to decide disputes between the government and taxpayers. It is actually pretty easy for anyone to go to Tax Court, and sometimes taxpayers even win cases against the IRS. Tax disputes can be also decided in U.S. District Courts and the Federal Court of Claims, but this is a much more expensive proposition than Tax Court. All decisions of those courts, for or against you, may be reviewed by higher courts.

See, that wasn't all that bad, was it? Now, venture forth into the rest of the book and into the entrepreneurial world, and may the small business gods be with you. ■

CHAPTER 1

Business Income and Tax-Deductible Expenses

"There is nothing sinister in arranging one's affairs as to keep taxes as low as possible...for nobody owes any public duty to pay more than the law demands."

— Judge Learned Hand

Every small business owner wants to know how to legally minimize his or her tax obligations. The key is understanding tax-deductible expenses, which are explained in this chapter. Chapter 2, Writing Off Long-Term Business Assets, completes the picture; it deals with the rules for deducting assets purchased for your business.

TAX-DEDUCTIBLE EXPENSES IN A NUTSHELL

1. Just about any expense that helps a business is tax-deductible as long as it is ordinary, necessary and reasonable.

2. Some business outlays can be deducted in the year they are paid. (They are called "current expenses.") Other expenditures must be capitalized—that is, spread out and deducted over several future years.

A. How the Tax Code Focuses on Profit

There are many systems of business taxation in use over the world. In much of Europe, the "value added tax," or VAT, is the rule. The VAT taxes the incremental value added to a product at each stage of manufacturing and distribution. Another approach is to tax a business on its gross receipts, whether or not it makes a profit.

The U.S. tax code zeros in on a business's profits: the more you make, the more you pay. So the American entrepreneur has a strong incentive to keep taxable profits low, while at the same time

taking home as much money and benefits as the law allows. Doing this legally has a price—you need to learn your ABCs (and even your DEFs) about how your enterprise is taxed. We'll start with some basic tax rules governing how expenses are deducted, to give you the greatest tax benefit.

Congress says just about any expense to produce income can be deducted from a business's receipts. But to get the deduction, you must follow the Internal Revenue Code (IRC).

Here's a very simple illustration of how taxable profits are determined.

Example: Sam and Jeannie own Smiths' Computer Sales and Service as a sole proprietorship. Because their business produces a good profit, they are in the highest federal tax bracket (39.6% in 1995). Here is how the 1995 income and expenses for Smiths' Computer Sales and Service determine the business's taxable profit.

Figuring Taxable Profit From a Business

Gross Sales (receipts from business)		$2,500,000
Less: Cost of Goods Sold (computers)	-	1,900,000
Gross Profit	=	600,000
Less: Deductible business expenses	-	300,000
Net Profit	=	$ 300,000

The $300,000 net profit is subject to income tax. How much tax the Smiths will actually owe on their business income depends on other factors: their other income, losses on any investments, personal deductions such as for home mortgage interest, and, most importantly, how much they can take out of the business in fringe benefits.

B. What Is Business Income?

Before getting into business deductions, let's make sure we all understand what the tax code means by the term "income." When it comes to sources of income, the tax law doesn't care whether you get it from your business, from wages paid by someone else's business, or from an investment: it is taxable to you as an individual. Of course, the subject of this book is business, but keep in mind that, as far as the tax code is concerned, income is income is income.

Actually, the better question for small business tax understanding is, "What is *gross* income?" IRC § 61 talks in terms of gross income, so we will, too. It reads: "Except as otherwise provided...gross income means all income from whatever source derived." You can't get much broader than that, can you?

Income for tax purposes doesn't mean just cash; it can take many forms. Goods, property or services received have all been held to be within the definition of income under IRC § 61. If you barter (exchange goods or services for the same), the fair market value of the item or service you received should be included in your income. I know—a lot of bartering goes on and the IRS isn't any the wiser, but getting away with it doesn't make it right. So, we start with the proposition that anything of value your business (or you individually) receives is income, and is therefore subject to the income tax laws.

Income also means anything you have the right to put your hands on, but don't for some reason. A legal doctrine called "constructive receipt" says that as soon as money or property is set aside for you to use, or is credited to your account, it becomes income—whether you grab it or not. So, you can't get a check for services in November 1996 and hold it for deposit until 1997 without being taxed on it in the year received.

Note that IRC § 61 is morally neutral; it doesn't distinguish between illegal and legal income. So, if you earn a living as a hit man for the mob, you still are earning income as far as the IRS is concerned, and had better declare it on your tax return. Al Capone wasn't sent to prison for murder, bootlegging or racketeering; he was convicted of tax evasion by not reporting the fruits of his labors to the IRS.

One last thing you should know about income: Americans are taxed on their worldwide income; no matter where you earn it, it is still income taxable.

There is one exception: if you make it and reside outside the U.S. for most of the year, some or all of your foreign income may be excludable, but this exception is beyond the scope of this book. See IRS Publication #54, "Tax Guide for U.S. Citizens and Resident Aliens Abroad," for more information on foreign income.

What Isn't Income. Some kinds of income fall into the "except as otherwise provided" exception of IRC § 61. For instance, the tax code excludes gifts and inheritances received from taxable income. There is no dollar limitation on how much you can get by these means without it being taxable to you. (Sorry, the $10,000,000 that is being dropped off by the Prize Patrol from Publisher's Clearing House is not legally a gift and is taxable.) But, thankfully, many fringe benefits provided by businesses to owners and employees are specifically excluded from income. (See Chapter 14, Fringe Benefits.) Most of the statutory exclusions from income granted by Congress are found in IRC §§ 101 to 150.

Of great importance to owners and investors in businesses is that the return of a capital investment is not taxable income. In other words, to the extent that you sell an asset and get back your money exchanged for the asset, you haven't earned any income. Of course, the profit, if any, is income.

Example: Toni invests $1,000 in the stock of Ronaldo's Rubber Fashions, a small business corporation, and later sells her stock for $1,500. Only $500 is considered income for tax purposes; the other $1,000 is a return of capital to Toni.

Tax-free withdrawals. If you borrow against an asset, whether it belongs to your business or to you personally, the loan proceeds are not income. This is a valuable tool for taking money tax-free out of an unincorporated business that holds an appreciated asset, such as real estate.

C. What Is Tax-Deductible in Business?

How tax savvy a businessperson you are has a great effect on how much money is in your pocket at the end of the year. I am sure you know that the tax code allows you to deduct costs of doing business from your gross income. What you are left with is your net business profit. This is the amount that gets taxed. So knowing how to maximize your deductible business expenses lowers your taxable profit. To boot, you may enjoy a personal benefit from a business expenditure—a nice car to drive, a combination business trip/vacation and a retirement savings plan—if you follow the myriad of tax rules. The balance of this chapter deals with the best ways to get the biggest business expense deduction bang for your buck. The chart on the next page, "Personal Income Tax Brackets," illustrates the value of a deduction to an individual, but the law works the same for business deductions as well.

For higher income taxpayers, there are two extra "gotchas" that pump your tax rate up still higher without actually saying so. You lose part of your personal exemptions (a graduated phase-out) if you are married filing jointly and have an adjusted gross income in excess of $176,950—or if you are single and the figure is more than $117,950. The same thing happens—a loss of part of your total itemized deductions (mortgage interest, property taxes, medical expenses and other expenses claimed on Schedule A)—if your adjusted gross income is more than $117,950, married or single. I understand that, Congress giveth and Congress taketh away, but I wish they wouldn't be so sneaky about it.

SOURCES OF TAX LAW

How to research tax law questions is covered in Chapter 22, Help Beyond the Book, but here's a brief description of the main sources of federal tax law.

Federal Statutes. Congress enacts laws, or codes, on taxes that are set forth in the Internal Revenue Code (IRC). Each tax provision (called a "code section") has its own number and title. For example, IRC § 183 refers to tax code section number 183, titled "Activities Not Engaged in for Profit."

Regulations. When Congress makes laws, it paints with a fairly broad brush. It's then up to the Treasury Department (the IRS is a part of it) to fill in the details of how the tax code is to be applied. The details are set forth in Treasury Regulations, called simply "regulations" or "regs." They are numbered to correspond with the IRC sections they explain. Regulations are published in volumes separate from the IRC. Most regs are numbered in the same order as their related tax code sections, but preceded by the numeral "1" to alert you that it's a regulation, not a tax code section. For example, the regulation explaining IRC § 183 is designated Reg. 1.183. (Not all IRC sections have corresponding regulations.)

Both the IRC and Treasury Regulations are available at most public libraries, larger bookstores and, of course, IRS offices.

Court Cases. When the IRS and taxpayers go to court, the judges' rulings containing the reasons for their decisions are collected and published in "case reporters," available in law libraries. These written opinions offer guidance on the correct interpretation of the tax code.

PERSONAL INCOME TAX BRACKETS

The easiest way to determine the tax effect of additional income or deductible expense is to use your marginal tax bracket—the rate at which any additional income would be taxed. If your tax bracket is 31%, 31¢ of every new dollar of income you earn will go to Uncle Sam. Conversely, you will save 31¢ in taxes on every additional dollar you are able to claim as a deductible expense. If you factor in state income taxes and the Self-Employment tax, your tax rate may exceed 50%.

Tax Bracket (1996)	Married Joint Filed Tax Return	Single
15%	up to $40,100	up to $24,000
28%	from 40,100–96,900	24,000–58,150
31%	96,900–147,700	58,150–121,300
36%	147,700–263,750	121,300–263,750
39.6%	on all over 263,750	Over 263,750

NOTE: Tax brackets for married people filing separately are somewhat different.

1. Business Expenses

I promise not to burden you with a lot of tax code sections, but hear me out on this one. IRC § 162 is the cornerstone for determining the tax-deductibility of every business expenditure. It is fairly lengthy, but the first hundred or so words are the ones that mean the most. Here they are:

"Internal Revenue Code § 162 'Trade or business expenses.'

(a) In general. There shall be allowed as a deduction all the ordinary and necessary expenses paid or incurred during the taxable year in carrying on any trade or business, including

(1) a reasonable allowance for salaries or other compensation for personal services actually rendered;

(2) traveling expenses (including amounts expended for meals and lodging other than amounts which are lavish or extravagant under the circumstances) while away from home in the pursuit of a trade or business; and

(3) rentals or other payments required to be made as a condition to the continued use or possession, for purposes of the trade or business, of property to which

the taxpayer has not taken or is not taking title or in which he has no equity."

Section 162 goes on—and on—but the rest of it deals with specific items that *can't* be deducted. Those with relevance to small businesses are covered later in this book. Not part of IRC § 162 are rules for deducting purchases of *assets* used in your business—machinery, cars and a thousand other things. We'll get to asset write-offs in the next chapter. Right now we are focusing on the day-to-day operating expenses of a business.

In most cases, a legitimate business expense under IRC § 162 is obvious. In some cases, such as outlays for travel, the IRS provides specific instructions for determining "ordinary and necessary." This is done through published income tax "regulations" noted throughout this book.

Like the rest of the tax code, IRC § 162 is far from crystal clear. Starting with the meaning of "ordinary and necessary," we suspect that things could go wrong for us. The tax code doesn't define these terms anywhere. Instead, myriads of federal courts have tried to figure out what Congress intended and apply it to a particular set of facts. "Ordinary" has been held by courts to mean "normal, common and accepted under the circumstances by the business community." "Necessary" means "appropriate and helpful." Taken together, the legal consensus is that "ordinary and necessary" refers to the *purpose* for which an expense is made. For instance, renting office space is ordinary and necessary for many business folks, but it is neither unless it is actually used in running an enterprise for profit.

Given these broad legal guidelines, it is not surprising that some folks have tried to push the envelope as to what is an "ordinary and necessary" business expense, and the IRS has pushed back. Sometimes a compromise is reached, and sometimes the issue is thrown into a court's lap.

Example: An accountant deducted his yacht expenses, contending that because the boat flew a pennant with the numbers "1040," it brought him recognition and clients. The matter ended up before the Tax Court. The court ruled that the yacht wasn't a normal business expense for a tax pro, and so it wasn't "ordinary" or "necessary." In short, the yacht expense was personal and nondeductible. (Henry v. CIR, 36 TC 879 (1961).)

The laugh test. Tax pros frequently rely on the "laugh test": Can you put down an expense for business without laughing? In the example above, the Tax Court laughed the accountant out of court!

2. Large Expenses

Because the IRS knows that people don't intentionally overpay for anything, amounts paid aren't usually questioned. IRS auditors do sometimes object to expenditures they deem to be unreasonably large under the circumstances. While the tax code itself contains no "too big" limitation, courts have ruled that it is inherent in IRC § 162. It might be reason-

able for a multi-state apparel company to lease a jet for travel between manufacturing plants, but not for a corner deli owner to fly to New York to meet with her pickle supplier.

3. Personal Expenses

The number-one concern of the IRS when auditing business deductions is whether purely *personal* expenditures are being claimed as business. For instance, you can't deduct the cost of commuting to work, because the tax code specifically says this is not a business expense. More common examples include using the company credit card for a vacation, or personal use of the company car. Because business people regularly try this, IRS auditors is ever watchful.

Fortunately, as discussed throughout this book, you can often arrange your affairs—legally—in a way that lets you derive considerable personal benefit and enjoyment from business expenditures.

Be careful if you deal with relatives. The IRS will probably be suspicious about expenses paid to a family member, or to another business in which your relatives have an ownership interest. In tax code parlance, these are termed "related parties." An IRS auditor may suspect that profits are being taken out of your business for direct or indirect personal benefit in the guise of expenses—for example, paying your spouse's father, who is in prison, $5,000 as a consultant's fee for your restaurant business.

BUSINESS COSTS THAT ARE NEVER DEDUCTIBLE

A few expenses are not deductible even if they are business-related because they violate "public policy." (IRC § 162.) This category includes:

- any type of government fine, such as a tax penalty paid to the IRS, or even a parking ticket

- bribes and kickbacks

- any kind of payment made for referring a client, patient or customer, if it is contrary to a state or federal law, and

- expenses for lobbying and social club dues.

Thankfully, very few other business expenses are affected by these rules.

D. Current or Capitalized Expense?

Tax rules cover not only what expenses can be deducted but also *when* they can be deducted. Some types of expenditures are deductible in the year they are incurred, while others must be taken over a number of years. The first category is called "current" expenses, and the second "capitalized" expenditures. You need to know the difference between the two, and the tax rules for each type of expenditure. I'll try to make it easy on you.

"Current expenses" are generally everyday costs of keeping your business going, such as the rent and electricity bills. Rules for deducting current expenses are fairly straightforward; you subtract the amounts spent from your business's gross income in the year the expense was incurred.

Other expenditures are made to generate revenue in future years. These are "capitalized"—that is, they become assets of the business. As they are used, their cost is "matched" to the revenue they help earn. This allows the business to more clearly account for its profitability from year to year.

Sometimes it is not clear what is a current expense and what is a capital expense. Normal repair costs, such as fixing a broken copy machine or a door, can be deducted in the year incurred. The cost of making improvements to a business asset must be capitalized if the enhancement:

- adds to its value, or

- appreciably lengthens the time you can use it, or

- adapts it to a different use.

"Improvements" are usually associated with real estate—for example, putting in new electrical wiring, plumbing and lighting—but the rule also applies to rebuilding valuable equipment.

Example: Gunther uses a specialized die stamping machine in his metal fabrication shop. After 15 years of constant use, the machine is on its last legs. His average yearly maintenance expenses on the machine have been $10,000, which Gunther has properly deducted as repair expenses. Now, Gunther is faced with either thoroughly rehabilitating the machine at a cost of $80,000, or buying a new one for $175,000. The rehabilitated machine will carry a warranty, so he goes for the rebuilding. The $80,000 expense must be capitalized—that is, it can't be taken all in the year the machine is rebuilt. The tax code says that metal fabricating machinery must be depreciated over five years.

Chapter 2, Writing Off Long-Term Business Assets, deals with writing off capitalized purchases in detail. Costs for items with a "useful life" of one year or longer cannot be deducted in the same way as current expenses. Rather, these costs are treated as investments in your business, and must be deducted over a number of years (with one important exception, discussed below). The deduction is usually called "depreciation," but in some cases it is called a "depletion" or "amortization" expense. All of these words describe the same thing: writing off or depreciating asset costs through tax deductions.

There are many rules for how different types of assets must be written off. The tax code dictates limits on depreciation deductions, and over how many future years a business must spread its depreciation deductions for asset purchases. All businesses, large and small, are affected by these provisions (IRC §§ 167, 168 and 179), which we discuss in detail in Chapter 2.

A valuable tax break creating an exception to the long-term write-off rules is found in IRC § 179. A small business owner can write off in one year most types of its capital expenditures, up to a grand total of $17,500. All profitable small businesses should take full advantage of this provision every year. See Chapter 2, Writing Off Long-Term Business Assets, for details on how IRC § 179 works.

E. Special Deduction Rules

Some common and not-so-common business expenses have special rules that govern how they must be tax deducted.

1. Vehicle Expenses

Fine-print tax rules for claiming car and truck expenses for your business are tricky, but well worth mastering; they can provide a jumbo payoff at tax time.

Records. The first set of rules are to make sure you keep the right records to know how to calculate your deduction—and defend it if you are ever audited.

Allocation. Keep in mind that if your automobile is used for both business and pleasure, only the business portion produces a tax deduction. So you must track the use of a dual-purpose vehicle and allocate business/personal use. The proper allocation will come from a year-end analysis of your records to come up with the percentage of each use, such as 62% business, 38% personal. If you own just one car or truck, no IRS auditor will allow you to claim that 100% of its use is business-related. (I have seen folks get away with as much as 90%, though.) Of course, if you have both business and personal vehicles, and the business one is obviously dedicated to a business use (a minivan with your logo painted on the side), it isn't necessary to do any allocation, and you can claim 100% business use.

Two methods to claim vehicle expense deductions. The tax code gives you a choice of two ways to calculate and deduct business vehicle expenses: the *standard mileage* and *actual expense*. With some qualifications explained below, you may switch between the two methods each year and choose the one that gives you the largest tax benefit. As a rule, if you use a newer car primarily for business, the actual expense method provides a larger deduction. But the mileage method works better for some folks and requires much less recordkeeping.

a. Standard Mileage Method

The simplest way for writing off business vehicle expenses is the *mileage* or *standard mileage rate* method. You just total up the number of business miles driven over the year and multiply by 31 cents (1996 tax code allowed rate). Commuting miles (getting to and from your business location) are personal miles, but if you're home-based, generally all travel from home for a job is considered "business." By choosing the mileage method, you cannot separately deduct your operating expenses—gas, repairs, license tags and insurance—but you can deduct parking fees, tolls and any state and local property taxes on the car or truck.

Example: In 1996, Morris drove 10,000 business miles in his practice of veterinary medicine. He also spent $700 in bridge and highway tolls and parking garages. Morris' vehicle expense deduction is $3,800—$3,100 (.31 x 10,000) + $700. If Morris' practice is incorporated, the business could deduct this sum and reimburse Morris the same amount. However, if the corporation paid Morris a car allowance of $4,000 per year for the use of his personal car for business, the excess over the proper business deduction ($200) would be reportable as income to Morris on his tax return.

The Basics

Primary disadvantage of mileage method. If this method for claiming auto expenses is used, you can't take a depreciation deduction on the vehicle—which could be substantial with newer cars. (See Chapter 2, Writing Off Long-Term Assets.)

Not everyone can choose the mileage method for deducting business vehicle expenses. If any of the following conditions apply to you, you must use the actual expense method:

- Your vehicle is leased

- You used more than one vehicle simultaneously in your business

- You ever used the actual expense method on this same vehicle and claimed an accelerated depreciation method. (See Chapter 2.)

- You ever claimed IRC § 179 to write off part of the vehicle's purchase price. (See Chapter 2.)

RECORDKEEPING FOR BUSINESS-USED VEHICLES

No matter which method you use to claim auto expenses, you will need to keep accurate records. The best way to keep auto use records I have found is with a log book, sold at most office supply and stationery stores. Or you can keep a notepad in your glove compartment. However you do it, whenever you drive a personal car for business, write down:

- The date of the trip
- Your destination
- Your mileage (round-trip), and
- Who you visited and your business relationship with that person.

Below is a sample page from a logbook, showing how to make these entries.

Also, make sure you keep vehicle-servicing receipts showing the mileage at the first servicing of the year and at the last servicing of the year. This is a good way to prove to a nosy auditor the number of total miles driven. Of course, if you are using the actual expense method, you should save all of the other car receipts, too.

SAMPLE VEHICLE MILEAGE LOG

| Date | Destination (City, Town or Area) | Business Purpose | Odometer Readings | | | Expenses | |
			Start	Stop	Miles this trip	Type (Gas, oil, tolls, etc.)	Amount
1/18/97	Local (St. Louis)	Sales calls	8,097	8,188	91	Gas	$18.25
1/19/97	Indianapolis	Sales calls	8,211	8,486	275	Parking	2.00
1/20/97	Louisville	See Bob Smith (Pot. Client)	8,486	8,599	113	Gas/ Repair flat tire	16.50
1/21/97	Return to St. Louis		8,599	8,875	276	Gas	17.25
1/22/97	Local (St. Louis)	Sales calls	8,914	9,005	91		
1/23/97							
///	WEEKLY TOTAL	///	8,097	9,005	846	///	$62.50
TOTAL YEAR TO DATE		///	///	///	6,236	///	$993.00

b. Actual Expense Method

The mileage method works well for some, but it doesn't cover the full cost of owning and operating most newer cars. If your auto costs more than $15,300, it may be better to use the *actual expense* method, primarily to get the depreciation deduction benefit. Total up your car operating expenses—gas, repairs, insurance and so on—and then add the depreciation deduction amount allowed in the tax code for that year. (See Chapter 2, Writing Off Long-Term Business Assets.)

Example: Sam buys a Plymouth minivan in 1995 for $15,000, to be used 100% for his business. He drives the van 10,000 miles the first year. Assume the tax code allows $3,060 for depreciation in the first year. Sam's actual operating expenses for the year for gas, maintenance and insurance total $2,600, plus $700 for parking and tolls. Sam can deduct a total of $6,360 for car expenses in 1995, including depreciation. With the mileage method, Sam's business deduction would have totaled only $3,700.

HOW TO CLAIM EXPENSES FOR AUTOS

A business claiming expenses for car use must file IRS Form 4562, Depreciation and Amortization. This form requires you to show a breakdown of the business, personal and commuting miles driven during the year. Even if you don't use the mileage method, you still must use this form and report the number of miles driven for business. See Chapter 2, Section C, for a sample filled-out Form 4562.

Do the math before you pick a way to claim auto expenses. Usually, the *actual expense* method results in higher tax deductions if you own a late model car, because you can take a depreciation deduction as well as claiming operating expenses. On the other hand, the standard mileage method may be better if you drive a lot of miles in a 50 mpg gas miser or in a faithful old clunker. Generally, you may switch back and forth between the standard mileage and actual expense methods each year to get the greatest tax deductions. However, if you use the *mileage method* the first year your auto is placed in service, you are not allowed to take accelerated depreciation deductions in any future years. If you switch, you must take a straight-line depreciation. If you qualify, figure your deduction both ways each year and then choose.

c. Business Corporations

Business expenses of vehicles in incorporated businesses are claimed in a slightly different fashion than the methods discussed above. How expenses are claimed depends on whether the corporation or its employee owns the car.

Company-Owned Vehicles. Incorporated businesses often buy cars and give employees—including shareholder owners—use of them for both work and play. Records must be kept as to how much the car is used for each purpose. Using the actual expense method, the entire car expense is tax-deductible to the corporation, but personal use of the car is taxable to the employee. The amount of income that must be reported is modest compared to the real cost of owning a newer car. See a tax pro for an accurate determination of the tax consequences here.

Corporate Employee Vehicles. To get tax deductions, a business corporation doesn't have to own the cars its employees drive. Alternatively, a shareholder/owner can buy a car and be reimbursed directly by the corporation for all expenses of using the car for business—gas, repairs and so on. Plus, the company can pay the car owner the amount of depreciation allowed in the tax code. (IRC § 168(b)(1).) This expense is deductible to the corporation and it is not income to the employee.

Example: Ralph's corporation reimburses him $3,812 for his actual cost of operating his personal car. It also gives him $1,675, the amount of the depreciation deduction allowed under the tax code for that particular car. (See Chapter 2, Writing Off Long-Term Business Assets, for how this amount is determined.) Ralph uses his car 90% of the time for business, so he must report, as extra income from his corporation, 10% of the reimbursements ($381 + $167 = $548).

In the above example, the result would be the same if all of the car expenses were paid directly by the corporation instead of reimbursed to Ralph. For example, if Ralph used a company check or credit card to pay expenses, he would still be entitled to the depreciation reimbursement.

d. Miscellaneous Auto and Commuting Expense Rules

Any taxpayer—whether in business or not—who itemizes deductions on their income tax return may deduct any state-imposed personal property taxes on autos. But parking fines and traffic tickets cannot be deducted; to do so would be against "public policy."

Generally, commuting expenses—getting to work and back home—are not deductible. Only if stops are made for business en route may some of your commuting travel expense be claimed as business.

Only incorporated businesses may deduct expenses for providing their employees transit passes, cash or vouchers for commuting—up to $60 per month per employee. This benefit must be offered to all employees using public transportation or a special "commuter vehicle." (Sorry, your family car probably won't qualify—and even if it does, a shareholder in the company can't be the driver.) The dollar limit is subject to inflation indexing. (See IRC § 132 for more details.)

Parking is tax-deductible for businesses and tax-free for employees—even if given only to some employees and not others. A business can either provide parking or reimburse an employee for

parking tax-free, up to $160 per month. Anything more than $160 is taxable income to the employee. The benefit is subject to inflation indexing, and increases slightly each year. (IRC § 132.)

Interest paid on a car loan is deductible in proportion to the business use percent. Otherwise, car loan interest is a nondeductible personal expense.

Special capitalization rules for manufacturers and contractors. Manufacturers, building contractors and agricultural producers are subject to a special set of deduction rules known as the "uniform capitalization rules." (IRC § 263A.) Under these provisions, certain costs you might otherwise think are current expenses must be treated as capitalized expenses and added to the tax basis of your product or inventory. In turn, these expenses figure into the "cost of goods sold" formula discussed in Chapter 2. The bottom line is that your deductions are calculated under fairly complex accounting rules. If your business is in a category that might be subject to these rules, see a tax pro.

2. Costs of Going Into Business

All costs of getting a business started *before* you actually commence operations are *capital* items—including advertising, travel, office supplies, utilities, repairs and employee wages. (IRC § 195.) This can be a bit of a shock, since these are the costs that can be immediately deducted as expenses once you are open for business. Under the tax code, these start-up expenses must be deducted ratably over the first 60 months you are in business. (For sole proprietors, partners and limited liability company members these deductions are claimed on IRS Form 4562, Depreciation and Amortization.)

Example: Bill and Betty set up Management Consulting Partners (MCP). During the first three months of 1995, they locate and fix up office space (with the help of a handyman) and have brochures printed and mailed to prospective clients. MCP spends a total of $6,000, and on April 1st, they open for business. Tax result: all of the pre-April expenses are capital expenditures and are deductible at the rate of $100 per month over the first 60 months MCP is in business. Therefore, in 1995, $900 can be deducted for the nine months the business was open, $1,200 in 1996, and so on until 60 months elapse. Expenses incurred after the business is in operation—April's rent and most other recurring monthly costs—are 100% deductible in 1995.

You can work around this rule. If it would benefit you to deduct start-up costs in the first year rather than over five years, you might legally be able to:

- delay paying costs until you start serving customers. (Whether or not your suppliers and workers will allow you this much time to pay is another matter.)

- do a trivial amount of business before you are officially open. That will probably be enough to get you by an IRS audit. Make a $75 sale to a friend or give a few people a bargain they can't resist, just to get some activity on the books.

Before rushing to get the deduction all in the first year, make sure this really helps your tax situation. If, like many businesses, you will suffer losses the first few years of operation, you might be better off taking the deduction over 60 months.

What happens if, after incurring start-up expenses, you back out and don't go into operation? Your costs may or may not be deductible, depending on the tax rules you fall under. The tax code (IRC § 195) divides expenses of trying, but failing, to establish a business into two categories:

- Costs of investigating whether to start a

business. Any expenses for a general search or preliminary investigation are not deductible.

- Costs of attempting to acquire or start a specific business. These are classified as "investment" expenses. All investment expenses are itemized deductions on Schedule A of your individual income tax return. They are not considered start-up expenses because you never went into any business.

3. Education Expenses

You can deduct education expenses if they are related to your *current* business, trade or occupation, but you must follow strict rules. To be deductible, the tax code (IRC § 162, Reg. 1.162-5) requires that an education expense must either be:

- to maintain or improve skills required in your (present) employment, or

- required by your employer or as a legal requirement of your job or profession.

Example: The State Contractor's Board requires Jim, a licensed building contractor, to attend and pay for 24 hours of continuing education programs as a precondition of renewing his license. In this case, both IRC conditions are met, so the expense is deductible for Jim's business. After Jim takes 24 hours of programs, any additional courses in his field would still be deductible under the first rule above.

However, education expenses that qualify you for a new job or business are not deductible under the tax code. This tax rule has been interpreted rather narrowly by the IRS and courts.

Example: Mary, a public school teacher, wants to open up a small private school. Her state requires her to take several college courses before granting her a license. Mary can't deduct the cost of these courses, because they are for a new job or business, even though it's in a related field.

4. Legal and Other Professional Fees

Professional fees for attorneys, tax pros or consultants generally can be deducted in the year incurred—as long as you actually go into operation. For instance, fees for forming the business—drawing up a partnership agreement or reviewing license requirements—are immediately deductible. However, when professional fees clearly relate to future years, they must be deducted over the life of the benefit. Some fees, however, fall into a gray area, and you can choose between deducting them all in the first year or spreading them over future years.

Example: Carlos and Teresa's attorney helps them negotiate and prepare a five-year lease for their restaurant. In this case, the lawyer's fees may be deducted either in the current year or in equal amounts over the lease's 60-month period. Carlos and Teresa should figure out which methods give them the best tax benefit. Taking the expense in the first year of operation may not be a good idea if they won't have sufficient income to offset it.

Tax assistance is deductible. But again, it can get sticky. Folks usually want tax advice covering both their business and individual taxes, which in most cases are intertwined. For instance, you might ask a tax pro how to minimize taxes on income from all sources—your sole proprietorship, investments and your spouse's income. Her fee qualifies as a business tax deduction in proportion to the business advice given. The remaining portion, for tax advice on investments and spouse's income, can be deducted (but not as a business expense—as a personal itemized deduction on Schedule A of your return).

Separate bill for business and personal expenses. If you see a lawyer or a tax pro, ask that the bill clearly show the extent the work was related to your business. The IRS rarely questions the apportionment used, so ask the advisor to be liberal in putting as much of the expense as possible to the business side.

5. Research and Experimentation Expenditures

The tax code provision allowing a tax credit for Research and Experimentation expenses expired on June 30, 1995 but was reinstated for qualified expenditures incurred from July 1, 1996 through June 30, 1997. (R & E expenditures made from July 1, 1995 through June 30, 1996 are not deductible under this special tax break.) Whether or not this provision will die again, or be extended by Congress beyond June 30, 1997, is anybody's guess. Be sure to check with a tax pro for further developments.

6. Business Bad Debts

If you are in business long enough, you will eventually be stiffed by a deadbeat. The resulting bad debt may or may not be a deductible expense. (IRC § 166, Reg. 1.166.)

If your business sells services, you cannot deduct an unpaid bill as a bad debt. No tax deduction is allowed for time you devoted to the client or customer who doesn't pay. The tax code rationale is that if you could deduct the value of unpaid services, it would be too easy to inflate your bills and claim large bad debt deductions—and too hard for the IRS to catch you.

If your business provides *goods,* however, you can deduct the costs of any goods sold, but not paid for, as an ordinary business expense.

The same is true if you actually lose dollars. For instance, you made a loan to a customer and didn't get paid back. To get the deduction, there must have been a *business*—not personal—reason for the loan, and you must have taken reasonable steps under the circumstances to collect the debt—such as, making a written demand for payment, going to court or turning the debt over to a collection agency.

Example: Ralph and Rhonda's incorporated print shop made a $2,000 loan to Susan, a friend and good customer, to keep her florist business afloat. Despite this help, Susan went into bankruptcy a year later before making any repayment. Result: As long as Ralph and Rhonda's made the loan to protect their business relationship—and not to help a friend—the bad debt is deductible for the corporation in the year Susan declares bankruptcy. In the case of bankruptcy, it's not necessary for Ralph and Rhonda to take any steps to collect the debt.

There are different tax rules for "nonbusiness" bad debts—ones that don't qualify as business expenses. A bad debt in your personal life can still produce a tax benefit, but under the much more restrictive short term capital loss rules for individuals. Generally this means that the loss can only be claimed to offset capital gains—plus up to another $3,000 in ordinary income (See Chapter 4, Business Losses.) To claim a nonbusiness bad debt deduction, file Schedule D, Capital Gains and Losses, with your tax return. A loan to Uncle Festus falls into this category, but not if it was really a gift to get him into alcohol rehab that you never expected to get back. To bulletproof the deduction, get a signed promissory note from your uncle and show you made some efforts to try to collect on it. Expect an auditor to be suspicious if a relative is the deadbeat.

A business or nonbusiness bad debt claimed on a tax return will likely increase your audit chances. So it's a good idea to attach a statement to the return referring to the bad debt with the date it became due, the name and address of the debtor and your reason for determining it was worthless—the guy skipped town, died, declared bankruptcy or whatever.

Of course there is no free lunch; if in a later year you collect wholly or in part a debt that you had deducted as worthless, you must then include it in your income in the year it is received.

Note: If your business is in the minority of operations using the accrual accounting basis, you have an alternative way to deduct bad debts, which may be more advantageous than the method described above. This is too technical to get into here, so see your tax pro or IRS Publication 535 for details.

7. Promotion Expenses and Business Entertaining

If you pick up the tab for entertaining present or prospective customers, clients or employees, the cost is partially—not wholly—deductible.

You may deduct 50% of a business entertainment expense if it satisfies one of two tax code tests. The expense must either be:

- "directly related" to the business. Business must actually be discussed during the entertainment. For example, a catered meeting at your office would qualify, or

- "associated with" the business. The entertainment must take place prior to or immediately after a business discussion. This is more common—no business has to be discussed while having fun (for example, if your meeting is followed by an evening out at a restaurant, play or sporting event).

The costs of transportation to the entertainment event are fully deductible, and so aren't subject to the 50% limit.

Corporate Employee's Expenses. If your enterprise is a C corporation (see Chapter 7), and you entertain customers or clients, you can either pay the expenses and claim reimbursement, or have the corporation pay the expenses directly. Direct corporate payment is better—for instance, using a credit card and letting the corporation pay the bill. If you are not reimbursed by the corporation, you must claim the expenses as deductions for "unreimbursed employee expenses" along with your other "itemized" deductions on your individual tax return, which is less advantageous tax-wise. Also, claiming unreimbursed employee expenses increases your audit chances.

Employee Parties. Holiday parties and picnics for employees and their families are recognized morale builders. These affairs are not subject to the regular entertainment rule and are 100% deductible. Don't overdo it though—employee get-togethers must be infrequent and everyone at work must be invited in order to be fully deductible. No business need be discussed.

Home Entertaining. You can get a deduction for home entertaining if you follow the rules. To qualify, guests must either be employees or have a business connection—that is, they must be a present or potential customer or client. If family or social friends are also present, their pro-rata share of party costs is not deductible. You are on the honor system here. If audited, it will help your cause to show you gave other (purely social) parties you did not claim as business expenses. For guests other than employees, keep notes showing who was present and the nature of the business discussed before, during or after the get-together.

Business Gifts. You may make deductible gifts to clients and customers as long as the value does not exceed $25 per person per year. You can also deduct the cost of wrapping, mailing or even engraving the gift, so the real limit is slightly higher than $25. And gifts of items costing less than $400 on which your business name is imprinted aren't counted against the $25 limit.

Keep good records for business entertainment. If you have a business party, keep a written guest list, along with your explanation of the business connection and general nature of business discussed. This should satisfy most IRS auditors, unless the amount spent was outrageous. I have never heard of an auditor contacting guests to see whether or not business was really discussed.

WHEN ARE ENTERTAINMENT EXPENSES DEDUCTIBLE?

General Rule

You can deduct expenses to entertain a client, customer or employee if the expenses meet the "directly related" test or the "associated" test.

Definitions

- Entertainment includes any activity generally considered to provide amusement or recreation, and includes meals provided to a customer or client.
- The type of expense must be common and accepted in your field of business, trade or profession.
- The expense must be helpful and appropriate, although not necessarily indispensable, for your business.

Two tests

"Directly related" test

- Entertainment took place in a clear business setting, or
- Main purpose of entertainment was the active conduct of business, and
- You did engage in business with the person during the entertainment period, and
- You had more than a general expectation of getting income or some other specific business benefit.

"Associated" test

- Entertainment is associated with your trade or business, and
- Entertainment directly precedes or follows a substantial business discussion.

Other rules

- You cannot deduct the cost of your meal as an entertainment expense if you are claiming the meal as a travel expense.
- You can deduct expenses only to the extent they are not lavish or extravagant under the circumstances.
- You generally can deduct only 50% of your business entertainment expenses.
- If your client brings along a spouse, you can bring yours too, and deduct the cost as entertainment expenses.

8. Business Travel

Below is a summary of deductible travel expenses.
Also see Chapter 14, Fringe Benefits, for the rules
on combining business and pleasure travel.

DEDUCTIBLE TRAVEL EXPENSES	
Transportation	The cost of travel by airplane, train or bus between your home and your out-of-town business destination (but not commuting to your place of business from home).
Taxi, Commuter Bus, and Limousine	Fares for these and other types of transportation between the airport or station and your hotel, or between the hotel and your work location away from home.
Baggage and Shipping	The cost of sending baggage and sample or display material between your regular and temporary work locations.
Car	The costs of operating and maintaining your car when traveling away from home on business. You may deduct actual expenses or the standard mileage rate, including business-related tolls and parking. If you lease a car while away from home on business, you can deduct business-related expenses only.
Lodging	The cost of lodging if your business trip is overnight or long enough to require you to get substantial sleep or rest to properly perform your duties.
Meals	The cost of meals only if your business trip is overnight or long enough to require you to stop to get substantial sleep or rest. Includes amounts spent for food, beverages, taxes and related tips.
Cleaning	Cleaning and laundry expenses while away from home overnight.
Telephone	The cost of business calls while on your business trip, including business communication by fax machine or other communication devices.
Tips	Tips you pay for any expenses listed in this chart.
Other	Other similar ordinary and necessary expenses related to your business travel, such as public stenographer's fees and computer rental fees.

9. Sick Pay

Disability and sick pay to employees (but *not* to business owners) are deductible business expenses—if they are for health-related work absences under a written wage continuation plan. The policy doesn't have to be in any particular legal form; any document setting out conditions of sick pay benefits is fine. Sick or disability pay is fully taxable income to the recipient. (IRC § 104, Reg. 1.104-1.)

10. Interest

If like many folks, you use credit to finance business purchases, the interest and carrying charges are fully tax deductible. The same is true if you take out a personal loan and use the proceeds for your business. However, in case the IRS comes calling, keep good records showing that the money was really put into your enterprise. Otherwise, an auditor may disallow an interest expense deduction as a personal expense. And, if you pay interest for an expense that is part business and part personal (such as a car loan for a dual purpose vehicle), you must prorate the interest expense between the two uses.

11. Moving Expenses

You may be able to deduct certain household moving costs that would otherwise be nondeductible personal living expenses. To qualify, you must have moved in connection with your business (or job, if you are an employee of your corporation or someone else's enterprise.) The new workplace must be at least 50 miles farther from your old home than your old home was from your old workplace. If you had no former workplace, the new one must be at least 50 miles from your old home. Technically, moving costs are not business expenses, and so aren't claimed on Schedule C (sole proprietors)

or other business tax reporting form when you have another form of business entity. Instead, use Form 3903, Moving Expenses, to calculate the amount of the deduction, and attach to your income tax return. Enter the deduction on the first page of your Form 1040, on line 24. (See IRS Publication 521, Moving Expenses, for details.)

12. Computer Software

As a general rule, software programs purchased for business use must be depreciated over a 36-month period. But there are three important exceptions:

- When the software is acquired with the computer and its cost is not separately stated, the software is treated as part of the computer hardware and is depreciated over the five-year recovery period for computers and peripherals.

- If you elect it, and all of your equipment purchases are less than $17,500 for the year, the whole system, including "bundled software," can qualify for first-year write-off under IRC § 179. (See Chapter 2, Writing Off Long-Term Business Assets.)

- Software with a useful life of less than one year may be deducted as a business expense in the year it is bought. Arguably, with the rapid changes in computer and software technology, many software programs are only good for a year or not much longer.

13. Charitable Contributions

Unless you are operating as a C corporation, you must deduct any of your charitable contributions by your business on your personal (not business) tax return. If you own an S corporation, partnership or LLC, it can make a charitable contribution and pass the deduction through to you to claim on your individual return. (The contribution is shown on the K-1 form that each shareholder or partner receives from the business each year.) Add the value of the business reported deduction to the rest of your charitable deductions and claim it on Schedule A of Form 1040. (There is an overall charitable deduction limit for individuals of 50% of your adjusted gross income.)

Donations of business-used items.. Giving away computers or office furniture you've replaced to a school or local nonprofit organization can yield goodwill plus a tax benefit. If, however, you have fully depreciated or used IRC § 179 to take business deductions, you can't double-dip—deduct for something you already wrote off. On the other hand, if that computer still has some unused depreciation, you may get a deduction for the value of the computer, but not greater than its tax basis (the remaining portion of depreciation that hasn't been claimed).

Example: Belinda buys a new computer for her software development business and donates her three-year-old computer to her church. She paid $2,000 for it and has claimed $1,000 in depreciation in the past. Unless Belinda is operating as a C corporation, she may claim a $1,000 charitable deduction if the computer has a value of at least $1,000. She cannot claim a deduction of $1,200 for it even if that is its value, however, because that exceeds its tax basis.

14. Taxes

Taxes incurred in operating your business are generally deductible. How and when to deduct taxes in your business depends on the type of tax.

Sales tax on items used in your day-to-day operation is deductible as part of the cost of the items—not deducted separately as taxes. On the other hand, sales tax (or federal luxury tax) on a business asset—such as an auto bought for your business—must be added to the car's cost basis. This means the tax is not deductible all in the year the car was purchased. (See Chapter 2, Writing Off Long-Term Business Assets.) Sales taxes that you collect as a merchant and pay over to the state are not deductible unless you included them in your business' gross receipts.

Excise and fuel taxes paid by qualifying businesses are deductible as separately stated tax expenses.

If your business pays *employment taxes,* the employer's share is deductible as a business expense.

Self-employment (SE) tax isn't a business expense. However, the owner can deduct one-half of the SE tax on the front page of his or her Form 1040 tax return.

Federal income tax paid on your business' income is never deductible.

State income tax can be deducted on your personal tax return as an itemized deduction on Schedule A, not as a business expense.

Real estate tax on business-used property is deductible, along with any special local assessments for repair or maintenance. However, if the assessment is for improvements (for example, to build a sewer or sidewalk), it is not immediately deductible; instead, it is added to the basis of the property and deducted over a period of years. (See Chapter 2.) Real estate tax for nonbusiness property is deductible as an itemized deduction on your personal tax return.

Penalties and fines paid to the IRS and any other governmental agencies are not deductible as business expenses—or as any other type of tax deduction.

15. Advertising and Promotion

The cost of ordinary advertising for your goods or services—business cards, yellow page ads and so on—is deductible as a current expense. Promotional costs that create business goodwill—for example, sponsoring a peewee football team—are also deductible as long as there is a clear connection between the sponsorship and your business. For example, naming the team the "Southwest Auto Parts Blues" or listing the business name in the program is evidence of the promotion effort.

A contest prize qualifies as a promotion expense, but not if an employee wins it.

Any cost that is *primarily* personal is not deductible. For example, you can't deduct the cost of inviting customers or clients to your son's wedding. Also not deductible are costs of lobbying a politico (with a few limited exceptions).

The cost of signs, if they have a useful life of over one year, must be capitalized and depreciation deductions taken over seven years.

16. Repairs and Improvements

Upkeep and improvements to your business and business property are, of course, tax deductible. However, it's not always clear whether an expenditure to keep a business asset maintained can be deducted all in one year or if it has to be depreciated (taken as a deduction over a period of future years).

There are also special deduction breaks for the rehabilitation of older buildings, improvements for the elderly and handicapped and for the costs of removing architectural or transportation barriers. If you can fit your expenditure within one of these tax code provisions, you can deduct an improvement currently instead of capitalizing it, or even better get a tax credit. Most small businesses don't qualify, so I won't go into details, which are very technical. If you think you might qualify, check this out with a tax pro, or look at the instructions accompanying IRS forms 3800 General Business Credit, 3468 Investment Tax Credit and 8826 Disabled Access Credit.

17. Health Benefits

See Chapter 14, Fringe Benefits, Section H, for the tricky rules of deductibility of health costs for owners and employees of a business.

F. How and Where Deductions are Claimed

Although the tax deductibility rules are basically the same, *how* you claim expenses on your tax return varies significantly, depending on how your business is organized. For now, the basics of business expense tax reporting are as follows:

Sole proprietors (including independent contractors) and *statutory employees* report business expenses on Schedule C of the individual income tax returns we all file (Form 1040). Always keep in mind that in the eyes of the tax code, a sole proprietor and his business are one and the same.

S corporations (Form 1120S), *partnerships* and *limited liability companies* (Form 1065) file their own returns showing expense deductions. In turn, these entities issue Form K-1 to their owners showing how much profit or loss is allocable to each individual. This amount is reported on Schedule E of their Form 1040s. So, with a few exceptions (called "separately stated" items, discussed in Chapters 8 and 9), an S corporation shareholder, partner or limited liability member's tax returns won't list any of their business expenses.

Non-owner employees of businesses who incur out-of-pocket expenses can also deduct them, but only under the restrictive "unreimbursed business expense" rules for their Schedule A of their Form 1040s. For this reason, a business should always either fully reimburse its employees for their expenses or should pay those expenses directly.

And, as mentioned above in Section E, some types of expenses that might seem to be business related, such as business charitable contributions and moving expenses, also must be claimed on Schedule A of the business owner's personal tax returns.

COMMONLY OVERLOOKED BUSINESS EXPENSES

Despite the fact that most people keep a sharp eye out for deductible expenses, it's not uncommon to miss a few. And some folks don't list a deduction because they can't find what category it fits into. Some overlooked routine deductions include:

advertising giveaways and promotion

audio- and videotapes related to business skills

bank service charges

business association dues

business gifts

business-related magazines and books (like the one in your hand)

casual labor and tips

casualty and theft losses

coffee and beverage service

commissions

consultant fees

credit bureau fees

education to improve business skills

office supplies

online computer services related to business

parking and meters

petty cash funds

postage

promotion and publicity

seminars and trade shows

taxi and bus fare

telephone calls away from the business

Note: Just because you didn't get a receipt doesn't mean you can't deduct the expense, so keep track of those small items and get big tax savings.

FEDERAL EXCISE TAXES

In addition to income taxes, some businesses are subject to special federal "excise taxes." For instance, an interstate trucking company may have to pay a federal excise tax on fuels or on each truck used on a federal highway. Unlike income taxes, excise taxes don't affect many small businesses, so we won't go into detail. Businesses most likely to be subject to excise taxes are in transportation or manufacturing. Even if you aren't in one of these fields, see IRC §§ 4041 to 5763 to find out whether you are affected. Otherwise, you may not discover it until it is too late—when you receive a notice that you owe excise taxes plus penalties and interest for several years, which could spell financial ruin.

RESOURCES

IRS Publication 529, *Miscellaneous Deductions*

IRS Publication 535, *Business Expenses.*

IRS Publication 334, *Tax Guide for Small Business.* A free 325-page book, indispensable for every small business person.

Master Tax Guide (Commerce Clearing House). A one-volume tax reference book with a lot of tax deduction materials for individuals and small business owners. Many IRS auditors use this book for quick answers to tax questions, too.

Small-Time Operator, Bernard Kamoroff (Bell Springs). A good small business guidebook, written by a CPA, that has tips on maximizing deductions.

Small Business Development Centers have small business tax publications and personal counseling available. Contact a federal Small Business Administration office or the nearest large university to find an SBDC near you. ■

C H A P T E R 2

Writing Off Long-Term Business Assets

"Of all debts men are least willing to pay the taxes."

— **Ralph Waldo Emerson**

As a business person, one of the few joys of spending money on a new computer, photocopier or even that great rosewood desk you have been coveting is knowing that the government is paying part of the expense—maybe as much as 50% or more. Just how much tax benefit you get from buying equipment depends on your business's earnings and your tax bracket; the more you make, the more your business purchases will be subsidized by Uncle Sam.

You can't deduct costs for equipment, building or other assets as ordinary business expenses, which were discussed in Chapter 1. Instead, you must "capitalize" these costs. (IRC § 263.) With one important exception, this means you must spread these expenditures by taking tax deductions (in tax lingo, "depreciate") over a number of years. Put another way, you recover your costs for these "fixed assets" of your business in future years' tax returns. (IRC §§ 167 and 168.) How many years depends upon which category of the tax code the particular asset falls into—it may be as few as three, or as many as 39 years.

There is, however, one very important exception to the rule that capital expenditures must be depreciated over a number of years. Section 179 of the tax code lets you write off, immediately, up to $17,500 of most capital expenditures.

This chapter explains how to use both IRC § 179 and depreciation procedures to benefit your small business.

WRITING OFF BUSINESS ASSETS IN A NUTSHELL

1. The tax code divides expenditures for business into "current expenses" and "capital items," and treats each type differently.

2. Capital expenditures must be deducted over a number of years under tax code depreciation rules.

3. A special tax code provision, IRC § 179, allows most business owners to tax-deduct up to $17,500 or more of capital expenditures as if they were current expenses.

4. Typically, assets are tax-deducted using one of two methods, called "accelerated" and "straight-line" depreciation. No matter which method is used, the entire cost of the asset may be written off over time.

5. There are several ways to tax-deduct the business use portion of an automobile.

A. Some Expenditures Must Be Capitalized

The most fundamental rule of deducting business expenditures is that they must first be divided up into two categories, called current "expenses" and "capitalized" costs.

Generally, money spent for things used up within a year are current expenses. These include ordinary operating costs of a business such as rent, equipment repair, telephone and utility bills for the current year. Garden variety supplies, such as stationery and postage stamps, are also considered expenses even though they may be around from one year to the next. All items that fall into the current expense category can be fully deducted in the tax year they are purchased. (See Chapter 1, Business Income and Tax-Deductible Expenses.)

Capitalized costs, on the other hand, are usually for things the tax code says have a *useful life of more than one year*—equipment, vehicles and buildings are the most common examples. (See Section 3, below, on inventory.) A capital cost may be to acquire an asset, or to improve one you already own so as to substantially prolong its life or adapt it to a different use. (Chapter 1, Business Income and Tax-Deductible Expenses, explains how to determine whether an expenditure should be categorized as a current expense or capital cost.)

No matter the size and scale of the business, all of these things come under the heading of "business assets." And while it's true that almost all assets can provide tax write-offs for a business owner, not all assets are treated equally by the tax code.

BUSINESS ASSETS THAT MUST BE CAPITALIZED

Buildings

Cellular phones and beepers*

Computer components and software*

Copyrights and patents

Equipment*

Improvements to business property

Inventory

Office furnishings and decorations*

Small tools and equipment*

Vehicles

Window coverings*

(See IRC § 263 and Reg. 1.263 for details about items that must be capitalized.)

[*May be subject to immediate deduction under IRC § 179 at your option. (See Section B.)]

---

1. Types of Property

Almost any kind of property can qualify for a tax write-off if it is used in a business. The one notable exception is land. The tax code categorizes assets as "tangible" and "intangible," and "real" and "per-

sonal." These distinctions are important because they dictate how you must deduct asset costs and how fast you can take the deductions.

Tangible property is simply things that can be felt or touched—warehouses, machines, desks, trucks, vans and tools are all tangible property. The vast majority of property owned by a small business is tangible. Intangible property is everything else—a trademark, franchise right or business goodwill, for example.

Long ago the English legal system divided the world of property into two broad kinds: real and personal property. *Real* property is land and anything permanently attached to it which are considered "improvements," such as fences, parking lots, buildings and trees. Everything else is *personal* property, such as furniture, equipment, cars and paper clips. These divisions are deeply imbedded in all our laws, including our tax law. In general, it takes much longer to write off real property than personal property. The rationale is that real property improvements wear out more slowly than personal property. Land itself is considered to never wear out, and so is nondeductible.

2. Tax Basis of Assets

"Basis" is a tax code term you should have more than a passing familiarity with. Tax basis, or just plain basis, is the amount the tax code says you have invested in an asset—which may be quite a different figure than you think. Your basis in an asset determines how much you can deduct each year when you write off a business asset. It is also used to determine your taxable gain or loss when you sell or dispose of the asset.

a. Property You Purchase

As a general rule, the beginning tax basis of an item of property is its original cost to you. (IRC § 1012.) So, if you pay $3,000 for a dry cleaning machine, that's your beginning tax basis. Related costs, such as $200 for freight and $150 for installation, are added to the basis—making it $3,350 in this example.

b. Property You Receive as a Gift

If you receive property as a gift, you take the same tax basis as the one who gave it to you had. This is termed a "transferred" basis. (IRC § 1015.)

Example: Ralph's father gives him a building worth $60,000. His father's tax basis in the property was $15,000; Ralph has a transferred basis the same as his father's—$15,000. So if Ralph immediately sells the building for $60,000, he will owe tax on a $45,000 gain (the sales price, $60,000, less his tax basis, $15,000).

If gift tax was paid on the gift by Ralph's father, the basis is "stepped-up," meaning that it will include the amount of tax paid. In the real world, it is unlikely that a gift tax was paid by the father.

c. Property You Receive for Services

If you receive property in exchange for your services, your basis in the property is its fair market value. (IRC § 7701.) The value of the property is considered barter income to you and is taxable in the year received. If the property is then used in your business, it may be tax deducted under the depreciation rules for the type of asset it is.

Example: In 1995, Woody refinished four antique chests for Zeke; in exchange he received one of them. Because it could be sold for $250, that's its fair market value, and becomes Woody's tax basis in the chest. He should report $250 as income on his 1995 tax return. Woody sells the chest for $350 in 1996, so he has a further taxable gain of $100 (less any costs of making the sale, such as a newspaper classified ad).

d. Property You Inherit

If you inherit property and subsequently use it in your business, the tax basis of the property is its fair market value at the time of death of the person who left it to you. (IRC § 1014.)

Example: Beth dies and leaves a warehouse to her son, Charles. She bought the property in 1970 for $50,000, and it was worth $200,000 on the real estate market when Beth died in 1994. Charles, who has an insurance agency, can't use the warehouse, but needs a small office building for his business. If Charles sells the warehouse for $200,000, he has no taxable gain or loss, because $200,000 was his tax basis. Charles can then buy a new building with the proceeds and begin taking depreciation deductions as soon as he starts using it for his insurance business.

CAPITAL GAINS TAX

There is a special top rate of 28% for long-term capital gains. (Congress is presently considering reducing or eliminating the capital gains tax.) This means if you own a capital asset for over one year and sell it at a gain, the gain will not be taxed at a rate greater than 28%, even if your individual rate is higher. If your ordinary income tax rate is lower than 28%, the gain will be taxed at the lower rate. However, gains on most property used in a trade or business are excluded from this special tax break and are taxed as ordinary income when sold by a business. (IRC § 1231.)

e. Property You Receive for Other Property

If you receive property in exchange for other property, the new property's basis is usually the same as the property you traded. This is called "substituted" basis.

WRITING OFF LONG-TERM BUSINESS ASSETS

Example: Janet, a cabinet maker, trades a table saw with a tax basis of $250 to Boffo for his industrial shop vac. Her basis in the shop vac is $250.

The tax code doesn't allow substituted basis treatment for all exchanges. To be nontaxable, the trade must be for a "like kind" property, which means that if you trade real estate, you must receive real estate in exchange. And, if you trade tangible property (such as Janet's table saw, above), you can't get intangible property, such as a copyright, in return. The tax code treats such a transaction as a sale of the table saw (normally resulting in a taxable profit or loss), followed by the purchase of the copyright, and not an exchange.

f. Property Exchanged With Money

If you trade property and throw in money to boot, your basis in the property received equals the basis of the property you exchanged, plus the amount you paid in cash.

Example: Kevin trades his business pickup truck (tax basis of $3,000) and $6,000 cash to Truck City for a new model. Kevin's basis in the new truck is $9,000. This would be true even if the cost of the new truck were higher than $9,000.

g. Property You Convert to Business Use

If you convert your nonbusiness property to business use, you must determine its basis at the time you make the switch. The tax basis of converted property is the *lesser* of:

a. the fair market value of the property on the date converted to business use, or

b. your adjusted basis in that property. (IRC § 167.)

Example 1: You bought that $3,000 computer a year ago for home study projects, but just now start using it in your business. The tax basis of the computer is the lesser of your cost or its current fair market value. Since the computer is used and has lost value, it is now worth only $2,000, which becomes its tax basis as a business asset.

Example 2: Theresa pays $60,000 to a contractor to have a home built on a lot she bought for $10,000. She lives in the home several years and spends $20,000 for improvements, and one year claims a $2,000 tax deduction for a casualty loss when a runaway car hits her living room. Over time, Theresa's neighborhood becomes a commercial area. Theresa moves out and converts the house into a health food store. The tax basis of the building is computed for the business as follows:

	$60,000	(cost of building)
+	20,000	(improvements)
-	2,000	(deductions taken in prior years)
=	$78,000	(tax basis)

(The $10,000 cost of the land is not part of the basis of the building, and it is not depreciable under the tax code.)

If the building's fair market value had decreased to $50,000 at the time of the conversion, Theresa's basis would have decreased to $50,000 as well. That's because she must use the fair market value as her basis whenever it is lower than her cost. (IRC § 167, Reg. 1.167.)

3. Inventories

Businesses selling goods rather than services usually maintain stock on hand, called "inventory." Money spent for goods to sell is *not* a general business expense. Instead, your inventory is considered a business asset and its cost is expensed as it is sold—or discarded.

You must value your "cost of goods sold" using an IRS-approved inventory accounting method. In effect, what you spend for inventory is deducted as it is sold from the revenue it generates, to come up with your gross profit. From this figure, your general business expenses are deducted to determine your net profit. It is the net profit that is taxed.

Tax rule. Inventory generally must be listed at the *lower* of cost or market value.

Example: At the end of its first year of operation, Rick's Music Store has an inventory of compact disks that cost him $50,000, and vinyl LP records that cost $30,000. Using the "cost method," Rick has an ending inventory of $80,000. Rick's cost of goods sold deduction:

	$0	(beginning inventory)
+	$300,000	(purchases)
-	$80,000	(ending inventory)
=	$220,000	(cost of goods sold).

You may reduce ("write-down") the value of any inventory that has become unsalable. This needs to be documented. For instance, if you write-down and destroy dead stock, keep evidence of the destruction—photos, videos, receipts or the statement of a reputable third party who can certify the goods were destroyed.

Example: At inventory time, Rick knows his inventory of CDs have held their value, but his LP records hardly sell any more. Rick asks a prominent music distributor to appraise the LP inventory and gets a written statement saying the market value is only $8,000. Accordingly, Rick reduces their retail prices and lowers the inventory on his books by $22,000. Now Rick's cost of goods sold deduction for tax reporting looks like this:

	$0	(beginning inventory)
+	$300,000	(purchases)
-	$58,000	(ending inventory)
=	$242,000	(cost of goods sold)

The difference between the two examples is the method of valuing the inventory. Using fair market value instead of cost reduces Rick's income for tax purposes by $22,000. Note that it is improper to reduce the book value of the inventory without some evidence of the loss in value and without reducing the retail price of the goods. With the taxes saved from the inventory write-down, Rick can build up his CD inventory or do anything he wants to with the extra money in his pocket.

B. Expensing Business Assets: IRC Section 179

Small business owners don't need to learn the Internal Revenue Code by section number, but it pays to remember at least one: IRC § 179, perhaps the best small business tax break of all. IRC § 179 allows— but doesn't require—a business owner or C corporation to deduct up to $17,500 (in 1996) of asset purchases each year as current expenses. This produces an immediate write-off of capital assets.

Using § 179 is referred to as "expensing an asset," as opposed to capitalizing it under normal tax code rules. Within the $17,500 limit, a business may buy assets at any time during the year and deduct the costs in full—as long as they are "placed in service" in that same year. I once bought, set up and started using a new copier on December 31, at a cost of $3,000, and wrote it off completely that year using this provision.

Example: Hal, a self-employed consultant, buys a computer for $5,000 in early 1995 . Hal plans on using IRC § 179 to write off the computer. Hal's business is very profitable and later in the year, while estimating how much he is going to owe in taxes for 1995, Hal finds he will owe $4,000 over the estimated quarterly tax payments he has made. Hal was planning to buy an $8,000 color printer in 1996. If, instead of waiting, Hal purchases and starts using the printer before December 31, he qualifies under § 179 to write off $13,000 in 1995 and wipe out his tax balance.

It works out like this: Hal is in a 40% combined federal and state income tax bracket and pays self-employment taxes of 15.3%. This means that every business deduction dollar saves him 55¢ in taxes. So the total tax savings resulting from the $8,000 copier purchase in 1995 wipes out Hal's projected $4,000 tax balance. Of course, Hal had to spend $8,000 to save $4,424 in taxes. But, Hal would still get the deduction even if he purchased the machine on credit, and as long as he needs the copier, this is still the next best thing to a free lunch.

When would you not want the fast deduction of IRC § 179? Answer: When you don't get any immediate tax benefit from it. For instance, you don't have enough business income to offset the Section 179 deduction, but you hope to have it in future years. In that case, choosing regular depreciation (discussed in Section C, below) and spreading the deduction over future years makes more sense.

Example: Hal's business loses money in 1995 when a major account declares bankruptcy after Hal buys a $5,000 computer. The tax code prescribes a five-year depreciation period for computers. Hal doesn't have any outside income, so spreading the deduction over five years makes more sense than writing off the whole cost under IRC § 179 in 1995.

A few other tax code sections let you choose whether to expense or capitalize certain assets. The majority of these provisions don't affect small businesses unless you engage in research (IRC § 174), agriculture (IRC §§ 175, 180 and 193), publishing (IRC § 173) or mining (IRC §§ 615 and 616). (See IRC § 263 and Reg. 1.263 or a tax pro for details.)

NEW LAW: INCREASING § 179 DEDUCTIONS TO $25,000

Beginning in 1997, the annual limit on expensing of business assets under IRC § 179 increases as follows: 1997: $18,000; 1998: $18,500; 1999: $19,000; 2000: $20,000; 2001: $24,000; 2002: $25,000.

---

1. Ineligible Property for Section 179

For some types of property and in some circumstances, you can't use IRC § 179. Ineligible property includes:

- Real estate
- Inventory bought for resale to customers (discussed above)

- Property received by gift or inheritance, and
- Property bought from a close relative—grandparent, parent, child, sibling or equivalent in-law—or another business in which you have an ownership interest

Property you already own can't be converted from personal to business use under Section 179; instead, it must be depreciated, as explained in Section C, below.

2. Listed Property—Special Rules

Using IRC § 179 to write off things designated in the tax code as "listed" property entails special rules. Three typical business assets are termed listed property:

- vehicles used wholly or partly for business
- cellular phones, and
- computers and peripherals.

Listed property qualifies for IRC § 179 only if it is used 50% or more of the time for business, both in the year acquired and years thereafter.

All listed property items have a potential for personal as well as business usage in the eyes of the IRS. And remember, the writers of the tax code don't want you deducting personal expenses against your business income. So, the IRS enforces strict recordkeeping rules for listed property if also utilized for personal purposes. (See Chapter 3, Recordkeeping and Accounting, Section D, for how to keep such records.)

Example: Joan paid $3,000 for a computer in 1996 and uses it 60% of the time for business. She can write off $1,800 as a business expense in 1995 (60% business usage x $3,000 cost) using IRC § 179. But if Joan used it only 45% of the time for business, she could not use IRC § 179. Instead, Joan would have to take depreciation deductions for the business portion ($1,350) over *the five-year period the tax code prescribes for computers.*

Autos used for business are subject to a different limitation under IRC § 179. The deduction for depreciation is currently limited to $3,060 in the year of purchase—even if the business usage is 100%. This means that there is no advantage to choosing IRC § 179 to write off a car, because the limit is the same as with regular depreciation rules (See Section D, below). And if you want to take the full $17,500 deduction under § 179, using part of it to claim an auto would be counterproductive.

3. Items Not Fully Paid For

An asset can be bought on credit—that is, not be fully paid for—and still be eligible for a full tax write-off under IRC § 179. This means you can buy on credit and get a tax deduction in that year larger than your cash outlay!

Example: Jack buys and starts using $30,000 of machinery for his tool and die shop with $10,000 down. The balance of $20,000 is to be paid over the next five years. Jack is nevertheless allowed to deduct up to $17,500 in the year of purchase, using IRC § 179. Jack can then claim depreciation deductions on the balance of $12,500 in subsequent years. (See Section C, below.) Jack cannot, however, carry over the $12,500 excess and use IRC § 179 to write it off in the following year. (Also, Jack can take a deduction for any interest paid on the unpaid balance of the note each year.)

4. Other Limitations on Using Section 179

Assuming you qualify under the rules discussed above, there are some limitations on using IRC § 179.

a. Income Limit and Carry Forward

Your *earned* income (meaning income from a trade or business you work in, as opposed to income from investments) must be at least as much as the total cost you write off under IRC § 179. However, the income does not have to come from the business the equipment is purchased for; it may be from another business you have.

If your IRC § 179 expenditures exceed your total earned income from all sources, you can carry the excess over to future years' tax returns. You can then claim the unused portion as long as the total in any one year is $17,500 (1996) or less.

Example: Joy is a sole proprietor who establishes an acting school in 1996. After deducting all operating expenses, her earned income is $6,000. Joy buys $15,000 of furnishings and stage props in 1996, paying for them from her savings. Result: Joy can deduct at least $6,000 of the costs using IRC § 179. If Joy had earned an additional $9,000 in 1996—say from managing a health food store—she could deduct the whole $15,000. Or, Joy can carry the $9,000 unused excess deduction over to her 1997 tax return and claim it along with any other IRC § 179 expenses—as long as she has enough income. Joy is still limited to taking a total of $17,500 in 1997.

b. Limits on Married Couples

Being married works against you when it comes to IRC § 179. A married couple is limited to an annual *total* write-off of $17,500 (1996). This is true even if both have separate businesses and whether they file tax returns jointly or separately. If they file separately, each is limited to $8,750 in IRC § 179 deductions. This is another example of "marriage penalties" built into the tax code.

c. Spending Too Much

IRC § 179 is really just for small businesses. You cannot take any IRC § 179 write-off if your busi-

ness spends $217,500 or more for equipment in one year. You can still take normal depreciation deductions, however. (See Section C, below.)

d. More Than One Owner

Most business owners, partners, limited liability company members or shareholders in an S corporation can use IRC § 179 only in proportion to their ownership share. The $17,500 limit applies to the business as a whole. So, if a business with four equal partners buys $30,000 of qualified IRC § 179 equipment, each owner can claim only one-fourth of the $17,500 (1996) deduction on his or her individual tax return.

There are two exceptions, however:

- Owners who are married to each other, as discussed above, and

- C corporations, where only the corporation (and not the shareholders) can take one IRC § 179 deduction.

e. Not for Passive Investors

Owners may use IRC § 179 if they are active in the business. They can't use § 179 if they are passive investors, unless they are employed or active in some other business.

Example 1: W & W partnership buys a $16,000 injection molding machine for manufacturing plastic toys. The partnership allocates $8,000 of the IRC § 179 deduction to each of the two partners, Wanda and Willie. Since they are both active in the business and earn at least $8,000, each can write off $8,000 against their earned income.

Example 2: Willie becomes disabled. He is still a partner in W & W, but gets no income from the partnership. Instead, he lives on his Social Security and monthly payments from the state lottery. He can't take an IRC § 179 deduction of any amount.

Example 3: Willie takes an outside job as a part-time toy designer for ToyCo and earns $12,000. He can take his share of the Section 179 deduction of $8,000.

f. Minimum Period of Business Use

You must use equipment written off under IRC § 179 in your business for at least the period over which it would have been depreciated. Also, as mentioned above, the asset must be used for business purposes at least 50% of the time. If you don't meet these rules, you face "recapture"—meaning you must report as income an IRC § 179 deduction taken in a prior year. You don't report the entire deduction, just the portion that would remain if you had depreciated the equipment instead of using § 179.

Example: In 1995, Hal elected IRC § 179 to write off a $4,000 computer for his business. In 1996 he got a new computer and took the old one home for video games. Hal must recapture income of $2,800 in 1996. This is the amount of depreciation deductions Hal would have gotten according to IRS tables. (You can find these tables in tax preparation guides and IRS Publication 946.)

What if instead Hal continues to use it for business 45% of the time, and to keep track of his stamp collection the rest of the time? Same result. Hal must report recapture income because business usage is less than 50%. On the other hand, if Hal uses the computer through half of the sixth year (the end of the period over which computers must be depreciated) for business only, he would not have any recapture income.

IRS auditors usually look at your purchase contracts and proofs of payment, but they rarely check if equipment is being used for business. Let your conscience be your guide.

5. Combining IRC Section 179 and Depreciation

After using IRC § 179 to immediately write off the first $17,500 (1996) of assets purchased, you can claim regular depreciation deductions for the balance.

Example: Miranda bought and started using a $30,000 instant printing press for her graphics business. She elected IRC § 179 and took the maximum deduction of $17,500 in the first year. She can claim the remaining $12,500 as depreciation expenses beginning with the following year. (See Section C, below.)

Section 179 deductions are reported on IRS Form 4562, Depreciation and Amortization. See Section C, below.

WATCH OUT FOR DEPRECIATION RECAPTURE!

Congress giveth, and in some cases taketh away. Depreciation deductions may come back to bite you when you quit using business property that has given you past tax benefits. Various tax code provisions mandate that in certain circumstances you must report as ordinary income some of your past tax deductions for depreciation (called "recapture") on your tax return when an asset is no longer used for business. (IRC §§ 1245, 1250.) This is true whether you just stop using the asset in your business or dispose of it.

Example: Rusty, a self-employed flooring contractor, closes his shop in 1997 and sells his 100% business-used Dodge pickup for $7,500. The truck cost $11,000, and Rusty took $4,200 of depreciation deductions in past years. He must report $700 as recapture income (the difference between his tax basis of $6,800 and the sale price of $7,500) on his 1997 tax return. Rusty should use IRS Form 4797, Sales of Business Property, to report the sale and the recapture income.

However, there are several exceptions to the rules requiring recapture. For instance, if you trade a business asset for another of like kind, no recapture results.

Example: Rusty's business is going great. Instead of selling his truck, he trades up to a $20,000 truck and is allowed $10,000 credit for his old pickup. There is no recapture income to report because this was a like-kind exchange.

Another exception to rules requiring recapture is if the asset had been damaged, stolen or destroyed and the loss was covered by insurance. In this case (called "involuntary conversion"), there is no recapture as long as all of the insurance proceeds are used to replace the asset.

Example: Rusty wrecks the old pickup and it is declared a total loss. Allsnake Insurance pays him $9,000 ($2,200 more than his tax basis in the truck). As long as he buys a replacement truck for at least $9,000, there is no recapture, but if he decides to buy a used truck for $5,000 instead of buy it, he must report $2,200 as recapture income.

C. Depreciating Business Assets

Because of its obvious advantages, most successful small business owners look first to IRC § 179 to write off assets. But you must go with tax code depreciation methods if:

- you don't have other earned income to offset, or
- the asset doesn't meet IRC § 179 qualifications (see Section B, above), or
- you've already used up your IRC § 179 deduction that year.

1. What Is Depreciation?

The tax code recognizes that almost everything wears out over time. So, property used in a trade or business or held for the production of income is entitled to a tax deduction for depreciation. A depreciation deduction is commonly called a "write-off"; the term favored by accountants is "cost recovery."

A tax deduction for depreciation works something like this. You buy and use a copy machine in your business. Under the tax code a copy machine is assigned a (rather arbitrary) five-year life expectancy. (IRC § 168, Reg. 1.168.) This means you can write off part of the cost of the copier in the year you bought it and in each of the following five years, by taking annual deductions. (Yes, I know—this is a total of six years, not five.) Eventually, the whole cost of the copier has been deducted from your business income. Just how much you can take each year and how to claim the deduction are explained next.

There is one important exception to the normal depreciation rule: land costs can never be deducted. Special rules also apply to deducting business inventories and natural resources.

KEEPING UP WITH CHANGING DEPRECIATION RULES

Congress changes the depreciation rules frequently—five times in the last 15 years. The good news is that if the rules change after you acquire something, you don't change how you depreciate it. The bad news is that you will have to learn and use the new rules for any new property. So, you may end up tracking depreciation of different business assets—computers, buildings, or whatever—under several sets of rules. A tax pro can come in handy to keep the process straight and even compare different methods available to see which one produces the best results. Computer software (such as Turbotax for Business or Macintax) also can analyze tax depreciation and help you keep things straight.

---

2. Depreciation Categories

The tax code establishes depreciation categories for all assets and assigns each category a "useful life" (the minimum time period over which the cost of an asset can be deducted—for example, five years for a computer). In tax lingo, this is called the "recovery period." IRS Publication 534 lists the categories and the depreciation periods for different assets.

Most small business assets fit into one of the following four classes (but this is only a summary of the rules, which are much more technical):

- *3-Year Property:* Manufacturing equipment (plastics, metal fabrication, glass).
- *5-Year Property:* Cars, trucks, small airplanes, trailers, computers and peripherals, copiers, typewriters, calculators, manufacturing equipment (apparel), assets used in construction activity and equipment used in research and experimentation.

- *7-Year Property:* Office furniture, manufacturing equipment (except types included in 3- and 5-year categories above), fixtures, oil, gas and mining assets, agricultural structures and personal property that doesn't fit into any other specific category.

- *Real Estate (varying periods):* Business-use real estate is depreciated over 39 years using the straight-line method only (discussed below) if placed in service after May 31, 1993. Residential rental real estate is allowed a 27.5-year recovery period. Some types of land improvement costs (sidewalks, roads, drainage facilities, fences and landscaping) are depreciable over 20 years.

There are also classes of 10, 15 and 20 years, which might apply if your business is agricultural or rather unusual, like breeding horses or operating tug boats. See IRC § 168 and IRS Publication 534 for more information and a description of all asset classes.

3. Methods of Depreciation

Once you find the correct category for an asset, you must determine the depreciation method to use. You may or may not have a choice of method, depending on the type of asset. Depreciation methods fall into two general types, which accountants call:

- *straight-line,* and
- *accelerated.*

The tax code makes it a little more complicated by offering four principal methods of depreciating most business assets—one straight-line and three accelerated—all of which result in the same total amount of deductions in the end. An additional method, for farm equipment only, isn't covered here. (See IRS Publication 946.)

a. Straight-Line: The Slowest and Simplest Depreciation Method

The straight-line method allows the cost of an asset to be deducted as a depreciation expense in equal amounts every year, except for the first and last years. In those two years, you get only half of a year's deduction.

For instance, with a $10,000 computer, straight-line depreciation allows these deductions:

Year 1	*$1,000*
Years 2, 3, 4 & 5	*2,000 each year*
Year 6	*1,000*
TOTAL	*$10,000*

See also Section 4b, below.

b. MACRS: The Fastest Accelerated Depreciation Method

The present tax code depreciation system is known by the acronym MACRS (pronounced "makers" by tax folks), which stands for "modified accelerated cost recovery system." Technically, this term covers all of the accelerated depreciation methods, but also refers to just the most widely chosen method—MACRS 200% Declining Balance. This is the fastest—that is, most "accelerated"—way to write off assets. It allows greater deductions in early years of ownership of an asset than in later ones. For instance, using this method to depreciate a $10,000 computer produces $7,120 in depreciation deductions in the first three years, versus $5,000 with the straight-line method.

To find the yearly deduction amounts, refer to the IRS tables that show the deduction as a percentage of the cost for each year of ownership. MACRS tables are found in your annual Form 1040 instruction booklet, IRS Publication 946 and annual tax preparation guides.

c. 150% ACRS: A Slower Accelerated Depreciation Method

The 150% ACRS method is identical to MACRS (200% Declining Balance method), except that it produces smaller depreciation deductions in earlier years. Because the rate of depreciation is slower, not many folks go for this method. If you want to compare the results of the 200% and 150% accelerated methods, see the table below and IRS Publication 946.

d. Alternative ACRS Depreciation: For Motor Vehicles

"Alternative ACRS" is the mandatory method of accelerated depreciation of motor vehicles. It combines the straight-line and accelerated methods by allowing accelerated deductions in early years and switching to a straight-line method roughly halfway through the depreciation period. It isn't necessary to understand the mechanics here, since the IRS provides tables that show you what you need to know.

Should you lease? Because of these limits, it may take longer than your life expectancy to fully write off a Mercedes-Benz or other valuable asset. Section E, below, describes leasing versus buying business assets.

The fastest depreciation method may not be the best. Don't automatically conclude that the quicker you can take a deduction, the better. If your business has been around a while and is quite profitable, you are probably right. But most start-up businesses are not money-makers, so they don't benefit by using accelerated depreciation in their early years. For them, the straight-line method, with smaller deductions in their formative years, produce the best long-term tax benefit.

4. Mechanics of Depreciation

Whether you use a straight-line or accelerated depreciation method, you must ascertain a number of facts to know how to take your deductions.

a. Basis for Depreciation

In addition to knowing an asset's useful life, you must know its tax basis before you can claim a deduction for depreciation on it. Section A, above, tells you how to calculate your tax basis in a business asset.

DEPRECIATION LIMITS FOR VEHICLES

The tax code imposes absolute dollar maximums on depreciation deductions for each year that you own a car used for business—no matter how much it cost. For 1996, you are limited to depreciation deductions of:

1st year: $3,060
2rd year: $4,900
3rd year: $2,950
4th, and all subsequent years $1,775

These amounts are adjusted annually for cost of living changes, so they usually increase every year. (IRC § 280F.)

BASIS INCLUDES STATE AND LOCAL TAXES

Any state or local sales type taxes paid on assets are deductible along with the item itself. Sales taxes become part of the basis of the asset and can be depreciated over the life of the asset. A sales tax cannot be completely written off in the year the item was bought (unless it qualifies for IRC § 179 treatment). For instance, an 8% state sales tax on a truck bought for $10,000 ($800) must be added to its cost ($10,800) and written off over the period the truck is depreciated, usually five years.

b. First-Year Depreciation Rules

You may start depreciating an asset the year it is "placed in service" in your operation. This means that you must not only acquire the asset, but start using it as well, to claim a depreciation deduction.

But when during the year does the depreciation period begin? Generally, assets are treated in the tax code as if they were bought in the middle of the year—July 1—for depreciation purposes. This is called the "half-year convention." It means you get one-half year's depreciation deduction the first year, and your final deduction comes in the year following the last year of the asset's useful life. So, the last year of deductions for five-year property, such as a computer, is really the sixth year.

Example: In April 1995, Julie buys a copier to use at her boutique for $2,000. If Julie depreciates it over five years on a straight-line basis, her deduction for the first year is $200. (1/2 year x $2,000 x 1/5.) In each of the next four years she takes a $400 deduction, and takes the remaining $200 in the sixth year. (200 + 400 + 400 + 400+ 400 + 200 = $2,000.)

Unless you are using IRC § 179, don't load up on new assets at the end of the year. Unfortunately, another tax quirk can further reduce your first-year depreciation deduction. If you make more than 40% of all your asset purchases for the whole year in the last three months, you get only 1.5 months of depreciation on the last-acquired portion.

Example: Now suppose Julie also purchases $25,000 of new display cases—classified as "five-year" property—in May 1995. If she uses the straight-line method of depreciation, the tax write-off for 1995 is $200 for the copier and $2,500 for the cases. In November, Julie buys $20,000 of racks and shelving, which is also five-year property. Since Julie's last purchase is more than 40% of the total assets bought during the year, she can write off only $500 of it the first year. (1.5 months of 60 months of depreciation of the $20,000 cost of the racks and shelving.) But she can still write off $2,700 for the copier and display cases purchased in 1995.

c. How to Report Depreciation and IRC § 179 Deductions

Whether you use one of the depreciation methods, IRC § 179, or combine the two, you must show the deduction on IRS Form 4562, Depreciation and Amortization. Sole proprietors, partners, LLC members and S corporation shareholders file this form with their individual returns, and C corporations with their income tax returns. Form 4562 must be used if you are either:

- depreciating any assets acquired that year,
- depreciating certain types of assets (such as vehicles, computers, cellular phones and a few others named in the tax code) acquired in a previous year, or
- operating as a C corporation and are depreciating any assets.

A sample Form 4562 is shown below.

Form **4562**	**Depreciation and Amortization** (Including Information on Listed Property)	OMB No. 1545-0172 **1994**
Department of the Treasury Internal Revenue Service (T)	▶ See separate instructions. ▶ Attach this form to your return.	Attachment Sequence No. **67**

Name(s) shown on return: Susan J. Brown   Identifying number: 111-00-1111

Business or activity to which this form relates: Milady Fashions

Part I — Election To Expense Certain Tangible Property (Section 179) (Note: *If you have any "Listed Property," complete Part V before you complete Part I.*)

1	Maximum dollar limitation (If an enterprise zone business, see instructions.)	1	$17,500
2	Total cost of section 179 property placed in service during the tax year (see instructions)	2	7500
3	Threshold cost of section 179 property before reduction in limitation	3	$200,000
4	Reduction in limitation. Subtract line 3 from line 2. If zero or less, enter -0-	4	0
5	Dollar limitation for tax year. Subtract line 4 from line 1. If zero or less, enter -0-. (If married filing separately, see instructions.)	5	17,500

(a) Description of property	(b) Cost	(c) Elected cost
6 Adding machine	200	200

7	Listed property. Enter amount from line 26.	7	0
8	Total elected cost of section 179 property. Add amounts in column (c), lines 6 and 7	8	200
9	Tentative deduction. Enter the smaller of line 5 or line 8	9	200
10	Carryover of disallowed deduction from 1993 (see instructions)	10	0
11	Taxable income limitation. Enter the smaller of taxable income (not less than zero) or line 5 (see instructions)	11	17,500
12	Section 179 expense deduction. Add lines 9 and 10, but do not enter more than line 11	12	200
13	Carryover of disallowed deduction to 1995. Add lines 9 and 10, less line 12 ▶ 13		

Note: *Do not use Part II or Part III below for listed property (automobiles, certain other vehicles, cellular telephones, certain computers, or property used for entertainment, recreation, or amusement). Instead, use Part V for listed property.*

Part II — MACRS Depreciation For Assets Placed in Service ONLY During Your 1994 Tax Year (Do Not Include Listed Property)

(a) Classification of property	(b) Month and year placed in service	(c) Basis for depreciation (business/investment use only—see instructions)	(d) Recovery period	(e) Convention	(f) Method	(g) Depreciation deduction
Section A—General Depreciation System (GDS) (see instructions)						
14a 3-year property						
b 5-year property						
c 7-year property		800	7	HY	200 DB	114
d 10-year property						
e 15-year property						
f 20-year property						
g Residential rental property			27.5 yrs.	MM	S/L	
			27.5 yrs.	MM	S/L	
h Nonresidential real property			39 yrs.	MM	S/L	
				MM	S/L	
Section B—Alternative Depreciation System (ADS) (see instructions)						
15a Class life					S/L	
b 12-year			12 yrs.		S/L	
c 40-year			40 yrs.	MM	S/L	

Part III — Other Depreciation (Do Not Include Listed Property)

16	GDS and ADS deductions for assets placed in service in tax years beginning before 1994 (see instructions)	16	
17	Property subject to section 168(f)(1) election (see instructions)	17	
18	ACRS and other depreciation (see instructions)	18	1,117

Part IV — Summary

19	Listed property. Enter amount from line 25.	19	1300
20	**Total.** Add deductions on line 12, lines 14 and 15 in column (g), and lines 16 through 19. Enter here and on the appropriate lines of your return. (Partnerships and S corporations—see instructions)	20	2,731
21	For assets shown above and placed in service during the current year, enter the portion of the basis attributable to section 263A costs (see instructions) 21		

For Paperwork Reduction Act Notice, see page 1 of the separate instructions.   Cat. No. 12906N   Form **4562** (1994)

Form 4562 (1994)   Page **2**

Part V — Listed Property—Automobiles, Certain Other Vehicles, Cellular Telephones, Certain Computers, and Property Used for Entertainment, Recreation, or Amusement

For any vehicle for which you are using the standard mileage rate or deducting lease expense, complete only 22a, 22b, columns (a) through (c) of Section A, all of Section B, and Section C if applicable.

Section A—Depreciation and Other Information (Caution: *See instructions for limitations for automobiles.*)

22a Do you have evidence to support the business/investment use claimed? ☒ Yes ☐ No 22b If "Yes," is the evidence written? ☒ Yes ☐ No

(a) Type of property (list vehicles first)	(b) Date placed in service	(c) Business/ investment use percentage	(d) Cost or other basis	(e) Basis for depreciation (business/investment use only)	(f) Recovery period	(g) Method/ Convention	(h) Depreciation deduction	(i) Elected section 179 cost
23 Property used more than 50% in a qualified business use (see instructions):								
USA 280 Van	3/20/94	75 %	8,667	6,500	5 yrs.	200DB/HY	1300	0
		%						
		%						
24 Property used 50% or less in a qualified business use (see instructions):								
		%			S/L –			
		%			S/L –			
		%			S/L –			

25 Add amounts in column (h). Enter the total here and on line 19, page 1 . . . . . **25** 1300

26 Add amounts in column (i). Enter the total here and on line 7, page 1 . . . . **26** 0

Section B—Information on Use of Vehicles—*If you deduct expenses for vehicles:*

- *Always complete this section for vehicles used by a sole proprietor, partner, or other "more than 5% owner," or related person.*
- *If you provided vehicles to your employees, first answer the questions in Section C to see if you meet an exception to completing this section for those vehicles.*

		(a) Vehicle 1	(b) Vehicle 2	(c) Vehicle 3	(d) Vehicle 4	(e) Vehicle 5	(f) Vehicle 6
27	Total business/investment miles driven during the year (DO NOT include commuting miles)	7,500					
28	Total commuting miles driven during the year	2,025					
29	Total other personal (noncommuting) miles driven	475					
30	Total miles driven during the year. Add lines 27 through 29	10,000					

		Yes	No	Yes	No	Yes	No	Yes	No	Yes	No	Yes	No
31	Was the vehicle available for personal use during off-duty hours?	✓											
32	Was the vehicle used primarily by a more than 5% owner or related person?	✓											
33	Is another vehicle available for personal use?	✓											

Section C—Questions for Employers Who Provide Vehicles for Use by Their Employees

Answer these questions to determine if you meet an exception to completing Section B. Note: Section B must always be completed for vehicles used by sole proprietors, partners, or other more than 5% owners or related persons.

		Yes	No
34	Do you maintain a written policy statement that prohibits all personal use of vehicles, including commuting, by your employees?		
35	Do you maintain a written policy statement that prohibits personal use of vehicles, except commuting, by your employees? (See instructions for vehicles used by corporate officers, directors, or 1% or more owners.)		
36	Do you treat all use of vehicles by employees as personal use?		
37	Do you provide more than five vehicles to your employees and retain the information received from your employees concerning the use of the vehicles?		
38	Do you meet the requirements concerning qualified automobile demonstration use (see instructions)? . .		

Note: *If your answer to 34, 35, 36, 37, or 38 is "Yes," you need not complete Section B for the covered vehicles.*

Part VI — Amortization

(a) Description of costs	(b) Date amortization begins	(c) Amortizable amount	(d) Code section	(e) Amortization period or percentage	(f) Amortization for this year
39 Amortization of costs that begins during your 1994 tax year:					

40 Amortization of costs that began before 1994 . . . . **40**

41 **Total.** Enter here and on "Other Deductions" or "Other Expenses" line of your return . . . **41**

♻ *Printed on recycled paper*

	DEPRECIATION WORKSHEET									
Description of Property	Date Placed in Service	Cost or Other Basis	Business/ Investment Use %	Section 179 Deduction	Depreciation Prior Years	Basis for Depreciation	Method/ Convention	Recovery Period	Rate or Table %	Depreciation Deduction
COMPUTER	3/31/95	3,200	100%	3,200	∅	∅	200DB/MY	5	20%	∅
CELLULAR PHONE	6/26/95	300	40%	∅	∅	120	SL/MY	5	10%	12
CHEVY PICK-UP	11/1/92	10,500	20%	0	525	2,100	SL/MQ	5	20%	420
TOTAL				3,200						432

Show the IRS how you figure depreciation. It is wise to attach a separate "depreciation schedule" or worksheet to your tax return whenever claiming depreciation or IRC § 179 deductions. This shows an IRS examiner how the deduction was calculated. If the schedule looks okay, it may ward off a further IRS inquiry or audit. It indicates that you are careful and aware of the tax rules on depreciation. Most good computer software tax preparation programs will make a depreciation schedule for you.

D. Depreciating Common Business Assets

These days, hardly any small business is without a computer, and most also need vehicles. Here are some special rules for depreciating these items, and a few other common business assets.

1. Business Vehicles

The cost of operating and owning a car used in business is deductible, as I am sure you know. (See Chapter 1, Business Income and Tax-Deductible

Expenses, for details on how to claim operating expense deductions on cars used for business.)

If your car is used *exclusively* for business, the entire costs of a car are deductible, including depreciation. The tax code imposes a dollar ceiling on the amount of depreciation you may claim for business use of a car. For cars placed in service in 1995, the limits are $3,060 for the first year, $4,900 for the second year, $2,950 for the third year and $1,775 for every year thereafter.

If vehicle business use is less than 100%, the maximum depreciation limits must be reduced to reflect the business-use percentage. (But, as shown in Chapter 1, you may not be able to claim auto depreciation deductions in all cases.)

What happens when you no longer want your business vehicle? If you sell the vehicle, the difference between its tax basis and the sale price is either a taxable gain or loss for the business. (But if the car was used for both business and pleasure, you can't take more than the allocable business portion as a gain or loss. See Chapter 4 for information on taking losses for tax purposes.) As a practical matter, because of the stingy tax code limits on depreciation deductions, it is more often than not a loss. However, the tax rule is different if you trade in your car for another business-used one. In this case your tax basis in the new car is increased by the remaining basis of the old one. So there isn't any gain or loss to report with a trade-in.

MAJOR LEAGUE LOOPHOLE FOR SPORT UTILITY VEHICLES (SUVS) & TRUCKS

Buying a truck or heavy sport utility vehicles (gross vehicle weight when loaded of over 6,000 pounds) lets you get around the business vehicle deduction limitations discussed above. Road yachts such as Chevy Suburbans, Toyota Land Cruisers and Range Rovers qualify. If your business vehicle falls into this category and costs over $30,000, you may fully write it off in six years. If you start using the SUV in the first nine months of the year, you may take 20% of the cost as depreciation (assuming business use is 100%) that year, followed by 32% in year two, then 19.2%, 11.52%, 11.52% and 5.76% in the last year. If you don't get the vehicle until the last three months of the year, however, you can take only a 5% deduction in the first year.

Three more tax benefits:

1. SUVs are exempt from the 10% luxury tax on vehicles over $32,000

2. IRC 179 allows a hefty $17,500 first year write-off if you elect it; and

3. SUVs are exempt from the IRS lease table income "add-backs." (See Section E, below.)

Example: Benecia buys an SUV and uses it 60% of the time for her property management company. She also uses the vehicle for weekend family camping trips to out-of-the way places where the four-wheel drive comes in handy. Benecia has the option of deducting $17,500 this year under IRC 179, and then writing off the balance of $6,500 over six years ($40,000 x 60% business use: $24,000 - $17,500: $6,500). Alternatively, if she bought and started using the SUV before the last quarter of the year, Benecia could claim a deduction of $4,800 ($40,000 x 60% x 20%: $4,800). Otherwise, under regular depreciation rules it would take Benecia about 14 years to fully depreciate the same vehicle.

2. Home Computers Used for Work

Many full- and part-time entrepreneurs use computers at home. The tax code allows you to deduct the costs of business-used computers no matter where they are kept. Section B, above, discusses how to get a fast write-off using IRC § 179.

If you decide instead to depreciate a computer used at home, here's how to proceed. The tax code says computers have a five-year depreciable life, and the fastest way to depreciate one is by using the MACRS 200% Declining Balance method (explained above in Section C3).

Example 1: Sue is a hospital nurse and has a part-time medical billing service in her home. Sue bought, and started using, a computer for her business in June for $5,000. She acquired no other assets that year. Computers have a useful life of five years under the tax code. Under the fastest depreciation method allowed, Sue deducts the computer's cost as follows: 20% in the first year ($1,000), 32% in the second year ($1,600), 19.2% in the third year ($960), 11.52% in the fourth and fifth years ($576 each year) and 5.76% in the sixth and last year ($288).

If Sue had chosen straight-line instead of accelerated depreciation, she would have a 10% deduction ($500) in the first and sixth years, and 20% ($1,000) depreciation deductions in years two, three and four.

Example 2: Sue uses the computer 20% of the time for personal things, so she must reduce the original cost basis by 20% (from $5,000 to $4,000), before taking depreciation deductions. This means an $800 deduction in year one, instead of $1,000, and so on.

If you use your computer for personal as well as business purposes, keep a diary or log. Record the dates, times and reason the computer was used, to distinguish the two uses in case an IRS auditor comes calling.

3. Other Items—Stereo, Camcorders, Etc.

Things you might not think of as tax-deductible can be, under the right circumstances. For example, I have a great stereo system in my home office, and if the volume is cranked up enough, it sounds nice throughout the rest of the house, too. My clients and I enjoy the background music while we ponder their tax problems. It sounds even sweeter knowing that I tax-deducted the entire cost. My home office also contains two aquariums, oriental rugs and antiques. All these are 100% tax-deductible business items.

Example: Herb owns and operates "Olde Tyme Quilts" to sell quilts that he makes or takes on consignment from other quiltmakers. To improve his skills, he buys and uses a VCR to watch tapes on quilt-making. Later Herb buys a camcorder to make tapes of quilt designs at craft shows, a video catalog of his stock, and him doing a quilt-making demonstration. These items are all depreciable or deductible under IRC § 179. But if he also uses the VCR and camcorder for pleasure, Herb is required to apportion between business and personal use.

You might have to defend asset purchases at an audit. You are on the honor system when it comes to claiming some business asset purchases—no one from the IRS is watching to see how you really use your camcorder. But if the IRS finds expenditures that are questionable, be ready to prove how these items were used for business. Otherwise, an auditor can disallow them as nondeductible personal expenses.

E. Leasing Instead of Buying Assets

To conserve cash, many businesses decide to lease equipment or autos instead of buying them. Lease payments are deductible as current business expenses, like electricity or office supplies. (See Chapter 1, Business Income and Tax-Deductible Expenses.) However, there are some special tax code rules for leasing vehicles.

1. Vehicles

Both tax and non-tax considerations determine whether its best to buy or lease a vehicle used for business. Here are some tax angles that apply to any form of enterprise, from sole proprietor to C corporation.

a. Keeping Track of Personal Use

If you, like most small business people, use your car both for business and personal transport, the tax code requires records tracking each use. This is true whether you lease or buy. (See Section D, above.)

b. Tax Rules That Favor Leasing

The tax advantage of leasing starts when your business usage is 50% or more and car cost exceeds $15,500. If you buy a more expensive car, your tax write-off period will necessarily extend beyond five years. For instance, it might take 20 years to fully depreciate a $60,000 Lexus. No one I know keeps a car that long. In effect, leasing gets around the stingy depreciation deduction limits.

The tax code, in its oblique fashion, favors leasing over buying expensive cars, through its leasing "inclusion" tables. You are required to include extra income, as stated on the table, on your tax return if you lease a business-used car costing more than $15,500. This is true even when the car is used 100% for business with no personal driving at all. This may sound unfair, but the imputed lease income is so small it is not really a problem. The IRS tables are adjusted annually for cost of living changes. Many computer tax programs can make the lease inclusion calculations for you.

Example: Phil, an independent sales representative for a furniture manufacturer, leases a $40,000 BMW in 1994. Assuming 100% business use, the IRS lease table directs Phil to report only $175 of extra income for 1994 and $384 for 1995. Phil can deduct his lease payments in full as a business expense as long as the car is 100% used for business. If Phil uses the car 80% of the time for business calls, he would discount the lease "inclusion amount" by 20%, meaning he would report only $307 (80% x $384) as additional income in 1995. Even if he were in the highest tax bracket, Phil's additional income tax would be less than $130 in 1995.

To further complicate the matter, in weighing a lease vs. a purchase, you must also consider the tax benefits of being able to deduct the interest on a business-used car loan. For instance, if you pay $2,000 in interest over a year for a car driven 80% for business, $1,600 is deductible off your business income. The other $400 is nondeductible personal interest.

Car leasing shouldn't be just a tax decision. The tax benefits of buying versus leasing may be only the tail of the dog. First, do a purely economic analysis—how much are the lease payments vs. financing costs, how much will the car cost to operate, and so on. There is no such thing as a "standard" lease; some have no down payments and others require more money down than if you had financed a purchase. All leases penalize drivers who put a lot of miles on their cars. Leases are difficult to get out of before the end of the lease term, without substantial penalties.

Don't rely on tax guidance from a car salesperson—even one who knows the right answer may not tell you. Car dealers make higher commissions by leasing a car than by selling it, and a dealer can disguise a higher sales price in a complex lease agreement. So, ask your tax pro or find a computer program that analyzes car lease tax benefits.

2. C Corporations

A business doesn't have to own all of its operating assets. Leasing personally owned property—a building, vehicle or equipment—to your C corporation business may provide a tax savings. Similarly, a leased asset may be owned by another corporation, a partnership or a family business in which you have an ownership interest. (As discussed in Chapter 12, Family Businesses, such arrangements can result in "income shifting"—transferring income to people in lower tax brackets to reduce overall taxes for the family unit.) Apart from taxes, business people—especially in endeavors where lawsuits are common—don't want their corporation to own a lot of assets. Leasing instead of owning is one way to insulate assets from potential creditors.

To avoid problems with the IRS, lease terms between an individual and his corporation must be fair to both sides. Lease payments are deductible expenses to the corporation, while lease income is taxable to the asset's owner, who in turn deducts costs of ownership—mortgage interest, maintenance, repairs and depreciation.

Example: Sam bought a store building in June 1994 for $100,000. The land has a fair market value of $20,000, and the structure $80,000. Sam does some minor repairs and leases it to Sam Smith, Inc. in 1995 for $16,000 per year. His expenses of ownership are $15,000 and he is entitled to a $2,052 depreciation deduction in 1995 (the second year's write-off of the building allowed in the tax code). Tax result: Sam gets $1,000 left over after expenses ($16,000 - $15,000), which is offset by his $2,052 depreciation deduction. He has a tax loss of $1,052 to "shelter" his other earned income in 1995, such as his salary from Sam Smith, Inc.

RESOURCES

IRS Publication 946, *How to Begin Depreciating Your Property*

IRS Publication 534, *Depreciation*

IRS Publication 917, *Business Use of a Car*

Master Tax Guide (Commerce Clearing House). This manual contains a good explanation of the depreciation process, covered in more detail than in this chapter. Although it's intended for tax professionals, it's more readable than the IRS materials.

Small-Time Operator, by Bernard Kamoroff (Bell Springs). This CPA-written self-help book covers the fundamentals of depreciating business assets and keeping depreciation records. ■

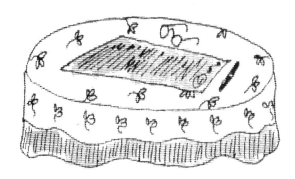

CHAPTER 3

Recordkeeping and Accounting

"The income tax has made more liars out of the American people than golf has."

— **Will Rogers**

Most ventures are started by enthusiastic people with ambition and drive. Whether they are hoping to build the next Fortune 500 company or simply to supplement their day job, it's usually what the business will buy, sell, make or fix that interests them most. They aren't intrigued by the back office details of how to run the business. You are not alone if you hate paperwork.

The good news is that the IRS does not require business records to be kept in any particular form, as long as they are reliable and paint an accurate picture of income and expenses. Since no two enterprises are alike, no two recordkeeping systems are exactly alike. Always keep in mind that the IRS has a legal right to audit your tax returns and see the records used to prepare them.

This chapter explains the maximum amount of record keeping you need to do to stay out of trouble with the IRS and ways to set up a good recordkeeping system and keep it current. It also touches on basic accounting principles you need to familiarize yourself with.

RECORDKEEPING IN A NUTSHELL

1. The IRS doesn't prescribe any particular format for keeping your business's records, as long as they clearly reflect your income and expenses.

2. You can choose a manual or computerized recordkeeping system, but a computer will save you time and be more accurate in the long run.

3. Small businesses are usually required to keep records and report business income on a calendar-year basis.

A. Why You Need a Good Bookkeeping System

Some fledging entrepreneurs think that if there is money in their business checking account at the end of the month, they must be making a profit. But only if you keep accurate records will you really know if your business is making or losing money. A recordkeeping system is also crucial to the preparation of your federal and state income tax returns.

Not surprisingly, a commandment of the tax code is thou shalt keep "records appropriate to your trade or business." (IRC § 6001.) The tax code doesn't require most records to be kept in any particular form, but they do have to be accurate. (Reg. 31.6001-1(a).)

Records can also serve as an early warning system to let you know whether changes need to be made in your operation. Indeed, operating without good records is like flying a small plane in dense fog with no instruments. I can almost hear you saying, "I think I'll skip this chapter; I hate bookkeeping. After all, if my business takes in enough money, all these paperwork matters will resolve themselves. If they don't, I'll hire someone to clean them up."

Take recordkeeping seriously. If you only get one thing out of this book, go away knowing that ignoring recordkeeping is just plain wrong. Take it from someone who has seen it—if the IRS audits and finds insufficient records or significant mistakes, it can force you out of business and wipe out your life savings as well.

Recordkeeping must become part of your everyday business routine, just like opening your doors each morning. Believe me, I am *not* an accountant, and I hate paperwork as much as any of you. I also hate shaving every morning, keeping fat out of my diet and carrying out the garbage in the rain, but these tasks never seem to go away. As we shall see, though, recordkeeping doesn't need to be drudgery, and you don't need to spend godawful amounts of time tracking every last penny.

RANDOM BUSINESS RECORD INSPECTIONS

You may be audited after written notice from the IRS, but there are no "IRS business record inspectors" roaming around spot-checking to see that records are being kept. In many states, however, employment or sales tax auditors do show up unannounced and demand to see records. So, just like the Boy Scouts, "be prepared."

B. Should You Hire a Bookkeeper?

When it comes to keeping small business records there are only two good choices: learn to do it yourself, or hire someone who truly knows how to do it. Don't make the mistake of doing this job badly or hiring the wrong person to do it for you.

Maybe you can't afford someone to keep records when starting off, but once you are solid, consider bookkeeping help. A lot of folks actually like doing other people's books! And someone else keeping records leaves you with time to utilize your business talents to the fullest.

Typically, part-time bookkeepers charge $10 to $25 per hour and can take care of your needs for as little as $50 to $100 a month. Remember, this is a tax-deductible expense, so Uncle Sam is paying part of the bookkeeper's salary.

Don't just hire the first person who comes along. Check references carefully and learn enough about your records so that you can periodically check to see that things are done right. The IRS holds *you* responsible for your bookkeeper's actions.

Let me tell you one sad but true story to make this point. Barney owned an auto body shop. He had no patience for bookkeeping, so he hired Lorraine, a prim and proper type, who came in once a week to do his books, pay the bills and fill out tax reports. She was a faithful worker and so Barney was upset when Lorraine suddenly quit after two years. Shortly thereafter an IRS collector came calling about unfiled and unpaid payroll taxes for Barney's employees. Only then did Barney discover that sweet Lorraine had embezzled $38,000, including all payroll taxes Barney owed over the last 18 months. Barney had to go into his savings for the unpaid taxes—plus penalties—or face padlocking of his body shop by the IRS.

Be safe; consult a tax pro. If you tackle the books yourself, have a tax pro review your system to make sure it is registering all necessary data. This costs a few dollars up front, but should pay dividends when it comes time for filing tax returns. And the tax pro's fees are deductible expenses.

C. Manual or Computer System?

There are two ways to keep your records: manually—the good old-fashioned way that has been around for thousands of years; and with a computer—the new-fangled, better way. The IRS doesn't care which one you use, just as long as the system accurately reflect your business's transactions. Of course, if you don't have any system, or just throw papers in a shoebox and forget them, the IRS will be delighted. You are an audit waiting to happen.

Whether you use a computer or pencil, the basics of a bookkeeping system are the same. You must track *transactions* to show your enterprise's financial activities. *Accounts* are where the transactions are noted in your records; they are simply categories in which the day-to-day dealings are written.

A microbusiness, such as a home-based consultant, might get by with a check register, lined ledger paper and an accordion file for paid bills. Contrary to how a lot of folks do it, receipts should be organized by category—rent, entertainment, travel, equipment, and so on—and not by month. This way you don't have to waste time sorting through the months, but can go directly to totaling up the different types of expenses at the end of the year for tax preparation. Every time you spend money in the business (or once a week or month), go through the receipts and write down on your ledger paper the amount, date, and a brief description of the business purpose of the transaction (office rent, new stapler, gas, etc.), whom you paid (Chevron, Kinko's). This manual system works fine for many small enterprises and requires an outlay of only $10 to $20 at an office supply store. Some more details on how to keep a good manual system follow below.

Computers accomplish the same thing as manual systems; they simply automate this whole process and save you a time if your business has a fair number of transactions over the year. Just how this is done is shown below.

1. Manual System

If you have enough initiative to go into business, you should be able to learn enough about recordkeeping in a few hours to start off on the right foot.

Adequate pads of records are kept by hand using widely available pads of ledger sheets for listing income and expense items. This columnar paper (usually colored light green like those eyeshades the money counters wear) is found in stationery and office supply stores.

On these ledger sheets you create a "chart of accounts" to list your expenses. This chart of ac-

counts is also called an "expense journal" by accountants.

As the example below illustrates, a *chart of accounts,* lists your business's different types of expenditures—such as cash, credit card and check payments. Next to the type of expenditure is the date on which it was paid. Going across the top of the paper are columns for listing the amounts of each type of expenditure. Each column covers one category, such as "rent," "supplies" or "utilities." (Ideally, every item of expense listed should be taken from an invoice, receipt, cash voucher, check register or other document showing it was incurred by the business.)

After each item of expense (or total of expenses in each category) is entered in its proper column, all of the columns are totaled. Typically, totals are run monthly and then the 12 months are totalled at the end of the year.

Good practice requires adding up your ledger sheets at least once a month. But you'll have better records if you do it more often—daily or weekly, when everything is fresh in your mind and before data is misplaced.

Don't throw away your ledger sheets. Your ledger sheets (and your receipts for expenses and canceled checks) should be kept at least three years after you file your tax return to satisfy a potential IRS auditor. Keep them for as long as you own your business. And, if you ever want to sell your business, a prospective buyer may want to see the ledger sheets to verify the financial performance of your business.

SAMPLE CHART OF EXPENSE ACCOUNTS

Ck	Cash	Cred	Date	Transaction	Advert	Util	Supplies	Rent
		VISA	4/1	DAILY NEWS	48.00			
122			4/15	PROP. MGMT. SERV.				782.75
	$		4/21	OFFICE WORLD			62.44	
123			4/30	CITY ELECTRIC		91.50		
124			4/30	KFOO RADIO	95.00			
APRIL 19XX		TOTALS			143.00	91.50	62.44	782.75

2. Computerized System

Recordkeeping on a computer works on the same principles as the manual system, but the computer automates the process. A simple software program like Quicken (published by Intuit) eliminates the need for a handwritten set of books. You can print out reports whenever you need them. It is a good idea to keep written records, too, until you are fully confident in your computer skills and have backed up your data on diskettes. This inexpensive program ($50 or less) works on both IBM PCs with DOS or Windows and Macintoshes. It is fine for most small service businesses, which don't have to keep inventory records. I have used Quicken for years in my law practice. If you know how to keep a checkbook register, you can use Quicken.

An example of a Quicken account is shown on the next page; you can see it looks exactly like your checkbook register—only more legible. Each transaction, such as a business expense or an item of income, is typed in as either a check from or deposit to your checking account. (You can also record cash and credit card expenses in Quicken.)

Then assign a number or category name to each transaction and type that in too. For instance, label "201" as office rent, or simply type the word "rent" to tell the computer how to group all rent payments in your records. Category 202 could be supplies,

and so on. You might keep track of all advertising costs under category 301, or break it into subcategories such as 302 for "ads—yellow pages," 303 for "ads—newspaper." The computer recognizes and groups the entries under each numbered or named category you create. This makes it easy to keep an up-to-date chart of accounts, which is the heart of your business bookkeeping.

QUICKEN SAMPLE 1/1/95 THROUGH 5/1/95

Category Description	
Income/Expense	
Income	
Business Acct.	2,000.00
Total Income	2,000.00
Expenses	
Advertising	143.00
Rent	782.75
Supplies	62.44
Utilities	91.50
Total Expenses	1,079.69
TOTAL INCOME/EXPENSE	920.31

QUICKEN SAMPLE						
DATE	NUM		TRANSACTION	PAYMENT	C	DEPOSIT	BALANCE
4/1/95	DEP		Opening Balance			2,000.00	2,000.00
	memo:						
	cat:	Business Act.					
4/1/95			Daily News	48.00			1,952.00
	memo:	VISA					
	cat:	Advertising					
4/15/95	122		Prop Mgt Services	782.75			1,169.25
	memo:	CASH					
	cat:	Rent					
4/21/95			Office World	62.44			1,106.81
	memo:	CASH					
	cat:	Supplies					
4/30/95	123		City Electric	91.50			1,015.31
	memo:						
	cat:	Utilities					
4/30/95	124		KFOO Radio	95.00			920.31
	memo:						
	cat:	Advertising					

Take it from someone who did not grow up in the computer age—these programs are easy to use, even if you type like a snail. An hour should get you up and running, no kidding. I no longer make math errors that used to drive me mad when I kept books by hand.

Just avoiding computation mistakes isn't the best reason to use a computer program to keep track of expenses—the categorization feature is! It eliminates the annual chore of going through (or paying someone to organize) a jumble of paper. A computerized system allows you to quickly see your income and expenses—by category—at any time during the year. Your business's "profit & loss" figures are only a keystroke or two away, so you can whip out a financial statement for a bank or creditor at any time. (See example on previous page.)

With the push of a button, you'll also have at least 90% of the data needed to prepare your business's tax schedule or return. If you do your own tax preparing, this feature makes it infinitely easier for you. Quicken, for instance, is compatible with popular tax preparation programs like TurboTax for Business (Windows and DOS) and MacIntax (Macintosh). (These two excellent computer programs published by Intuit will prepare any typed business tax return: sole proprietor, C or S corporations, partnerships or limited liability. A version of this book is included in the CD-ROM versions of this software.) You can move your business's financial data from Quicken into many tax return programs, without having to reenter any figures by hand. These programs can also keep track of your personal finances too.

Simple programs like Quicken are not adequate for some small businesses, especially those with an inventory. QuickBooks (also published by Intuit) handles more complex small business bookkeeping tasks. Other programs, such as Peachtree Accounting, also do the job. They sell in discount stores in the $100 range.

A tiny sideline business probably doesn't justify purchasing a computer and learning how to use it, but if you are serious, then you should come into the 1990s. Not only is a computer a nearly foolproof bookkeeping tool, it can keep track of your billing and invoices much better than any manual system. At the end of the year it takes minutes instead of hours to produce data to prepare a tax return. Don't take my word for it; talk to fellow businesspeople about their computers and programs that they use.

Example: Jack Johnson is a medical technology consultant who is paid by only one or two clients through the year. So, like many independent business people, keeping track of Jack's income is no problem. To ply his trade, Jack maintains an office, and occasionally hires support staff. He travels in the U.S. and abroad, drives his car for business, pays insurance and so on. Over the course of a year, he incurs hundreds of expenses of many different types. So, Jack needs a good expense recordkeeping system. Jack keeps a business check register separate from his personal account. He writes business checks for most expenses and uses a business-only credit card and pays the balance from his business account. Jack is advised to convert his business to a computerized check register system such as Quicken.

D. What Kinds of Records to Keep

Business records can be divided into three categories: *income*, *expenses* and *capital expenditures*. Income and expenses are pretty much self-explanatory, but "capital expenditures" may be something new for you. We'll go over each in order.

1. Income Records

Your operation may take in money from one or many sources, depending on what line of work you are in. Most of what you receive are taxable receipts—also called "gross" income or receipts—for goods or services sold. Your records should account for all gross income and also show the *source* of each item—for instance, "retail sales" or "services." This added step is necessary because money you put into your business's bank account may not always be taxable income—for example, a loan to the business from a relative.

There are several ways to track income. For instance, retail stores typically use cash registers that produce tapes or printouts of sales. Some businesses keep track of income from bank deposit records, which can lead to problems. If you do it this way, keep copies of deposit slips listing the monies put into your business bank account, as well as the bank statements showing the deposits. Deposit slips indicate the form of items received—cash, checks, credit card payments—which is not always reflected on the bank statements.

COMMON SENSE TIPS ON KEEPING BUSINESS RECORDS

File paid bills, canceled checks and other business documents in an orderly fashion and keep them in a safe place. Some people use a bunch of manila folders or an accordion file labeled "car," "utilities," "entertainment" and so on. Stuff receipts in the proper categories throughout the year and total them up at tax time. Attach the adding machine tape to the outside of each. If this works, good for you. You aren't required to keep records in a bound "set of books."

A perfectly adequate recordkeeping system for a small business might include some or all of the following items:

- Check register—preferably separate from your personal account

- Daily summary of receipts of gross income—totalled daily, weekly or monthly

- Monthly summary of receipts

- Disbursements record (check register or journal) showing purchases and payments of bills

- Asset listing (equipment used in business), and

- Employee compensation record.

Keep track of where your money comes from. Make notes explaining the origin of all money put into your business and personal bank accounts. Write down the source of the deposit on the slip or in your checkbook. If you can't adequately explain a bank deposit, an IRS auditor will call it "income." When the IRS conducts an audit, they usually ask for bank statements, deposit slips and cancelled checks.

If you don't furnish copies to the IRS, they can get them from your bank—whether you agree or not. If bank deposits are greater than your reported income, and you can't show why, the auditor will assume the difference was unreported income—and assess tax, interest and penalties. There may be a perfectly good explanation of why an item was not taxable income. For instance, say you transferred $10,000 from your personal bank account into your business bank account to buy inventory. This is not taxable income. Likewise, you may have sold a personal item or put inherited money in your business. So, keep notes.

If you had income from selling your services, you may get Form 1099s from the payors showing how much you received. Make sure you include this 1099 income on your tax return—the IRS has these forms and can easily check this. The IRS computer routinely matches Form 1099 as well as W-2 income data to tax returns. If the 1099 is wrong, make sure you get the issuer to send a corrected form to you and the IRS.

Example: Dr. No was snagged by the IRS on a computer check of 1099-form payments to him. He had claimed less gross income than Medicare alone reported to the IRS they paid him—not even taking into account his other patients! (How Dr. No thought he could get away with this is beyond me.) This was costly for the doctor; when he was audited, heavy penalties and interest were added to his tax bill. He could have also been (but lucky for him, wasn't) charged criminally with tax evasion.

2. Expense Records

To make money in your business, undoubtedly you will have to spend money. The good news is that most "ordinary and necessary" business expenditures are deductible against your gross receipts each year. (This is discussed in detail in Chapter 1.) And most asset purchases are deductible over several years and require special recordkeeping treatment. (See Chapter 2, Writing Off Long-Term Business Assets.)

Recording expenses is only part of the job. You also need to keep some proof the expenditures were made—such as receipts, invoices, credit charge slips, canceled checks or lease agreements. An easy way to do this is to put paid bills and invoices into accordion folders or envelopes according to expense category ("supplies," "travel" and so on).

Canceled checks and paid receipts are the standard ways to verify business expenses. The IRS now also accepts statements from financial institutions showing check clearing or electronic funds transfers, without the actual canceled checks or charge slips. This rule covers credit card statements and banks that do not return canceled checks. To satisfy an IRS auditor, the financial institution's statement must show the date, name of the payee and amount of expense. However, you may have to order copies of the checks from the bank in the event that the auditor is not satisfied with the statement for some reason. (My advice is to keep your original credit card slips too, especially for travel and entertainment expenses. See "Business Entertainment, Meals and Travel Records," below.)

Bear in mind that proof of payment by itself does not establish that you are entitled to a business expense deduction. If audited, you also need to show how the expense was related to the business. Many items (rent, advertising) are pretty much self-explanatory. For others that might not look business-related to the IRS (travel, entertainment), you should make notes at the time of the expense—in your diary, or on the receipt—to explain the business purpose. (See "Business Entertainment, Meals and Travel Records," below.)

BUSINESS ENTERTAINMENT, MEALS AND TRAVEL RECORDS

With certain expenses, the tax code requires more stringent recordkeeping. Primarily, these are business expenses for travel, meals and entertainment. (IRC § 274.)

For each such expense you must document five elements:

1. Date
2. Amount
3. Place
4. Business purpose, and
5. Business relationship.

Get in the habit of making notes to cover these five items on the back of receipts and on your business diary or calendar. For example, write on your calendar or in your appointment book something like "Lunch with Bill Jones, client, to discuss new advertising campaign. Ritz Restaurant, $60 with tip." If you charged it on your American Express card, write "Bill Jones" and note the type of business discussed ("television advertising on Channel 5") on the back of the charge slip, and put it with your other business receipts.

---

3. Asset Records

Whenever an expenditure provides a benefit beyond the year you make it—such as for a copy machine, building, car or office furniture—the item must be categorized as a business "asset."

Assets must be tracked separately from other business expenses by your record system. Accountants call these records the "fixed asset schedule" or "asset log." You don't have to know the terminology, just keep a separate file for each asset or category of assets your business acquires. Show the date of purchase and the type of asset—computer, truck, machinery and so on. And unless it is obvious, write a short explanation of how the asset is used in the business.

Assets must be tax-deducted in a different manner than everyday operating expenses like rent or telephone bills. Generally, you can't deduct the whole cost in the year of purchase; instead, you must take "depreciation" or "amortization" deductions over several years. There is one important exception to this rule; up to $17,500 of assets may be written off in the year of purchase under a special tax code provision, IRC § 179. (See Chapter 2, Writing Off Long-Term Business Assets, for details.)

a. Standard Records to Keep

If you have business assets, keep records showing:

1. A description of the asset, the date acquired and how you acquired it, usually by purchasing it. Typically, all this information is shown on an invoice or receipt from the seller. It is important to note the kind of asset acquired because the tax code has different rules for different categories of assets. For instance, office furniture is deductible over seven years, but computers take five. (These categories are discussed in Chapter 2, Writing Off Long-Term Business Assets.)

2. When you started using the asset—the date it was "placed in service." Ordinarily you start using an asset as soon as you acquire it, but not always, so note it in your asset records.

3. Your tax basis in the asset. Usually, this means what you paid for it, including sales tax and delivery. But the basis could be larger if you spent money on improvements or modifications—such as a larger hard drive added to a computer. (See Chapter 2 for a discussion of determining the basis of assets.) And there may be a reduction to the basis. For instance, depreciation deductions may have been taken on your prior years' tax returns, if you used the equipment in another venture.

4. The sales price of the asset when you dispose of it or, if it becomes worthless or obsolete, the date you discarded it.

5. Any costs of selling the asset—for instance, a newspaper ad for your old computer.

Either keep track of assets manually, using ledger sheets or asset log books sold in stationery and office supply stores, or with a computer program such as QuickBooks, discussed above.

b. Special Records for Listed or Mixed-Use Property

Listed or *mixed-use* property are tax terms for certain assets used in your business. This category was created for assets that Congress believed have a high potential for personal use. If you use listed property strictly for business and keep it on the premises, then this recordkeeping rule does not apply to you. But, if it's used for some personal benefit, or if you keep the property at your home, you must keep track of all personal use. As you might expect, you can't claim any tax benefit for the personal portion.

Listed property includes:

1. Autos, airplanes and other forms of transportation.

2. Entertainment-type property such as VCRs, cameras and camcorders.

3. Cellular telephones and similar communications equipment.

4. Computers and related peripheral equipment (if not used exclusively at a regular business location). This limitation targets the growing popularity of the portable laptop and notebook computers.

The best way to meet this requirement is to keep a log book showing dates, times and projects. Or, you can keep this record by notes in a calendar or business diary. (For more information on listed property see IRS Publication 534, *Depreciation*.)

Example: Joan bought a computer she keeps at her home. She uses it 60% of the time for her direct marketing business. Her son, Jason, uses it the rest of the time for school projects and games. Joan should keep a log showing the time the computer was used for her business and personal purposes.

If you want to immediately deduct the cost of listed property under IRC § 179, your records must show that it is used 50% or more of the time for business. (See Chapter 2 for a full explanation of IRC § 179.)

Example: Joan paid $3,000 for her computer in 1995. Because she uses it 60% for business, she can write off $1,800 as an IRC § 179 expense. But if Joan only used it 45% of the time for business, she could not claim it as an IRC § 179 write-off. (She would have to take depreciation deductions instead over a number of years.)

RECORDKEEPING IF YOU HAVE SEVERAL SMALL BUSINESSES

If you report income from more than one business on a tax return—say, you are a part-time coin dealer and own a bicycle shop, and your spouse has a sideline home decorating business—keep separate records for each activity. Each venture requires separate tax reporting. If you operate three businesses as a sole proprietor, for example, you need to file three IRS Schedule C forms with your tax return each year. (See Chapter 6, Sole Proprietorships.)

E. Bookkeeping Methods of Tracking Income and Expenses

There are two methods for keeping your set of business records, called "single-entry" and "double-entry" bookkeeping. If you are doing books by hand and don't have a lot of transactions, the single-entry method is okay. A much better way is the double-entry method because it is inherently more accurate. Let's briefly look at each method, and then move quickly into how can forget the differences by using a computer.

1. Single-Entry System

Single-entry bookkeeping is the easiest way to go and is acceptable to the IRS. Single-entry means you write down each transaction in your records once, preferably on a ledger sheet. You record the flow of income and expenses through your business by making a running total of money taken in (gross receipts) and money paid out (disbursements.) Gross receipts should be kept and summarized daily and weekly, and then totaled along with summaries of categories of expenses, monthly. At the end of the year the twelve monthly summaries are totalled up. You are ready for tax time.

2. Double-Entry System

Many small businesses start out with a single-entry method, but later convert to double-entry. Like it sounds, this bookkeeping system requires two entries for each transaction, which provides built-in checks and balances to assure accuracy. Each transaction requires an entry as a "debit" and as a "credit." I know this is beginning to sound like Accounting 101, but you only need to get the general idea.

A double-entry system is more complicated and time-consuming if done by hand, since everything is recorded twice. And, if done manually, this method requires a formal set of books—"journals" and "ledgers." As illustrated below, all transactions are first entered into a journal, then are posted (written) on a ledger sheet—the same amount is written down in two different places. Typical ledger accounts are titled *income, expenses, assets* and *liabilities (debts)*. There also may be an account called *net worth*, which shows the excess value of all of your business assets over your liabilities, or vice versa if you are in the hole.

Income and expense accounts are totalled up and your books are "closed" at the end of each tax year. Then you start over again for the new business year. Asset, liability and net worth accounts, however, are "open" as long as you are in business.

Computers make it easy. If you are using a computer program, the double-entry is done automatically for you. You only have to enter a transaction once, and the computer does the rest. Programs such as Quicken (Intuit) and MS Money (Microsoft) work this way.

Here is a sample of a double-entry system, showing a payment of rent.

General Journal of Sam's Computer Sales & Service

Date	Description of Entry	Debit	Credit
10/5/94	Rent Expense	$1000	
	Cash		$1000

As you can see, payment of rent resulted in two separate journal entries—a debit for the expense of $1,000, and a corresponding credit of $1,000—a double entry. The debits in a double-entry method (here, $1,000) must always equal the credits ($1,000). If they don't, you know there is an error somewhere. So, double-entry allows you to "balance your books," which you can't do with the single-entry method.

With a computer, the $1,000 rent expenditure is input as an expense (a debit), then the computer automatically posts it to the "rent" account as a credit. In effect, the computer eliminates the extra step or the need to master the difference between debits and credits—and it doesn't make math errors.

F. Timing Methods of Accounting: Cash and Accrual

Besides recordkeeping systems, there are also two accounting methods of timing the recording of income and expenses of a business, called the

"cash" and "accrual" methods. These are two sets of rules for recording *when* you have income and expenses for tax purposes.

A business must choose one of these methods and notify the IRS which one it is using on its tax return (a box on the form must be checked). Once chosen, that method must be used in all subsequent tax returns unless the IRS grants you permission to switch to another method.

The tax code requires a venture's income and expenses to be reported in the year in which they occur.

Example: Monique bought $7,000 in supplies for her hairdressing salon in January 1995. But Monique hasn't filed her 1994 income taxes yet—can she deduct the $7,000 expense on her 1994 tax return? No, because the expense was incurred in 1995. Monique cannot shift it to another year.

What if Monique had bought the supplies in 1994, but didn't pay for them until 1995? In which year does Monique take the deduction? To answer, you need to know the difference between cash and accrual methods of accounting.

1. Cash Method

The term "cash method" refers to *when* an expense is paid (or income received) for tax reporting purposes rather than *how* it is paid. So, don't take the word "cash" here literally; it covers other kinds of payments—check, barter, credit card, etc.—as well as the green stuff. Most businesses selling services use the cash method of accounting for income and expenses, which is logical even to us non-accountants. Generally, you simply report income in the year you receive it and an expense in the year you pay it.

The cash method seems simple, but there are a few special tax rules to watch out for. One involves a legal doctrine called "constructive receipt," which requires counting some items as income before you actually receive them. This rule states that you have income as soon as it is available or credited to your account—even if you don't take it at that time.

Example: Ray got a $3,000 check for his consulting business in December 1996, but didn't get around to depositing it until January 1997. Since Ray could have cashed the check in 1996, 1996 is the year in which the business "constructively received" the $3,000 and should be accounted for as income.

The corollary of the constructive receipt rule is that you are not allowed a deduction in the current year for items you have paid for but not yet received.

Example: Ray got a special deal on "Consulting Times," a monthly business publication. He paid $360 for a three-year subscription in July of 1994. He can tax-deduct only $60 in 1994 (1/6 of the total); the balance must be prorated over the term of the subscription and deducted $120 (1/3) in 1995, $120 (1/3) in 1996, and $60 (1/6) in 1997.

Watch the calendar. There is some flexibility allowed by the IRS with cash method accounting for those who prepay expenses at the end of the year. The last week of every December, I get the income and expense figures of my law practice together to see if I can shave some money off my tax bill. For instance, if I pay January's office rent on December 27, I'll get the deduction a year earlier. As long as I don't prepay an expense more than 30 days in advance, I'm okay if an auditor calls. Or, if I had an especially good year (meaning a big tax bill), I can stock up on office supplies or buy new equipment to write off under IRC § 179. And, sometimes I've found the converse is true—my accounting shows a disappointing year, so I put off paying December's creditors until January.

2. Accrual Method

Under tax code rules, C corporations and businesses with inventories of goods must use the more complex accrual method of accounting instead of the cash method. The accrual method requires some getting used to for us non-accountants.

With accrual accounting, income is treated as received when it is *earned*—not when it is actually received. And for tax purposes, an expense is recorded at the time the obligation arose—not when it is paid. Expenses and income are considered accrued at the moment they become "fixed."

Both income and expenses must meet what the tax code calls the "all events" test to become fixed. This means that everything required—all events—to secure a right to receive the income, or for a liability for the expense, must have happened. At that point in time it becomes fixed if known with reasonable certainty—whether any cash has changed hands or not.

Example: George's Foundry, which uses the accrual method, receives $4,500 in 1996 for custom ironwork to be manufactured in 1997. The business won't record $4,500 as income in 1996 because it hasn't been earned yet. On the expense side, if the business receives a $1,000 bill in 1996 for raw materials to be used in the same job, it is deducted in 1996—even if not paid for until 1997.

Get help setting up accrual accounting. If your operation keeps inventories or is a C corporation, consult a tax pro in setting up your accounting system. Find someone familiar with your type of operation, whether it is a gas station, a loan company or a medical practice. Don't try to change your accounting method without running it by a tax pro first.

Computer programs work equally well with either method, but obviously the accrual method requires more thought.

3. Hybrid and Special Accounting Methods

Some businesses may need to use a combination of the cash and accrual methods of accounting. For instance, a business may sell both goods and services and operate on the cash basis for all purposes except for keeping records of its stock. Inventories, under tax code rules, always must be accounted for on the accrual basis, so both methods may be necessary.

Special methods are available to farmers and businesses working on long-term contracts, as well as to manufacturers and building contractors.

Permission from the IRS is usually required before choosing a hybrid or special method of accounting for tax reporting. (See a tax pro or IRS Publication 538, *Accounting Periods and Methods*.)

4. Changing Accounting Methods

The IRS is concerned that whenever an accounting method is changed the business could obtain an unfair tax advantage—or some expenses or income could get lost in the transition. So, if you want to change your venture's accounting method, ordinarily you need permission from the IRS. However, if there is a fundamental change in the operation of your business—say, from selling goods to offering services—then permission is not required.

Example: Kate's Electronics Repair Service, which has been using the cash method, starts stocking and selling TVs. The business now has an inventory, so it must use an accrual accounting method for the retail portion of the business. Permission from the IRS is not required because there was only a change in operation. However, if Kate's business remains just a repair shop but wants to change accounting methods, it must get written permission from the IRS.

If you need permission, you must request it before you change methods. File Form 3115, Application for Change in Accounting Method, within 180 days before the end of the year for which you want to make the change. There is a $500 application fee but there are some exemptions from having to pay the fee.

G. Accounting Periods: Calendar Year or Fiscal Year

For tax purposes, an enterprise must keep its books for accounting periods, called "tax years." For individuals, the tax year is the same as the good old calendar year—starting on January 1 and ending on December 31. Generally, most small businesses are required to use the calendar year, too.

However, some businesses can use an alternative tax-reporting period called the "fiscal year." This is any one-year period that does *not* end on December 31 (with one minor exception, discussed below). A business notifies the IRS of its accounting period by check-marking the appropriate box on its tax return form. Once chosen, the accounting period usually cannot be changed without written approval from the IRS.

Regardless of which accounting tax year is used by your business, your payroll and excise taxes must always be reported on a calendar year basis.

1. Calendar Year

Most small businesses are either required by IRS rules to use a calendar year as their tax year or choose to do so voluntarily. The tax code directs sole proprietors, partnerships, limited liability companies, S corporations and personal service corporations to report on a calendar-year basis, unless they can convince the IRS they qualify for an exception. (See Section 2, below.)

The Basics

2. Fiscal Year

A minority of small businesses use a fiscal year instead of a calendar tax year. The fiscal year is any one-year period ending on the last day of any month except December. The fiscal year is not favored by the tax code and when allowed, it is usually for C corporations. Other small businesses can use fiscal year only by showing a business reason for it, such as a cyclical or seasonable business—for instance, farming. To get permission, file Form 8716, Election to Have a Tax Year Other Than a Required Tax Year.

3. Short Tax Years

A "short tax year" occurs whenever a business starts up any day but January 1—which is usually the case. For instance, if you open on July 15 and use a calendar tax year reporting period, your first tax year was only 5 1/2 months and ends on December 31. Likewise, a short year occurs whenever a business terminates at any time other than the year end. Generally, this requires you to prorate certain tax deductions, such as depreciation of assets, to match the short period.

RESOURCES

IRS Publication 334, *Tax Guide for Small Business*. A very handy, several-hundred-page book with all kinds of small business tax information.

IRS Publication 55, *RecordKeeping for Individuals*. Helpful especially if you are new in business or are keeping your own books, as it contains details and examples.

IRS Publication 583, *Starting a Business and Keeping Records* (new 1996); 551, *Basis of Assets;* 534, *Depreciation;* 538, *Accounting Periods and Methods;* and 535, *Business Expenses*. These booklets can get fairly technical, but if you are hungry for tax knowledge or are bent on tackling your business's tax return preparation, this is stuff you must know.

Keeping the Books, Pinson & Jinnett (Upstart Publishing). A basic primer written by accountants for those of you keeping your books manually.

Small-Time Operator, Bernard Kamoroff (Bell Springs Publishing). A wealth of practical recordkeeping and accounting tips from a longtime CPA.

Business Owner's Guide to Accounting & Bookkeeping, Placencia, Welge & Oliver (Oasis Press). A more detailed and complex small business accounting book for those who are really serious about the subject.

Accounting and Recordkeeping Made Easy for the Self-Employed, by Jack Fox (John Wiley & Sons). This book offers case studies, worksheets and sample forms to help you work through basic accounting in a small business.

Auto Mileage Log and *Travel & Entertainment Log*, Research Institute of America, 800-742-3348. These are good recording tools and also contain basic tax rules.

Basic accounting system information is available free through the Small Business Administration (SBA). Send for the *Directory of Business Development Publications*: SBA Publications, P.O. Box 1000, Ft. Worth, TX 76119. ■

CHAPTER 4

Tax Benefits of Business Losses

"There is no such thing as justice—in or out of court."

— Clarence Darrow

The term "risky business" comes to mind whenever I see another brave soul take the plunge into a new venture. Most operations lose money during their start-up phase. Some folks stick in there until the business turns the corner, while most others throw in the towel after a year or two. A significant number will go under because they lose money—and a few of these will have done so badly that they will be forced to file for bankruptcy.

Fortunately, the tax code softens the blow for people who lose money in business. Congress has long believed that one way to encourage new enterprises is to give a tax break to those who try. After all, when the business flourishes, the government shares in profits, so why shouldn't it absorb part of the losses as well? The help that you will get from Uncle Sam, however, depends on whether or not your business is incorporated, and whether you are active in the business operation or just an investor. The basics on taking tax benefits from business losses are the subject of this chapter. By "losses," we are not talking about bad debts that you incur in your business operation. For the tax treatment of bad debts, see Chapter 1.

BUSINESS LOSSES IN A NUTSHELL

1. The law allows, but limits, tax losses that can be claimed by owners and investors in a business.

2. Your ability to claim a tax benefit for a business loss may depend on whether or not your business is incorporated.

3. Because a C corporation is a separate tax entity, its operating losses belong to the corporation, not the shareholders.

4. Corporate shareholders get a tax break for their business's losses, but only in the year that the corporation fails, or when they sell their stock at a loss.

A. Unincorporated Businesses

Congress extends a helping hand by allowing struggling sole proprietors, partners, limited liability company members and shareholders of S corporations to deduct any business losses directly against their other income. The tax code, however, provides rules that dictate how and when you can take the losses for a tax benefit.

1. Owners

Owners of an unincorporated business—a sole proprietorship, partnership or limited liability company—can deduct business losses on their individual tax returns. Such a loss is called a "net operating loss" or NOL, and can be used to offset other income to lower the total amount subject to income tax. Of course, the loss can't reduce their income to below zero for tax purposes.

Example: John Jones Hardware shuts its doors in 1995. The business had profits in its first two years, 1993 and 1994, but lost $100,000 in its third and final year of operation. In 1995, John's wife, Jean, worked at the phone company to keep the family afloat and earned $25,000. The Joneses also sold mutual funds they had owned for several years at a $10,000 gain, so their total family income was $35,000. The Joneses can claim $35,000 of the net operating loss on their tax return in 1995. The balance of $65,000 must be used in other tax years.

An NOL is first taken to offset your other income in the year it occurred. But if your business operating loss (NOL) exceeds your other total income for the year, you can amend up to three past tax returns and perhaps qualify for a tax refund. An unused loss must first be carried back three years and the tax return amended to show the loss. From there, any unused business loss is carried forward to each of the preceding two years. (The example below should help make this clear.)

If there's still more loss you haven't claimed, you can carry it forward to future years. Any unused NOL expires after 15 years. The overall effect is to spread out the tax benefit of business losses over as many as 19 years.

Example: Harry started Nebula Graphic Designs in 1994 and lost $40,000 that year. Harry also worked as a printer's representative, netting $12,000 in commissions. Harry claims $12,000 of the loss to wipe out his commission income. Then Harry must carry the balance of the net operating loss of $28,000 back three years to 1991 to offset income and hopefully entitle him to a refund of taxes paid that year. If he still has any unused loss, Harry will amend his 1992 return, and if necessary his return for 1993. He can keep claiming the loss against income until it is fully used up or the 15-year period expires.

Be sure to claim your business operating losses. You must notify the IRS that you intend to carry over your outfit's net operating loss in the year the loss is incurred. Either attach a written statement to the loss year's tax return, or attach IRS Form 3621, Net

Operating Loss Carry-Over. Use this form to determine how much loss is left over after the first tax year.

2. Investors

If you are an investor in someone else's unincorporated enterprise (sole proprietorship, partnership or limited liability company), the tax result is different than if you operated the business yourself. An investor is *not* entitled to any tax benefit from operating losses of an ongoing business.

However, if the venture fails completely, you can take your loss on the investment to offset other income for that year. Any excess loss can be carried forward to future years, but the investment loss cannot be carried back to past years. Your loss is termed "capital loss" and is treated under different rules than operating losses (NOLs) for business owners. (IRC § 1212.)

Capital losses are first deducted dollar-for-dollar from your other capital gains, if any. A capital gain results from an investment held for more than one year—for example, a $10,000 capital gain from selling stock on the New York Stock Exchange. Any excess capital loss (after deducting your capital gain) can then be deducted against ordinary income (compensation earned from your labor), but *only* up to $3,000 in any year. Any capital loss left over can be carried forward until your death. In case I have already lost you, let's go to another example.

Example: Jake and Mona Willow invest $45,000 in Jake, Jr.'s digital imaging business. The business fails in 1994, and the Willows lose their entire investment—a $45,000 capital loss. If they have other income but no capital gains to offset this loss, it will take them 15 years (at $3,000 per year) to tax-deduct the whole amount.

If, however, the Willows sold stock in Microsoft in 1995, realizing an $8,000 capital gain, they can claim $11,000 of the loss (the $8,000 capital gain plus $3,000 of ordinary income). After taking $3,000 as a tax loss in 1994 and $11,000 in 1995, the Willows have $31,000 in capital losses remaining to be taken in future years.

They will only be able to deduct $3,000 per year against ordinary income unless they have some more capital gains.

There is a way to get beyond these limitations—if the business is incorporated. See the next section.

B. Corporations

Whether tax benefits from a corporation's losses can be taken by the shareholders individually, or only by the corporation, depends on several factors, discussed below.

1. Shareholder Losses When a Business Fails

One of the handful of tax code provisions you should know by number if you incorporate is IRC § 1244. This provision allows stockholders in small business corporations—whether they are active in the business or not—to deduct their loss in the year the business fails, or when they sell their stock. This option is available if, when the corporation was formed, the total money or property it received for stock was less than $1 million.

This means that most individual shareholders in Section 1244 companies may take losses beyond the $3,000 annual limit that applies to investors in unincorporated businesses. (See Section A, above.) A tax loss up to $100,000 (for a married couple filing jointly or a single taxpayer), or $50,000 for a married person filing separately, may be claimed against the shareholder's ordinary income in the year of the loss.

Any excess loss (over $100,000) can be carried forward and claimed in future years. However, in future years, a $3,000 per year limit applies; over that amount, the loss can be used only to offset any other capital gains from investments, not ordinary income from earnings.

Example: Gordon and Joella Hall buy $150,000 in stock in LowTech, a § 1244 corporation. LowTech does poorly (customers wanted high-tech, I guess), and in 1995, the Halls sell their stock for $20,000, losing $130,000 of their investment. If they have income of at least $100,000 in 1995, the Halls can offset $100,000 of their investment as a tax loss in 1995.

The remaining $30,000 must be carried forward to the Halls' future tax returns. The Halls can use $3,000 of the loss in 1996 and subsequent years to offset ordinary income, or they can claim the whole $30,000 to offset any capital gains in any one year. If the Halls don't have any capital gains, it will take them ten years to use up the whole loss.

Make sure your corporation qualifies for § 1244 treatment. The details on forming a § 1244 corporation are in Chapter 7, C Corporations.

If you take a loss under IRC § 1244, you must file a statement with your individual tax return telling the IRS this is what you are doing. If the IRS audits and finds that IRC § 1244 wasn't applicable, your loss is treated instead under "capital loss" rules, discussed in Section A, above. This means you can't take your loss against ordinary income beyond the $3,000 capital loss annual limit, and you will face an audit bill for the disallowed loss claim.

IRC § 1244 stock sales between related parties are suspect. If you claim a tax loss from a transaction with someone related to you, an IRS auditor can disallow it. "Related parties" means parents, children and in-laws, as well as other businesses controlled by family members. To be safe, deal with a non-relative, if possible. For instance, if the corporation stock you own is worthless, sell it to a friend for a dollar. Your buddy has nothing to lose by helping you out—except the dollar.

2. C Corporation Operating Losses

As with most S corporations, very few small business C corporations pay corporate income taxes; instead, their shareholders take out profits as salaries, bonuses and fringe benefits. (See Chapter 7, C Corporations.) The ideal tax result is to break even, or maybe have a small loss. And corporate income taxes must be paid in one year, it may be possible to get them refunded in another year that the corporation loses money. This is called a corporate net operating loss (NOL). (Net operating loss is discussed in Section A, above.)

This corporation NOL can be carried back to get refunds of corporate income taxes paid in the past. Keep in mind that the tax refunds go to the corporation, not to its shareholders.

The fastest way to get a corporate tax refund is to file IRS Form 1139, Corporation Application for Tentative Refund. The IRS is required to process this form within 90 days, and issue a refund. If your corporation hasn't yet filed its prior year's tax return, use Form 1138, Extension of Time for Payment of Taxes by a Corporation Expecting a Net Operating Loss Carryback instead.

RESOURCES

All of the following IRS publication shed light on the topic of reaping tax benefits from business losses. The titles are descriptive of the contents.

IRS Publication 550, *Investment Income and Expenses*

IRS Publication 925, *Passive Activity and At-Risk Rules*

IRS Publication 536, *Net Operating Losses*

IRS Publication 541, *Tax Information on Partnerships*

IRS Publication 908, *Bankruptcy and Other Debt Cancellation.* ■

CHAPTER 5

Tax Concerns of Employers

"If there isn't a law, there will be."

—Harold Farber

Chances are if your venture is successful, you won't be able to do all the work yourself. If you can do it all on your lonesome, more power to you—you don't have to worry about this chapter. Being an employer carries a whole new set of tax responsibilities. Once you have employees, the IRS will be looking over your shoulder to see if you are filing payroll tax returns and making required tax deposits.

If your business uses independent contractors, you can avoid payroll taxes and paperwork. However, the IRS may audit to see if anyone you call an "independent contractor" rather than an "employee" is classified correctly. If you lose, the consequences can be very expensive, as we shall see.

Every employer has an obligation to:

• withhold payroll taxes from employees' wages

• remit these taxes, together with the business share of employment taxes, to the IRS, and

• make periodic employment tax reports to the IRS. (IRC § 3509.)

According to the IRS, the majority of small businesses fall behind in filing reports or making federal tax deposits at one time or another. (I have to confess that my office missed getting an employment tax form filed on time on at least one occasion.) While many of these delinquencies are oversights—like missing a deadline—others reflect poor office management.

It is tempting, when you experience a "cash crunch," to pay rent, utilities and key suppliers instead of making a required payroll tax deposit. Folks rationalize that since it may take the IRS months (if not years) to find out, employment taxes can wait. Too often, however, the business keeps struggling or goes under altogether, but the tax obligation survives.

Under all circumstances, pay your payroll taxes, in full and on time. If you don't, the IRS *will* knock at the door, and when it does, it won't be gentle. The IRS tacks on interest and penalties to delinquent payroll taxes, the bill can skyrocket so fast that, often, businesses fail as a result. And unlike ordinary debts, payroll taxes survive the death of the owner or bankruptcy of the enterprise to become personal liabilities of its owner(s) or heirs. (IRC § 6502.) (See Chapter 18, When You Can't Pay Your Taxes, for strategies to deal with a tax debt.)

EMPLOYER TAX CONCERNS IN A NUTSHELL

1. If your business has employees, you will have to become familiar with your obligations for withholding taxes and filing payroll tax reports.

2. IRS auditors are on the alert for businesses that misclassify employees as independent contractors, and they can levy heavy penalties on violators.

3. Business owners, and sometimes employees, too, can be held personally liable for unpaid payroll taxes of the business. (You may, however, appeal IRS findings of responsibility.)

A. Payroll Taxes

The term "payroll taxes" encompasses three different types of taxes that every employer must pay:

• Income tax withheld from each employee's paycheck throughout the year. You must send an IRS W-2 form to each employee showing all payments and all withholdings from their wages. W-2 forms must be furnished by January 31 of each following year. By February 28, you must also file IRS Form W-3 (summary and transmittal form) and copies of all the W-2s to the Social Security Administration, which transmits the data to the IRS.

• Social Security and Medicare tax (FICA). The employee's share is withheld from each paycheck; the employer must match this amount.

• Federal Unemployment Tax (FUTA). This tax goes to the unemployment insurance system and must be paid by the employe. The employee pays no part of FUTA.

There are several ways to figure correct income tax withholding for employees. For instructions, see IRS Publication 15, *Circular E, Employers Tax Guide.*

On the other hand, one look at that publication might convince you to hire a payroll tax service or get your accountant to figure it out for you—at least the first time around.

Generally, the employee's income and FICA taxes are paid to the IRS monthly, by making federal tax deposits at specified banks. (If the total owed is $500 or less, the deposits are due quarterly.) An IRS Federal Tax Deposit coupon (Form 8109-B) must be submitted with each payroll tax payment.

In turn, these payments are reported to the IRS on Form 941, Employer's Quarterly Federal Tax Return, after each calendar quarter that you have employees. Form 941 shows how many employees you had, how much you paid them and the amount of Social Security, Medicare and federal income tax withheld during the three-month period. (A sample 941 form is on the following page.)

The last federal form required is an annual report detailing FUTA taxes due (Form 940). This shows how much federal unemployment tax is owed. A credit is allowed for any state unemployment taxes paid. (You don't get any credit unless you paid the state unemployment tax on time.)

Most states that tax income also require employers to withhold employees' taxes similar to the federal law. Some cities, such as New York City, have payroll taxes, too.

By law, payroll tax collection is based on a "trust fund" theory. The employer initially acts as a tax collector by holding employees' taxes in trust for the IRS. Violation of this trust can bring on both civil and criminal punishments. Although the IRS seldom throws anyone in jail, it can—and often does—seize a business's assets and force it to close down if it owes back payroll taxes.

1. Personal Responsibility for Payroll Taxes

The IRS can hold people associated with a small business personally responsible if the operation fails to meet its payroll tax obligations. (IRC § 6672.) This unusual power is authorized by the law known as the Trust Fund Recovery Penalty.

To enforce this law, a Revenue Officer—an experienced IRS collector—investigates people associated with an active business (or, more likely, a defunct one) that owes payroll taxes. Anyone found responsible has the "trust fund" portion of unpaid payroll taxes treated as a personal debt. The trust fund portion is all of the income tax that should have been withheld from an employee's wages, plus one-half of the FICA tax (7.65% of the first $62,700 of wages paid). The other half of the FICA tax (7.65%) and the employer's federal unemployment tax (FUTA) are not trust fund taxes, and are not treated as personal debts.

HOW TO GET A TAX ID NUMBER

If your business has employees or is a partnership, limited liability company or corporation, you must have an "employer identification number," or EIN for short. If you are a sole proprietorship without employees, your tax ID number can be your Social Security number.

To get an EIN, file IRS Form SS-4, Application for Employer Identification Number, with the IRS center listed in the instructions to the form. You can get this form at all IRS or Social Security offices. Or, call 1-800-829-1040 and request that it be mailed to you. There is no charge to get an EIN, and it usually take several weeks to process your application. If there are any tax filings due before you get your number back, write "applied for" on the filing in the space for the EIN.

If you have more than one business, you need a different EIN for each distinct venture. If you change the form of your entity, such as from a sole proprietorship to a corporation, or from a partnership to a limited liability company, you must get a new EIN.

Form **SS-4** (Rev. December 1993) Department of the Treasury Internal Revenue Service	**Application for Employer Identification Number** (For use by employers, corporations, partnerships, trusts, estates, churches, government agencies, certain individuals, and others. See Instructions.)	EIN OMB No. 1545-0003 Expires 12-31-96

1 Name of applicant (Legal name) (See instructions.)
Alpha Bean Cromwell

2 Trade name of business, if different from name in line 1 ABC Plumbing	**3** Executor, trustee, "care of" name

4a Mailing address (street address) (room, apt., or suite no.) 1234 Rooter Place	**5a** Business address, if different from address in lines 4a and 4b 1234 Rooter Place
4b City, state, and ZIP code Nowheresville, CA 95555	**5b** City, state, and ZIP code Nowheresville, CA 95555

6 County and state where principal business is located
Somewherestown

7 Name of principal officer, general partner, grantor, owner, or trustor – SSN required (See instructions.) ▶ 555-55-5555
Alpha Bean cromwell

8a Type of entity (Check only one box.) (See instructions.)

☒ Sole Proprietor (SSN) 555-55-5555   ☐ Estate (SSN of decedent) _____   ☐ Trust
☐ REMIC   ☐ Personal service corp.   ☐ Plan administrator-SSN _____   ☐ Partnership
☐ State/local government   ☐ National guard   ☐ Other corporation (specify) _____   ☐ Farmers' cooperative
☐ Other nonprofit organization (specify) _____   ☐ Federal government/military   ☐ Church or church controlled organization
☐ Other (specify) ▶ _____   (enter GEN if applicable) _____

8b If a corporation, name the state or foreign country (if applicable) where incorporated ▶ | State | Foreign country

9 Reason for applying (Check only one box.)

☒ Started new business (specify) ▶ _____   ☐ Changed type of organization (specify) ▶ _____
☐ Hired employees   ☐ Purchased going business
☐ Created a pension plan (specify type) ▶ _____   ☐ Created a trust (specify) ▶ _____
☐ Banking purpose (specify) ▶ _____   ☐ Other (specify) ▶

10 Date business started or acquired (Mo., day, year) (See instructions.) 01/01/97	**11** Enter closing month of accounting year. (See instructions.) DECEMBER

12 First date wages or annuities were paid or will be paid (Mo., day, year). **Note:** If applicant is a withholding agent, enter date income will first be paid to nonresident alien. (Mo., day, year) . . . . ▶ N/A

13 Enter highest number of employees expected in the next 12 months. **Note:** If the applicant does not expect to have any employees during the period, enter "0." . . . . ▶

	Nonagricultural	Agricultural	Household
	1	0	0

14 Principal activity (See instructions.) ▶ Plumbing

15 Is the principal business activity manufacturing? . . . . ☐ Yes ☒ No
If "Yes," principal product and raw material used ▶

16 To whom are most of the products or services sold? Please check the appropriate box.   ☐ Business (wholesale)
☒ Public (retail)   ☐ Other (specify) ▶   ☐ N/A

17a Has the applicant ever applied for an identification number for this or any other business? . . . . ☐ Yes ☒ No
Note: If "Yes," please complete lines 17b and 17c.

17b If you checked the "Yes" box in line 17a, give applicant's legal name and trade name, if different than name shown on prior application.

Legal name ▶   Trade name ▶

17c Enter approximate date, city, and state where the application was filed and the previous employer identification number if known.

Approximate date when filed (Mo., day, year)	City and state where filed	Previous EIN

Under penalties of perjury, I declare that I have examined this application, and to the best of my knowledge and belief, it is true, correct, and complete.

Name and title (Please type or print clearly.) ▶ Alpha Bean Cromwell	Business telephone number (include area code) (415) 555-5555

Signature ▶   Date ▶

Note: Do not write below this line. For official use only.

Please leave blank ▶	Geo.	Ind.	Class	Size	Reason for applying

For Paperwork Reduction Act Notice, see attached Instructions.   Form **SS-4** (Rev. 12-93)

Beware of the Trust Fund Recovery Penalty (TFRP).
The IRS legally has 10 years to collect payroll (or any other federal) taxes after they become due against a business or individual. (IRC § 6502.) The IRS can seize almost any of your assets—bank accounts, wages, cars and even your home. You can't wipe out a payroll tax debt even if you file for bankruptcy.

To hold you personally liable for the Trust Fund Recovery Penalty (TFRP), the IRS must find that: (1) you were responsible to make the missed payments and that (2) you acted willfully in not seeing that payroll tax obligations were paid.

Entrepreneurs are almost always held personally responsible for paying payroll taxes, so they can seldom avoid the TFRP if the taxes aren't paid. Included are sole proprietors, general partners, limited liability company members and officers of corporations, whether or not they were stockholders.

If a staff member or outside accountant screws up—or worse, steals the money that should have gone to the government—you, the owner, are still on the hook. The IRS reckons that since you chose the person responsible for tax reporting and paying, you have the duty of supervising them. (On rare occasions, however, an owner or part owner of a business may escape liability for the TFRP if the IRS finds that someone else acted without the business owner's knowledge and beyond their control.)

When it comes to pinning on the personal responsibility tag, the IRS does not always stop with the head people. Non-owner employees, such as a bookkeeper or office manager, can also be held responsible. Even outside accountants and attorneys for the business may be found responsible.

Because the IRS is eager to find as many people responsible as possible, Revenue Officers are given wide latitude in assigning personal responsibility for failure to pay payroll taxes. As part of its investigation, the IRS may question anyone it remotely

suspects may be responsible. In determining who is to blame for the missed payments, the IRS looks at a number of factors, including:

- Who made the business's financial decisions?
- Who signed, or had authority to sign, checks? (This is the factor the IRS seems most impressed with.)
- Who had power to direct payment (or nonpayment) of bills?
- Who had the duty of tax reporting?

Willfulness—one of those legal terms that keep lawyers and judges fully employed—triggers a TFRP. You were willful if you knew payroll taxes were owed and didn't do anything about it—even if you never intended to cheat the IRS. In short, if you're responsible for making payments, the IRS regards your failure to do so as a willful act.

Protect yourself from co-owners' carelessness or misdeeds. If you share financial responsibilities with others—that is, you're a partner, limited liability company member or corporation shareholder—get a written agreement with the other owners that contains a TFRP "indemnification clause." This means that your co-owners promise to reimburse any payroll tax penalty assessed against you personally, plus any costs of fighting the IRS, beyond your proportionate ownership share.

A suitable clause looks like this:

"All co-owners or shareholders agree to indemnify any of the others that may be held liable for any unpaid payroll tax liabilities of the business that are proposed or assessed against them personally, together with legal costs in contesting the taxes, except amounts in proportion to their ownership shares in the business."

Even with this clause, you are still liable for the whole thing if the others don't pay; this simply obliges them to pay you back some of what the IRS collects from you. It helps as long as the other owners are still solvent (or become so).

Form **941**		**Employer's Quarterly Federal Tax Return**		
(Rev. April 1994) Department of the Treasury Internal Revenue Service	4141	▶ See separate instructions for information on completing this return. Please type or print.		

Enter state code for state in which deposits made ▶ [:]
(see page 2 of instructions).

Name (as distinguished from trade name)	Date quarter ended	OMB No. 1545-0029
Peter Cone	Dec. 31, 1994	T
Trade name, if any	Employer identification number	FF
	10-1234567	FD
Address (number and street)	City, state, and ZIP code	FP
362 Main Street	Pinetown, VA 23000	I
		T

If address is different from prior return, check here ▶ [ ]

IRS Use

1 1 1 1 1 1 1 1 1 1 1   2   3 3 3 3 3 3   4 4 4
5 5 5   6   7   8 8 8 8 8   9 9 9   10 10 10 10 10 10 10 10 10

If you do not have to file returns in the future, check here ▶ [ ] and enter date final wages paid ▶

If you are a seasonal employer, see **Seasonal employers** on page 2 and check here (see instructions) ▶ [ ]

1	Number of employees (except household) employed in the pay period that includes March 12th ▶			
2	Total wages and tips subject to withholding, plus other compensation	2	19500	00
3	Total income tax withheld from wages, tips, and sick pay	3	1820	00
4	Adjustment of withheld income tax for preceding quarters of calendar year	4		
5	Adjusted total of income tax withheld (line 3 as adjusted by line 4—see instructions) . .	5	1820	00
6a	Taxable social security wages . . . . . . $ 19500 00 × 12.4% (.124) =	6a	2418	00
b	Taxable social security tips . . . . $ × 12.4% (.124) =	6b		
7	Taxable Medicare wages and tips . . . . $ 19500 00 × 2.9% (.029) =	7	565	50
8	Total social security and Medicare taxes (add lines 6a, 6b, and 7). Check here if wages are not subject to social security and/or Medicare tax . . . . ▶ [ ]	8	2983	50
9	Adjustment of social security and Medicare taxes (see instructions for required explanation) Sick Pay $ _____ ± Fractions of Cents $ _____ ± Other $ _____ =	9		
10	Adjusted total of social security and Medicare taxes (line 8 as adjusted by line 9—see instructions)	10	2983	50
11	**Total taxes** (add lines 5 and 10)	11	4803	50
12	Advance earned income credit (EIC) payments made to employees, if any	12		
13	Net taxes (subtract line 12 from line 11). **This should equal line 17, column (d) below** (or line D of Schedule B (Form 941))	13	4803	50
14	Total deposits for quarter, including overpayment applied from a prior quarter	14	4803	50
15	**Balance due** (subtract line 14 from line 13). Pay to Internal Revenue Service	15		
16	**Overpayment,** if line 14 is more than line 13, enter excess here ▶ $ _____ and check if to be: [ ] Applied to next return **OR** [ ] Refunded.			

- **All filers:** If line 13 is less than $500, you need not complete line 17 or Schedule B.
- **Semiweekly depositors:** Complete Schedule B and check here . . . . ▶ [ ]
- **Monthly depositors:** Complete line 17, columns (a) through (d) and check here . . . . ▶ [X]

17	**Monthly Summary of Federal Tax Liability.**			
	(a) First month liability	**(b)** Second month liability	**(c)** Third month liability	**(d)** Total liability for quarter
	1847.50	1478.00	1478.00	4803.50

Sign Here

Under penalties of perjury, I declare that I have examined this return, including accompanying schedules and statements, and to the best of my knowledge and belief, it is true, correct, and complete.

Signature ▶ *Peter Cone*   Print Your Name and Title ▶ Peter Cone, owner   Date ▶ 2/5/95

For Paperwork Reduction Act Notice, see page 1 of separate instructions.   Cat. No. 17001Z   Form **941** (Rev. 4-94)

Form **940-EZ**

Department of the Treasury
Internal Revenue Service

Employer's Annual Federal Unemployment (FUTA) Tax Return

OMB No. 1545-1110

19**94**

T	
FF	
FD	
FP	
I	
T	

If incorrect, make any necessary changes. ►

Name (as distinguished from trade name)
Peter Cone

Trade name, if any

Address and ZIP code
362 Main Street
Pinetown, VA 23000

Calendar year
1994

Employer identification number
10:1234567

Follow the chart under **Who May Use Form 940-EZ** *on page 2. If you cannot use Form 940-EZ, you must use Form 940 instead.*

A Enter the amount of contributions paid to your state unemployment fund. (See instructions for line A on page 4.)► $ 630. 00

B (1) Enter the name of the state where you have to pay contributions .... ► .... Virginia
(2) Enter your state reporting number as shown on state unemployment tax return. ► 0-0000000-0

If you will not have to file returns in the future, check here (see **Who Must File**, on page 2) **complete, and sign the return** . . . . . ► ☐

If this is an Amended Return check here . . . . ► ☐

Part I **Taxable Wages and FUTA Tax**

1	Total payments (including payments shown on lines 2 and 3) during the calendar year for services of employees	**1**	78000	00

Amount paid

2 Exempt payments. (Explain all exempt payments, attaching additional sheets if necessary.) ► ....
....

| **2** | | |

3 Payments for services of more than $7,000. Enter only amounts over the first $7,000 paid to each employee. Do not include any exempt payments from line 2. Do not use your state wage limitation. The $7,000 amount is the Federal wage base. Your state wage base may be different . . . .

| **3** | 57000 | 00 |

4	Total exempt payments (add lines 2 and 3)	**4**	57000	00
5	**Total taxable wages** (subtract line 4 from line 1) . . . . ►	**5**	21000	00
6	**FUTA tax.** Multiply the wages on line 5 by .008 and enter here. (If the result is over $100, also complete Part II.)	**6**	168	00
7	Total FUTA tax deposited for the year, including any overpayment applied from a prior year (from your records)	**7**	149	60
8	**Amount you owe** (subtract line 7 from line 6). This should be $100 or less. Pay to "Internal Revenue Service" ►	**8**	18	40
9	**Overpayment** (subtract line 6 from line 7). Check if it is to be: ☐ **Applied to next return, or** ☐ **Refunded** ►	**9**		

Part II **Record of Quarterly Federal Unemployment Tax Liability** (Do not include state liability.) Complete only if line 6 is over $100.

Quarter	First (Jan. 1 – Mar. 31)	Second (Apr. 1 – June 30)	Third (July 1 – Sept. 30)	Fourth (Oct. 1 – Dec. 31)	Total for year
Liability for quarter	149.60	18.40	-0-	-0-	168.00

Under penalties of perjury, I declare that I have examined this return, including accompanying schedules and statements, and, to the best of my knowledge and belief, it is true, correct, and complete, and that no part of any payment made to a state unemployment fund claimed as a credit was, or is to be, deducted from the payments to employees.

Signature ► *Peter Cone*   Title (Owner, etc.) ► Owner   Date ► 1/25/95

Cat. No. 10983G

Form **940-EZ** (1994)

2. If You Get Behind on Payroll Tax Payments

If your enterprise gets behind in payroll taxes, the obvious advice is to catch up as fast as possible. If you can't do it all at once, first bring payments current for the tax quarter you are in. Then, start paying the overdue taxes. Paying—if you still have employees. Then pay off the older payroll taxes. Paying quarterly taxes on time stops interest and penalties from accumulating. More importantly, the IRS is much more likely to work with you for past payroll tax delinquencies if your current quarter's payroll tax deposits have been made.

a. Designating Tax Payments

Whenever you pay past employment taxes, tell the IRS how you want back payments credited—the type of tax and tax periods. Specifically designating the application of your payments ensures they don't get credited to a different tax account, such as your personal income taxes. Also, if the payments don't cover the whole past due payroll tax bill—which is frequently the case—state that you want the trust fund portion of payroll taxes to be paid first. Here's how to designate your payments:

Step 1. Write a letter, like the one below, to the IRS office where you file your employment tax returns. If you're in doubt as to where to send it, call the IRS at 1-800-829-1040

SAMPLE LETTER TO THE IRS

XYZ CORPORATION
September 15, 1995

Dear IRS:

Please apply the enclosed payment of $1529 to the account of XYZ Corporation, EIN 94-5555555, for payroll tax Form 941 liability, 3rd Quarter of 1994. Apply to Trust Fund portion only.

Signed,

Sandra Shoestein

Sandra Shoestein, President

Step 2. Enclose your check. Write in the lower left hand corner: "Apply to Trust Fund portion only." Under this, write your employer identification number, the tax type and period the payment is for, such as: "EIN 94-5555555—941, for payroll tax Form 941 liability, 3rd quarter, 1994."

Step 3. Send the letter and check to the IRS, by registered mail.

Get IRS payroll tax records. If you are ever in doubt as to whether the IRS has given you proper credit for your payroll tax payments, order a printout of your account. Call a taxpayer service representative at 1-800-829-1040 and ask for your "BMF," which in IRS lingo means Business Master File. Tell them the specific tax periods you want to see, such as "3rd and 4th quarters of 1994." You should be able to get this information within a week or two and can compare their records with yours. If the printout is too full of codes for it to make sense, call the IRS and ask for an explanation, or show it to a tax pro.

3. If You Are Liable for Payroll Taxes

If you are found personally liable for payroll taxes, you are entitled to appeal within the IRS and have a hearing if you don't believe you are liable, or if you just want to delay the inevitable for some reason. Take heart; IRS Appeals Officers can reverse a TFRP finding. If you lose the appeal, you may contest further by going into court, but this will be very costly. (See Chapter 20, Appealing IRS Audits.)

Payroll taxes are one of the few tax debts that cannot be legally discharged in bankruptcy. Normally, this means you will either have to pay, or live with a payroll tax debt hanging over your head for 10 years.

Your best bet to reduce a payroll tax debt may be through a negotiation process called an Offer in Compromise. The IRS will sometimes accept a settlement on a tax bill if it is convinced that you don't have the assets or income to pay it in full. (See Chapter 18, When You Can't Pay Your Taxes.)

B. Employee or Independent Contractor?

Individuals who perform services for your small business are usually classified as either regular employees (legally termed "common law employees") or independent contractors (usually meaning they are "self employed" for tax purposes). A small percentage of people may fall into two other categories recognized by the IRS: statutory employees and statutory non-employees. We'll talk about all of these categories of workers in more detail below.

It may not make much difference to you what the individual is called as long as the work gets done. The distinctions, however, are very important to the IRS, and can be very costly if you don't pay attention to them. Let me warn you: the law is muddled in this area, and legal experts and courts regularly disagree as to whether someone is an employee or independent contractor.

From the standpoint of tax reporting, you should know by now that you have payroll tax withholding and reporting obligations for all of your employees. You report your employees to the IRS on quarterly 941 forms and W-2 forms issued annually. On the other hand, with a true independent contractor, you don't have any withholding or contributions for payroll taxes, and your only duty to the IRS is to issue a 1099 form once a year. (There are 11 versions of the 1099 form; the "1099-Misc." is the one that must be issued to an independent contractor.) And you don't have to make any report at all if you pay the independent contractor less than $600 a year, or the services were performed for you personally and not for your business. (See Section D, below, for the dates for filing and details on reporting workers to the IRS.)

This determination is crucial. This stuff may seem dull or technical, but the most important advice that you read in this book might turn out to be this: You must make a determination (hopefully, a correct one) of whether or not the person you hire is an employee or independent contractor at the time work begins.

Calling someone an independent contractor saves a tremendous amount of time that would otherwise be spent on complying with IRS reporting requirements. Even more significant to your bottom line is that you won't have to make the employer's share of the FICA contributions for each worker; this saves you 7.65% of each paycheck. Of course, you won't have to pay unemployment compensation tax either. The IRS is *very aware* of the benefits of misclassifying an employee as an independent contractor, and has wide powers to make life miserable for all those they catch doing it. (See Section C, below.)

Sole proprietors, limited liability company members and partners are neither employees nor independent contractors. These folks are owners, and as such are not subject to payroll tax withholding and paying. They should pay and file quarterly Estimated Taxes instead. This amounts to about the same amount of tax being paid, but with a lot less accounting and IRS paperwork required. Small business shareholders/owners of corporations—C or S type—who work for the corporation, and are employees, are subject to the payroll tax rules.

No other classifications of workers are recognized by the IRS. Many employers mistakenly believe that a short-term worker is not an employee for tax purposes. Sorry, whether part-time or temporary, called a consultant or subcontractor, a worker must fit into one of the four types for tax purposes. Period.

1. "Common Law" Employees

According to the IRS, anyone who performs services that can be controlled by an employer (what work will be done and how it will be done) is a common law employee. This is true even if an employer doesn't actually exercise control, but gives the employee freedom of action. As long as an employer has the legal right to control the method and result of the work done, there's an employer-employee relationship. Under this definition, most working people who do not own their businesses are classed by the IRS as common law employees.

Here are the factors the IRS says that show a worker is a common law employee:

1. The worker can be required to comply with instructions about when, where and how to work.

2. The worker is trained by the employer to perform services in a particular manner.

3. The worker's services are integrated into the business operation, or a continuing relationship exists.

4. The worker is required to render services personally.

5. Assistants to the worker are hired by the business, not the worker.

6. The worker has set hours of work.

7. The worker is required to devote substantially full time to the employer.

8. Work is done on business premises.

9. The worker is required to submit reports regularly.

10. The worker is paid by the hour, the week or month, unless these are installments of a lump sum amount agreed for the job.

11. The business pays the worker's business or travel expenses.

12. The business furnishes tools, equipment and materials.

13. The business has the right to fire, and the worker has the right to quit at will.

2. Independent Contractors

The IRS says that people in business for themselves—not subject to control by those who pay them—are independent contractors, not employees. When you hire an independent contractor to accomplish a task for your business, you don't have an employer-employee relationship and don't, therefore, have to pay employment taxes. Independent contractors (ICs) are responsible for their own tax reporting and paying.

The IRS says these factors tend to show a person is an independent contractor:

1. The worker hires, supervises and pays her assistants.

2. The worker is free to work when and for whom she wants.

3. The work is done on the worker's premises.

4. The worker is paid by the job or on straight commission.

5. The worker has the risk of profit or loss.

6. The worker does work for several businesses at one time.

7. The worker's services are available to the general public.

8. The worker can't be fired except for breach of contract.

Protect yourself from potential IRS claims that you misclassified employees as independent contractors.
Make sure that any independent contractor you hire:

- is paid by the job, not by the hour.
- works on his or her premises only, if possible.
- shows you a business license and workers' compensation insurance coverage (if applicable).
- signs a contract spelling out the terms of the work relationship. (See "Contracts With Independent Contractors," below.)

CONTRACTS WITH INDEPENDENT CONTRACTORS

If an IRS auditor attempts to reclassify a worker from independent contractor (IC) to employee, a written contract with the IC may sway the auditor. A signed contract won't help if the worker in question is obviously an employee, but it can be persuasive in borderline situations. A written agreement with an independent contractor should acknowledge that he or she is an IC, spelling out his or her responsibilities. (Pay attention to the IRS list of factors.) Include a clause stating that all payments to the IC will be reported to the IRS on Form 1099. If you regularly use independent contractors, develop blank contract forms and keep them on hand.

---

3. Statutory Employees

Federal law automatically classifies some people as "statutory employees." (IRC § 3121(d)(3).) Statutory employees are subject to tax withholding by businesses that pay them, in *all* cases; they can never be treated as independent contractors. Employers must issue W-2 forms to statutory employees; however, these people are allowed to deduct business expenses for their statutory employee income. This is a tax break not granted to regular wage earners, who receive W-2 forms. Workers who fall in this small category include:

- Corporate officers who provide services to the corporation.
- Delivery drivers of food, laundry and similar products, even if they are paid strictly on a commission basis.
- Full-time, business-to-business sales people, who may be paid on commission—such as manufacturer's representatives and other traveling salespeople, who do not sell directly to the public.
- Full-time life insurance agents working mainly for one company.
- Home workers who do piecework according to business specifications and with the business materials.

Example: Mary is an on-the-road salesperson for RoofCo, a roofing materials manufacturer selling to building contractors. She works out of her car and an office at home, visiting the RoofCo headquarters only twice a month, to pick up samples and commission checks. RoofCo has little control over how and where Mary does her work. Although her work meets some requirements of an independent contractor, Mary is classified as a statutory employee.

If you are a statutory employee, you should report wages and expenses on Schedule C, the same form used by sole proprietors. (See Chapter 6.)

4. Statutory Non-Employees

The fourth legal category for working people is the statutory non-employee, also known as the "exempt employee." (IRC § 3508.) Primarily, this classification covers two types of salespeople:

- Licensed real estate agents working on commission only.
- Direct (to the customer) sellers of consumer products—if the sales took place somewhere other than a retail store or showroom.

These individuals are always treated as self-employed, just like independent contractors, and aren't subject to tax withholding. To qualify, a statutory non-employee's income must be directly related to sales—not to hours worked.

Example: Lorenzo runs a wholesale cosmetics business and claims his sales people are statutory non-employees. This will stand up to an IRS audit if sales were all made off the premises, to consumers of the cosmetics, and the sales people were paid strictly on commission.

C. Misclassifying Employees as Independent Contractors

Small businesses often run up against IRS auditors when they classify workers as independent contractors instead of employees. The interests of the business person and the IRS are diametrically opposed: the IRS wants to collect employment taxes for as many workers as possible, and the business person wants to keep employment taxes at a minimum. It's obvious that a small business can save a bundle by not having workers on the payroll—according to the U.S. Chamber of Commerce, it costs a business from 20% to 33% more per worker to treat them as employees for tax purposes. The simple way to do this is to run a one-person (or a husband and wife) business, with no outside help. Because this won't work for most business people, some try to be "creative" in their hiring practices, which can be disastrous.

1. Penalties for Misclassification

If your business is audited for any reason, the IRS automatically checks for employees you claimed as independent contractors. Also, special IRS teams search for misclassified workers under the ETE (employment tax examination) program. Typically these ETE audits focus on industries where abuses are suspected to be common. Recent targets include temporary employment agencies, nursing registries and building contractors. Other businesses can be selected for the ETE simply because they file a lot of 1099 forms for independent contractors.

The tax code authorizes the IRS to force the offending business owner to pay all taxes that should have been paid, plus a special penalty that ranges from 12% to 35% of the tax bill. The *Wall Street Journal* reported that between 1988 and 1994 the IRS performed more than 11,000 audits of companies using independent contractors. The results: 483,000 reclassifications (independent contractor to employee status) and $751 million in back taxes and penalties. Ouch!

Unfortunately, the IRS is very selective in its enforcement of worker classification rules. It picks on small businesses while major corporations openly flaunt the worker classification rules. Two of the largest local employers in the San Francisco Bay area frequently hire independent contractors in addition to their regular employees. These corporate giants furnish offices, require regular work hours and pay these ICs in other respects like their regular employees—except they do not pay employee benefits and, more importantly, do not pay employment taxes. An attorney I know has worked on this basis for years; he is well paid enough not to complain about this obvious misclassification. I have reported these companies to the IRS, but nothing ever comes of it; politics, I guess. In the tax world, we all know that life is unfair.

Here's how easily a small business person can get in trouble.

Example: Ray, who wholesales American-made bathing suits, faces stiff competition from cheap imports. To survive, he must keep prices low by cutting overhead to the bone. Ray decides to classify his secretary, warehouse person, delivery person and two salespersons as independent contractors, to realize the following savings:

- *Administrative work, including completing tax-reporting forms, withholding employees' pay and making federal tax deposits.*
- *Social Security and Medicare tax matching. Unlike employees, with independent contractors there is no need to pay 7.65% of their wages for the employer's share of Social Security and Medicare taxes.*
- *Federal and state unemployment tax costs.*
- *Non-tax expenses like workers compensation insurance and employee benefits such as sick leave and vacation pay.*

Ray is saving a hefty sum by calling these workers independent contractors. The problem is that Ray's workers are all legally employees, not ICs.

Let's say the IRS audits Ray and reclassifies his secretary, Faye, as an employee. Faye was paid $20,000 per year for three years. Ray's audit bill, with interest and penalties, could be as much as $30,000 if the auditor finds that Ray intentionally disregarded the law. If, however, the IRS auditor concludes Ray made an "innocent" mistake, the tax bill could be half that amount. It's a judgment call, but either way it is still a lot of money.

NEW IRS CLASSIFICATION SETTLEMENT PROGRAM

In 1996, the IRS offered an olive branch to small business owners charged with misclassifying employees, with the Classification Settlement Program (CSP). This is a relatively inexpensive way to settle with the IRS over past misclassification of workers. In order to qualify for this program, a business owner must:

1. Have an open case with the IRS at the time, either in an audit or in Appeals. (In other words, you can't call up and volunteer for the program: you must have first been selected for audit.)

2. Specifically request CSP treatment.

3. Have been in compliance with § 530 of the 1978 Revenue Act. That means you must have:

- Filed all tax returns, including 1099 forms showing independent contractor treatment,
- Treated all similarly situated workers as independent contractors
- Had a reasonable basis for your misclassification, such as: reliance on court rulings, an IRS ruling or written technical advice; a past audit that resulted in no employment tax liability for workers in positions substantially similar to the workers in question, or a long-standing practice of a significant segment of your industry.

If you qualify, you will be offered one of three settlement deals:

1. Pay no tax assessment for past misclassifications.

2. Pay the most recent year of taxes for worker classification deficiencies and the IRS will drop demands for assessments for prior years.

3. Pay 25% of the latest audit year deficiency. In all cases, you must further agree to classify the workers as employees in the future. The IRS says it will monitor your case for five years to make sure you don't fall back into your old ways.

Which one of the three deals you will get will depends on the judgment of the IRS—and your ability to convince the IRS that you acted "reasonably" but incorrectly in misclassifying workers. Excuses that may work: your reliance on the advice of an attorney or tax pro, industry practice even if not widespread, or your misinterpretation of the 20 IRS factors.

Always issue a 1099 form for a qualifying independent contractor you pay. Some sly types will tell you it isn't necessary to give them one. Undoubtedly these are the folks who aren't playing it straight with Uncle Sam. The IRS can penalize you $50 for each 1099 not issued, but much more importantly, you can be assessed all of the income taxes due and not paid for each individual not given a 1099—if they are found to be employees instead of ICs. This could be hundreds of thousands of dollars if you had a lot of workers over several years! There is no penalty for filing a 1099 if it was not required, so if in doubt, do it.

State employment tax agencies also get into the employee classification act. Suppose a worker who was misclassified as an independent contractor is laid off and makes a claim for unemployment benefits. This triggers a state agency inquiry, and the state may turn the employer in to the IRS. If either the IRS or the state reclassifies a worker as an employee, the employer will also be liable for state payroll taxes that should have been paid, plus penalties. So, not only might you have to pony up for the IRS, the state will put a gun to your head, too.

LEASING EMPLOYEES

Larger businesses may sidestep employee classification challenges—and save on employee fringe benefits—by leasing workers. The lease company, not you, withholds and does payroll tax reporting. It is all legal as long as you deal with a bona fide employee leasing company.

Weigh whether the cost markup of leasing is worth any fringe benefit or administrative savings for your business. Generally, this idea makes sense only for certain types of successful businesses with fluctuating needs for workers.

---

2. Should You Ask the IRS to Classify Your Workers?

If you are in doubt as to how to classify a particular worker, you can ask the IRS to determine the worker's status. Just fill out and send to the IRS Form SS-8, Determination of Employee Work Status for Purposes of Federal Employment Taxes and Income Tax Withholding. The IRS will respond within several months.

Think twice before you ask the IRS to classify workers. The IRS is very likely to rule them employees no matter what the circumstances are. And by using this form you have put yourself on record, which can work against you if you decide not to follow the IRS's determination and are audited.

3. Appealing a Ruling that You Misclassified Workers

As IRS auditors have a bias towards classifying workers as employees, it shouldn't be a surprise that business owners more times than not lose out at the audit on this issue. Fortunately, just as with any audit issue, you may appeal a misclassification finding. (See Chapter 20 on how to appeal an IRS ruling.) What's more, the IRS allows you to appeal a worker classification issue even before the rest of the audit of your business is complete. (Rev. Proc. 96-9).

Before starting your appeal might be a good time to consult a tax pro, who could help you analyze your position. There are four possible grounds for winning your appeal:
- The IRS didn't properly consider the 20 factors.
- The "safe harbor" rule may apply. Even if the IRS properly classified a worker as an em-

ployee, you can claim "industry standard" relief in your independent contractor treatment—if you did at least what 25% or more of the other businesses in your industry are doing (§ 530 of the Revenue Act of 1978).

- You can raise the "previous audit" defense if you were audited at any time in the past and no IRS challenge was made to how you classified your workers—assuming you are still in the same line of business with similar workers.

- If you still can't convince an Appeals Officer you are right, suggest a settlement based on your written agreement to change your classification of workers to employees in the future, if the IRS will drop the challenge for the past years. This "future compliance" offer might be accepted if your workers are in a gray area and the Appeals Officer is concerned that you might win in court. (For more on negotiating strategy, see Part 6, Dealing with the IRS.)

D. IRS Filing and Payment Requirements for Employers

As mentioned, the IRS imposes a lot of form filing duties on employers. If you fail to file a required form—or file it late—at the very least it will generate troublesome inquiries from the IRS and at worst will result in expensive penalties. If you miss a payment date it will almost certainly cost you extra. The following is a list of important dates you will want to mark on your calendar. Make sure that either you or your employee, an accountant or payroll service meets these deadlines.

Note: For any due date, the "file" or "furnish" requirement is met if the form is properly addressed, mailed first class and postmarked on or before the due date. If any deadline falls on a weekend or legal holiday, use the next business day.

Get any forms you need to comply with these requirements from your local IRS office or call 1 800-829-FORM (3676).

- *Each Payday: Withhold Income Taxes and Employees' Share of Social Security and Medicare.* See Section A, "Payroll Taxes," above. No report needs to be made to the IRS at the time of the withholding.

- *Annually on January 31: Reporting of Payments to Workers, FUTA.* January 31st is a key date for businesses with employees and independent contractors. That is the deadline for mailing these people either a "Form W-2" to report wages (no minimum) paid for the prior year or "Form 1099" to report independent contractor payments ($600 or more only). Copies of the 1099s and W-2s you issue must be sent to the IRS by the last day of February (see below). Get these forms from the IRS and follow the instructions in IRS Circular E, "Employer's Tax Guide" if you are not using a tax pro or payroll tax service.

  Also, "Form 940 (or 940EZ), Employer's Annual Federal Unemployment Tax Return," is due on January 31, along with payment of any balance due. You get until February 12 to file if all FUTA taxes were deposited when due.

- *Annually on February 28: Forms 1099 (and 8027) to IRS.* Mail copy "A" of all the Forms 1099 you issued, along with "Form 1096, Annual Summary and Transmittal of U.S. Information Returns," to your IRS Service Center. If applicable to your business, file "Form 8027, Employer's Annual Information Return of Tip Income," as well.

- *Annually on February 29: Forms W-2 to Social Security Administration.* Mail copy "A" of all the Forms W-2 you issued, along with "Form W-3, Transmittal of Wage and Tax Statements," with the Social Security Administration (address on the forms).

E. Keeping Employer Tax Records for the IRS

As with most tax records, I suggest that you keep records of employees and others who have provided services to your business for at least four, and preferably *six years* after you file the tax return for that year. The reason is that the IRS always has at least three years to audit you after you file your tax returns, and in some cases six years. Also, your state tax agency and the IRS sometimes spot-checks employment tax records without subjecting your business to a full scale audit. So, take the Boy Scout motto to heart.

The minimum records that should be kept available for IRS review are originals or copies of the following:

- Amounts and dates of all wages, pensions or other benefits paid to employees and monies paid to independent contractors. Also, keep the dates of employment, social security numbers, names and addresses of these folks and their W-4 Employee's Withholding Allowance Certificate.

- All 1099s, W-2s issued to workers, along with proof of payment (such as canceled checks) showing that any taxes due the IRS were withheld. Also keep any employee copies of W-2s and 1099s that were returned to you by the Post Office as undeliverable.

- Tax deposit forms with dates and proof of deposit (deposit slip, canceled check).

- All Forms 941, 940 and the income tax returns for these years.

- Records of fringe benefits provided, including substantiation.

RESOURCES

- *IRS Publication 937, Employment Taxes and Information Returns.* Every employer should be familiar with this publication; it shows how to fill out employment tax forms.

- *IRS Circular E, Employer's Tax Guide.* This is a useful booklet with forms and charts for determining how much to withhold from employees' pay checks.

- *Hiring Independent Contractors: The Employer's Legal Guide,* by Stephen Fishman (Nolo Press). Everything you need to know about federal and state laws for working with independent contractors.

- *Stand Up to the IRS,* by Fred Daily (Nolo Press). This book should be helpful in the event you want to contest adverse IRS decisions.

- *The Employer's Legal Handbook,* by Fred Steingold (Nolo Press). This book details all the legal issues involved with being an employer. I heartily recommend it. ■

Sole Proprietorships

"The most enlightened judicial policy is to let people manage their own business in their own way."
— Oliver Wendell Holmes, Jr., U.S. Supreme Court Justice

For tax purposes, the term "sole proprietor" refers to a single person (or husband and wife) who owns a business. (IRC § 6231.) The term also includes individuals who are treated as independent contrac-tors. (See Chapter 5.) According to the IRS, there are 15 to 20 million sole proprietorships in the U.S., comprising over 80% of all businesses. Most folks choose this way of operating because it is the easiest, fastest and cheapest way to go.

For most legal purposes, a sole proprietor and her business are indistinguishable. Business profits and losses are reported on the owner's personal tax return every year, and the sole proprietor is person-ally responsible for business debts. And when the owner dies, a sole proprietorship venture terminates for federal tax purposes.

Sole proprietorships aren't just shopkeepers—they may offer any type of goods or services, have multiple employees, lose money or make millions. In most parts of the country you can start a sole proprietorship for the cost of printing a business card or flier advertising your goods or services. You may have to get a local business license and possibly a sales tax permit as well, but that's about it.

TAXES AND SOLE PROPRIETORSHIPS IN A NUTSHELL

1. The tax code does not consider a sole proprietor a separate entity from its owner, so the business does not file its own tax return. Its income or loss is reported on the owner's tax return.

2. Sole proprietors, as self-employed individuals, must file and pay quarterly estimated income taxes, as well as Social Security and Medicare taxes.

3. The great majority of small businesses begin as sole proprietorships, but many sole proprietors eventually convert to a partnership, limited liability company or corporation.

A. Business Expenses

All legitimate business expenses can be tax-deducted no matter what form your business takes—sole proprietorship or major corporation. The types of expenses and rules for deducting them are covered in Chapters 1 and 2. If you have a home-based business, also see Chapter 13, Microbusinesses and Home-Based Businesses, for special rules on writing off home expenses.

B. Profits Left in the Business

The following bit of tax news comes as a shock to most sole proprietors: You are taxed on all profits in the year they are earned—*whether you take the money out of the business or not.* Any profits remaining in a business bank account at the end of the year are taxed as if you had put them in your personal bank account. Remember, under the tax code a sole proprietor and the business are one.

For retailers and manufacturers, this means if you put profits into building your inventory—which is almost inevitable—you first will be taxed on them. In other words, you will have to use "after-tax" dollars to expand your business.

Example: Jose made a net profit of $85,000 in his magic and novelty shop in 1995. He took $50,000 out of the business bank account for living expenses and spent the remaining $35,000 on inventory. Jose pays income and self-employment tax on the full $85,000.

If your small business is incorporated, you may pay less tax on profits put into inventory. This is because owners of C corporations do not report profits left in the business on their personal tax returns. Although profits left in a corporation are taxable to the corporation, initial rates of taxation are lower than for most individuals, producing a tax saving for most small businesses. (See Chapter 7, C Corporations, for the tax advantages of incorporation.)

START-UP PERMITS

Although it is easy to start a sole proprietorship, certain types of businesses and professions (bars and restaurants, and attorneys and accountants, for example) may need state or local licenses and are subject to added taxes and fees. For more information, see *The Legal Guide for Starting and Running a Small Business,* by Fred Steingold (Nolo Press), and *Small-Time Operator,* by Bernard Kamoroff (Bell Springs).

C. How Sole Proprietors Tax Report

As far as the IRS is concerned, a sole proprietorship starts the day you begin taking in income for goods or services. No IRS licensing or even form-filing is required. A sole proprietorship and its owner (or married couple filing a joint tax return) are one and the same for tax purposes.

1. Schedule C (or Schedule F, for Farming)

Business income is reported on a separate "schedule" (form) attached to the proprietor's annual Form 1040 individual tax return. The IRS provides Schedule C, Profit or Loss From Business (Sole Proprietorship), or Schedule F if your business is farming, just for this purpose. A sample of Schedule C is shown below.

You must file Schedule C if your net income (after deducting expenses) from all sole proprietorship ventures exceeds $400 in a year. But you should file one even if you make less than $400 or lose money. One reason is that if you have a loss, it will usually produce a tax benefit. And reporting starts the statute of limitations (the period during which the IRS legally can audit you) running. If you don't report, theoretically the IRS has forever to audit you for the business operation.

Example: In December 1995, Sam and Jeannie Smith open Smith's Computer Sales and Service as a sole proprietorship, and they just about break even in that year. Even though they didn't make or lose money, good practice dictates that by April 15, 1996, they should file their income tax return, including a Schedule C.

A sample Schedule C is shown below.

2. Schedule C-EZ

If you run a really small side business, you may be able to use a simplified form, Schedule C-EZ. You are eligible to use it if you:

- claim less than $2,500 in business expenses,
- have no inventory,
- have no employees,
- use the cash method of accounting,
- don't claim IRC § 179 or depreciation expenses to write off any assets, and
- don't have an overall loss in operation.

Most businesses worthy of the name can either claim much more than $2,500 in business expenses or will not otherwise qualify for Schedule C-EZ.

MORE THAN ONE SOLE PROPRIETORSHIP

If you have more than one sole proprietorship, you must file a different Schedule C, or C-EZ, for each business. You might have multiple C's on one tax return if you have your finger in many pies.

Example: Jeannie and Sam Smith own Smith's Computer Sales and Service. Besides helping run to run their business, Jeannie has an Amway distributorship and Sam buys and sells sports cards. The Smiths file one 1040 form, with three Schedule C's. Since the sports card venture takes in more than $25,000, they must use a regular C form, even though the other, smaller, businesses qualify for the EZ form.

SCHEDULE C
(Form 1040)

Department of the Treasury
Internal Revenue Service   (T)

Profit or Loss From Business
(Sole Proprietorship)

▶ Partnerships, joint ventures, etc., must file Form 1065.

▶ Attach to Form 1040 or Form 1041.   ▶ See Instructions for Schedule C (Form 1040).

OMB No. 1545-0074

1994

Attachment
Sequence No. **09**

Name of proprietor	Social security number (SSN)
Susan J. Brown	111 00 1111

A Principal business or profession, including product or service (see page C-1)
Retail, ladies' apparel

B Enter principal business code
(see page C-6) ▶ 3 9 1 3

C Business name. If no separate business name, leave blank.
Milady Fashions

D Employer ID number (EIN), if any
1 0 1 2 3 4 5 6 7

E Business address (including suite or room no.) ▶ 725 Big Sur Drive
City, town or post office, state, and ZIP code   Franklin, NY 18725

F Accounting method: (1) ☐ Cash   (2) ☑ Accrual   (3) ☐ Other (specify) ▶ ....

G Method(s) used to value closing inventory: (1) ☑ Cost   (2) ☐ Lower of cost or market   (3) ☐ Other (attach explanation)   (4) ☐ Does not apply (if checked, skip line H) | Yes | No |

H Was there any change in determining quantities, costs, or valuations between opening and closing inventory? If "Yes," attach explanation   No ✔

I Did you "materially participate" in the operation of this business during 1994? If "No," see page C-2 for limit on losses.   Yes ✔

J If you started or acquired this business during 1994, check here ▶ ☐

Part I   **Income**

1	Gross receipts or sales. **Caution:** If this income was reported to you on Form W-2 and the "Statutory employee" box on that form was checked, see page C-2 and check here ▶ ☐	**1** 397,742
2	Returns and allowances	**2** 1,442
3	Subtract line 2 from line 1	**3** 396,300
4	Cost of goods sold (from line 40 on page 2)	**4** 239,349
5	**Gross profit.** Subtract line 4 from line 3	**5** 156,951
6	Other income, including Federal and state gasoline or fuel tax credit or refund (see page C-2)	**6** 0
7	**Gross income.** Add lines 5 and 6 ▶	**7** 156,951

Part II   **Expenses.** Enter expenses for business use of your home **only** on line 30.

8	Advertising	**8** 3,500	**19**	Pension and profit-sharing plans	**19**
9	Bad debts from sales or services (see page C-3)	**9** 479	**20**	Rent or lease (see page C-4):	
10	Car and truck expenses (see page C-3)	**10** 3,850	**a**	Vehicles, machinery, and equipment	**20a**
11	Commissions and fees	**11**	**b**	Other business property	**20b** 12,000
12	Depletion	**12**	**21**	Repairs and maintenance	**21** 964
13	Depreciation and section 179 expense deduction (not included in Part III) (see page C-3)	**13** 2,731	**22**	Supplies (not included in Part III)	**22** 1,203
14	Employee benefit programs (other than on line 19)	**14**	**23**	Taxes and licenses	**23** 5,727
15	Insurance (other than health)	**15** 238	**24**	Travel, meals, and entertainment:	
16	Interest:		**a**	Travel	**24a**
a	Mortgage (paid to banks, etc.)	**16a**	**b**	Meals and entertainment	
b	Other	**16b** 2,633	**c**	Enter 50% of line 24b subject to limitations (see page C-4)	
17	Legal and professional services	**17**	**d**	Subtract line 24c from line 24b	**24d**
18	Office expense	**18** 216	**25**	Utilities	**25** 3,570
			26	Wages (less employment credits)	**26** 59,050
			27	Other expenses (from line 46 on page 2)	**27** 8,078

28	**Total expenses** before expenses for business use of home. Add lines 8 through 27 in columns ▶	**28** 104,239
29	**Tentative profit (loss).** Subtract line 28 from line 7	**29** 52,712
30	Expenses for business use of your home. Attach **Form 8829**	**30**
31	**Net profit or (loss).** Subtract line 30 from line 29. ● If a profit, enter on **Form 1040, line 12,** and ALSO on **Schedule SE, line 2** (statutory employees, see page C-5). Estates and trusts, enter on Form 1041, line 3. ● If a loss, you MUST go on to line 32.	**31** 52,712
32	If you have a loss, check the box that describes your investment in this activity (see page C-5). ● If you checked 32a, enter the loss on **Form 1040, line 12,** and ALSO on **Schedule SE, line 2** (statutory employees, see page C-5). Estates and trusts, enter on Form 1041, line 3. ● If you checked 32b, you MUST attach **Form 6198.**	**32a** ☐ All investment is at risk. **32b** ☐ Some investment is not at risk.

For Paperwork Reduction Act Notice, see Form 1040 instructions.   Cat. No. 11334P   Schedule C (Form 1040) 1994

Schedule C (Form 1040) 1994   Page **2**

Part III   Cost of Goods Sold (see page C-5)

33	Inventory at beginning of year. If different from last year's closing inventory, attach explanation . .	33	42,843
34	Purchases less cost of items withdrawn for personal use	34	240,252
35	Cost of labor. Do not include salary paid to yourself	35	0
36	Materials and supplies	36	0
37	Other costs	37	0
38	Add lines 33 through 37	38	283,095
39	Inventory at end of year	39	43,746
40	**Cost of goods sold.** Subtract line 39 from line 38. Enter the result here and on page 1, line 4 . .	40	239,349

Part IV   **Information on Your Vehicle.** Complete this part **ONLY** if you are claiming car or truck expenses on line 10 and are not required to file Form 4562 for this business. See the instructions for line 13 on page C-3 to find out if you must file.

41   When did you place your vehicle in service for business purposes? (month, day, year) ▶ ..../........./........ .

42   Of the total number of miles you drove your vehicle during 1994, enter the number of miles you used your vehicle for:

a   Business ....   b Commuting ....   c Other ....

43   Do you (or your spouse) have another vehicle available for personal use? . . . . ☐ Yes   ☐ No

44   Was your vehicle available for use during off-duty hours? . . . . ☐ Yes   ☐ No

45a Do you have evidence to support your deduction? . . . . ☐ Yes   ☐ No
  b If "Yes," is the evidence written? . . . . ☐ Yes   ☐ No

Part V   **Other Expenses.** List below business expenses not included on lines 8–26 or line 30.

Bank service charges	180
Chamber of Commerce	60
Free Credit Card Co.	6,000
Trash removal	1,600
Window washing	238
46 **Total other expenses.** Enter here and on page 1, line 27 . . . . **46**	8,078

PART **2**

The Form
of Your Business

3. How Sole Proprietor Income Is Taxed

Schedule C, line 31, shows the profit or loss from your sole proprietorship. This figure is entered on the front page of your Form 1040 tax return and is added to your income (or losses) from all sources—regular jobs, dividends, capital gains and so on. This combined figure is taxed at whatever overall tax bracket you are in—currently from 15% to 39.6%. In addition, you are subject to self-employment taxes (discussed in Chapter 13, Microbusinesses and Home-Based Businesses), which currently take 15.3% of the first $65,400 of your total self-employment income and 2.9% of everything over $65,400 (1996 rate).

If your business loses money, you can use the loss to offset your other earnings in that year—say from a regular job—or, if you don't have enough other earnings, carry the loss over to the following year. If the business makes a profit in a future year, you can use the previous unused losses to offset it and reduce your taxes. (See Chapter 4, Business Losses.)

D. Recordkeeping

Poor recordkeeping—such as scribbling cash expenses on scraps of paper, trusting your memory, or mixing up personal and business records—is the chief tax bugaboo of small businesses. Without accurate records, you will never be able to know, let alone properly tax report, your income and expenses.

Basic recordkeeping principles are really the same for all businesses, including sole proprietorships. Of course, bookkeeping becomes more involved as your business grows.

To summarize, the tax code says a business must keep track of its income and expenses, so it must have some system to accurately record its transactions. The IRS doesn't dictate any particular way to do it—just that records be kept and available for an audit.

Beware of mixing business and pleasure. Keep business records separate from your personal ones. Sole proprietors tend to run the loosest ships in the business world and have a bad habit of keeping everything in the same pot. If you mix things up, you will have a mess at tax preparation time, not to mention an audit. If you haven't set up a real recordkeeping system, you should at least maintain a separate checking account and credit card just for business transactions. If you take money from the business for personal use, write a check (signed by you, of course) from your business account to your personal account.

Another, better, approach—one I use myself—is to use a computer program such as Quicken, which distinguishes business from personal expenses in one checking account. It also tracks credit card and even cash expenditures.

For more on how to keep good business records for tax purposes, and for an explanation of simple computer recordkeeping programs, see Chapter 3, Recordkeeping and Accounting.

E. Estimated Tax Payments

Wage-earners have their income taxes siphoned off by their employer every paycheck. It's not so simple for a sole proprietor, who must make income tax payments to the IRS four times a year. If you wait until April 15, you will incur a penalty. The chief difficulty for most people with estimated taxes is knowing how much to pay. In effect, a self-employed person is required to project how much he or she will earn for the whole year ahead of time. To avoid the estimated tax penalty, you should make payments equal to your tax liability for the previous year.

If you will have at least $400 in profits, you must make four quarterly "estimated tax" payments throughout the year, using IRS Form 1040-ES. These four equal payments are due on April 15, June 15, September 15, and January 15 (of the following year). Estimated tax payments cover Self-Employment taxes (better known as SE or Social Security and Medicare taxes) as well as plain old income taxes.

SPOUSE'S SELF-EMPLOYMENT TAXES

Even though spouses who co-own a sole proprietorship are taxed as one on income of the business, they are treated as two individuals for purposes of self-employment tax. (IRC § 1402 (a) (5) (A), Reg. 1.1402(a)(8).) So, a separate SE tax form must be filed—and taxes paid—based on an allocation of each spouse's share of the net income. The allocation should be based on how much each spouse contributed to the operation of the business. This rule has more significance than just filing another form. It means that listing your spouse as a co-owner can cost you extra taxes if the business profit exceeds $65,400 (1996). (See Chapter 12, Section C, for an explanation of how this tax provision works against you.) Because of this, you might want to list only one spouse as an owner and the other as an unpaid "volunteer."

If estimated tax payments are too small or aren't made on time, the IRS will assess an underpayment penalty. Currently this penalty is based on an annual interest rate of 9% of the underpaid amount for each quarter. Some cash-strapped entrepreneurs skip quarterly ES payments, waiting to pay in one lump sum with their annual Form 1040 income tax return. If you're running this close to the edge, you may not have the needed funds at tax time. And if you don't pay all the estimated taxes by April 15, the IRS will tack on yet another tax penalty and interest for paying late.

Most states also require quarterly estimated income tax payments. Get forms and information from your state's tax agency.

F. Employee Taxes

Sole proprietorships are not necessarily one-person or mom-and-pop operations. Many solos have employees—and if they do, they must pay federal employment taxes. Employment taxes cover Social Security and Medicare for the employees as well as Unemployment Compensation insurance. (IRC §§ 101, 3111.)

A sole proprietor with employees must follow these employment tax rules:

- Report federal payroll tax information.
- Make federal payroll tax deposits.
- Report and pay annual federal unemployment tax (FUTA).
- Report annual wages for employees, and
- Report annual payments to independent contractors.

All these rules are explained in Chapter 5, Tax Concerns of Employers.

Sole proprietors (including a husband and wife team) are not employees of the business under the tax law, so no employment taxes are due on their income. Instead, as discussed in Section E, above, sole proprietors pay estimated taxes, which include self-employment taxes covering Social Security and Medicare.

PART **2**

The Form of Your Business

G. Outgrowing the Sole Proprietorship

As we've emphasized, a sole proprietor and the business are one in the eyes of the IRS. This simplicity alone is a compelling reason to choose this form. While most businesspeople start and finish their business lives as sole proprietors, others take on partners, incorporate or form a limited liability company later on down the road. For instance, if your business becomes quite profitable and can afford fringe benefit packages, it may make tax sense to incorporate. Incorporating can pose tax problems, however. For instance, if you shut the business down, you must formally liquidate a corporation, which might bring extra tax costs a sole proprietor wouldn't face. (See Chapter 7, C Corporations.)

Seldom will tax reasons alone justify changing the legal structure of your business. More often, people who go beyond the sole proprietorship are influenced by non-tax issues, such as the fact that corporations and limited liability companies can shield owners from personal liability for business debts. Also, partnerships, corporations and limited liability companies allow bringing others into the business. And some folks believe the letters "Inc." after a business name projects a larger business image, which may impress customers, investors and lenders.

New expenses. Don't change the form of your sole proprietorship business entity without factoring in the added costs of accounting and legal services that will probably be needed.

H. Ending the Business

Just as the sole proprietorship is the easiest business to start, it is also the easiest to end. Simply stop doing business, file a Schedule C for the final year of operation with the words "Final Return" across the top.

Things are not so easy when it comes to disposing of your enterprise's assets; you may need to report a gain (or loss) on your tax return. (See Chapter 17, Selling a Business or Its Assets, for the tax consequences of selling a business or its assets.)

I. Death

If you die owning a sole proprietorship, the business dies with you in the eyes of the tax law. (One exception is when a husband and wife are co-proprietors.) Remember, you and your sole proprietorship business are one and the same for the IRS. Your business is an asset of your estate that becomes the property of your heirs, so there may be estate tax and probate consequences. (See Chapter 12, Family Businesses, for a brief discussion of estate planning for a small business.) If your heirs (other than your spouse) carry on the business, they will report its income and expenses on Schedule C of their own tax return. They will need to get a new Employer Identification Numbers from the IRS and have all licenses and permits transferred into their names.

RESOURCES

- Chapter 27 of IRS Publication 334, *Tax Guide for Small Business*. There are no IRS publications devoted strictly to sole proprietors, but this is a good one and covers the tax basics for all businesses. If you are a farmer, see Publication 225, *Farmer's Tax Guide*; if you are a commercial fisherman, see Publication 595.
- IRS Publication 533, *Self-Employment Tax*.
- IRS *Circular E, Employer's Tax Guide*. This booklet gives a detailed explanation of the payroll tax process and the forms used.

Several good books thoroughly discuss factors to consider when choosing the legal form for your business. Two of the best are:

- *Legal Guide for Starting & Running a Small Business*, by Fred Steingold (Nolo Press).
- *Small-Time Operator*, by Bernard Kamoroff (Bell Springs). ■

CHAPTER 7

C Corporations

"You can have a lord, you can have a king, but the man to fear is the tax collector."

— **Sumerian Proverb**

The word "corporation" brings to mind IBM, GM or AT&T—businesses so big and familiar we know them by their initials. But corporations don't have to be huge; anyone can form one. Incorporating is more popular than ever in the U.S.; in 1994, 737,000 new businesses incorporated, which was an all-time high.

Big business obviously has a great deal to say about how tax law is written. As a result, much of our tax code favors corporate America. Fortunately, small incorporated businesses can also qualify for many of these favorable tax breaks, some of which are unavailable to partnerships, LLCs and sole proprietorships. Incorporating offers potential tax savings, but any tax advantages must be balanced against the more complex tax rules corporations must follow.

A corporation is the most costly way of doing business. You must pay an initial incorporation charge, as well as annual fees to the state, to maintain a corporation—whether or not it is active or makes a profit. Additional accounting costs and fees can put a significant dent in a new business's cash flow. Professional help needed to deal with federal and state corporation tax reporting forms in future years will cost you as well.

Another consideration is that most corporate tax breaks involve fringe benefits. This means that only solidly profitable businesses stand to gain by incorporating. The majority of small enterprises don't reap tax advantages from incorporating and typically find the relative simplicity of being a sole proprietorship, limited liability company or partnership preferable. Later, if the business grows and becomes as profitable as you hope it will, you can always incorporate.

C CORPORATIONS IN A NUTSHELL

1. A C corporation is a completely separate tax entity from its owners, who are treated as employees of the corporation by the tax laws.

2. C corporations are subject to corporate income taxes, but most small business C corporations can legally avoid paying corporation income taxes.

3. C corporations are the most complex business entity to set up, and they have significant tax reporting responsibilities.

4. C corporations allow you to keep profits in the business for expansion or inventory and have them taxed at lower rates than if your business were not incorporated.

Tax considerations are only one factor in deciding whether to incorporate. For most businesses, other reasons—primarily the limited personal liability that a corporation provides—are more important. For instance, if your business carries high risks that can't be adequately recovered by insurance, a corporation can protect your personal assets from business creditors. Don't get so carried away with comparing the tax advantages and disadvantages of the different forms of business that you overlook these other issues.

A. Types of Corporations

For federal tax purposes, most small profit-making corporations are classified as either "C" or "S" types. These names come from the subchapters of the tax code that govern the different kinds of corporations. This chapter discusses tax treatment of "C" corporations; "S" corporations are covered in Chapter 8. An additional kind of corporation, called the "professional corporation," is covered in Chapter 11, Personal Service Corporations.

All corporations begin life as C corporations. After incorporating, the shareholders may choose "S" corporation status, so the business will be taxed more like a partnership than like a standard C corporation. It is a good idea to read the S corporation chapter as well as this one to fully understand your options.

B. How C Corporations Are Taxed

A corporation is considered an "artificial person" because it is a legal entity distinct from its owners, who are called "stockholders" or "shareholders." As a separate entity, a corporation may own property, enter into contracts, borrow money and sue and be sued. In most states, corporations are allowed as few as one stockholder, who can also be the sole legal manager of the corporation's business. This person is called a "director."

PART 2

The Form of Your Business

HOW TO SET UP A CORPORATION

Small business corporations are chartered by the 50 states, not the federal government. While there are differences in the details, corporation organization law and procedures are remarkably similar throughout the U.S.

Some states, such as Delaware or Nevada, have very low incorporation fees, seemingly making them more attractive than your home state. And these two states do not tax corporations that do not do business in that state. Be warned: Though another state's plan may seem attractive, it usually isn't, for several reasons. For starters, your state probably requires out-of-state corporations to register and pay a fee there before doing business. For instance, California charges the same amount for an out-of-state corporation to register as it does to a California corporation. So a California resident forming a Nevada corporation must pay both Nevada's annual corporation fees and California's, if the company does any business in California. What's more, any income from the Nevada corporation paid to the California resident is subject to California's state income tax. In this case, there is a tax cost, not a savings, for incorporating out of state.

Incorporating is not a terribly difficult process. You can do it yourself using a self-help book containing forms and instructions, or a private incorporation service such as Corporation Service Center 800-638-2320, or software that prepares the forms for you. Or you can hire a local lawyer. This last is the best—but most expensive—way to do it.

First, choose your corporate name (after making sure it is available by checking with your state's corporate filing office). Then, prepare a document called the "Articles of Incorporation," usually available as a fill-in-the-blanks form. In the Articles, you list the name of your corporation, where it is headquartered, its general purpose, and additional information such as who can be served with legal papers in case of a lawsuit. Send this paperwork to your state's corporate filing office, along with the filing fee—usually $50 to $1,000. You will get back your corporate charter and, congratulations, you are officially incorporated.

After you incorporate, you must hold a meeting of stockholders and adopt "bylaws"—rules that govern the corporation's operation. Again, you can use fill-in-the-blanks preprinted bylaws forms. Nolo Press sells corporate form books for California, New York , Florida and Texas. (See "Resources" at the end of the chapter.) "Corporate kits" that contain blank stock certificates and forms for minutes of corporate meetings are available in office supply and stationery stores. You must keep a corporate record book to prove to the world (including an IRS auditor) that you really are a corporation.

CLOSELY-HELD CORPORATIONS

The corporations discussed in this chapter are referred to in the tax code as "closely-held" corporations. Almost all small business corporations fall into this category. A closely-held corporation is defined as a corporation that:

- Sells stock privately and has fewer than 35 shareholders, and

- Has shareholders who all work in the business, or are closely related to people who do, or are experienced investors.

If a corporation offers shares to the public or has more than 35 investors, it is not closely-held. In this case more complicated state and federal tax and securities laws come into play.

Whether a corporation has just one or dozens of shareholders, it is a completely separate legal and tax entity. So if your business operates as a corporation, you will be its employee—you are not self-employed in the eyes of the tax law. Consequently, throughout this chapter, the term "employee" usually includes owners (the stockholders).

Example: Sam Smith and his wife Jeannie incorporate Smith's Computer Sales & Service. All stock is owned by Sam, Jeannie and two key employees who are actively involved in the business. For most legal purposes, including paying taxes, the Smiths and the business are now separate entities. Both the Smiths and their corporation must file income tax returns, and if Smith's Computer Sales & Service is sued, the Smiths will probably not be personally liable. This is a huge change from when Sam and Jeannie were sole proprietors; then the Smiths and their business were legally one.

1. Avoiding Double Taxation

A "C" corporation is subject to federal and state corporation income tax laws totally different from those laws governing sole proprietorships, limited liability companies or partnerships. The key difference is that before any profits are paid to shareholders, the corporation must pay income tax at the corporate rate. (See Section 3, below.) Any profits that are distributed to shareholders via dividends are then subject to individual income tax. This amounts to double taxation, with business profits taxed at both the corporate and personal levels.

Fortunately, small C corporations rarely have to pay taxes. The simple reason is that a small C corporation's earnings typically are paid out to its employees as wages and benefits, and deducted from corporate income as a business expense. After everyone is paid for their labor, there is usually no income for the corporation to owe tax upon.

Example: Ned's corporation, Men's Den, Inc., has profits of $70,000 one year. But after the corporation pays Ned $50,000 as a salary, provides him with $10,000 in tax-free fringe benefits, including retirement plan contributions, and gives him a year-end bonus of $18,000, the corporation has no net profit; so it owes no corporate income tax. Ned, however, pays taxes on $60,000 of earned income. The fringe benefits of $10,000 aren't subject to tax.

If any corporate income is left in the business, it is usually tied up in inventory or retained to fund future growth. It is taxed, but at corporate tax rates that are, in most cases, lower than personal income tax rates.

Example: Instead of giving Ned a year-end bonus of $15,000, Men's Den, Inc., retains it all for expansion in the next year. This amount is subject to federal corporate income tax at 15%, resulting in a $2,250 tax bill to the corporation. Ned pays taxes on $50,000 of earned income at his individual income tax rate.

Although double taxation of C corporations is not the norm, it can occur, especially when some shareholders don't work for the business, and therefore can't take salaries and fringe benefits. The way to get profits out of the corporation and into the pockets of these investors/shareholders is by paying dividends. But keep in mind, dividends are not paid until *after* corporate income taxes are calculated, and are therefore taxed again to the recipients on their individual tax returns.

Example: Ned's sisters, Shirley and Sally, each invest $100,000 in Men's Den, Inc., in return for 100 shares of stock each. Sally works in the business and receives a yearly salary of $50,000; Shirley doesn't work in the business. After paying all wages and all other business expenses, the corporation has $30,000 in profits. Its directors decide to pay out this profit as a dividend to shareholders. First, the corporation must pay income tax of $4,500 (15% corporation tax rate x $30,000), leaving $25,500 for the dividend. The amount each shareholder receives is subject to income tax on the shareholder's individual tax return. (See Section F, below, for a discussion of dividends.)

Getting around double taxation is not difficult. Amounts paid to a non-active shareholder who's treated as a "consultant" isn't a dividend. However, there is a trade-off; the consultant and the corporation must pay Social Security and Medicare taxes on compensation paid to that shareholder. The point is that you must consider the tax situations of both shareholders and the corporation to determine whether to pay salaries or dividends. If you are in this situation, have a tax pro run the figures.

NO SHAREHOLDER BENEFIT FOR "C" CORPORATION LOSSES

Just as corporate profits don't flow through directly to shareholders, neither do losses. While losses of a C corporation in one year can be offset against future or past years profits, individual shareholders can't claim operating losses of a C corporation business. Why? Because the corporation is a separate tax entity.

Example: Men's Den, Inc., loses $20,000. Ned received no compensation for his year's work, living off his savings. The corporation's loss provides no tax benefit to Ned when he files his individual tax return, but the loss can be used to offset any corporate profits in future years.

2. Tax Reporting for C Corporations

C corporations must file annual tax returns, either IRS Form 1120, U.S. Corporation Income Tax Return, or the short form 1120A. The return is due by the 15th day of the third month after the close of their tax year. So if the corporation uses a calendar year, its tax return is due every March 15.

A corporation is entitled to a six-month extension to file its tax return (using IRS Form 7004), until September 15 if on a calendar year reporting schedule. (See Chapter 3, Section F.) If your corporation owes any corporate tax, it must be paid along with the extension filing to avoid penalty and interest charges.

Corporations must make quarterly estimated tax payments, similar to self-employed individuals, if the corporation will owe taxes. (But, as discussed in Section B1, most small business corporations do not owe income taxes.)

3. C Corporation Income Tax Rates and Retained Earnings

Most small corporations aren't concerned with corporate tax rates because most profits are paid out as tax-deductible salaries and fringe benefits. But there are times when paying out all profits isn't desirable. For example, a business may need to retain money to expand, or it may have profits tied up in inventory. Fortunately, profits kept in the business are taxed at the initial tax rate of 15%, which is usually lower than the individual income tax rates of its owners. (IRC § 11.) This ability to retain earnings in the business is a major tax advantage that growing small C corporations have over unincorporated businesses.

FEDERAL CORPORATE TAX RATES	
Net Income	Tax Rate
First $50,000	15%
Next $25,000	25%
Next $25,000	35%
Next $225,000	40%
Everything else	35%

[Note: States also impose corporate income taxes.]

Example 1: Henry's engine-rebuilding corporation, Top Value Motors, Inc., plans to expand. To do so, it retains $100,000 of net profit in the business one year. Top Value owes corporate income taxes as follows:

$$\$50,000 \times 15\% = \$\ 7,500$$
$$\$25,000 \times 25\% = \$\ 6,250$$
$$\$25,000 \times 35\% = \underline{\$\ 8,750}$$
$$\$22,500$$

This is an effective tax rate of 22½%. By contrast, if Top Value paid Henry this $100,000, depending on his tax bracket, as much as an additional $39,600 could be added to his tax bill, as tax rate of 39.6%.

Paying some profits to shareholders and keeping the rest in the business is a form of "income splitting." But once a corporation reaches the $100,000 profit level (after paying salaries and benefits), retaining earnings produces smaller tax savings. This is because corporate profits between $100,001 and $335,000 are hit with a 5% tax surcharge, which effectively eliminates the benefits of the initial lower tax rates.

Example 2: Top Value Motors, Inc. retains a $200,000 net profit after paying salaries and fringe benefits. The corporation owes $61,500 tax to the IRS ($22,500 on the first $100,000 and $39,000 on the second $100,000). This is an average tax rate of about 31%. By contrast, if all the money had been paid to Henry as salary, he most likely would have been in the top individual tax bracket (39.6%). If his income had exceeded $300,000 before this addition, he would have had to pay an extra $79,200 in income taxes.

In addition, there are three other potential federal taxes that a C corporation might be subject to and which the other types of business entities don't have to worry about:

- the accumulated earnings tax
- personal holding company tax, and
- the corporate alternative minimum tax.

All of these are discussed in Section G, below.

Get help with corporate tax matters. This chapter covers only the basics—not the details—of the tax rules. Because the learning curve to master corporate tax intricacies is steep, I encourage you to involve a tax expert in your corporate tax matters, and to prepare corporate tax returns.

Form 1120-A

Department of the Treasury
Internal Revenue Service

U.S. Corporation Short-Form Income Tax Return

See separate instructions to make sure the corporation qualifies to file Form 1120-A.
For calendar year 1994 or tax year beginning .... , 1994, ending .... , 19 .....

OMB No. 1545-0890

1994

A Check this box if the corp. is a personal service corp. (as defined in Temporary Regs. section 1.441-4T—see instructions) ▶ ☐

Use IRS label. Other-wise, please print c type.

10-2134567   DEC94   5995
Rose Flower Shop, Inc.
38 Superior Lane
Fair City, MD   20715

B Employer identification number

C Date incorporated
7-1-82

D Total assets (see Specific Instructions)
$ 65,987

E Check applicable boxes: (1) ☐ Initial return   (2) ☐ Change of address

F Check method of accounting: (1) ☐ Cash   (2) ☑ Accrual   (3) ☐ Other (specify) · · ▶

Income

1a Gross receipts or sales 248,000	b Less returns and allowances 7,500	c Balance ▶	1c 240,500
2 Cost of goods sold (see instructions)			2 144,000
3 Gross profit. Subtract line 2 from line 1c			3 96,500
4 Domestic corporation dividends subject to the 70% deduction			4
5 Interest			5 942
6 Gross rents			6
7 Gross royalties			7
8 Capital gain net income (attach Schedule D (Form 1120))			8
9 Net gain or (loss) from Form 4797, Part II, line 20 (attach Form 4797)			9
10 Other income (see instructions)			10
11 **Total income.** Add lines 3 through 10 ▶			11 97,442

Deductions (See instructions for limitations on deductions.)

12 Compensation of officers (see instructions)			12 23,000
13 Salaries and wages (less employment credits)			13 24,320
14 Repairs and maintenance			14
15 Bad debts			15
16 Rents			16 6,000
17 Taxes and licenses			17 3,320
18 Interest			18 1,340
19 Charitable contributions (see instructions for 10% limitation)			19 1,820
20 Depreciation (attach Form 4562)	20		
21 Less depreciation claimed elsewhere on return	21a		21b
22 Other deductions (attach schedule) Advertising			22 3,000
23 **Total deductions.** Add lines 12 through 22 ▶			23 62,800
24 Taxable income before net operating loss deduction and special deductions. Subtract line 23 from line 11			24 34,642
25 **Less:** a Net operating loss deduction (see instructions)	25a		
b Special deductions (see instructions)	25b		25c

Tax and Payments

26 **Taxable income.** Subtract line 25c from line 24			26 34,642
27 **Total tax** (from page 2, Part I, line 7)			27 5,196
28 Payments:			
a 1993 overpayment credited to 1994	28a		
b 1994 estimated tax payments	28b 6,000		
c Less 1994 refund applied for on Form 4466	28c ( )	Bal ▶	28d 6,000
e Tax deposited with Form 7004			28e
f Credit from regulated investment companies (attach Form 2439)			28f
g Credit for Federal tax on fuels (attach Form 4136). See instructions			28g
h Total payments. Add lines 28d through 28g			28h 6,000
29 Estimated tax penalty (see instructions). Check if Form 2220 is attached ▶ ☐			29
30 **Tax due.** If line 28h is smaller than the total of lines 27 and 29, enter amount owed			30
31 **Overpayment.** If line 28h is larger than the total of lines 27 and 29, enter amount overpaid			31 804
32 Enter amount of line 31 you want: **Credited to 1995 estimated tax ▶** 804 **Refunded ▶**			32

Please Sign Here

Under penalties of perjury, I declare that I have examined this return, including accompanying schedules and statements, and to the best of my knowledge and belief, it is true, correct, and complete. Declaration of preparer (other than taxpayer) is based on all information of which preparer has any knowledge.

▶ George Rose   2-15-95   ▶ President

Signature of officer   Date   Title

Paid Preparer's Use Only

Preparer's signature ▶   Date   Check if self-employed ▶ ☐   Preparer's social security number

Firm's name (or yours if self-employed) and address ▶   E.I. No. ▶   ZIP code ▶

For Paperwork Reduction Act Notice, see page 1 of the instructions.   Cat. No. 11456E   Form **1120-A** (1994)

Form 1120-A (1994)   Page **2**

Part I   Tax Computation (See instructions.)

1	Income tax. If the corporation is a qualified personal service corporation (see page 14), check here ▶ ☐	**1**	5,196
2a	General business credit. Check if from: ☐ Form 3800 ☐ Form 3468 ☐ Form 5884 ☐ Form 6478 ☐ Form 6765 ☐ Form 8586 ☐ Form 8830 ☐ Form 8826 ☐ Form 8835 ☐ Form 8844 ☐ Form 8845 ☐ Form 8846 ☐ Form 8847 **2a**		
b	Credit for prior year minimum tax (attach Form 8827) **2b**		
3	Total credits. Add lines 2a and 2b	**3**	
4	Subtract line 3 from line 1	**4**	5,196
5	Recapture taxes. Check if from: ☐ Form 4255 ☐ Form 8611	**5**	
6	Alternative minimum tax (attach Form 4626)	**6**	
7	Total tax. Add lines 4 through 6. Enter here and on line 27, page 1	**7**	5,196

Part II   Other Information (See instructions.)

1 Refer to page 19 of the instructions and state the principal:

   a Business activity code no. ▶ 5995

   b Business activity ▶ Flower shop

   c Product or service ▶ Flowers

2 Did any individual, partnership, estate, or trust at the end of the tax year own, directly or indirectly, 50% or more of the corporation's voting stock? (For rules of attribution, see section 267(c).) *Schedule not shown.* ☑ Yes ☐ No

If "Yes," attach a schedule showing name and identifying number.

3 Enter the amount of tax-exempt interest received or accrued during the tax year   ▶ |$ –0–|

4 Enter amount of cash distributions and the book value of property (other than cash) distributions made in this tax year.   ▶ |$ –0–|

5a If an amount is entered on line 2, page 1, see the worksheet on page 12 for amounts to enter below:

   (1) Purchases   134,014

   (2) Additional sec. 263A costs (see instructions—attach schedule)

   (3) Other costs (attach schedule)   9,466

b Do the rules of section 263A (for property produced or acquired for resale) apply to the corporation?   ☐ Yes ☑ No

6 At any time during the 1994 calendar year, did the corporation have an interest in or a signature or other authority over a financial account in a foreign country (such as a bank account, securities account, or other financial account)? If "Yes," the corporation may have to file Form TD F 90-22.1   ☐ Yes ☑ No

If "Yes," enter the name of the foreign country ▶

Part III   Balance Sheets

		(a) Beginning of tax year	(b) End of tax year
Assets	1 Cash	20,540	18,498
	2a Trade notes and accounts receivable		
	b Less allowance for bad debts	( )	( )
	3 Inventories	2,530	2,010
	4 U.S. government obligations	13,807	45,479
	5 Tax-exempt securities (see instructions)		
	6 Other current assets (attach schedule)		
	7 Loans to stockholders		
	8 Mortgage and real estate loans		
	9a Depreciable, depletable, and intangible assets		
	b Less accumulated depreciation, depletion, and amortization	( )	( )
	10 Land (net of any amortization)		
	11 Other assets (attach schedule)		
	12 Total assets	36,877	65,987
Liabilities and Stockholders' Equity	13 Accounts payable	6,415	6,079
	14 Other current liabilities (attach schedule)		
	15 Loans from stockholders		
	16 Mortgages, notes, bonds payable		
	17 Other liabilities (attach schedule)		
	18 Capital stock (preferred and common stock)	20,000	20,000
	19 Paid-in or capital surplus		
	20 Retained earnings	10,462	39,908
	21 Less cost of treasury stock	( )	( )
	22 Total liabilities and stockholders' equity	36,877	65,987

Part IV   Reconciliation of Income (Loss) per Books With Income per Return (You are not required to complete Part IV if the total assets on line 12, column (b), Part III are less than $25,000.)

1 Net income (loss) per books	29,446	6 Income recorded on books this year not included on this return (itemize)
2 Federal income tax	5,196	
3 Excess of capital losses over capital gains		7 Deductions on this return not charged against book income this year (itemize)
4 Income subject to tax not recorded on books this year (itemize)		
5 Expenses recorded on books this year not deducted on this return (itemize)		8 Income (line 24, page 1). Enter the sum of lines 1 through 5 less the sum of lines 6 and 7 34,642

ANOTHER INCORPORATION ADVANTAGE: FEWER AUDITS

One of the best unofficial tax reasons for incorporating a small business is that it lowers your audit odds. Corporations reporting under $100,000 of gross receipts per year are audited at one-third the rate of unincorporated businesses with the same income. Only when a business brings in over $1 million per year do the audit odds turn against corporations. The IRS keeps threatening to step up small corporation audits, but never quite gets around to it.

C. Tax Benefits of C Corporations

Although you may incorporate for reasons that have nothing to do with taxes, C corporations offer several tax planning benefits once you are making a good profit.

1. Income Splitting

An inherent tax benefit of a C corporation is the ability to engage in "income splitting"—that is, dividing income between the corporation and the shareholders in a way that lowers overall taxes. This helps more lucrative small businesses with shareholders in the higher tax brackets, and is discussed in Section B3, above.

2. Fringe Benefits

Maybe the best tax reason to form a C corporation is that it allows the greatest tax-favored fringe benefits of all business entities. New ventures typically can't afford fringes, so this is not an advantage for start-ups. But once your business is thriving, favorable tax treatment for fringes is a reason to consider incorporating.

Two C corporation fringe benefits worth considering are more generous corporate retirement and medical plans. While any business person can establish a tax-advantaged retirement plan, C corporations offer somewhat greater contribution limits and more flexibility.

And sole proprietors, partners and limited liability company members can deduct only 30% of their medical insurance premiums, whereas a C corporation with a medical plan can deduct 100% of insurance premiums. On top of that, the corporation can adopt a medical reimbursement plan and deduct any medical expense not covered by insurance. This is usually far more advantageous than taking the medical expense deductions on your individual income tax return.

The principal drawback, as with most corporate fringe benefits, is that ordinarily they must be given to most, if not all, employees of the corporation. (See Chapter 14, Fringe Benefits, and Chapter 15, Retirement Plans, for details.)

3. Business Losses

There are essentially no limits or restrictions on the amount of capital or operating losses of a C corporation that may be carried back or forward to other corporate tax years. Other businesspeople—sole proprietors, partners and limited liability company owners—are subject to more restrictive rules on individuals for claiming tax benefits of losses. For instance, in most circumstances, an individual cannot claim a capital loss greater than $3,000 unless he has offsetting capital gains. (See Chapter 4, Business Losses, for details.)

4. Dividends from Other Corporations

Another tax break for C corporations is the "dividends received" exclusion. This won't affect many of you, but it should be kept in mind if your corporation is cash-heavy and you don't want to take out profits right away. A C corporation may receive dividends from stock it owns in another unrelated corporation 70% tax-free. In other words, while you as an individual would have to pay taxes on 100% of a $1,000 corporate stock dividend, a C corporation is taxed on only $300. This could produce a savings if you are investing in other corporations. But don't try this without seeing your tax pro first; there are some highly technical rules to be aware of.

LIMITED LIABILITY: A NON-TAX REASON TO INCORPORATE

Most small business owners who incorporate do so to limit their personal liability for debts of their business—not for tax purposes. The U.S. is the most "sue-happy" place in the world. If you are in business long enough you will be sued, and if you lose, life as you know it could be over.

Incorporating provides a "corporate shield" that separates your business assets and liabilities from your personal finances. For instance, if a customer is injured in your store, she can only sue the corporation—not you personally. If she wins, she can collect only from corporate assets—not your house or personal bank account. Ditto if your business fails and can't pay its creditors. Of course, you lose this advantage if you personally guarantee corporate obligations.

So deciding to incorporate (and whether to be a C or S corporation) usually involves weighing a number of pros and cons. I recommend you read *The Legal Guide for Starting and Running a Small Business*, by Fred Steingold (Nolo Press), which discusses the non-tax issues involved in making this decision. Then, once you've done your reading, sit down with a tax pro to confirm whether your choice makes good tax sense.

D. Incorporating Your Business

You may jump right into operation as a C corporation, but most folks incorporate after being in business a while. Remember, a corporation is a separate tax entity from its owners, and normally when two entities transfer assets between themselves there are some potential taxes to pay. The tax code, however, allows a going business to incorporate without tax consequences. In effect, you can defer taxes on gains for any property transferred to the corporation until your shares of stock are sold or the corporation is dissolved.

1. Putting Cash Into a New Corporation

Typically, incorporators (shareholders) put money into a corporate bank account in return for shares of stock. There is no minimum amount of cash that must be invested for federal tax purposes, but there might be under your state's law. Some states require corporations to have sufficient cash and other assets to show that they are not empty "shell" corporations.

Whether you are buying shares of Microsoft or starting your own Minisoft corporation, there are no immediate tax consequences of purchasing stock; this is called an "equity" investment. The taxes come later, when you sell or otherwise dispose of your stock.

Example: Marty incorporates her newsletter business and puts $10,000 into its bank account. In return, Marty, Inc., gives her 1,000 shares of stock. This is an equity investment and has no tax consequences. Later, when Marty sells her shares or dissolves her corporation, she will be taxed only if she has a gain—that is, she receives more than her tax basis in the stock, which is presently $10,000.

2. Lending Money to Your New Corporation

In the past, incorporators could put money into a new corporation as a loan, not as a purchase of stock. This meant the first money they took out of the business was a repayment of their loan and therefore a tax-free return on their investment. This no longer works; changes in the tax code have all but eliminated shareholder loans to fund a corporate start-up. A shareholder now can make only a cash or property investment in return for stock. (IRC § 351.) However, once established and profitable, you can legally make loans to fund your corporation's operation or expansion. (See Section F, below.)

3. Putting Property Into a New Corporation

You may transfer property other than cash—such as a building, vehicle or patent you own—to a corporation in exchange for its stock. Normally, transferring a personal asset to your corporation is a taxable event for you. However, § 351 of the tax code grants an exception, making transfers nontaxable when you first incorporate, *if* you follow certain rules.

a. When IRC § 351 Can Help

Transferring appreciated property (property that has a fair market value greater than your tax basis in it) to a corporation in exchange for stock is potentially taxable, just as if you sold it for cash.

IRC § 351 lets you defer any taxes that otherwise would be due if the transfer were taxable. No taxes are due until you sell the stock received in exchange for the property or until the corporation is dissolved.

Example: Mario transfers his warehouse (which he has owned for a number of years and which has a tax basis of $50,000), to Mario Brothers, Inc., in exchange for stock. (See Chapter 2, Writing Off Long-Term Business Assets, if you need an explanation of how the tax basis of property is determined.) At the time of the transfer, the warehouse has a fair market value of $100,000.

Without IRC § 351, the tax code would treat this as Mario's selling the warehouse to the corporation, with a taxable gain to Mario of $50,000—the difference between his $50,000 basis and the $100,000 market value. Fortunately, Mario can elect non-taxable treatment of the transfer by invoking IRC § 351.

Conversely, if property has gone down in value, IRC § 351 may not be the way to go. It takes away the tax benefit of a loss, because it does not allow a shareholder to claim a taxable loss when transferring property to his own corporation. IRC § 351 makes all transfers "tax-neutral."

Example: Since Mario bought his warehouse for $50,000, its value has dropped to $30,000. He has lost $20,000 on paper. Because IRC § 351 does not allow a tax loss on a transfer of a shareholder's property to his corporation, Mario cannot get a tax benefit of a $20,000 loss if he transfers the property to Mario Brothers, Inc.

Watch out for IRS rules on these sales. Selling property to your corporation and claiming a loss on the sale on your individual tax return is verboten under the "related party" rules of the tax code. IRC § 267 prohibits tax losses on transactions between shareholders and their corporation if they own 50% or more of the stock in the corporation. In this case, you and your corporation are related parties.

Example: Mario, in the example above, can claim a $20,000 tax loss resulting from the warehouse's decline in value only by selling the warehouse to an unrelated party. If his business really needs the warehouse, Mario could lease it back from the new owner after the sale.

b. How to Meet the Conditions of IRC § 351

Generally, if you are transferring property that has gone up in value since you acquired it, use IRC § 351 so that the transaction won't be taxed. To do so, four conditions must be met:

- *The corporation must receive property in exchange for stock.* Real estate and equipment are the most common types of property transferred, but it could be just about anything of value.

- *Shareholders must receive only stock in exchange for the property.* Stockholders can't take back any items such as cash, bonds, corporate promissory notes or more complicated instruments like stock warrants or stock rights (options to acquire stock in the future). And each shareholder must receive stock in proportion to the fair market value of the property he or she transfers.

Example: If Joe transfers $20,000 worth of equipment and Jill transfers $20,000 worth of real estate to Joe & Jill, Inc., each must get an equal number of shares of stock in return.

If any shareholders get anything else but stock, the value of these items is taxable income to that shareholder—but the rest of the IRC § 351 transfer is still nontaxable. So if in addition to stock, a stockholder receives a promissory note from the corporation, the value of the note is taxable to her in the year received.

- *The shareholders who transfer property must be in control.* Taken as a group, shareholders who transfer property for stock must own at least 80% of the new corporation's shares after the transfer. Since the stock of most small business corporations is held by a few investors, ordinarily this rule does not pose a problem.

Example: Paul, Ringo and John want to incorporate and take advantage of IRC § 351. Paul and Ringo transfer $170,000 in biotech research equipment, previously used by the P & R partnership, in return for 75% of the shares of BioResearch, Inc. John, who is retired and does not intend to work in the business, is internationally known in this field; the corporation gives him 25% of the shares outright on condition that it can advertise his name as a shareholder. This transaction fails IRC § 351 rules because after the transfer, Paul and Ringo own less than 80% of the stock.

- *No stock may be given in exchange for future services.* This condition often causes the most problems. The no work for stock rule precludes some people from corporation ownership. Any shareholders who got stock for their service must pay tax on the value of the stock received.

Example: Wanda and Perry form Galaxy Inc. to help businesses use the Internet. Perry contributes $100,000, but Wanda, instead of paying money, promises to apply her skill with online electronic networks. They each receive 250 shares of Galaxy Inc. Wanda's transaction doesn't qualify as nontaxable under IRC § 351, so she is taxed on $50,000, the value of her half of the corporation's stock.

c. Value of Stock in an IRC § 351 Transfer

When you get shares of stock for property, IRC § 351 gives them the same tax basis the property had. In tax lingo, this is referred to as "substituted basis." It follows that to value your stock, refer to the value of the property exchanged for it. For tax purposes, you have the same amount invested in the stock as you did in the asset transferred.

Example: When he forms Jones, Inc., Jason transfers a building he owns for stock under IRC § 351. Jason's tax basis in the building was $75,000. His basis in his Jones, Inc., stock is $75,000, since, in effect, Jason substituted the building for the corporate stock.

d. IRS Filing Requirements on Corporations and Shareholders

IRS rules require a corporation and each shareholder to report all IRC § 351 transfers. A statement listing all property transferred to the corporation should be attached to the tax returns of the individual shareholders, and of the corporation its first year. There is no IRS preprinted form, so you'll need help from a tax pro here.

Keep permanent records of IRC § 351 transfers in the corporate minutes book. Individual shareholders should also keep records of assets transferred for as long as they own their shares, and for at least three years after they dispose of them. (Reg. 1.351-3.)

Transfers to a corporation may be taxed under state and local laws. IRC § 351 is only a federal tax rule. State and local laws may treat IRC § 351 transfers as sales of assets, and tax them. For example, a retail clothier who transfers clothing racks and his inventory of men's suits to his new corporation may be subject to his state's 5% sales tax, which may negate the federal tax savings of an IRC § 351 incorporation.

There may be other adverse results from an IRC § 351 transfer. For instance, real estate transferred may trigger a property tax reassessment. In states such as California, transferring appreciated real estate to a corporation means a property tax hike. In short, check with state and local tax agencies before transferring property. You might be better off leasing your property to your corporation, instead of having it owned by the corporation. (See Section F4, below.)

E. Issuing IRC § 1244 Stock to Protect Shareholders

A small business C corporation should always issue what is called "Section 1244 stock." (S corporations don't qualify for IRC § 1244.) This enables shareholders to get a more generous tax treatment if they lose money when disposing of their investment in C corporation stock. (See Chapter 4 for an explanation of business losses.) There is no downside to IRC § 1244 stock. It is easy to qualify an investment in a corporation for IRC § 1244 treatment if you follow the rules—none of which should be a problem for most folks:

1. IRC § 1244 corporate shares may be issued only in return for money or property. So, you can't exchange stocks or bonds from another corporation or contribute services in return for IRC § 1244 stock. And stock can't be issued in return for canceling a prior debt to the shareholder.

2. Investors must be individuals—not other business entities, such as partnerships or other corporations.

3. No more than 50% of the corporation's gross receipts during the preceding five years (or the life of the corporation, if less than five years) was "passive" income. Passive income is royalties, dividends, interest, rents, annuities or gains from securities or stock. So IRC § 1244 corporation losses must be from business operations, not investments.

4. The total money or property received by the corporation for IRC § 1244 stock cannot exceed $1 million.

5. The corporation must be a domestic (U.S.) company.

6. The shareholder must be the original purchaser of the stock.

Subsequent investments in the corporation by a IRC § 1244 shareholder. In reality, it is not always possible to put a large chunk of money into a new corporation at the outset. The tax code says that a shareholder can't claim that any contributions made after the initial shares were issued are qualified under IRC § 1244. However, it may be possible to treat any money put in after the first shares were issued as § 1244 stock if it is payment for § 1244 qualified stock that was authorized but not initially issued.

Example: HairCo, a new corporation, authorized 1,000 shares of IRC § 1244 stock be issued to Morey at $100 per share. At the time the corporation was formed, Morey paid $40,000 and was issued 400 shares. The next year Morey paid $60,000 for the remaining balance of 600 authorized shares, a total of $100,000. All of Morey's stock is IRC § 1244 stock.

Always adopt a written corporate resolution at the time the corporation first issues stock, stating it is IRC § 1244 stock. It is possible to qualify without a resolution if you meet the other conditions, but it's best to put it in writing. Even a postdated resolution made after the stock was issued is better than none. Neither the corporation nor shareholders have to file the resolution with the IRS. However, keep this resolution in your corporate records in case the IRS decides to question the investment loss during an audit. A sample IRC § 1244 resolution is shown below.

SAMPLE IRC § 1244 RESOLUTION

The Board next considered the advisability of qualifying the stock of this corporation as IRC § 1244 stock as defined in the Internal Revenue Code, and of organizing and managing the corporation so that it is a Small Business Corporation as defined in that section. Upon motion duly made and seconded, it was unanimously

RESOLVED, that the proper officers of the corporation are, subject to the requirements of federal law and the law of this state, authorized to sell and issue shares of stock in return for the receipt of the aggregate amount of money and other property, as a contribution to capital and paid in surplus, which does not exceed $1,000,000.

RESOLVED FURTHER, the sale and issuance of shares of stock shall be conducted in compliance with IRC § 1244 so that the corporation and its shareholders may obtain the benefits of that section.

RESOLVED FURTHER, that the proper officers of the corporation are directed to maintain such records as are necessary pursuant to IRC § 1244 so that any shareholder who experiences a loss on the transfer of shares of stock of the corporation may determine whether he or she qualifies for ordinary loss deduction treatment on his or her individual income tax return.

Since there was no further business to come before the meeting, on motion duly made and seconded, the meeting was adjourned.

Date _____   x_____
                        Secretary

An IRC § 1244 loss is claimed on IRS Form 4797, which is filed with your individual income tax return for the year of the loss.

F. Taking Money Out of a C Corporation

A C corporation offers more flexibility in taking money out of a business than any other type of business organization. This stems from the fact that a corporation is a separate legal and tax entity from its owners—unlike a sole proprietorship, limited liability company or partnership. One effect is that, within limits, you and your corporation may engage in formal financial dealings, such as loans between each other.

Pay attention to corporate formalities; the IRS does.
Always make and keep corporate minutes (records) showing any significant financial transactions—loans, compensation of officers, and so forth. IRS auditors frequently ask to inspect corporate minutes to see if corporate formalities have been followed. If you haven't kept up your paperwork, an auditor may not recognize your business's corporate status. Any corporation tax benefits can be disallowed because corporate minute books were not up-to-date.

1. Compensation for Services

Remember that if you incorporate your business, you are not self-employed in the eyes of the IRS. Instead, you are an employee of your corporation—unless you are just an investor and have nothing to do with its day-to-day operations. As an employee, you earn wages, just as if you didn't own the business.

Small corporations often put the owner's spouse and kids on the payroll as part-time employees. Spreading family income over lower tax brackets in this manner is legal—as long as everyone does real work and isn't overpaid. (See Chapter 12, Family Businesses.) But chances are the IRS won't care unless the pay is outrageous for the hours worked.

In theory, the tax law limits how much pay you can receive from your corporation. (IRC §§ 162, 274.) Corporations paying "unreasonable compensation for personal services" can have this (otherwise deductible) expense disallowed on an IRS audit. All compensation deemed to be unreasonable is then treated as a stock dividend, which is taxable to the corporation and then again to the recipient. An unreasonable compensation challenge by the IRS is unlikely, but it can happen.

Be ready for an IRS audit challenge for "unreasonable compensation." Assuming you do significant work for the corporation, draw up an employment contract stating your salary and duties. This shows that your pay was a well thought-out business decision.

Keep your stated salary fairly consistent from year to year—even if the corporation does not have enough funds to pay it. The more closely a salary is tied to profits, the more it looks like a corporate dividend—and not wages. If the corporation has a down year and doesn't have funds to pay your stated salary, get a promissory note and have the corporation pay it when the funds are available in the future.

2. Dividends: Rarely a Good Idea

A C corporation can pay dividends to shareholders if it has enough current and retained earnings to pay its debts and stay solvent. Paying dividends brings up the bugaboo of double taxation—the corporation is taxed on its profits before the dividend is paid, and the shareholder is taxed again as income when it is received. While it seldom makes sense for a small corporation to pay dividends, this may be the only way to compensate investors who don't work in the business. Before doing so, consider putting these folks on the payroll as consultants or electing them as corporate directors and paying for their service.

3. Loans to Shareholders

A profitable C corporation (only) may lend money to its shareholders. A loan from your C corporation isn't taxable income to you and doesn't have tax consequences to the corporation, except that interest received on the loan is income.

Shareholder loans must be bona fide: the borrowers must obligate themselves in writing to repay the loan at a specific date, and the loans should be secured by pledging property, which will be turned over to the corporation if it is not repaid. Loans for less than $10,000 can be interest-free; larger loans must carry a commercially reasonable rate of interest—at least the minimum legal interest rate. (See "How to Make Sure a Loan Is Treated as Legitimate by the IRS," below.)

The IRS knows shareholders would like to label all withdrawals from their corporation as "loans," because compensation is income to the shareholders and loans are not. Even worse, if called a dividend, it would mean taxes to both the corporation and shareholders. So, if a loan doesn't look legit, an IRS auditor can rename and tax it as compensation or a dividend payment to the shareholder.

CHECKLIST: HOW TO MAKE SURE A LOAN FROM A CORPORATION IS TREATED AS LEGITIMATE BY THE IRS

The more a loan to a shareholder meets the criteria of a bank loan, the less likely it is that an IRS auditor will challenge it. Not only must the loan look legitimate, the parties must abide by its terms. The corporation shouldn't give the shareholder any breaks—such as forgiving part of the loan—that a bank wouldn't give. Specifically, loans between corporations and shareholders should meet these requirements:

• The shareholder should sign a promissory note for a specific amount.

• The note should obligate the shareholder to repay the loan unconditionally on a specific date or in regular installments.

• The corporation should charge at least the minimum legal interest rate. The Treasury Department sets this rate once a month; call the nearest Federal Reserve Bank office to get the current rate. If a corporation doesn't charge at least this rate, an IRS auditor can attack it as a "below market" loan (IRC § 7872) and the borrower will be taxed on the value of the undercharged interest.

• The note should be transferable by the corporation to a third party.

• The loan should be secured by collateral such as a house, building or other property.

• The note should stand on equal footing with debts of others to the corporation.

• The note should give the corporation the right to sue and take the collateral if the shareholder does not repay the loan on time.

4. Leasing Property to Your Corporation

Leasing your individually-owned property to your corporation is another way to remove money from your business—without paying dividends or worrying about the unreasonable compensation issues inherent in paying a large salary.

Real estate is the most common kind of property leased to a corporation by shareholders. However, leasing can work just as well for other things, like equipment or machinery. Commonly, renting property to a small business corporation produces a tax loss for the shareholder—either as a paper loss resulting from the shareholder's taking a depreciation deduction on the property, or an out-of-pocket loss (cash expenses exceeded cash income). Either type of loss can be used to offset or "shelter" other income on the shareholder's tax return. You may need a tax pro to help you make this analysis.

Example: On January 1, 1995, Bart buys a small building for $100,000, which he leases to his C corporation, Homer, Inc., at the market rate of $12,000 per year. The building is assessed at $80,000 (the lot is worth $20,000), so Bart is allowed to take depreciation deductions of $2,051 per year. (See Chapter 2, Writing Off Long-Term Business Assets.) He pays expenses for real estate taxes, maintenance and mortgage interest on the building of $11,400. After applying the rent payments, Bart has an overall loss of $1,451, which he can claim on his individual tax return. ($12,000 - $11,400 - $2,051 = $1,451 loss.) In reality, Bart ends up with $600 in his pocket, because most of his "loss" was from the depreciation deduction.

To pass IRS audit muster, a lease between a shareholder and the corporation must be a realistic deal. The lease payment must be at, or close to, fair market value. Since rents for similar properties can vary considerably, you can charge your corporation a bit more than you might get from others. How much more depends on several factors. Some tax pros say a 25% premium is defensible—especially if you can back it up with a written statement from a real estate professional that the rent your corporation has agreed to pay is within the market range.

Example: Brenda owns a small building and rents it to her incorporated bakery business. While the building might rent for $500 a month on the open market, no one knows for sure; like all real estate, Brenda's building, given its size, amenities and location, is unique, making precise valuation difficult. Brenda is probably safe renting it to her corporation for $625 a month, but $2,000 is not likely to fly at an IRS audit.

Leasing property limits your liability. A good non-tax reason for leasing your property to your corporation, rather than having the corporation own it, is to protect your personal assets from corporate liabilities. For instance, suppose your corporation is successfully sued for sexual harassment and the judgment is not covered by insurance. It can be collected only against the corporation's property, not yours. Even if the corporation declares bankruptcy, the leased property is not a corporate asset; it still belongs to you.

5. Selling Your Corporate Stock

A share of corporate stock—a fractional ownership interest in a business—is an asset. As with any asset, its sale is a taxable event, usually producing a gain or loss to the seller. However, because stock held in a C corporation is a "capital asset" if it has been held at least one year and a day, profit from its sale is taxed at special tax code capital gains rates. (See Chapter 2, Writing Off Long-Term Business Assets, for an explanation of capital gains rates.)

Example 1: Robin forms RRR, Inc., and transfers his warehouse to the corporation in exchange for stock. He elects IRC § 351 treatment, so the transfer is not a taxable event. (See Section D3, above.) His basis in the warehouse—$75,000—becomes his basis in his stock. Two years later, when the fair market value of the *warehouse is $125,000, Robin sells his stock to Wanda for $175,000. Robin has a taxable gain of $100,000 ($175,000 minus his basis in his stock of $75,000). The capital gains tax on Robin's profit is 28% (IRC § 1(h)), making his tax liability $28,000. (Robin's state tax agency will probably want a cut of the action, too.) Without the capital gains tax rate, Robin's tax could have been as high as $39,600.*

Losses on the sale of stock are treated under different tax rules than are gains. Unless the corporate stock is qualified under IRC § 1244 (discussed in Section E, above), a shareholder's capital losses can only partly offset his ordinary income. Any capital losses may, however, be fully used to offset any of the shareholder's capital gains. (See Chapter 4, Business Losses, for a detailed explanation.)

**TAX BREAKS FOR QUALIFIED
SMALL BUSINESS CORPORATION INVESTORS**

Investors in C corporations formed after August 10, 1993, may be eligible for a special tax break if they sell their stock at a gain. Fifty percent of any gain on the sale of stock in these "qualified" corporations is not taxed.

What corporations qualify? The rules are complex, but one is that at least 80% of the corporation's assets must be used in the active conduct of the business. This eliminates corporations with significant income from investments. And businesses that sell services, or a mix of goods and services—for example, hotels or restaurants—are excluded. See IRC § 1202 for details.

G. Tax Pitfalls of C Corporations

When you operate as a C corporation, you are playing with the big boys as far as the tax law is concerned. Mind-boggling corporate tax complexities occasionally trap small business people. One of the biggest potential worries—double taxation—has been discussed; here are three others worth mentioning.

1. Personal Holding Company Tax

The tax code imposes a special penalty tax on C corporations that are deemed incorporated "pocketbooks." This provision targets corporations that derive 60% or more of their income from investments, such as dividends and royalties.

This "personal holding company" tax doesn't affect many small businesses, which are active operations, rather than passive investment entities. For more information, see IRC § 541 and following sections.

2. Accumulated Earnings Tax

An advantage of a C corporation over other business entities is the ability to accumulate earnings (roughly meaning "profits") to fund future growth. These earnings are taxed to the corporation, but at lower rates than if they were first distributed to shareholders who then put the money back into the corporation.

If, however, a C corporation accumulates too much money, it is subject to an "accumulated earnings" (AE) tax of 39.6%. Most small C corporations can breathe easy—this tax does not kick in until accumulated earnings exceed $250,000. (IRC § 531.)

3. Corporate Alternative Minimum Tax

A corporation that takes advantage of certain tax code provisions can't avoid taxes altogether; the corporation must pay a minimum amount of tax, called the "corporate alternative minimum tax." The goal of the nicknamed "alt min" tax is to disallow some tax breaks by requiring a minimum amount of income taxes be paid by companies using these provisions. (IRC § 55-58, Reg. 1.56-.58.) Fortunately, few small business corporations ever have to deal with it.

The tax breaks that cause the alternate minimum tax to come into play are called "tax preference" items. They include out-of-the-ordinary things like income from life insurance or from a corporation spreading its tax liabilities into the future by using the installment method of reporting some of its income.

H. Dissolving a C Corporation

The procedures governing how a corporation goes out of business depend on your state's law—just like the formation of the corporation. Generally, a corporation can close down voluntarily by agreement of its shareholders if more than 50% of the shareholders vote to quit. Or, a corporation can cease to exist involuntarily, what is usually called "by operation of law"—such as from a deadlock of shareholders or nonpayment of annual corporation state filings and payment of fees. Simply neglecting to keep up with state filings is by far the most common way small corporations cease to exist. However, this doesn't mean that the IRS will go away. While it is relatively easy to kill a corporation or let it die, if you suddenly stop filing corporation tax returns, expect an IRS letter of inquiry.

The tax issue comes from tax code provisions dealing with corporate liquidations. Typically, the problem is this: if the corporation has any significant assets when it dissolved, and these assets were distributed to the shareholders, the specter of "double taxation" arises. A sale of the business' assets followed by a distribution of the proceeds to the shareholders means the corporation owes tax on any gain on the sale, and the shareholders owe tax again on the money received. Keep in mind that if any tax benefits, such as depreciation, have been claimed by the corporation in the past, the basis on which gain is figured may be very low or even zero. Technically, deductions previously taken are considered "recaptured," and are now taxed. The result is an unexpected taxable gain even when assets are disposed of at relatively low prices. If the business

failed miserably and everyone took a bath, it may be that no one has a gain, so double taxation isn't a problem. In any case, this is probably a time you'll want to bring in a tax pro.

Consider switching to S corporation status on your way out. One way around the double taxation problem may be for a dissolving C corporation to elect S corporation status before it liquidates—but don't try this without first consulting a good tax pro.

IRS Form 966, Corporate Dissolution or Liquidation, must be filed with the IRS whenever a corporation is terminated. (For more information, see IRC § 331 and following sections (recipients), 336 and following sections (corporations), Reg. 1.331, 336.)

RESOURCES

IRS Publication 334, *Tax Guide for Small Business*. This is an indispensable book for any small business, including C corporations.

IRS Publication 542, *Tax Information for Corporations*. This booklet is especially useful if you are preparing and filing corporate tax forms without professional assistance.

How to Form Your Own Corporation (California, Texas, New York, Florida editions), by Anthony Mancuso (Nolo Press). This book takes you through the incorporation process step by step. The forms are also available on disk.

Taking Care of Your Corporation, Volumes I and II, by Anthony Mancuso (Nolo Press). These books show you how to write up minutes of corporate meetings and document corporate decisions and transactions, which are often important to withstand IRS scrutiny.

The Legal Guide For Starting and Running a Small Business, by Fred Steingold (Nolo Press). This excellent book deals with all of the ramifications of operating as a C corporation. ■

CHAPTER 8

S Corporations

"Corporations cannot commit treason, nor be outlawed, nor excommunicated, for they have no souls."

— Sir Edward Coke

Before reading this chapter, you should be familiar with the previous one (Chapter 7) on C Corporations. That's because all corporations are born as C corporations under the tax code. Becoming an S corporation requires an extra step, called an "election," which has many tax implications. This chapter explains the tax treatment of S corporations and how to become one.

S CORPORATIONS IN A NUTSHELL

1. All corporations begin as C corporations, but may elect S status with the IRS.

2. S status allows corporations to be treated much like partnerships, for tax purposes. The corporation itself doesn't pay taxes; instead, shareholders pay taxes on business income, at their individual tax rates.

3. Electing S corporation status means losing some of the tax benefits available to a C corporation.

4. Because business start-ups typically lose money in their early years, electing S corporation status is advantageous. It allows shareholders to take business losses directly on their personal tax returns.

A. An Overview of S Corporations

The Internal Revenue Code recognizes a number of different types of corporations, including nonprofits, financial institutions and personal service corporations. Luckily, most small business owners need not worry about the tax rules for these specialized corporations. For most businesses offering goods or services, the tax choice is limited to two types—C and S corporations.

C and S corporations (the letters refer to subchapters of the Internal Revenue Code) are distinguished by *how* their income is taxed. In broad outline, S corporations pass their income through to their shareholders, who then pay tax on it at their individual income tax rates. C corporations, as explained in Chapter 7, are separate tax entities that pay a corporate income tax on profits. (Taxation of professional corporations for certain, mostly service professions—doctors, lawyers—is explained in Chapter 11, Personal Service Corporations.)

A primary tax advantage of electing S corporation status is to eliminate the possibility of double taxation. (C corporations may pay income tax at the corporate level, and then again when that income is paid to shareholders.) Because S corporations are termed "pass-through" entities, their profits are taxed directly to the business's owners. S corporations pay no separate corporate income tax.

Similarly, S corporation shareholders take most business operating losses on their individual returns, since losses pass through as well. (There are, however, restrictions on loss-taking by shareholders who aren't active in the business; see Section D, below.) By contrast, C corporation losses remain in the corporation, so shareholders cannot claim them on their individual tax returns.

When business income and losses pass through to S corporation owners, they retain their tax "characteristics." For instance, S corporation profits are ordinary income to shareholders, and S corporation capital gains are capital gains to the shareholder. This is beneficial because capital gains are taxed at a lower rate than ordinary income to top bracket taxpayers.

Although an S corporation is not a tax-paying entity, it is most definitely a tax-reporting entity. It must file an annual corporation tax return, Form 1120-S, showing income and expenses and the resulting profits or losses. Individual S corporation shareholders then report income (or loss) on their individual tax returns. In addition, an S corporation must file and pay employment taxes on its employees just like a C corporation. (See Chapter 5 for an explanation of employment taxes.) S corporations generally must file state tax returns, too.

B. Should You Choose S Corporation Status?

Most people incorporate for non-tax reasons—principally, to shield their personal assets from liability for business debts. Corporate shareholders, unlike partners and sole proprietors, aren't personally liable for business debts. The S corporation combines this limited liability with pass-through tax treatment—allowing corporation income and loss benefits to flow directly to shareholders. This is the same tax result as with a sole proprietorship, partnership or limited liability company.

If you form an S corporation, you may get tax benefits from business losses, which are common in a business's start-up phase. S corporations, unlike C corporations, allow shareholders who are active in the business to take operating losses against their other income each year. For this reason, new enterprises often elect S corporation status for the business's early years, later converting to a C corporation after they become profitable to get C corporation fringe benefit tax-savings. (See Chapter 14, Fringe Benefits.)

Example: Jeannie Smith works as a loan officer for First Bank, earning $25,000 in 1995. She and her husband, Sam, also run a small S corporation business, selling computers. The Smiths file their tax returns jointly. The computer business loses $15,000 in 1995. By offsetting this $15,000 operating loss against Jeannie's $25,000 salary, the Smiths' total taxable income is reduced to $10,000. After taking into account their exemptions and personal deductions, the Smiths probably won't owe any income taxes. If this had been a regular C corporation, the business loss wouldn't have cut the Smiths' personal tax bill.

Consider forming a limited liability company. Even if an S corporation sounds good, consider a limited liability company (LLC) instead. All 50 states now allow this new form of business entity, which lets you "pass through" business income and losses to owners for tax reporting purposes. LLCs also offer the personal liability shield of corporations, but can be easier to form and operate than S corporations. However, unlike S corporations, a one-person LLC

may not be recognized by the IRS. See Chapter 10, Limited Liability Companies.

1. Eligibility for S Corporation Status

Assuming you have decided that being an S corporation is for you, first you must have been granted a corporate charter under the laws of a state. The corporation will probably—but doesn't necessarily have to—be formed in the state that you are doing business in. In all likelihood, you will qualify to file for S status with the IRS, but first check these technical rules to make sure your corproation is eligible. You qualify if:

- It is a U.S. corporation with no more than 75 shareholders. Before 1997, the limit was 35 shareholders. (Husband and wife are one shareholder if they own their stock jointly.)
- All shareholders are individual U.S. citizens or resident aliens. Starting in 1997, other S corporations, and a new kind of tax code-recognized entity called an "electing small business trust" can also own S corporation shares.
- The corporation has only one "class" of stock. There can't be any "preferred" or other types of shares that give special privilege to some shareholders—for example, one class of stock with voting rights and another without.
- The corporation doesn't own 80% or more of the shares of stock in another corporation.
- All shareholders consent in writing to S corporation status by signing a form filed with the IRS. (See Sample Form 2553, below.)

2. S Corporation Disadvantages

S corporations offer advantages to many small business owners, but they are not for everybody. Here are some tax disadvantages of S corporations you should be aware of.

a. No Retained Earnings

A successful incorporated business may want to keep some of its earnings as a fund for future needs, such as expansion. Profits kept in corporations are called "retained earnings." An S corporation, however, cannot retain earnings without them being fully taxed. Remember, its profits pass through to the shareholders even if they aren't taken out of the business. A C corporation, on the other hand, can keep its profits in the business in return for paying a relatively small amount of tax. (This point is discussed in detail in Chapter 7, C Corporations.)

Example: Sam and Jeannie Smith's incorporated computer retail store earns a $50,000 profit after paying the Smiths $200,000 in salary. They keep the $50,000 in the business bank account for future growth. If the business were a C corporation, the corporation would pay income tax on the $50,000 at a rate of 15% ($7,500). By contrast, as an S corporation, it would be taxed at the Smiths' personal income tax rate, which may be as high as 39.6%, meaning an additional tax bill of $19,800.

b. Limited Employee Benefits

S corporations don't have as great a range of fringe benefits for owners and other employees as do C corporations. Rarely can new businesses afford fringes, so this makes a difference only for more mature corporations. But for businesses with substantial earnings to fund benefits, a C corporation offers tax-savings opportunities over an S corporation. (Chapter 14, Fringe Benefits, and Chapter 15, Retirement Plans, discuss tax-advantaged fringe benefits.)

c. Converting From a C Corporation

It is possible to change a C corporation to an S corporation; however, tax complications may arise. This is more than a little complex, but a converted S corporation will have taxable income if it had passive income, if it used the LIFO method to report inventory or if it had gains related to depreciated assets of the C corporation. The point here is that before converting your C to an S corporation, see a savvy tax pro.

C. Tax Reporting for S Corporations

An S corporation must file U.S. Corporation Income Tax Form 1120-S every year of its operation, showing its profit or loss. If the tax year is the calendar year, the return is due on March 15; otherwise it is due on the 15th day of the third month following the close of its fiscal year.

It is easy to get a six-month extension to file the return. Just submit IRS Form 7004, Application for Automatic Extension of Time to File Corporation Income Tax Return, before the original due date.

A filled-in 1120-S form is included in this chapter to give you an idea of the kinds of things that must be reported. This is not to suggest that you prepare your corporation tax return yourself. To the contrary, corporate returns are the stuff that tax pros were made for.

STATE S CORPORATION TAX RULES

Most states recognize S corporation status, but their tax rules may differ from the federal tax law. Check with your state's corporation office to find out how an S corporation files and pays state taxes. Typically, states impose a minimum annual corporate tax or franchise fee that applies whether your business is active or inactive. You may also face a state corporation tax on S corporation income. California, a particularly tax-hungry state, imposes a 2.5% tax on S corporation profits—in addition to a minimum annual franchise tax of $800. The bright side (if you can call it that) is that you can deduct any state and local taxes as business expenses against business income.

D. How Shareholders Are Taxed

It is a bit of an oversimplification to say that corporation profits and losses simply flow though to shareholders. The tax code adds a twist, but one that is generally beneficial to S corporation owners. In addition to overall profit or loss of the corporation, some items of S corporation income, loss or deductions are "separately stated" on the shareholder's tax return.

For instance, if the corporation sells an asset at a gain, and the item qualifies for capital gain treatment for the business, the shareholder gets capital gain treatment. And, if the corporation is entitled to use the fast write-off of assets under IRC § 179 (see Chapter 2, Writing Off Long-Term Business Assets), the deduction flows through to each shareholder as a separately stated item. (IRC § 1366.)

An S corporation reports each stockholder's share of its profit (or loss) on annual IRS K-1 forms. K-1s are filed with the IRS and given to each shareholder. In turn, each shareholder reports the K-1 information on his or her individual Form 1040 tax return. As we all know, April 15 is the date for filing your individual income tax return, but you can get an automatic four-month extension to August 15 and a further two-month discretionary extension, which gives you until October 15 to file. S corporation owners are subject to employment taxes payable by the corporation's partners. Sole proprietors, on the other hand, pay the self-employment tax.

1. Profits

Typically, S corporation shareholders take profits out of their business usually as compensation for services, or sometimes as dividends on their investment in the corporation. Either way—or even if all profits are retained by the corporation instead of being paid out—the corporation's earnings are treated as ordinary income to the shareholders. In this regard, an S corporation business owner is taxed much the same as a sole proprietor, partner or limited liability company member is.

Example: Rusty's S corporation, Rustco, makes a profit of $17,000 in 1995. It issues a Form K-1 to Rusty, who owns 100% of its stock, reporting $17,000 of income. The corporation owes no income tax. Instead, Rusty enters the $17,000 on the first page of his 1995 Form 1040 income tax return, and pays income taxes according to his overall income tax bracket.

2. Losses

S corporation losses are also passed through to shareholders, and can offset their other income. The loss is claimed on the front page of the S shareholder's individual tax return, just like a profit. However, a shareholder can deduct no more than the amount of his or her tax "basis" in the stock. Generally, a shareholder's tax basis is the total of money and property he or she put into the corporation for shares of stock plus any corporate debts he or she personally guaranteed.

Example: Jerrie paid $5,000 for 100% of the stock in her S corporation, JerriCo. In its first year of operation, the business lost $7,000, which was reported on the corporate income tax form and on Jerrie's Form K-1. Of this amount, Jerrie can claim only $5,000 as a loss, because this is the amount of her basis (investment) in her S corporation stock.

SCHEDULE K-1 (Form 1120S) Department of the Treasury Internal Revenue Service	**Shareholder's Share of Income, Credits, Deductions, etc.** ▶ See separate instructions. For calendar year 1994 or tax year beginning _____ , 1994, and ending _____ , 19 ___	OMB No. 1545-0130 **1994**

Shareholder's identifying number ▶	Corporation's identifying number ▶ *10 : 4487965*

Shareholder's name, address, and ZIP code *John H. Green* *4340 Holmes Parkway* *Metro City, OH 43704*	Corporation's name, address, and ZIP code *Strato Tech, Inc.* *482 Winston Street* *Metro City, OH 43705*

A Shareholder's percentage of stock ownership for tax year (see Instructions for Schedule K-1) . . . . . ▶ *45* %
B Internal Revenue Service Center where corporation filed its return ▶ *Cincinnati, OH*
C Tax shelter registration number (see Instructions for Schedule K-1) . . . . ▶ ....
D Check applicable boxes: (1) ☐ Final K-1 (2) ☐ Amended K-1

		(a) Pro rata share items		(b) Amount	(c) Form 1040 filers enter the amount in column (b) on:
Income (Loss)	1	Ordinary income (loss) from trade or business activities . . .	1	*53,550*	See Shareholder's Instructions for Schedule K-1 (Form 1120S).
	2	Net income (loss) from rental real estate activities	2		
	3	Net income (loss) from other rental activities	3		
	4	Portfolio income (loss):			
	a	Interest	4a	*1,800*	Sch. B, Part I, line 1
	b	Dividends	4b	*7,200*	Sch. B, Part II, line 5
	c	Royalties	4c		Sch. E, Part I, line 4
	d	Net short-term capital gain (loss)	4d		Sch. D, line 5, col. (f) or (g)
	e	Net long-term capital gain (loss)	4e		Sch. D, line 13, col. (f) or (g)
	f	Other portfolio income (loss) *(attach schedule)*	4f		(Enter on applicable line of your return.)
	5	Net gain (loss) under section 1231 (other than due to casualty or theft)	5		See Shareholder's Instructions for Schedule K-1 (Form 1120S)
	6	Other income (loss) *(attach schedule)*	6		(Enter on applicable line of your return.)
Deductions	7	Charitable contributions (see instructions) *(attach schedule)* . .	7	*10,800*	Sch. A, line 15 or 16
	8	Section 179 expense deduction	8		See Shareholder's Instructions for Schedule K-1 (Form 1120S)
	9	Deductions related to portfolio income (loss) *(attach schedule)*	9		
	10	Other deductions *(attach schedule)*	10		
Investment Interest	11a	Interest expense on investment debts	11a	*1,350*	Form 4952, line 1
	b (1)	Investment income included on lines 4a, 4b, 4c, and 4f above	b(1)	*9,000*	See Shareholder's Instructions for Schedule K-1 (Form 1120S)
	(2)	Investment expenses included on line 9 above	b(2)		
Credits	12a	Credit for alcohol used as fuel	12a		Form 6478, line 10
	b	Low-income housing credit:			
		(1) From section 42(j)(5) partnerships for property placed in service before 1990.	b(1)		Form 8586, line 5
		(2) Other than on line 12b(1) for property placed in service before 1990	b(2)		
		(3) From section 42(j)(5) partnerships for property placed in service after 1989	b(3)		
		(4) Other than on line 12b(3) for property placed in service after 1989	b(4)		
	c	Qualified rehabilitation expenditures related to rental real estate activities (see instructions)	12c		
	d	Credits (other than credits shown on lines 12b and 12c) related to rental real estate activities (see instructions)	12d		See Shareholder's Instructions for Schedule K-1 (Form 1120S)
	e	Credits related to other rental activities (see instructions) . . .	12e		
	13	Other credits (see instructions)	13	*2,700*	
Adjustments and Tax Preference Items	14a	Depreciation adjustment on property placed in service after 1986	14a		See Shareholder's Instructions for Schedule K-1 (Form 1120S) and Instructions for Form 6251
	b	Adjusted gain or loss	14b		
	c	Depletion (other than oil and gas)	14c		
	d (1)	Gross income from oil, gas, or geothermal properties . . .	d(1)		
		(2) Deductions allocable to oil, gas, or geothermal properties . .	d(2)		
	e	Other adjustments and tax preference items *(attach schedule)*	14e		

For Paperwork Reduction Act Notice, see page 1 of Instructions for Form 1120S.   Cat. No. 11520D   **Schedule K-1 (Form 1120S) 1994**

Schedule K-1 (Form 1120S) (1994)   Page **2**

	(a) Pro rata share items	(b) Amount	(c) Form 1040 filers enter the amount in column (b) on:
Foreign Taxes	**15a** Type of income ▶ ....:		Form 1116, Check boxes
	b Name of foreign country or U.S. possession ▶		
	c Total gross income from sources outside the United States (attach schedule)	15c	Form 1116, Part I
	d Total applicable deductions and losses (attach schedule) . . .	15d	
	e Total foreign taxes (check one): ▶ ☐ Paid ☐ Accrued . .	15e	Form 1116, Part II
	f Reduction in taxes available for credit (attach schedule) . . .	15f	Form 1116, Part III
	g Other foreign tax information (attach schedule)	15g	See Instructions for Form 1116
Other	**16a** Total expenditures to which a section 59(e) election may apply	16a	See Shareholder's Instructions for Schedule K-1 (Form 1120S).
	b Type of expenditures ▶		
	17 Tax-exempt interest income	17	2,250	Form 1040, line 8b
	18 Other tax-exempt income	18	
	19 Nondeductible expenses	19	7,358	See Shareholder's Instructions for Schedule K-1 (Form 1120S).
	20 Property distributions (including cash) other than dividend distributions reported to you on Form 1099-DIV	20	29,250	
	21 Amount of loan repayments for "Loans From Shareholders" . .	21	
	22 Recapture of low-income housing credit:		
	a From section 42(j)(5) partnerships	22a	Form 8611, line 8
	b Other than on line 22a	22b	

23 Supplemental information required to be reported separately to each shareholder (attach additional schedules if more space is needed):

....
....
....
....
....
....
....
....
....
....
....
....
....
....
....
....
....
....
....
....

Supplemental Information

PART **2**

The Form of Your Business

MATERIAL PARTICIPATION

For an S corporation shareholder to deduct losses against other income, he or she must "materially participate" in the business. Being an investor in an S corporation is not enough; you must also be active in the business. If you are challenged by the IRS at an audit to show material participation, you'll be okay if:

• you put in at least 500 hours per year working in the business, or

• you worked at least 100 hours, if no other shareholder puts in more time, or

• the "facts and circumstances" show that you worked on a regular, continuous and substantial basis. (IRC § 469 and Reg. 1.469.)

E. Social Security and Unemployment Taxes

The tax code intends that all small business owners—no matter what the form of their business—pay the same amount of Social Security and Medicare (FICA) taxes, generally called employment taxes. (See Chapter 5, Tax Concerns of Employers, on how these taxes are computed and paid.) Despite the stated intent of a level playing field, there is a potential tax saving here for S corporation shareholders. Salaries and bonuses paid by an S corporation for work are subject to FICA taxes, but corporate dividends are "investment" income and are not subject to employment tax.

Taking a combination of salary and dividends from an S corporation can reduce your self-employment (SE) taxes.

Example: Gordon manages his S corporation business and takes an annual salary of $40,000. He pays self-employment taxes of 15.3% on this compensation ($6,120). Gordon also takes $14,000 from the business as a dividend on his stock in the corporation. If the $14,000 were instead labeled as salary or a bonus, he would have had to pay an additional $2,142 in employment taxes (15.3% of $14,000).

IRS auditors question low owner salaries. It hasn't escaped the notice of the IRS that S corporation owners minimize their SE taxes by labeling compensation as "dividends." If you are audited, and the IRS claims your dividends were really wages, you'll have to show your salary was reasonable and other money you took from the corporation was a return on your investment. One way to show your salary wasn't unreasonably low would be to compare compensation paid to managers of similar businesses, who weren't owners.

F. How to Become an S Corporation

If you decide to become an S corporation after you have incorporated, here is how to accomplish it:

• Get IRS Form 2553, Election by Small Business Corporation. You'll find a filled-in sample below. Get the most current form by calling the IRS at 800-829-FORM or 800-829-1040, or by going to your nearest IRS office or from your tax pro.

• Pay attention to filing deadlines. You must file Form 2553 with the IRS no later than three months after your corporation's taxable year begins—whether your corporation is brand new or is an operating C corporation. If you miss the deadline one year, you must wait until the next year. You cannot, however, file Form 2553 until your corporation charter has been granted by your state.

| Form **2553**
(Rev. September 1993)
Department of the Treasury
Internal Revenue Service | **Election by a Small Business Corporation**
(Under section 1362 of the Internal Revenue Code)
▶ **For Paperwork Reduction Act Notice, see page 1 of instructions.**
▶ **See separate instructions.** | OMB No. 1545-0146
Expires 8-31-96 |

Notes: 1. *This election, to be an "S corporation," can be accepted only if all the tests are met under **Who May Elect** on page 1 of the instructions; all signatures in Parts I and III are originals (no photocopies); and the exact name and address of the corporation and other required form information are provided.*

2. *Do not file **Form 1120S**, U.S. Income Tax Return for an S Corporation, until you are notified that your election is accepted.*

| **Part I** | **Election Information** | | |

Please Type or Print	Name of corporation (see instructions) XTC Incorporated	**A** Employer identification number (EIN) 94 : 000 0000
	Number, street, and room or suite no. (If a P.O. box, see instructions.) 123 Main St.	**B** Date incorporated 1/1/95
	City or town, state, and ZIP code Anytown, CA 90210	**C** State of incorporation CA

D Election is to be effective for tax year beginning (month, day, year) . . . . ▶ 1 / 1 / 95

E Name and title of officer or legal representative who the IRS may call for more information

Joe Smegola, President

F Telephone number of officer or legal representative
(555) 555-5555

G If the corporation changed its name or address after applying for the EIN shown in **A**, check this box . . . . ▶ ☐

H If this election takes effect for the first tax year the corporation exists, enter month, day, and year of the **earliest** of the following: (1) date the corporation first had shareholders, (2) date the corporation first had assets, or (3) date the corporation began doing business . . . . ▶ 1 / 1 / 95

I Selected tax year: Annual return will be filed for tax year ending (month and day) ▶ 12/31

If the tax year ends on any date other than December 31, except for an automatic 52-53-week tax year ending with reference to the month of December, you **must** complete Part II on the back. If the date you enter is the ending date of an automatic 52-53-week tax year, write "52-53-week year" to the right of the date. See Temporary Regulations section 1.441-2T(e)(3).

J Name and address of each shareholder, shareholder's spouse having a community property interest in the corporation's stock, and each tenant in common, joint tenant, and tenant by the entirety. (A husband and wife (and their estates) are counted as one shareholder in determining the number of shareholders without regard to the manner in which the stock is owned.)	**K** Shareholders' Consent Statement. Under penalties of perjury, we declare that we consent to the election of the above-named corporation to be an "S corporation" under section 1362(a) and that we have examined this consent statement, including accompanying schedules and statements, and to the best of our knowledge and belief, it is true, correct, and complete. (Shareholders sign and date below.)*		**L** Stock owned		**M** Social security number or employer identification number (see instructions)	**N** Shareholder's tax year ends (month and day)
	Signature	Date	Number of shares	Dates acquired		
Joe Smegola 123 Main St. Anytown, CA 90210	*Joe Smegola*	2/10/95	100	1/1/95	123-45-6789	12/31
Francine Schwartzkopf 666 B St. Anytown, CA 90000	*Francine Schwartzkopf*	2/15/95	100	1/1/95	987-65-4321	12/31

*For this election to be valid, the consent of each shareholder, shareholder's spouse having a community property interest in the corporation's stock, and each tenant in common, joint tenant, and tenant by the entirety must either appear above or be attached to this form. (See instructions for Column K if a continuation sheet or a separate consent statement is needed.)

Under penalties of perjury, I declare that I have examined this election, including accompanying schedules and statements, and to the best of my knowledge and belief, it is true, correct, and complete.

Signature of officer ▶ *Francine Schwartzkopf, Secretary*   Title ▶ Secretary   Date ▶ 2/30/95

See Parts II and III on back.   Form **2553** (Rev. 9-93)

PART **2**
The Form of Your Business

- Have Form 2553 completed by a person authorized to sign the corporation's tax returns—usually the president or any other corporate officer.

- Get written consents from all shareholders (or if you are about to incorporate, prospective shareholders) by having each sign Form 2553 at the appropriate place. Unless every shareholder signs, your S election is invalid. In a new corporation, if there is any doubt as to who will become a shareholder, have every possible shareholder sign. There is no penalty if someone who signs doesn't ever become a shareholder.

- Mail your completed Form 2553 to the IRS Service Center where you file your individual tax returns. Include an extra copy and self-addressed stamped envelope and request that the IRS return the copy file-stamped on the date received. Or, hand-deliver it to your nearest IRS office and get a copy file-stamped for your records. The IRS won't normally make a copy for you; you must send or bring your own photocopy for IRS stamping.

G. Revoking S Corporation Status

Once elected, S corporation status continues until revoked by stockholders (who hold more than 50% of its shares) or by the IRS. The IRS can revoke S status for various misdeeds, such as failing to file tax returns or keep corporate records. If a corporation loses S status—voluntarily or involuntarily—it can't be reinstated for five years. Once S corporation status is revoked, the corporation is taxed as a C corporation. (See Chapter 7, C Corporations.)

There is no IRS form to revoke S status. Send a letter titled "Revocation of S status" to the IRS Service Center where you filed your S election form. In it, state the name of the corporation, the tax identification number and the number of shares outstanding. Have the letter signed by all of the shareholders. A sample letter is shown below.

SAMPLE LETTER REVOKING S CORPORATION STATUS

To: Your IRS Service Center

REVOCATION OF S CORPORATION STATUS OF BONE CORPORATION

FEDERAL IDENTIFICATION NUMBER #94–0000000

1. Bone Corporation hereby voluntarily revokes its prior election to be treated as an S corporation under IRC § 1362 (a).

2. The revocation is to be effective January 1, 1997.

3. At the time of revocation there are 1000 shares outstanding in the corporation.

STATEMENT OF CONSENT

The following shareholders, who own all of the shares of the corporation, under penalty of perjury, consent to the revocation of the election of S corporation status:

Dated: 12/20/96. Hamilton Bone, 111 Main St., Juneau, AK, SSN 555-55-5555, 1000 shares acquired 1/1/87, 12/31/96

Hamilton Bone
_____
Shareholder

H. Dissolving an S Corporation

When a corporation ceases business and disposes of its assets, it is deemed to have been "liquidated" or "dissolved." When this occurs, S corporation shareholders receive whatever money or property the corporation owns. They are each taxed on the money and the value of any property they receive if it is greater than their pro rata basis in the corporation's assets.

Example: Ted, the sole shareholder of TYVM Inc., an S corporation, decides to close up and move to Costa Rica. After selling off its inventory of goods and paying its bills, the corporation's sole asset is the building it has been in for years. The property, with a tax basis of $1 million to the corporation, is sold for $2 million, so Ted, the 100% shareholder, has a $1 million gain. This profit is taxed at the 28% capital gains tax rate, producing a $280,000 tax bill for Ted. He may also have a state tax bill, depending on where he lives.

If TYVM were a C corporation, it would have to pay tax on the gain at the corporate tax rate of 34% ($340,000), and Ted would have a 28% tax on what was left over ($660,000), for total taxes of $592,800.

It's a good idea to confer with a tax pro if you are dissolving a corporation with assets. But whether or not your corporation has assets, the 1120-S tax return you file for the year you shut down must say "FINAL RETURN" across the top of the first page.

RESOURCES

IRS Publication 589, *Tax Information for S Corporations.* This 25-page booklet about S corporation taxes is updated annually. Although it is overly detailed and technical, it may be instructive. To get a free copy, call 800-TAX-FORM or stop by your nearest IRS office.

IRS S Corporation Income Tax Package (annually updated). Includes most of the current year's tax forms and instructions.

Taking Money Out of Your Corporation, by John Storey (John Wiley & Sons). This book, written by a business owner, discusses a number of tax-wise techniques for taking money out of S and C corporations. ■

PART 2

The Form of Your Business

Form **1120S**	U.S. Income Tax Return for an S Corporation	OMB No. 1545-0130

Department of the Treasury
Internal Revenue Service

► Do not file this form unless the corporation has timely filed Form 2553 to elect to be an S corporation.
► See separate instructions.

19**94**

For calendar year 1994, or tax year beginning _____ , 1994, and ending _____ , 19____

A Date of election as an S corporation **12-1-93**

B Business code no. (see Specific Instructions) **5008**

Use IRS label. Otherwise, please print or type.

10-4487965   DEC94   D74   3070
StratoTech, Inc.
482 Winston Street
Metro City, OH 43705

C Employer identification number 10 : 4487965

D Date incorporated **3-1-75**

E Total assets (see Specific Instructions) $ **771,334**

F Check applicable boxes: (1) ☒ Initial return (2) ☐ Final return (3) ☐ Change in address (4) ☐ Amended return

G Check this box if this S corporation is subject to the consolidated audit procedures of sections 6241 through 6245 (see instructions before checking this box) . ► ☐

H Enter number of shareholders in the corporation at end of the tax year . . . . ► **6**

Caution: *Include **only** trade or business income and expenses on lines 1a through 21. See the instructions for more information.*

Income

1a	Gross receipts or sales **1,545,700**	b Less returns and allowances **21,000**	c Bal ► **1c** **1,524,700**
2	Cost of goods sold (Schedule A, line 8)		**2** **954,700**
3	Gross profit. Subtract line 2 from line 1c		**3** **570,000**
4	Net gain (loss) from Form 4797, Part II, line 20 (attach Form 4797)		**4**
5	Other income (loss) (see instructions) (attach schedule) . . .		**5**
6	**Total income (loss).** Combine lines 3 through 5 . . . . ►		**6** **570,000**

Deductions (See instructions for limitations.)

7	Compensation of officers		**7** **170,000**
8	Salaries and wages (less employment credits)		**8** **138,000**
9	Repairs and maintenance		**9** **800**
10	Bad debts		**10** **1,600**
11	Rents		**11** **9,200**
12	Taxes and licenses		**12** **15,000**
13	Interest		**13** **14,200**
14a	Depreciation (see instructions)	**14a** **15,200**	
b	Depreciation claimed on Schedule A and elsewhere on return	**14b**	
c	Subtract line 14b from line 14a		**14c** **15,200**
15	Depletion **(Do not deduct oil and gas depletion.)** . . .		**15**
16	Advertising		**16** **8,700**
17	Pension, profit-sharing, etc., plans		**17**
18	Employee benefit programs		**18**
19	Other deductions (see instructions) (attach schedule) . . .		**19** **78,300**
20	**Total deductions.** Add the amounts shown in the far right column for lines 7 through 19 . . ►		**20** **451,000**
21	Ordinary income (loss) from trade or business activities. Subtract line 20 from line 6 . . .		**21** **119,000**

Tax and Payments

22	**Tax: a** Excess net passive income tax (attach schedule) . . .	**22a**	
b	Tax from Schedule D (Form 1120S)	**22b**	
c	Add lines 22a and 22b (see instructions for additional taxes) . .		**22c**
23	**Payments: a** 1994 estimated tax payments and amount applied from 1993 return	**23a**	
b	Tax deposited with Form 7004	**23b**	
c	Credit for Federal tax paid on fuels (attach Form 4136) . . .	**23c**	
d	Add lines 23a through 23c		**23d**
24	Estimated tax penalty (see instructions). Check if Form 2220 is attached . . ► ☐		**24**
25	**Tax due.** If the total of lines 22c and 24 is larger than line 23d, enter amount owed. See instructions for depositary method of payment . . . . ►		**25**
26	**Overpayment.** If line 23d is larger than the total of lines 22c and 24, enter amount overpaid ►		**26**
27	Enter amount of line 26 you want: **Credited to 1995 estimated tax** ► _____ **Refunded** ►		**27**

Please Sign Here

Under penalties of perjury, I declare that I have examined this return, including accompanying schedules and statements, and to the best of my knowledge and belief, it is true, correct, and complete. Declaration of preparer (other than taxpayer) is based on all information of which preparer has any knowledge.

► *John H. Green*   Signature of officer   **3-10-95** Date   ► *President* Title

Paid Preparer's Use Only

Preparer's signature ►		Date	Check if self-employed ► ☐	Preparer's social security number
Firm's name (or yours if self-employed) and address ►			E.I. No. ►	
			ZIP code ►	

For Paperwork Reduction Act Notice, see page 1 of separate instructions.   Cat. No. 11510H   Form **1120S** (1994)

Form 1120S (1994)   Page **2**

Schedule A   Cost of Goods Sold (See instructions.)

1	Inventory at beginning of year	126,000
2	Purchases	1,127,100
3	Cost of labor	
4	Additional section 263A costs (see instructions) *(attach schedule)*	
5	Other costs *(attach schedule)*	
6	**Total.** Add lines 1 through 5	1,253,100
7	Inventory at end of year	298,400
8	**Cost of goods sold.** Subtract line 7 from line 6. Enter here and on page 1, line 2	954,700

9a Check all methods used for valuing closing inventory:

    (i) ☐ Cost

    (ii) ☑ Lower of cost or market as described in Regulations section 1.471-4

    (iii) ☐ Writedown of "subnormal" goods as described in Regulations section 1.471-2(c)

    (iv) ☐ Other (specify method used and attach explanation) ▶ ....

  b Check if the LIFO inventory method was adopted this tax year for any goods *(if checked, attach Form 970).* . . . . . ▶ ☐

  c If the LIFO inventory method was used for this tax year, enter percentage (or amounts) of closing

    inventory computed under LIFO . . . . | 9c |

  d Do the rules of section 263A (for property produced or acquired for resale) apply to the corporation? . . . ☐ Yes ☑ No

  e Was there any change in determining quantities, cost, or valuations between opening and closing inventory? . . ☐ Yes ☑ No

    If "Yes," attach explanation.

Schedule B   Other Information

		Yes	No
1	Check method of accounting: (a) ☐ Cash (b) ☑ Accrual (c) ☐ Other (specify) ▶		
2	Refer to the list in the instructions and state the corporation's principal:		
	(a) Business activity ▶ 5008 Distributor **(b)** Product or service ▶ heavy equipment		
3	Did the corporation at the end of the tax year own, directly or indirectly, 50% or more of the voting stock of a domestic corporation? (For rules of attribution, see section 267(c).) If "Yes," attach a schedule showing: **(a)** name, address, and employer identification number and **(b)** percentage owned.		✔
4	Was the corporation a member of a controlled group subject to the provisions of section 1561?		✔
5	At any time during calendar year 1994, did the corporation have an interest in or a signature or other authority over a financial account in a foreign country (such as a bank account, securities account, or other financial account)? (See instructions for exceptions and filing requirements for Form TD F 90-22.1.)		✔
	If "Yes," enter the name of the foreign country ▶		
6	Was the corporation the grantor of, or transferor to, a foreign trust that existed during the current tax year, whether or not the corporation has any beneficial interest in it? If "Yes," the corporation may have to file Forms 3520, 3520-A, or 926		✔
7	Check this box if the corporation has filed or is required to file **Form 8264,** Application for Registration of a Tax Shelter . . . . ▶ ☐		
8	Check this box if the corporation issued publicly offered debt instruments with original issue discount . . ▶ ☐		
	If so, the corporation may have to file **Form 8281,** Information Return for Publicly Offered Original Issue Discount Instruments.		
9	If the corporation: **(a)** filed its election to be an S corporation after 1986, **(b)** was a C corporation before it elected to be an S corporation **or** the corporation acquired an asset with a basis determined by reference to its basis (or the basis of any other property) in the hands of a C corporation, and **(c)** has net unrealized built-in gain (defined in section 1374(d)(1)) in excess of the net recognized built-in gain from prior years, enter the net unrealized built-in gain reduced by net recognized built-in gain from prior years (see instructions) . . . . . . ▶ $ 37,200		
10	Check this box if the corporation had subchapter C earnings and profits at the close of the tax year (see instructions) . . . . ▶ ☐		

Designation of Tax Matters Person (See instructions.)

Enter below the shareholder designated as the tax matters person (TMP) for the tax year of this return:

Name of designated TMP ▶ John H. Green

Identifying number of TMP ▶ 458-00-0327

Address of designated TMP ▶ 4340 Holmes Parkway, Metro City, OH 43704

PART **2**

The Form of Your Business

CHAPTER 9

Partnerships

"We must not read either law or history backwards."

— Helen M. Cam

PARTNERSHIPS IN A NUTSHELL

1. Partnerships do not pay taxes; they pass profit and loss through to individual partners. Partnerships must, however, file annual tax returns.

2. Profits and losses in a partnership may be allocated unequally among partners, so as to distribute tax benefits favorably.

3. Partnership accounting and tax law is very complex, and researching the law or seeing a tax pro early on may prevent headaches later.

4. Contributing services to a partnership in return for a partnership interest creates a tax problem, but there is a way to get around it.

5. Terminating a partnership may result in tax liability for the partners.

We are all familiar with the idea of a partnership—two or more people (or legal entities) running a business and splitting the profits or losses. Typically, partners begin by contributing money or property and their efforts to the partnership. They must have an agreement to form a partnership. Legally it doesn't have to be in writing, but of course, it is always a good idea.

Like sole proprietors, each partner is *personally* responsible for all of the liabilities of the business, which makes many folks wary of partnerships. An exception to the rule of personal liability is offered by a limited partnership—however, most active small businesses are "general," not "limited," partnerships. (See "General and Limited Partnerships," below.)

From a tax standpoint, partners are treated much like sole proprietors; both must report their share of the business's profits or losses on their personal tax returns. Partnerships also bear a tax resemblance to S corporations and limited liability companies. All three are "pass-through" entities, which means that the business owners—not the entity—pay taxes on business income. And all three must file their own tax returns.

There is no federal partnership law; each state's law governs partnership formation and operation. However, all states have adopted the Uniform Partnership Act and Uniform Limited Partnership Act, so partnership laws are very similar in each state.

GENERAL AND LIMITED PARTNERSHIPS

Partnerships come in two varieties: general and limited. The vast majority of small business partnerships are general partnerships. Legally, in a general partnership each partner has a voice in the management of the business and can obligate the partnership to any contract, debt or other transaction within the scope of the partnership business. The corollary is that each general partner is responsible for *all* of the debts of the partnership—liability is not limited just to the partner's proportionate interest in the partnership.

The rules are different for limited partnerships (LPs), which are primarily used to raise money from "passive" investors (the limited partners). LPs have two categories of partners: one or more general partners, who are personally liable for all partnership obligations, and one (or more) limited partners, who have no liability at all for partnership debts.

LPs usually must register with the state agency that regulates securities (in most states, the Secretary of State or Corporations Commissioner), and in some cases with the federal Securities and Exchange Commission as well. LPs are most often found in the small business world as family limited partnerships. (See Chapter 12, Family Businesses.)

Example 1: Serendipity Partners, a limited partnership, formed to design and market 1970's sportswear, incurs debts of $17,000 to various creditors. Raul, the general partner, is liable for the whole amount if Serendipity goes under. Chessie, a limited partner, who put $6,200 into the partnership for her share, is not liable for any of the debt, except for the amount she contributed for her interest in Serendipity.

Example 2: If Serendipity was a general partnership, both Raul and Chessie would be each liable for the whole $17,000. Creditors could go after each of the partner's personal assets to collect the whole debt, not just $8,500 each. Of course, the creditors would not be entitled to collect more than a total of $17,000.

A. Partnership Tax Status

Partnership provisions of the tax code apply even if two or more people go into business together on nothing more than a handshake, and never sign a formal partnership agreement. As long as costs and profits of a venture are split, a partnership exists as far as the IRS is concerned.

The only exception is for spouses who operate an unincorporated business together. The tax code gives them a choice of either reporting taxes as partners, or as co-sole proprietors on a joint tax return. If they file as partners they will have to file a partnership tax return, too. As long as they file a joint individual tax return, their tax liability is the same either way, so a partnership provides no tax benefits. Since a partnership requires extra paperwork, most spouse-partners choose to tax report as co-sole proprietors. If spouses file tax returns separately, usually to keep their tax liabilities separate, though, they might want to tax report as a partnership. It is possible that separate tax filings for a married couple might result in a lower overall income tax liability. Check it out both ways with a tax pro who knows your complete family tax picture.

PART **2**

The Form of Your Business

PARTNERSHIP TAX DECISIONS

When you form a partnership, you have some tax-related decisions to make, including: choosing a method of accounting for income and losses, the type of tax year and the depreciation method to adopt. Depending on your needs and what the tax code allows, some of these decisions may be changed as your partnership goes along. Others cannot be, so don't make these choices lightly. See a tax pro. (See Chapter 3, Recordkeeping and Accounting.)

Put your agreement in writing. A partnership agreement should be in writing. It should include basics such as how much ownership interest each partner has (for instance, 1/3 or 22%), and how much investment each partner has in the business. A lawyer will charge about $400 to $1,000 to help you design a partnership agreement, or you can do it yourself using a guide book or software. (See the "Resources" list at the end of the chapter.) A cost-effective approach is to use a self-help resource to draft an agreement, and then have it polished by an experienced small business lawyer—and reviewed by a tax pro.

B. Tax Reporting by Partnerships

A partnership is a legal entity separate from its owners, but it is not a federal *tax-paying* entity. (IRC §§ 701, 761.) Instead, a partnership's profit or loss passes through to the partners, who must report their share on their individual Form 1040 tax returns (or joint returns, if they file with a spouse).

Still, a partnership must keep accurate track of income and expenses, just like any business. To satisfy the IRS, a partnership must make tax filings—both initially and annually—for as long as it is in operation.

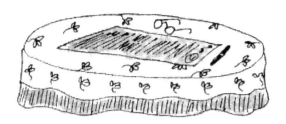

1. Annual Partnership Tax Return

Even though it pays no tax, a partnership must file an annual tax return, showing the venture's income and expenses, on IRS Form 1065, U.S. Partnership Return of Income. This form is due on the 15th day of the 4th month after the end of the partnership tax year—April 15 for most partnerships—the same date individual income returns are due. (See Chapter 3, Recordkeeping and Accounting.)

No tax payment is due with Form 1065; it is what the IRS calls an "information" return. Nevertheless, the IRS can penalize you for not filing a partnership tax return on time or for never filing it. The late filing penalty is $50 per month for each partner, to a maximum of $250, and applies to each year the partnership is delinquent.

STATE PARTNERSHIP TAXES

Most states treat partnerships the same way, tax-wise, as does the federal government—that is, they tax individual partners, not partnerships. States usually require that a state partnership tax return, similar to Form 1065, be filed annually. In addition, a few states require partnerships to pay an annual tax or fee for the privilege of operating in the state. Check with your state tax department or ask a tax pro what forms and fees are required.

---

2. Partner's Profit or Loss Statements

Active business partnerships must also issue IRS Form K-1 to each partner and file a copy with the IRS every year. As discussed in Section C, below, this form shows each partner's share of profits or losses and is used by the IRS computers to keep track of the income of partners. If your partnership didn't engage in any business during the year, you don't have to issue any K-1s.

3. Partnership Federal Identification Number

A partnership must get its own tax ID number, called the federal Employer Identification Number (EIN), from the IRS. (IRS Form SS-4 is used to apply for the EIN.) The terminology might lead you to believe that your partnership needs an EIN only if you have employees, but this is not the case. This ID number must be used on a partnership's annual partnership tax return and on K-1 forms filed with the IRS. (Instructions on getting a tax ID number are in Chapter 5.)

Example: Brenda and Betty apply for a tax ID number by filling in and sending Form SS-4 to the IRS. They are assigned 94-1234567 as the Employer Identification Number of the B & B partnership. They must use it on all tax returns and K-1 form filings and other dealings with the IRS. The partnership should also receive a copy of the Employer's Tax Guide *from the IRS (Publication 15) with forms and instructions for making required payroll tax reports.*

Form **1065**

Department of the Treasury
Internal Revenue Service

U.S. Partnership Return of Income

For calendar year 1994, or tax year beginning .... , 1994, and ending .... , 19 .... .
▶ See separate instructions.

1994

OMB No. 1545-0099

A Principal business activity
Retail

B Principal product or service
Books

C Business code number
5942

Use the IRS label. Otherwise, please print or type.

10-9876543   DEC94   D71
AbleBaker Book Store
334 West Main Street
Orange, MD 20904

D Employer identification number

E Date business started
10-1-79

F Total assets (see Specific Instructions)
$ 45,391

PART 2

The Form of Your Business

G Check applicable boxes: **(1)** ☐ Initial return   **(2)** ☐ Final return   **(3)** ☐ Change in address   **(4)** ☐ Amended return
H Check accounting method: **(1)** ☐ Cash   **(2)** ☑ Accrual   **(3)** ☐ Other (specify) ▶ ....
I Number of Schedules K-1. Attach one for each person who was a partner at any time during the tax year ▶ 2

Caution: *Include **only** trade or business income and expenses on lines 1a through 22 below. See the instructions for more information.*

Income	**1a** Gross receipts or sales	1a	409,465		
	b Less returns and allowances	1b	3,365	**1c**	406,100
	2 Cost of goods sold (Schedule A, line 8)			**2**	267,641
	3 Gross profit. Subtract line 2 from line 1c			**3**	138,459
	4 Ordinary income (loss) from other partnerships, estates, and trusts *(attach schedule)*			**4**	
	5 Net farm profit (loss) *(attach Schedule F (Form 1040))*			**5**	
	6 Net gain (loss) from Form 4797, Part II, line 20			**6**	
	7 Other income (loss) (see instructions) *(attach schedule)*			**7**	559
	8 **Total income (loss).** Combine lines 3 through 7			**8**	139,018
Deductions (see instructions for limitations)	**9** Salaries and wages (other than to partners) (less employment credits)			**9**	29,350
	10 Guaranteed payments to partners			**10**	25,000
	11 Repairs and maintenance			**11**	1,125
	12 Bad debts			**12**	250
	13 Rent			**13**	20,000
	14 Taxes and licenses			**14**	3,295
	15 Interest			**15**	1,451
	16a Depreciation (see instructions)	16a	1,174		
	b Less depreciation reported on Schedule A and elsewhere on return	16b		**16c**	1,174
	17 Depletion **(Do not deduct oil and gas depletion.)**			**17**	
	18 Retirement plans, etc.			**18**	
	19 Employee benefit programs			**19**	
	20 Other deductions *(attach schedule)*			**20**	8,003
	21 **Total deductions.** Add the amounts shown in the far right column for lines 9 through 20			**21**	89,648
	22 **Ordinary income (loss)** from trade or business activities. Subtract line 21 from line 8			**22**	49,370

Please Sign Here

Under penalties of perjury, I declare that I have examined this return, including accompanying schedules and statements, and to the best of my knowledge and belief, it is true, correct, and complete. Declaration of preparer (other than general partner) is based on all information of which preparer has any knowledge.

▶ *Frank W. Able*
Signature of general partner or limited liability company member

▶ 3-12-95
Date

Paid Preparer's Use Only

Preparer's signature ▶	Date	Check if self-employed ▶ ☐	Preparer's social security no.
Firm's name (or yours if self-employed) and address ▶		E.I. No. ▶	
		ZIP code ▶	

For Paperwork Reduction Act Notice, see page 1 of separate instructions.   Cat. No. 11390Z   Form **1065** (1994)

Form 1065 (1994)   Page **2**

Schedule A   **Cost of Goods Sold**

1 Inventory at beginning of year	**1**	*18,125*
2 Purchases less cost of items withdrawn for personal use	**2**	*268,741*
3 Cost of labor	**3**	*-0-*
4 Additional section 263A costs (see instructions) *(attach schedule)*	**4**	*-0-*
5 Other costs *(attach schedule)*	**5**	*-0-*
6 **Total.** Add lines 1 through 5	**6**	*286,866*
7 Inventory at end of year	**7**	*19,225*
8 **Cost of goods sold.** Subtract line 7 from line 6. Enter here and on page 1, line 2	**8**	*267,641*

9a Check all methods used for valuing closing inventory:

   (i) ☐ Cost

   (ii) ☑ Lower of cost or market as described in Regulations section 1.471-4

   (iii) ☐ Writedown of "subnormal" goods as described in Regulations section 1.471-2(c)

   (iv) ☐ Other (specify method used and attach explanation) ▶ ....

  b Check this box if the LIFO inventory method was adopted this tax year for any goods *(if checked, attach Form 970)* . ▶ ☐

  c Do the rules of section 263A (for property produced or acquired for resale) apply to the partnership? . . ☐Yes ☑No

  d Was there any change in determining quantities, cost, or valuations between opening and closing inventory? ☐Yes ☑No

    If "Yes," attach explanation.

Schedule B   **Other Information**

	Yes	No
1 What type of entity is filing this return?		
Check the applicable box ▶ ☑ General partnership ☐ Limited partnership ☐ Limited liability company		
2 Are any partners in this partnership also partnerships?		✓
3 Is this partnership a partner in another partnership?		✓
4 Is this partnership subject to the consolidated audit procedures of sections 6221 through 6233? If "Yes," see **Designation of Tax Matters Partner** below		✓
5 Does this partnership meet **ALL THREE** of the following requirements?		
a The partnership's total receipts for the tax year were less than $250,000;		
b The partnership's total assets at the end of the tax year were less than $600,000; **AND**		
c Schedules K-1 are filed with the return and furnished to the partners on or before the due date (including extensions) for the partnership return.		
If "Yes," the partnership is not required to complete Schedules L, M-1, and M-2; Item F on page 1 of Form 1065; or Item J on Schedule K-1		✓
6 Does this partnership have any foreign partners?		✓
7 Is this partnership a publicly traded partnership as defined in section 469(k)(2)?		✓
8 Has this partnership filed, or is it required to file, **Form 8264,** Application for Registration of a Tax Shelter? . .		✓
9 At any time during calendar year 1994, did the partnership have an interest in or a signature or other authority over a financial account in a foreign country (such as a bank account, securities account, or other financial account)? (See the instructions for exceptions and filing requirements for Form TD F 90-22.1.) If "Yes," enter the name of the foreign country. ▶		✓
10 Was the partnership the grantor of, or transferor to, a foreign trust that existed during the current tax year, whether or not the partnership or any partner has any beneficial interest in it? If "Yes," you may have to file Forms 3520, 3520-A, or 926		✓
11 Was there a distribution of property or a transfer (e.g., by sale or death) of a partnership interest during the tax year? If "Yes," you may elect to adjust the basis of the partnership's assets under section 754 by attaching the statement described under **Elections Made By the Partnership**		✓

Designation of Tax Matters Partner (See instructions.)

Enter below the general partner designated as the tax matters partner (TMP) for the tax year of this return:

Name of
designated TMP ▶ _____   Identifying
number of TMP ▶ _____

Address of
designated TMP ▶ _____

C. Tax Reporting for Partners

Partners are *not* employees of their business for tax reporting purposes. They don't get wages, and the business is not subject to payroll taxes on partners' income. Typically, partners take income through periodic partnership "draws."

At the end of each year, each partner's share of business profits (or losses) must be computed and reported to the IRS on form K-1. This shows each partner's "distributive share" of income, tax credits or tax deductions. Partners use the K-1 information to report their distributive share on the front page of their individual income tax returns. A sample K-1 form is shown above.

1. Estimated Tax Payments

Partners must pay income tax on partnership income throughout the year, just like sole proprietors. These are called "estimated tax payments." Of course, if the business loses money, no income taxes are due. (And, as explained below in Section 2, withdrawing money from a partnership is not always equivalent to taking taxable income.)

Partners use Form 1040-ES to report and pay estimated taxes four times a year. (See Chapter 6, Sole Proprietorships, for information on this form.) This once-every-quarter payment must also cover the partner's self-employment taxes (Social Security and Medicare). All general partners are subject to this tax, which is reported on the Form SE filed annually with their 1040 tax return. Limited partners are not subject to the self-employment tax, so aren't required to file this form.

2. Reporting a Partner's Income

The tax code makes calculating a partner's taxable income or loss more difficult than you might think. Most of the time, the cash a partner takes out isn't the same as that partner's taxable income from the business. Hopefully, this will become clear after you have read the remainder of this section.

a. The Distributive Share

Here we go; hang on. The law taxes a partner on the amount he or she is *deemed* to have gotten from the partnership under complex accounting rules. (IRC § 704.) This is called a "distributive share." (IRC § 703.)

A distributive share of profit or loss is normally based on the percentage of the partnership each partner owns—which might range from 1% to 99%. Unless a partnership agreement says otherwise, the tax code presumes all partners have an equal interest in the business. For instance, if two people are doing business as partners without any written agreement, it's considered a 50-50 partnership.

Example: Brenda and Betty's partnership agreement calls for each to get 50% of the profits (or losses) of the B & B partnership. If B & B makes a profit of $70,000 in 1995, each partner would get a distributive share of $35,000 to report on her individual 1040 tax return. In reality, Brenda or Betty may have taken different amounts out of the partnership.

b. Special Allocations

If a written partnership agreement authorizes it, unequal distributive shares, called "special allocations," may be made. A special allocation is any distribution of profits or losses that is not proportionate to a partner's ownership share. For instance, giving 65% of profits to one 50-50 partner and 35% to the other would be a special allocation. Also, a partnership agreement could provide a different ratio for splitting losses of the business than for profits—such as 80-20 for losses and 65-35 for profits.

Partners agree to special allocations for many reasons. For instance, one partner works full-time and others only part-time, or one partner brings special skills into the business or generates more income.

PART **2**

The Form of Your Business

SCHEDULE K-1 (Form 1065) Department of the Treasury Internal Revenue Service	Partner's Share of Income, Credits, Deductions, etc. ▶ See separate instructions.	OMB No. 1545-0099
	For calendar year 1994 or tax year beginning _____, 1994, and ending _____, 19__	**1994**

Partner's identifying number ▶ *123-00-6789*	Partnership's identifying number ▶ *10 9876543*
Partner's name, address, and ZIP code *Frank W. Able* *10 Green Street* *Orange, MD 20904*	Partnership's name, address, and ZIP code *Able Baker Book Store* *334 West Main Street* *Orange, MD 20904*

A This partner is a ☑ general partner ☐ limited partner
☐ limited liability company member

B What type of entity is this partner? ▶ *Individual*

C Is this partner a ☑ domestic or a ☐ foreign partner?

D Enter partner's percentage of:

	(i) Before change or termination	(ii) End of year
Profit sharing	%	*50* %
Loss sharing	%	*50* %
Ownership of capital	%	*50* %

E IRS Center where partnership filed return: *Philadelphia*

F Partner's share of liabilities (see instructions):

Nonrecourse	$ ....
Qualified nonrecourse financing	$ ....
Other	$ ...*10,900*

G Tax shelter registration number . ▶ ......*N/A*......

H Check here if this partnership is a publicly traded partnership as defined in section 469(k)(2) . . . . . ☐

I Check applicable boxes: (1) ☐ Final K-1 (2) ☐ Amended K-1

J Analysis of partner's capital account:

(a) Capital account at beginning of year	(b) Capital contributed during year	(c) Partner's share of lines 3, 4, and 7, Form 1065, Schedule M-2	(d) Withdrawals and distributions	(e) Capital account at end of year (combine columns (a) through (d))
14,050		*24,460*	(*26,440*)	*12,070*

	(a) Distributive share item		(b) Amount	(c) 1040 filers enter the amount in column (b) on:
Income (Loss)	**1** Ordinary income (loss) from trade or business activities . . .	**1**	*24,685*	See Partner's Instructions for Schedule K-1 (Form 1065).
	2 Net income (loss) from rental real estate activities	**2**		
	3 Net income (loss) from other rental activities	**3**		
	4 Portfolio income (loss):			
	a Interest	**4a**		Sch. B, Part I, line 1
	b Dividends	**4b**	*75*	Sch. B, Part II, line 5
	c Royalties	**4c**		Sch. E, Part I, line 4
	d Net short-term capital gain (loss)	**4d**		Sch. D, line 5, col. (f) or (g)
	e Net long-term capital gain (loss)	**4e**		Sch. D, line 13, col. (f) or (g)
	f Other portfolio income (loss) (attach schedule)	**4f**		Enter on applicable line of your return
	5 Guaranteed payments to partner	**5**	*20,000*	See Partner's Instructions for Schedule K-1 (Form 1065).
	6 Net gain (loss) under section 1231 (other than due to casualty or theft)	**6**		
	7 Other income (loss) (attach schedule)	**7**		Enter on applicable line of your return
Deduc-tions	**8** Charitable contributions (see instructions) (attach schedule) . .	**8**	*325*	Sch. A, line 15 or 16
	9 Section 179 expense deduction	**9**		See Partner's Instructions for Schedule K-1 (Form 1065).
	10 Deductions related to portfolio income (attach schedule) . . .	**10**		
	11 Other deductions (attach schedule)	**11**		
Investment Interest	**12a** Interest expense on investment debts	**12a**		Form 4952, line 1
	b (1) Investment income included on lines 4a, 4b, 4c, and 4f above	**b(1)**	*75*	See Partner's Instructions for Schedule K-1 (Form 1065).
	(2) Investment expenses included on line 10 above	**b(2)**		
Credits	**13a** Credit for income tax withheld	**13a**		See Partner's Instructions for Schedule K-1 (Form 1065).
	b Low-income housing credit:			
	(1) From section 42(j)(5) partnerships for property placed in service before 1990	**b(1)**		
	(2) Other than on line 13b(1) for property placed in service before 1990	**b(2)**		
	(3) From section 42(j)(5) partnerships for property placed in service after 1989	**b(3)**		Form 8586, line 5
	(4) Other than on line 13b(3) for property placed in service after 1989	**b(4)**		
	c Qualified rehabilitation expenditures related to rental real estate activities (see instructions)	**13c**		
	d Credits (other than credits shown on lines 13b and 13c) related to rental real estate activities (see instructions)	**13d**		See Partner's Instructions for Schedule K-1 (Form 1065).
	e Credits related to other rental activities (see instructions) . . .	**13e**		
	14 Other credits (see instructions)	**14**		

For Paperwork Reduction Act Notice, see Instructions for Form 1065.   Cat. No. 11394R   Schedule K-1 (Form 1065) 1994

Schedule K-1 (Form 1065) 1994

Page **2**

(a) Distributive share item		(b) Amount	(c) 1040 filers enter the amount in column (b) on:
Self-employment			
15a Net earnings (loss) from self-employment	**15a**	44,685	Sch. SE, Section A or B
b Gross farming or fishing income.	**15b**		See Partner's Instructions for Schedule K-1 (Form 1065).
c Gross nonfarm income.	**15c**		
Adjustments and Tax Preference Items			
16a Depreciation adjustment on property placed in service after 1986	**16a**		
b Adjusted gain or loss	**16b**		See Partner's Instructions for Schedule K-1 (Form 1065) and Instructions for Form 6251.
c Depletion (other than oil and gas)	**16c**		
d (1) Gross income from oil, gas, and geothermal properties . .	**d(1)**		
(2) Deductions allocable to oil, gas, and geothermal properties	**d(2)**		
e Other adjustments and tax preference items (attach schedule)	**16e**		
Foreign Taxes			
17a Type of income ▶			Form 1116, check boxes
b Name of foreign country or U.S. possession ▶			
c Total gross income from sources outside the United States (attach schedule)	**17c**		Form 1116, Part I
d Total applicable deductions and losses (attach schedule). .	**17d**		
e Total foreign taxes (check one): ▶ ☐ Paid ☐ Accrued . . .	**17e**		Form 1116, Part II
f Reduction in taxes available for credit (attach schedule) . . .	**17f**		Form 1116, Part III
g Other foreign tax information (attach schedule)	**17g**		See Instructions for Form 1116.
Other			
18a Total expenditures to which a section 59(e) election may apply	**18a**		See Partner's Instructions for Schedule K-1 (Form 1065).
b Type of expenditures ▶			
19 Tax-exempt interest income	**19**	25	Form 1040, line 8b
20 Other tax-exempt income.	**20**		See Partner's Instructions for Schedule K-1 (Form 1065).
21 Nondeductible expenses	**21**		
22 Recapture of low-income housing credit:			
a From section 42(j)(5) partnerships	**22a**		Form 8611, line 8
b Other than on line 22a.	**22b**		

23 Supplemental information required to be reported separately to each partner (attach additional schedules if more space is needed):

....
....
....
....
....
....
....
....
....
....
....
....
....
....
....
....
....
....
....

Supplemental Information

PART 2

The Form of Your Business

Example: Betty plans to work more hours for B & B partnership than does Brenda, who intends to spend part of her time authoring a travel book. The two agree in writing that Betty will receive 70% of the profits. Now Betty's distributive share of the $70,000 profit is $49,000, and Brenda's is $21,000.

A partner's income taxes depend on her overall tax situation—not just on what she gets from the partnership. Since no two people have the same tax situation, it's unlikely that two partners will pay the same amount of taxes. Special allocations may be used to give different tax benefits to different partners.

Example: In its second year, Brenda and Betty's partnership makes a profit of $70,000. By the terms of the partnership agreement, Brenda is entitled to a special allocation of a 60% distributive share of the profits, or $42,000. Taking into account other income, exemptions and deductions, Brenda falls into the 28% tax bracket. So, Brenda's income tax on the B & B income is $11,760.

Betty, on the other hand, is independently wealthy and has investment income besides her partnership profits. Her share of the partnership profits puts her into the 39.6% tax bracket, so the tax due on Betty's share ($11,088) is almost as much as Brenda's tax on her larger share of partnership income. If there had been a 50-50 division of partnership profits, Brenda would have paid $9,800 and Betty $13,860 in taxes—$23,660, a total of $812 more.

Special allocations can be tricky. Our discussion doesn't take into account other highly technical tax code rules for making special partnership allocations. Make sure you are on firm ground before making special allocations. Check out the law with a tax pro. (IRC §§ 703, 704 and Regs. 1.703, 1.704.)

c. Money Left in the Partnership

If a partnership keeps profits in the business at the end of the tax year for expansion or any other purpose, the partners are still taxed on that money. It doesn't matter that they never, as individuals, got their hands on the funds.

Example: Carl and Hector's equal partnership makes a $70,000 profit, but they only take $30,000 each out of the partnership, leaving $10,000 in the bank as working capital. For tax purposes, they are each taxed on receiving a distributive share of $35,000.

If your business needs to retain profits, consider incorporating. Forming a C corporation may be the best way to go, if you want to keep profits in your business (for future expansion or to expand your inventory). Remember that partnerships (as well as S corporations and limited liability companies) are tax pass-through entities, so any profits left in the partnership bank account—or as inventory—are fully taxed at each business partners' tax rate. C corporations can offer some relief from this tax bite. (See Chapter 7, C Corporations, to see how this works.)

D. Partnership Losses

For tax purposes, partnership *losses* are similar to profits—they pass through to each partner in proportion to her ownership share, unless a different scheme is in the partnership agreement. Tax reporting losses is, however, more complicated than reporting profits. A positive feature is that a partner can use her share of a partnership loss in a present—or future—tax year. This can lower her tax bill by offsetting her present income to get a tax refund. See Chapter 4, Business Losses, for an explanation of the rules of loss carryovers.

Example: Betty and Brenda formed the B & B Partnership in 1995. They lost $40,000 in the business operation that year, largely because their bed and breakfast inn was not yet listed in travel guides. Brenda is entitled to a distributive share of 60% of the loss ($24,000) under their partnership agreement. In 1994, Brenda earned $70,000 working for HotelCo, and paid taxes in the 28% tax bracket. By amending her 1994 individual tax return to claim her share of the 1995 partnership loss, Brenda can get a tax refund. It should be about $6,700 (28% x $24,000), plus interest. Brenda uses IRS Form 1040X to claim the refund.

PASSIVE PARTNERS

If you are only a "money" partner—that is, you invested in a partnership business but are not involved in its day-to-day business affairs, you are deemed a "passive" investor. As such, tax rules limit your taking partnership losses on your individual tax return. A primary rule is that you can't claim more than $25,000 per year on your individual tax return for passive investment losses. (IRC § 469, Reg. 1.469.) If your losses are greater, the balance can be carried forward to claim on future years' tax returns—but never back to past years'. The $25,000 limit applies each year. Typically, you might be affected by these rules if you invest in—but are not otherwise involved in—a money-losing real estate partnership or a business run by one of your children.

E. Partnership Contributions

When folks form a partnership, they typically contribute a combination of money, property and services to the business. These contributions may have unexpected tax consequences, however.

Tax and accounting rules for partnerships are especially baffling to those of us who are not accountants. Be warned that we are nearing deep waters, but will stop before we are over our heads. If your situation is more complicated than the ones covered here, go to one of the resources listed at the end of this chapter, or see a tax pro.

1. Keeping Track of Partners' Contributions

Each partner's total contribution to the partnership is referred to as his "capital account." This is a listing of contributions and withdrawals of each partner, plus his or her annual share of income or losses from the partnership. So a partnership's capital account is a kind of a financial history, starting at the beginning and continuing through the life of the partnership.

You must keep track of your contributions in order to figure out the tax consequences of taking money or property out of the partnership. Keep in mind that your partnership share is an asset—an investment in your business. For tax purposes, you need to establish and track the value of your partnership interest for as long as the partnership is in operation or has any assets.

No income tax is due from a partner on money or property taken out of the partnership until his capital account is reduced to zero. Until that point, the partner is just recouping his investment. Another way of stating this is that a partner's capital account balance is equal to his tax basis in his partnership interest. And until he recovers his tax basis by taking distributions from his partnership, he doesn't have any tax liability. The following example illustrates a point made early in this chapter (Section C): that the amount of cash taken out of a partnership is not always the same as a partner's taxable income from the business.

PART 2

The Form of Your Business

Example: Moe contributes $14,000 and six seltzer bottles worth $200 to the Stooges Partnership in 1995. So, $14,200 is the amount of Moe's capital account balance and his tax basis in his partnership interest. In 1996 Moe takes $12,000 as his distributive share from the partnership. He has no tax liability because he has not recovered all of his investment in the partnership. His tax basis and capital account balance stand at $2,200 at the end of 1996. As is shown in Section F1 below, anything taken by Moe over $2,200 will likely be taxable.

a. Cash Contributions

If each partner contributes just cash for his or her partnership interest, then things are simple, tax-wise. Each partner's capital account equals the cash contributed.

Example: Moe puts $14,000 cash (nothing else) into the Stooges partnership. His capital account balance is $14,000.

b. Property Contributions

If a partner transfers anything other than money—such as real estate, vehicles or copyrights—to the partnership, more complicated tax rules come into play. A partner's existing tax basis in the property transferred to the partnership becomes his tax basis in the partnership interest he receives in exchange for the property. As long as property hasn't changed in value from the time the partner acquired it to the time he contributes it to his partnership, his tax basis is easy to track.

Example: Ken transfers an office condominium he owns to VideoPro, the partnership that he and Barbara are setting up to rent video conferencing equipment to small businesses. In exchange for the office condo, Ken receives a 50% share of VideoPro partnership. At the time of its transfer, Ken had owned the condo for a short period and his tax basis in it (what he paid, minus depreciation, plus the value of his improvements) was

$50,000. This was also its fair market value, so Ken's tax basis in his partnership share is $50,000.

This example is clear-cut, but real life is often more complex. If property contributed to a partnership has changed in value from the time the partner acquired it, the tax result may be quite different. For instance, the contributing partner's basis in his partnership interest is the same, but he is subject to taxes on any gain in value of that property since he acquired it. He doesn't have immediate tax liability, but it will come later, when the property is disposed of or when the partnership is dissolved.

Example: Let's say that instead of being worth $50,000 (Ken's basis), Ken's condo office is worth $100,000 when he transfers it to VideoPro partnership. Ken's partner, Barbara, puts $100,000 cash into the partnership bank account for her one-half share. Shortly thereafter, VideoPro decides the office condo is unsuitable and sells it for $100,000. Ken has a taxable gain of the whole $50,000, even though the partnership, not Ken, now owns and sold the property.

Another tax trap may await contributing partners when there is a mortgage on real estate transferred to a partnership. As long as the mortgage is less than the transferring partner's basis in the property, there is no problem. But if the mortgage is greater than the partner's basis, the tax code treats the transfer to the partnership as a sale of the property, with the difference between the mortgage and the partner's basis as taxable gains.

Example 1: Assume Ken owned the office condo for several years and used it in another business before putting it into VideoPro. Before transferring it to the partnership, Ken mortgaged it for $60,000. His basis in the property was only $40,000—less than the loan amount—due to depreciation deductions Ken took for a prior business use. Because the mortgage is greater than his tax basis, Ken has a taxable gain of $20,000 when he transfers the condo into the partnership. (In case you are wondering, the fair market value of the building at the time of the transfer does not affect Ken's tax liability.)

The tax code logic is that Ken made a profit of $20,000 when he mortgaged the condo for more than his basis. He wasn't required to pay taxes then, but he must pay when he transfers it to the partnership. If, as in the previous example, VideoPro sold the property for $100,000 shortly after acquiring it, Ken would also have a taxable gain of $40,000.

Example 2: Assume that Ken's mortgage is $30,000 instead of $60,000. There is no tax liability because his basis ($40,000) is greater than his mortgage liability.

c. Contributions of Services to the Partnership

Often one partner has cash, while another has an empty wallet but possesses the expertise to make the business go. This may create a tax problem because services are not considered "property" when contributed to a partnership in return for an ownership interest. The tax code says you can't get ownership in a partnership in return for a promise to work in the business without a tax cost. Someone who gets a partnership share under these circumstances is immediately liable for income tax on the value of the ownership interest.

A way out. You can add a "profits partner" clause to your partnership agreement to reward a partner who wants to work but can't make a financial contribution. This clause states that the partner contributing services has no ownership, and instead gets a share of partnership profits—if any—in exchange for his work. (This doesn't prevent that partner from buying into the partnership later and becoming a full partner.)

Example 1: Brenda and Betty form the B & B partnership to operate a Bed & Breakfast Inn. Betty has $100,000 in cash but no business experience. Brenda has 20 years in the hospitality field—but no money—so promises to contribute managerial savvy. If they are both

50% owners, Brenda is immediately liable for income tax on the fair market value of her share in the partnership. Since Betty contributed $100,000, and Brenda (who the IRS views as contributing nothing) got a 50% interest, Brenda owes tax on $50,000 income.

Example 2: If Brenda and Betty draw up their partnership agreement stating Brenda is entitled to 50% of the profits, but is not a partner for other purposes, then there is no tax problem.

Two additional tax rules restrict profits partners:

- A profits partner can't sell her profits interest in the partnership within two years after receiving it.

- A profits partner can't be promised any fixed amount of money; she must bear a genuine risk of getting nothing if the partnership doesn't make a profit. (IRS Rev. Proc. 93-27.)

The legal status of profit partners is unsettled. Whether or not a profits partner is a general partner for other purposes—such as legal liability for partnership debts—depends on the law of your state.

One potential tax disadvantage to being a profits partner is that if the partnership suffers a loss, a profits partner—who may have put blood, sweat and tears into the business—can't take any of the loss on her tax return. Partnership tax losses belong to the "real" partners.

2. Adjustments to Partners' Accounts

Once a partnership venture is up and operating, continuous adjustments add to or subtract from a partner's basis in his capital account.

Three different events require making adjustments to a partner's basis:

- A partner withdraws cash or property from the partnership. This decreases the basis in his partnership interest.

  Example: Sylvester, who invested $50,000 in Sylvester & Son, takes $10,000 cash from the partnership in the first year. So starting year two, his partnership basis in Sylvester & Son is $40,000. (There are no taxes due from Sylvester on this withdrawal, because he was only recovering part of his original investment in the partnership.)

- A partner contributes cash or property to the partnership. If you have been with me this far, you'll understand that contributions increase a partner's basis in his partnership interest.

  Example: Midway in the first year of business, the Sylvester & Son partnership needs operating capital, so Sylvester, instead of withdrawing money, puts in an additional $10,000 above his $50,000 initial investment. Starting year two, Sylvester's tax basis in his partnership interest (capital account) has increased to $60,000.

- A partner is allocated his annual "distributive share" of partnership loss or profit or incurs a share of partnership liabilities. These events also change a partner's tax basis in his partnership interest.

  Example: The Sylvester & Son partnership takes out a $10,000 bank loan. Sylvester, a 50% partner, has his $50,000 basis in the partnership increased by half of the debt—that is, $5,000 of the $10,000 total debt. Sylvester's basis is now $55,000.

- If a partnership borrows money to buy an asset, no adjustment is made to the individual partner's capital accounts. The increase in value of partnership assets is offset by the increased partnership liabilities.

  Example: Sylvester & Sons borrows $15,000 from the bank to buy factory equipment. The effect is that Sylvester's $50,000 capital account is increased by 50% of the debt, $7,500, but is then decreased by the same amount once the equipment is purchased. The net result is a "wash"— Sylvester's capital account, the amount the tax code deems that he has invested in the partnership, remains at $50,000.

F. Money Withdrawn From a Partnership

Since you went into business to put money in your pocket, you should know the tax effect of withdrawing money or property from your partnership. Taking money out of a partnership is made complicated by the tax code.

1. Taxation of Withdrawals

Let's recap where we have been so far. Each partner has a unique tax basis in his or her partnership interest. This figure is called the partner's "capital account," and represents the amount of his or her investment in the partnership for tax purposes. The tax basis for each partner in his or her partnership interest is adjusted throughout the life of the business; withdrawals decrease a partner's tax basis, and contributions increase it.

A welcome tax principle is that withdrawals from a partnership are initially treated as a nontaxable return of your partnership investment. Only after you have recovered your entire investment (meaning that your basis in your partnership interest has been reduced to zero), are any further partnership withdrawals taxable to you.

Example: Sylvester put $50,000 into Sylvester & Sons. The partnership is profitable, and Sylvester is entitled to a distributive share of $60,000 at the end of the year. Sylvester must pay income tax on $10,000 of it, the amount he received in excess of his basis ($50,000). Since Sylvester has gotten back all of his contributions to the partnership, his basis in his partnership interest (capital account) is reduced to zero. Unless Sylvester makes any additional contributions, all money or property he takes out in the future from Sylvester & Sons will be fully taxable to him.

2. Loans to Partners

Unlike sole proprietorships, partnerships are separate entities and can legally lend money to their owners. This presents an opportunity to get money out of your partnership, at least for the short term, without it being taxed. Loans aren't income to you if there is a legal obligation to repay them. Likewise, borrowing from your partnership doesn't affect your tax basis in your partnership interest.

A true loan, however, must meet tax code requirements. In general, the borrowing partner must have a written, legally enforceable obligation to repay the partnership at a determinable date and at a reasonable rate of interest. (See Chapter 7, C Corporations, for all of the legal requisites of a corporate loan, which apply to partnerships too.)

G. Partnership Expenses

Tax rules for expenses of a partnership are the same as for other businesses: an expense related to the trade or business can be deducted if ordinary and necessary. (See IRC § 162 and Chapter 1, Tax-Deductible Expenses.) Expense deductions are taken each year on the partnership's tax returns (Form 1065), not on the individual partners' returns.

Partnership start-up expenses—money spent before a business begins operating—are not deductible in the year incurred but must be capitalized and deducted equally over the first five years of business. If the partnership dissolves before five years is up, any balance not yet deducted can be taken in the final year. (IRC § 709.)

Delay some expenses until your doors are open. As soon as your partnership begins taking in money, you are in business. This means you can begin deducting expenses that might otherwise be considered of the start-up variety. So, engineer a way to open up—take in a little money—as soon as possible, and delay incurring and paying expenses until you do.

H. Selling or Transferring a Partnership Interest

Sooner or later you will likely be ready to move on and dispose of your interest in a partnership business. As you should have guessed, this will have tax ramifications that depend on a number of factors, including how you transfer the partnership interest.

1. Sale

If one partner sells his partnership interest to another partner—or to anyone else, for that matter—there is no tax impact on the partnership itself. It's like a shareholder selling stock in a corporation; it doesn't affect the corporation's taxes one way or the other.

On the other hand, for the *seller* there is likely a gain or loss to be reported. A selling partner's basis in her partnership interest determines the amount of her taxable gain or loss. Gain is computed by subtracting the partner's tax basis in her interest from money and/or property she received. If the partner has owned her interest for over a year, her gain qualifies for "capital gains" tax rates—meaning a top tax rate of 28% on any profit from the sale. (See "Favorable Capital Gains Tax Rate," below, and IRC §§ 704, 706, 732.)

Example: Ken sells his VideoPro partnership interest to Jackie for $75,000. Ken initially put $40,000 into VideoPro, contributed another $15,000 when the business needed cash for expansion, and took out a total of $50,000 over several years, which represented his distributive share of earnings. Thus, Ken's basis in his partnership interest was $5,000 when he sold to Jackie.

	$40,000	*original basis*
+	$15,000	*additional investment*
-	$50,000	*withdrawals*
=	$ 5,000	*adjusted basis*

This means Ken has a taxable gain of $70,000 when he sells to Jackie ($75,000 received, less $5,000 basis). At the current capital gains tax rate of 28%, his tax liability is $19,600 for the sale. (If Ken's tax bracket were lower than 28%, his tax would be less.)

When an interest is sold or exchanged, a partnership must, however, file IRS Form 8308, Report of a Sale or Exchange of Certain Partnership Interests. This form is filed with its annual partnership tax reporting form. (IRS Form 1065.)

2. Retirement

If the partnership itself buys a partner's interest, the tax result is usually the same as selling to a third party. The tax code terms this a "retirement." Payments a withdrawing partner receives for the sale are treated first as a distribution of her partnership capital account. She first gets back her investment—which has no tax consequences. Anything more is a taxable gain, and anything less is a taxable loss. There is no effect on the basis of the remaining partners in the partnership.

Example: Starsky retires from the Starsky & Hutch partnership, which pays him $60,000 for his interest. Starsky's tax basis in his partnership interest is $80,000. So, the $60,000 Starsky gets is just getting part of his money back. The balance, $20,000, is treated as a loss on his investment in the partnership.

Death of a partner is discussed in Section I, below.

FAVORABLE CAPITAL GAINS TAX RATE

Profits on investments are currently taxed at a maximum capital gains rate of 28%, as long as they have been held for at least one year and a day. Most other income, including gains on investments held less than one year, is termed ordinary income and is taxed at an individual's tax bracket rate, which currently ranges as high as 39.6%. If an individual's tax rate is lower than 28%, then the lower rate will apply. Some state income tax laws follow the federal law on taxing capital gains at a reduced rate, but some do not.

---

3. Special Rules to Watch Out For

Two more tricky tax rules come into play when you transfer a partnership interest. These provisions deal with "relief of debt" for the transferring partner, and partnership income to the partner for the year of sale.

a. Relief of Debt

For tax purposes, the amount realized by a selling partner includes, in addition to cash and any property received, her share of any partnership liability she is leaving behind. For instance, if a three-person equal partnership owes $150,000 to its creditors when one partner withdraws, the withdrawing partner is treated as receiving $50,000 because she no longer owes that amount of the debts. This "relief of debt" income is not obvious to most of us, but it can produce an unexpected tax bill, even exceeding the amount a partner gets from selling her interest.

Example: Brenda, a 50% partner in the B & B partnership, retires. Brenda takes partnership assets—a car worth $10,000 and $25,000 cash—in return for her share. Brenda is also relieved of half of the $40,000 owed by B & B to its creditors. The tax code says Brenda got a total of $55,000 for her partnership interest. How much, if any, is taxable gain is determined by Brenda's basis in the partnership.

b. Date-of-Sale Adjustment

The selling partner's basis in her interest is subject to a final adjustment for any partnership gains or losses for the year-to-date. A profit must be reported on her individual tax return as ordinary income—not part of a capital gain on the sale of her interest. If the year-to-date figure is a loss, it is deducted from her basis.

Example: On July 1, 1995, Betty sells her 50% partnership interest for $100,000. Her basis is $50,000. The B & B partnership has a profit of $40,000 so far during 1995. Betty must report $20,000, half of the profit, as her distributive share for that year—plus any gain or loss on the sale of her partnership interest. She owes regular income tax on the partnership profits ($20,000), meaning it can be taxed at a rate as high as 39.6%. Her partnership share, however, is taxed no higher than at the capital gains tax rate of 28%, assuming she was a partner for longer than one year.

I. Ending a Partnership

Unless the partnership agreement provides otherwise, a partnership terminates automatically by law on the death or withdrawal of a partner. For IRS purposes, *all* partnership assets—including equipment and all other partnership property—are then considered to have been distributed to the individual partners. (IRC § 708(b).) As we know, each partner must pay tax on anything received in excess of the tax basis of his interest (capital account balance). The deceased partner's share goes into his or her estate.

If property is sold before ending the partnership, money received is simply divided among the partners and taxed to them accordingly. It's also common to divvy up property—equipment or real estate—among partners. The value of the property is taxed to the recipient in the year distributed. Tax is due on the difference between the partner's tax basis and its fair market value, whether the partner sells or retains the property.

Example: Ken dies, and his VideoPro partnership terminates. His partner Barbara takes the business equipment, with a value of $120,000, to use in a new business. Ken's estate takes the partnership bank account of $120,000. At the date the partnership ends, Barbara's basis in her partnership interest is $50,000. So, Barbara has a taxable gain of $70,000 ($120,000 value of equipment less her basis in her interest, $50,000). Whether or not Ken's heirs will have to pay estate taxes on this distribution will depend on the size of his estate. (See Chapter 12, Family Businesses, for an explanation of estate tax.)

PART 2

The Form
of Your Business

You may need cash to pay your tax liability if you receive property when a partnership ends. Implicit in the above example is the danger of a tax liability for Barbara without cash to pay it. If you take non-cash assets—especially property, like real estate, that is hard to liquidate, or that you want to keep—make sure you have enough to pay the tax man.

PARTNERSHIPS AND IRS AUDITS

Small general partnerships are audited only about one-third as often as sole proprietorships with the same income. The IRS apparently reasons that since partnerships don't pay taxes (partners do, remember), auditing them won't directly result in more revenue. Of course, if a business partner's tax return is audited, chances are the IRS will look at his partnership's tax return too. And if problems are found—such as an improper tax deduction being taken on the partnership tax return—it can lead to the audit of all of the other partners' income tax returns as well.

RESOURCES

IRS Publication 334, *Tax Guide for Small Business*

IRS Publication 541, *Tax Information for Partnerships*

IRS Form 1065, *U.S. Partnership Return of Income*, and instructions

The Partnership Book, by Denis Clifford & Ralph Warner (Nolo Press), contains a wealth of details about setting up and running a partnership business.

Partnership Maker (Nolo Press) is a computer program that lets you draft your own partnership agreement with both standard and special partnership provisions. ■

Limited Liability Companies

"I stay within the law only because the law is maneuverable, it can be manipulated."

— William M. Kunstler

A new way to organize a small business, the limited liability company (LLC for short), may be in your future. They first cropped up in Wyoming in 1977, and have since been authorized in every state and the District of Columbia.

Doing business as an LLC offers several advantages over a partnership or a corporation. Unlike general partnerships, LLCs give owners (called "members") protection from claims of business creditors. Individual LLC members' liability for business debts is limited to the value of their ownership interest in the business—hence the name "limited liability." And all LLC members can take an active role in the operation of the business without exposing themselves to personal liability, which limited partners can't do.

Limited liability companies usually identify themselves with an "LLC" after the name of the business.

<table>
<tr><td>

LIMITED LIABILITY COMPANIES IN A NUTSHELL

1. The limited liability company offers a personal liability shield to its owners, much like a corporation does.

2. State law regulates the formation and operation of LLCs.

3. LLCs are taxed by the IRS like general partnerships; the LLC does not pay taxes, but instead passes its profits and losses through to its owners.

4. New IRS rules allow LLCs to choose to be taxed like a corporation, but there is little or no reason to choose this option.

5. The LLC is a relatively new form of business entity, and some tax and legal issues must be resolved.

</td></tr>
</table>

A. Limited Liability Company Income

The LLC, like a partnership or S corporation, is normally a pass-through tax entity. It doesn't pay taxes, but must file a tax return. Owners ("members") report and pay taxes on LLC income on their individual tax returns. The members are usually working in the business, but they may be just investors.

1. Federal Tax Reporting

At present, the IRS does not have a separate tax form for LLCs, so they file Form 1065, U.S. Partnership Return of Income. The LLC must also issue each member IRS Form K-1 at the end of each year, showing his or her proportionate share of the business's profit or loss. The LLC must file all K-1 forms with its tax return every year it's in operation.

Because LLCs, like partnerships and S corporations, do not pay federal income taxes, their income is taxed at a single level—to the members. The LLC members report the business income or loss from the K-1 form on their individual income tax returns, and pay federal taxes on it, along with the rest of their income. Members are subject to the self-employment tax (a total of 15.3% for Social Security and Medicare) if they are active in the business operation of the LLC. If they are just investors in the LLC, their income is not subject to the SE tax.

So an LLC and its owners (unless they elect to be taxed like a corporation) don't face the prospect of double taxation that C corporations do. But there's a downside as well. A C corporation can keep some of its earnings in inventory or in cash for future growth. These retained earnings are taxed, but at corporate tax rates that are usually lower than individual shareholders' tax rates. LLC members, on the other hand, can't leave profits in the business without paying taxes at their individual tax brackets, which might be as high as 39.6%. (See Chapter 7, C Corporations.)

2. State Taxes on LLCs

Most state taxing authorities require similar tax reporting on their own forms from LLCs. However, be aware that your state may impose taxes on profitable LLCs even though the IRS doesn't. For example, in California, LLCs are subject to annual income taxes between $800 and $4,500, even though California does not tax the income of general partnerships. This doesn't sound fair—but I didn't write the law.

B. Comparing LLCs With Other Entities

The primary attraction of the LLC is that if the business is sued or incurs obligations it can't meet, the creditor can only go after the assets of the business—not property owned by the individual co-owners (members). There is one notable exception: the IRS (and probably your state tax authority, too) can collect payroll taxes directly from members. (See Chapter 5, Tax Concerns of Employers.)

Example: Alex and Cathy form Fishworld, LLC, as a wholesale tropical fish enterprise. Two years later, their main customer declares bankruptcy, owing Fishworld $70,000. At about the same time, most of their fish stock die from an outbreak of parasites. The LLC owes $43,000 in general debts and $8,000 in payroll taxes. It has no cash but owns $10,000 of equipment. Fishworld's creditors can sue and get the equipment to satisfy their claims, but that's it. Alex and Cathy, however, will be jointly liable to the IRS for the $8,000 in employees' payroll taxes.

This limited liability feature, not taxes, is the reason most folks choose an LLC. Specifically, here's a summary of how LLCs stack up against the other business entity types:

- *Sole proprietorship.* The IRS has ruled that an LLC can be a one-man band, but most states still require at least two members to form an LLC. A spouse could be the other owner, however states will no doubt quickly move to change their restrictions on formation of one-person LLCs.

- *General partnership.* For tax purposes, the LLC is a partnership, so the only advantage is that LLC owners aren't personally liable for business debts as are general partners. In the example of the Fishworld, LLC, above, if Alex and Cathy had been general partners, they would be responsible for paying all of the debts out of their personal assets—bank accounts, autos, or just about anything they owned as individuals.

- *Limited partnership.* As with a general partnership, there is no tax benefit of limited partnerships over LLCs. While limited partners enjoy a shield from personal liability, they can lose this protection if they participate in the management of the business; limited liability company members have no restrictions on participation. And each limited partnership must by law have at least one general partner with liability for business debts.

- *S corporation.* LLCs and S corporations are both tax "pass through" entities, meaning that business profits and losses flow through the business to its owners, so this comparison is tax neutral. LLCs, however, enjoy fewer state organization restrictions, fewer formalities, and are generally cheaper to operate than corporations.

- *C corporation.* As with S corporations, because they are separate entities from their owners, C corporation businesses offer protection from creditors. There is a clear tax advantage to LLCs here, because C corporations—unlike all of the other entity forms—are taxpaying entities. So there could be a double taxation of profits.

Since LLCs are relatively new, a lot of legal and tax issues are not yet settled. Here are some murky areas:

- Switching from a corporation to an LLC may have unwanted tax consequences. (See Section C2, below.)

- Legal uncertainties. Just as a radically new model of car might have some problems, so LLCs might be more likely to have legal difficulties, at least until the law is settled. This is a risk, albeit a small one.

PART 2

The Form of Your Business

PROFESSIONAL LIMITED LIABILITY PARTNERSHIP AND LLCS

Most states now allow professionals to form LLCs, which some states call Limited Liability Partnerships (LLPs). In the five states that haven't provided for professional LLCs, the alternative is the Personal Service Corporation. (See Chapter 11.) Only certain state-licensed occupations—such as doctors, lawyers and accountants—may form these LLCs or LLPs. For example, California provides that an LLP may be formed only by accounting or law firms. A California LLP is a general partnership that is registered with the state, on a provided form, with the payment of a $70 fee. The designations "LLP" or "RLP" or "Registered Limited Liability Partnership" become part of the firm name and must be used in all legal transactions and advertising to the public. Once properly registered, the partners of the LLP do not have liability for the malpractice of the other partners, but of course, remain liable for their own acts. This limited liability feature is the primary reason why professionals form LLPs.

If you provide services of any kind and are thinking about an LLC, check with your state for restrictions and requirements. A few states may allow a one-person firm to form an LLC, but the IRS has not yet approved a one-person LLC and may never do so.

C. Forming and Operating a Limited Liability Company

As with most business entities, limited liability companies are creatures of the individual states. Most state laws tend to be similar—for example, most states have adopted the Uniform Partnership Act—but none has yet adopted a Uniform Limited Liability Company Act. So for now, LLC laws, procedures, paperwork and expenses vary widely from state to state.

1. Formalities

To form an LLC, you or your attorney must prepare written "Articles of Organization" and send them to your state's filing office, often called the Secretary of State. The articles may be just a simple one-page form, similar to Articles of Incorporation. The filing fee depends on your state and generally ranges from $50 on up. (California, for example, is on the high side; it charges $800. New York charges a more reasonable $200.)

A written LLC Operating Agreement and Bylaws may also be required by your state. These documents are similar to partnership agreements or bylaws that govern a corporation. The LLC operating agreement sets out the internal rules for governing the LLC, such as voting rights, check-signing authority and other vital matters. Even if a written agreement is not required by your state, it is certainly a good idea to have one, to help avoid or settle disputes about the management of the business later down the road. Check your local bookstore or library to see if they have LLC formbooks for your state. These will have examples of how such agreements are written.

LLCs don't require you to follow common corporate formalities such as keeping minutes, passing resolutions and holding annual meetings, under most states' laws.

Some states may require extra steps before your LLC can start business. In New York, for instance, you must publish notice of your LLC formation in a newspaper.

To qualify for pass-through taxation, LLCs used to have to jump through a number of hoops set up by the IRS. The goal was to distinguish LLCs from corporations. The IRS dumped these requirements when it adopted its 1997 rules that allowed LLCs to choose either pass-through taxation or taxation as an entity (like a corporation). But if your state law still contains these technical requirements, be sure to meet them when you set up your LLC. Otherwise, it's possible that a business creditor could sue you personally, claiming that your LLC wasn't properly formed under state law.

For tax purposes, the only step after forming the LLC that you must take is to get a new federal identification number (EIN) for the LLC from the IRS. (See Chapter 9, Partnerships, for details on how to get the new EIN.)

WHERE TO GET HELP

Check with your Secretary of State's office for LLC fee and filing rules. Some states may provide sample LLC articles or fill-in forms. Business lawyers can help you form an LLC, and tax pros have the IRS tax reporting information. Professional fees should be about the same as for forming a partnership or corporation—generally ranging from $500 to $1,500.

---

2. Converting to a Limited Liability Company

Before converting an existing business to an LLC, there are some important tax consequences to consider.

Changing an existing S or C corporation business to an LLC may carry too heavy a tax price. A corporation must be formally "liquidated" under tax code rules before its assets are put into an LLC, and corporate liquidations are potentially taxable and legally complex. Liquidating a C corporation with significant assets might mean taxes for the corporation, because this is treated as a sale of the corporation's assets. Then the funds from the sale of assets are deemed to have been distributed to the shareholders, who are taxed again. (See Chapter 7, C Corporations.) Whatever is left after taxes goes into the LLC.

If you convert an S corporation to an LLC, you'll fare slightly better, because any taxes on liquidation are placed only on the shareholders. There is no double taxation, as with C corporations.

A relatively new corporation, or one that has not been successful or that doesn't have any assets to speak of, may be able to convert to an LLC without a tax cost. If you are tempted to convert to an LLC, see a tax pro first.

3. Restrictions on Limited Liability Company Membership and Rights

The tax code does not limit the number or kinds of owners (members) an LLC can have. By contrast, an S corporation may have no more than 75 shareholders, including individuals and estates. And S corporation shareholders can't be nonresident aliens—which rules out any foreign shareholders. Because LLCs aren't under the ownership restrictions of S corporations, it may be easier for them to bring in more owners to raise capital.

Unlike general partners or S corporation owners, LLC members may be legally excluded from having a say in the management of the business, as long as the LLC articles of agreement say it and the powerless member agrees. In this respect, an LLC member is like a limited partner or the holder of nonvoting corporate stock. Typically, this kind of LLC member would be a passive investor in the LLC.

4. Transferring Ownership by Sale or Death

Members' interests are "shares" of the LLC, similar to a partnership interest or share of corporate stock. Transferring ownership in an LLC is relatively easy—a share document is signed over to the new owner, like a stock certificate.

The tax consequences to the selling or transferring member are the same as with a partnership—the gain or loss is determined by the member's tax basis in his share. (See Chapter 9, Partnerships.)

Small business owners don't want a co-owner forced on them without their approval. So, LLC articles of organization should contain restrictions on transfers of LLC shares. Typically, a retiring member of an LLC may be required to first offer his share to the remaining members before selling to anyone else. Usually a predetermined price for a share or a formula for valuing it is written into the articles.

A separate buy-sell agreement binding all members should be part of the LLC formation process, in addition to the provision mentioned above for limitations on share transfers in the articles. Apart from non-tax reasons for doing this (primarily to avoid disputes between members as to the value of a share if one member wants to sell out), the IRS will stick its ugly nose into the picture when a member dies. Keep in mind that the LLC share will be an asset in the estate of the dearly departed member, and there may be an estate tax to worry about. Valuation of business interests is a number one concern to an IRS estate tax auditor, and many executors end up in IRS battles over just what a small business interest is worth. (See Nolo's *Stand Up to the IRS* for more information about estate tax audits and business valuations.)

The good news is that the IRS usually respects the terms of a buy-sell agreement for fixing a fair price of a member's share. If the LLC members don't provide for some valuation formula for shares, it will be necessary to hire an (expensive) appraiser. If the IRS audits, it may or may not accept the professional appraiser's opinion. On the other hand, if there was a valuation formula (or maybe even a fixed price) for a member's LLC share, and the LLC had been around for several years, the IRS is likely just to go along with it.

5. Passing Profit and Loss Through to Members

LLCs must file tax returns and issue Form K-1s each year to members showing their respective portion of business income or loss. As mentioned, the IRS has not yet come up with a separate form for limited liability company tax returns, so you will use Form 1065, the federal partnership tax return form. (Chapter 9, Partnerships, contains a sample partnership tax return and Form K-1.)

One very valuable feature of LLCs is that they allow distributions of profits (or losses) that are disproportionate to the owners' shares in the business. This must be spelled out in the LLC agreement beforehand, however.

Example: Bruce owns 50% of Central Carpet Cleaners, LLC, along with two friends who own 25% each. Their LLC agreement provides that because Bruce devotes full-time to the business while the other members work part-time, Bruce is entitled to 75% of the LLC profits.

Partnerships, on the other hand, can distribute profits unequally only if they meet some technical tax code rules. For instance, partners who contribute services—but not capital—to the partnership can't claim a tax benefit for any business losses. And S corporation shareholders can't get profits or losses except in direct proportion to their ownership of shares. (These points are discussed in Chapter 9, Partnerships, and Chapter 8, S Corporations.)

D. Terminating a Limited Liability Company

Generally, the procedure for terminating an LLC is similar to closing up a partnership. It is governed by the state law and is typically provided for in standard form LLC articles of organization.

For tax purposes, tax treatment of the members is the same as if they were general partners. (See Chapter 9, Partnerships.)

RESOURCES

IRS Revenue Procedure 95-10. This IRS document spells out the requirements for a ruling request relating to classification of an LLC as a partnership for tax purposes.

A Guide to Limited Liability Companies (Commerce Clearing House), and *The Limited Liability Company,* by James Bagley (James Publishing). These are technical books written for CPAs and attorneys.

Limited Liability Companies, by Robert W. Wood (John Wiley & Sons). This book discusses in depth the implications and mechanics of converting existing small businesses to LLCs.

Form Your Own Limited Liability Company, by Anthony Mancuso (Nolo Press). This book provides step-by-step forms and instructions for setting up an LLC without costly legal fees.

The Essential Limited Liability Company Handbook (Oasis Press, 800-228-2275, 1995, $19.95). By Corporate Agents, a company that specializes in handling incorporation issues. Besides offering a good discussion of the pros and cons of LLCs, the guide provides a valuable state-by-state breakdown of key rules and fees. ■

PART 2

The Form of Your Business

Personal Service Corporations

PART **2**

The Form of Your Business

"There is no magic in parchment or in wax."

— **William Henry Ashhurst**

Professionals—physicians, lawyers, accountants and others—are treated as small businesses under the tax code. Most of them operate as sole proprietorships or partnerships, and are subject to the same tax rules as other similar entities. However, certain professionals who offer services may form and oper-ate a special type of entity, called a "professional corporation." Moreover, state laws require certain categories of professionals, if they want to incorpo-rate, to do so as a professional corporation. These professionals aren't allowed to form regular corpo-rations. Owners of professional corporations are its shareholders, who perform services for the corpora-tion as employees.

Most professional corporations are classified by the federal tax code as "personal service corpora-tions" (PSCs) and taxed differently from other busi-ness entities.

PERSONAL SERVICE CORPORATIONS IN A NUTSHELL

1. In most states, certain specified profession-als who want to incorporate their businesses or practices must form "professional corporations"; they may not form regular corporations.

2. The IRS recognizes specified professional corporations as separate tax entities called personal service corporations (PSCs).

3. For a successful professional, incorporating offers a few tax advantages, including a greater range of fringe benefits.

A. Professional Corporations That Qualify as Personal Service Corporations

Each state licenses and regulates numerous profes-sions, and also determines who may—or may not—form a professional corporation in that state. For example, a group of attorneys and paralegals may not form a single professional corporation if under their state's law a non-lawyer can't hold stock in a professional legal services corporation.

A professional must be incorporated under his or her state's law in order to be treated as a personal service corporation under the federal tax code. But as you shall see, just forming a professional corpo-ration doesn't always mean it qualifies as a PSC. (IRC § 448.) If a professional corporation does not qualify as a PSC, then it is treated under the tax code as a general partnership. (See Chapter 9, Part-nerships.)

Under the tax code, a PSC is a state-formed corporation in which substantially all of the activi-ties involve services in the fields of "health, law, engineering, accounting, actuarial science, perform-ing arts or consulting." IRS regulations elaborate on the types of occupations that fall within these groupings.

For example, health care professionals include physicians, nurses, dentists and others, but not people who operate health or exercise clubs. "Con-sulting" covers giving advice, but not working as a salesperson or any kind of broker. Performing arts covers actors, entertainers and musicians but not their promoters or managers. Interestingly enough, professional athletes are not allowed to form PSCs. (Reg. 1.448-1T (e)(4).)

The IRS imposes two tests to make sure a corpo-ration under state law qualifies as a personal service corporation. These tests focus on what the corpora-tion does (the "function test") and how it's owned (the "ownership test"). Generally, neither of these tests is a problem for most professional corpora-tions, but you should be aware of them.

1. Function Test

Substantially all of the activities of the PSC must involve rendering personal services. IRS regulations say that "substantially all" means 95% of work time expended by employees. (Reg. 1.448-IT(e).)

Example: Jack and Jill are fresh out of law school, but they cannot find full-time work as attorneys. To keep bread on the table, they form an S corporation, Sweetstuff, Inc., to operate a yogurt store. In addition, they find part-time employment, about 10 hours a week, with a law firm. Can they convert their S corporation into a PSC? No. The Sweetstuff employees do not devote 95% of their time to the profession of law, so the corporation can't be a PSC.

2. Ownership Test

Substantially all stock in a PSC must be held directly or indirectly (through one or more partnerships, S corporations or other qualified PSCs) by either:

- employees performing professional services for the corporation, or

- retired employees who performed services in the past, or

- the estates of such individuals, or

- any person who acquired stock by reason of the death of any such persons.

As with the function test, "substantially all" means 95% of the value of all outstanding stock.

Example: Ralph and Connie are physical therapists who are approached by Gino, the owner of Costa La health spa, to offer services at the spa. If Ralph and Connie will incorporate as a professional corporation with him, Gino will invest $20,000 in return for its stock. Ralph and Connie agree to this, and they all form a professional corporation, with Ralph and Connie owning 75% of the stock and Gino 25%. This may qualify as a professional corporation under their state's law, but it fails to meet the tax code 95% ownership rule, because Gino, who is not a health professional providing services, owns 25% of the stock.

B. Taxation of Personal Service Corporations and Shareholders

In theory, a personal service corporation is taxed at a flat rate of 35% of its net income. In practice, as with most small corporations, the shareholders take out profits as tax-deductible (to the corporation) salaries, bonuses and fringe benefits. So, typically the shareholders pay income taxes on their individual tax returns and the PSC pays nothing. The PSC income tax applies only to money left in the corporation at the end of the tax year—if any. And who would ever leave money in the corporation under these circumstances?

NON-TAX BENEFITS OF PROFESSIONAL CORPORATIONS

Professionals may find that a corporation is a desirable form of business operation for a variety of non-tax-related reasons. Like any corporation, a PSC has perpetual existence. If one shareholder dies or withdraws, a PSC business can often carry on with minimal legal disruption.

Often the most important advantage is that professional corporations offer a measure of limited personal liability. The extent of this protection depends on state law. Even an incorporated professional can't legally escape personal liability for her own negligent acts. However, an incorporated professional practicing with other professionals can usually avoid personal liability resulting from another's misdeeds.

Example: Allison and Bill, both psychiatrists, form a professional corporation to practice medicine together, sharing a receptionist and other common expenses. If Dr. Bill loses a malpractice lawsuit, both the corporation's assets and Dr. Bill's, personally, can be in jeopardy. However, Dr. Allison will not be personally liable—meaning her house and savings cannot be grabbed to pay the judgment. If, on the other hand, their business were a partnership, Dr. Allison would be personally liable for Dr. Bill's acts in their practice of medicine.

PART 2

The Form of Your Business

C. Special Tax Rules for Personal Service Corporations

For tax purposes, a PSC is a separate entity from its owners, similar to a C corporation. So, it must file its own corporate tax return every year, and may offer many of the fringe benefits available to a C corporation. (See Chapter 14, Fringe Benefits, and Chapter 15, Retirement Plans, for a discussion of corporate fringe benefits.)

A PSC may elect to be an S corporation, but it will not be able to qualify for corporate fringe benefits. (See Chapter 8, S Corporations.) Because the tax code does not provide the same flow-through tax treatment to PSC shareholders as S corporation shareholders get, PSCs seldom elect S status.

A PSC may adopt IRC § 1244 status when it is formed (if it has not elected to be an S corporation). This allows advantageous tax treatment to shareholders if they sell their stock in the PSC for a loss. (See Chapter 4, Tax Benefits of Business Losses.)

A PSC that has not elected S corporation status can give its shareholders/employees tax benefits not available to unincorporated professionals, mainly in the area of corporate fringe benefits, discussed next.

1. Retirement Plans

A PSC may establish corporate retirement plans and a 401(k) plan, allowing greater contributions than plans available to unincorporated professionals. (See Chapter 15, Retirement Plans.)

2. Health and Life Insurance Benefits

A PSC with more than two shareholders may establish a "Voluntary Employees' Beneficiary Association" (VEBA). This allows the PSC to tax deduct and provide health and life insurance coverage to all PSC employees, including shareholders, as a tax-free benefit. VEBAs are usually administered by banks or insurance companies. (See IRC § 501(c)(9) for details, or consult a tax or pension professional.)

3. Other Fringe Benefits

Generally, PSCs can offer life and disability insurance, death benefits, dependent care and other fringes, without establishing a VEBA. (See Chapter 14, Fringe Benefits.)

4. Tax Year

A PSC must keep its records on an annual basis, and can choose between a calendar year or fiscal year. (See Chapter 3, Recordkeeping and Accounting.) While it is possible for a PSC to tax report on a fiscal year basis instead of a calendar year, it may be more trouble than it is worth. A PSC must get permission to use a fiscal year by showing the IRS a "business purpose" for it. (Rev. Procs. 87-32 and 87-57 have details and examples.) To apply for permission from the IRS to use a fiscal year, you must file IRS Form 1128.

ALTERNATIVES TO THE PROFESSIONAL CORPORATION

A few states recognize professional limited liability companies (LLCs) for certain professions, as an alternative to the professional corporation. At this time, the states are Arizona, Kansas, Louisiana, Minnesota, Oklahoma, Texas, Utah and Virginia. Three states (Texas, Delaware and Louisiana) allow a variation of the professional LLC, called limited liability partnerships (LLPs). See Chapter 10, Limited Liability Companies, for more information about the pros and cons of forming an LLC.

D. Potential Tax Problems With Personal Service Corporations

There are a few tax concerns that may creep up on an unsuspecting PSC shareholder. These probably won't affect your PSC, but you should be aware of them.

1. Passive Loss Limitations

A tax code rule on "passive loss limitations" may restrict some PSC shareholders from taking tax deductions for corporation losses. This is not a problem unless the PSC loses money in its operation and wants to pass the loss along to *non-active* shareholders. In reality, most PSCs are composed of active owners and don't lose money. This rule means the majority of PSC shareholders must actively perform services for the corporation—they can't be part-timers or shareholders who have retired. (IRC § 469.)

2. Income Splitting and Retained Earnings

Historically, a reason to form a C corporation is that creating a separate tax allows dividing income between the corporation and a shareholder to take advantage of their different tax rates. (See Chapter 7, C Corporations.) However, income splitting between PSCs and their shareholders is *not* allowed.

A flat 35% PSC tax applies to all profits left in the corporation at the end of the year, so retaining earnings in a PSC rarely makes tax sense. (See Chapter 7, C Corporations.)

E. Transferring Shares or Dissolving a Personal Service Corporation

In most states, laws prohibit transferring PSC stock to anyone who is not qualified as a member of the profession. So, PSC shares usually can't be left to a spouse or other family member when you die; doing so could also violate the tax code's requirement that "substantially all" of the stock be held by those who are performing services. For this reason, PSCs typically have written agreements, binding on both the shareholders and their estates, providing for the purchase of deceased shareholders' stock by the PSC. Often, this "cross purchase" agreement is funded by a life insurance policy. The PSC takes out life insurance policies on its members and uses the death benefit to purchase the deceased owner's share from his or her estate.

A PSC may be dissolved voluntarily, by a majority of the shareholders, or it may be dissolved involuntarily by the state or because of legal action against it. The tax rules for dissolving a PSC are basically the same as for a C corporation. (See Chapter 7, C Corporations.) The important thing to know is that a taxable gain or loss for each shareholder may result when a corporation is closed down.

RESOURCES

IRS Publication 542, *Tax Information on Corporations.* Part of this booklet gives some tax details of the PSC.

IRS Publication 334, *Tax Guide for Small Business.* A small portion of this substantial booklet covers PSCs.

The California Professional Corporation Handbook, by Anthony Mancuso (Nolo Press). While this book is geared for California, much of it applies to other states too, and it contains many valuable professional corporation forms. ■

PART **2**

The Form of Your Business

Family Businesses

PART 3

Thinking Small

"Don't tax you, don't tax me; tax the fellow behind the tree."

— Senator Russell B. Long

Many small businesses get the whole family involved. Typically, parents bring children into a family business because they need the help and want the kids to learn money-making skills. When the kids grow up, they can work in the business with the goal of taking it over, and maybe even passing it on to their offspring.

Most tax provisions apply uniformly to businesses whether the family is involved or not, but some special rules and tax-saving opportunities are inherent in family businesses. And when it comes to passing ownership on to the next generation, the law contains both tax traps and opportunities.

FAMILY BUSINESSES IN A NUTSHELL

1. Family businesses allow "income splitting" to reduce the family's overall tax bill.

2. It is okay to hire your spouse and kids and take tax deductions for payments to them, as long as they do real work and their pay is reasonable.

3. A corporation or a family limited partnership allows you to transfer a valuable family business to a younger generation during your life, while reducing or eliminating your estate tax liability after death.

A. The Legal Structure of a Family Business

A husband and wife can own a business together and still have it treated, legally, as a sole proprietorship. But if other family members share ownership, too, the operation must be organized instead as a partnership, limited liability company or corporation.

These more complex forms of doing business may offer families both tax and non-tax advantages. These entities allow more tax and estate planning flexibility than do sole proprietorships. For instance, incorporating allows family members, other than the business principals, to receive ownership benefits (such as stock dividends) even if they don't work for the enterprise. (See Section B, below.) And incorporating or forming a family limited partnership makes it easier to transfer business ownership to family members gradually over time and save estate taxes.

Another, more exotic, alternative is to combine several different organizational forms to best distribute tax benefits. For instance, a partnership consisting of several children can own and rent a building to a corporation owned by their parents. Whether or not multiple entities make sense depends on the tax situations of all the individuals in the family. If this sounds intriguing, check it out with a top tax pro, who can best evaluate your family's unique circumstances. Generally, in light of tax possibilities, whether or not forming several entities results in significant tax savings hinges on the "income splitting" ideas discussed below—shifting income from family members in the highest tax brackets to those in the lowest.

B. Income Splitting to Lower Taxes

Family members often pool their efforts and resources to run small businesses. For many, this provides not only a good living, but also a sense of security and closeness. Family ventures can also bring tax savings for the family unit. A planning technique known as "income splitting" shifts income from higher bracket taxpayers—usually parents—to lower ones—usually children or retired grandparents. Obviously, these strategies depend on cooperation and trust between family members. If done carefully and legally, real tax savings can result.

It's perfectly legal to hire the family. However, some business owners, determined to cut their taxes, "pay" their spouses and children hefty salaries, whether they work or not. The IRS has frowned on this type of family income splitting, but hasn't yet said "no" to this tax-saving opportunity altogether. Court decisions support operators who legitimately hire their minor children and other family members and give them *real work* to do. By and large, work that relatives do or how much they are paid is not a problem at IRS audits—as long as some work was done and pay wasn't outrageous. Following are the basic tax code rules on hiring your children.

1. Tax Benefits of Hiring Your Kids

Putting your children to work in your business can reduce your income taxes. Paying them, of course, reduces the amount of business income available for you to pay yourself, which is the main tax benefit.

Also, the tax code says that employment for FICA (Social Security and Medicare taxes) can exclude services performed by a child *under 18* in the employ of her or his mother or father. Likewise, there is an exclusion from FUTA (unemployment tax) for a business paying the owner's child who is *under 21*. This means there is no extra payroll tax incurred for putting junior on the payroll. (IRC § 3121 (b)(3)(A), IRC § 3306(c)(5).) This FICA and FUTA tax exclusion applies only to *unincorporated* businesses. Assuming that the child uses the money for things the parents would be buying anyway, this is money in the bank.

Example: Laura, the sole proprietor of PhotoLand, a wholesale film processing company, earns $300,000 per year, putting her in the top tax bracket (39.6%). Her 17-year-old daughter, Louisa, helps out at the plant after school, on weekends and all summer. Louisa is paid $20,000 over the year, which puts her in the lowest (15%) tax bracket. The overall tax on the family unit is reduced about $6,500. This is because of the difference in the mother's and daughter's tax rates. It works out like this:

Louisa, who will file a tax return, takes her personal exemption and claims the standard deduction. Louisa owes $2,040 in income taxes. If Laura doesn't hire Louisa, and instead took the $20,000 in income for herself, she'd pay extra taxes of $8,500 ($7,920 income taxes based on her tax bracket of 39.6% plus $580 in self-employment taxes of 2.9% for Medicare). Total family tax savings: almost $6,500. The tax deal can be even better if Louisa opens an IRA. (See below.)

TAX RULES WHEN YOUR CHILDREN WORK FOR YOU

- Child labor laws. While I've never heard of any agency applying child labor laws against parents putting their minor kids to work, I suppose it is possible. Of course, if you hire kids other than your own, you are breaking the law. I've hired my teenager and nothing happened to me, but you might want to check your state's law.

- Taxation. Currently, a minor child can earn up to $3,800 without any income tax liability. After that, the tax rate starts at 15%. As long as the income is earned by the child performing services for the business, the "kiddie tax" (tax on a child's investment income, discussed in Section 2, below) doesn't apply.

- Real work. Kids as young as seven can get paid for simple chores like taking phone messages or cleaning the business premises for a parent. (I don't know about your kids, but I shudder at the thought of a seven-year-old answering a business phone.) Children can be paid a reasonable sum for their work, but what is reasonable depends on the facts and circumstances of each case. I'd say don't try to pay and deduct more than $3,000 per year to any of your children under age 10.

PART **3**

Thinking Small

Example: Dr. Moriarty (his real name—not Sherlock Holmes' nemesis), hired his four teenagers to do clerical work for his medical practice. An IRS auditor said this was a mere subterfuge to deduct the kids' allowances as a business expense. The U.S. Tax Court overruled the IRS, saying it was all legal as long as the kids did real work and were paid reasonable wages. (James Moriarty, TC Memo 1984-249.)

Type of work. The kind of work done by the child—such as washing the company car, filing or going to the mailbox—doesn't matter, as long as it's a task a business customarily would pay someone else to do. Duties should reflect the age and training of the children. While it is fine to pay a 16-year-old to do computer inputting, it wouldn't wash for an eight-year-old. You could hire your precocious 13-year-old to do filing even if you might not hire someone else's 13-year-old for the job.

Rate of pay. Generally, don't pay your child more than you would a stranger, but there is some wiggle room. If you pay little Susie $7 per hour, and you could realistically find someone else to do it for $5.50, an auditor will likely let it pass. But, you are pushing the envelope if you pay Susie $20 per hour.

When paid. The payments to your kids should reflect some kind of regular work schedule. This can be tied to school vacations, after school time or holidays. If you make only one or two lump sum payments in a year, this may look suspiciously to an auditor like you are trying to fudge on your taxes instead of legitimately employing junior.

Save even more with an IRA for your child. An Individual Retirement Account can be established for any child who earns wages. So $2,000 of earnings can be put aside each year tax-deferred—meaning that junior may earn $5,800 before incurring any income tax liability. And any amount earned by the child over that is taxed starting at the lowest income tax rate, 15%.

Putting money into an IRA can make tax sense even if the child takes it out long before retirement, say for college. Yes, there is a 10% tax penalty for removing funds from an IRA before age 59 1/2. Nevertheless, the dual advantages of deferring tax on money put in the child's IRA, and the fact that the IRA earnings aren't currently taxed, outweighs the penalty if the IRA exists for at least eight years.

2. Making Your Kids Co-Owners

An alternative way to shift business income from higher-bracket family members to lower ones is by giving them stock in your incorporated business. (There are other ways to transfer ownership through a family limited partnership; see Section D, below.)

Stock ownership is tax-treated as an investment in the business by the family member, even if they didn't pay for it. The primary drawback is that you must irrevocably transfer the stock to the family members. If you change your mind later, you have no legal right to take it back. If you are the cautious type, transfer only shares of non-voting stock, so that family members holding them have no vote in the management of the business—including whether they will get any dividends each year.

Example: Wally and Wanda incorporate their business, House of Shoes, and give their children each $20,000 worth of stock every year ($10,000 from each parent). The gift is not subject to federal gift tax. (See the discussion in Section D about estate and gift tax basics.) The stock is non-voting, so Wally and Wanda maintain control of the management of the business, as long as they own any shares at all.

Children who own stock can receive dividends on their ownership interests in the business, which are taxed according to how old the kids are. This is treated as investment income under the tax code. Here are the rules:

Under 14 Rule. An under-14-year-old child's "net unearned income"—such as stock dividends from a family-owned corporation—is taxed at the parent's tax rate. This is the so-called "kiddie tax," which forecloses income splitting when kids are very young and don't work in the business. However, the first $1,300 of the child's income is exempt from the kiddie tax in 1995.

Over 14 Rule. If your child is 14 or over and gets dividends from the family corporation, the kiddie tax limit of $1,300 does not apply. (Don't ask me why 14 is the magic age.) The family unit may still get an advantage because the child is taxed at a lower rate than the parents, thereby lowering the family tax bill.

A corporation can pay your kid for services and also pay him dividends on stock ownership. As long as a child's tax bracket remains lower than his parents', an overall income tax saving results. However, watch out for double taxation. A family corporation paying dividends to any shareholder—including kids—may have already incurred corporate income tax on this money, so tax savings will be lower than you might first think. You should run this by a tax pro to see if it makes sense for your family. (See Chapter 7, C Corporations, for a discussion of the taxation of corporations.)

3. Putting Older Parents on the Payroll

An income-splitting strategy can also work with retired parents and their grown children. For example, a contractor who might otherwise help his retired father financially might instead put him on his business payroll part-time. Not only does the business benefit from the older man's experience, but the father's pay is likely to be taxed in a lower bracket.

Normally, shifting income to parents makes sense only if they are in a lower tax bracket than you are and need income. Before doing this, check to see what effect earnings will have on your parents' Social Security benefits, and tailor their pay accordingly. If a retiree is under age 70, her Social Security benefits can be reduced in the following year if earned income is over a "threshold" amount. However, benefits are reduced only as a result of *earned* income; other income—investment, annuities, private pensions, unemployment, gifts and rents—don't count toward the threshold. One more thing you should take into account, which might sound strange: compensation of a person who receives Social Security benefits is still subject to Social Security and Medicare taxes.

HOW WORKING REDUCES SOCIAL SECURITY BENEFITS		
AGE	ANNUAL EARNINGS LIMIT	REDUCTION IN BENEFITS
62-65	$8,280	$1 for every $2 earned
65-69	$12,500	$1 for every $3 earned
70 or older	No limit	None

(These amounts are for 1996, and are subject to an annual adjustment. The ceiling for taxpayers aged 65-69 is scheduled to increase to $30,000 in 2002.)

Example: Marina retired at age 62, but went to work for her son, Manny, at his Motel Five as a part-time desk clerk. In 1996, Marina earned $12,000. In 1997, she will lose $1,980 in Social Security benefits under tax code above ($12,000–$8,280, divided by 2= $1,860), and Marina's wages are subject to Social Security and Medicare taxes. If Marina continues to work after age 65, she'll lose $1 for every $3 over the threshold until she turns 70. After that, her Social Security won't be reduced no matter how much she makes.

PART **3**

Thinking Small

Don't enlarge a parent's large estate. Think twice before paying your parent if she is single and has an estate that is worth over $600,000, or is married and has a combined worth, with her spouse, of more than $1.2 million. The reason is that at the parent's death, any surplus *above* these amounts will be subject to federal estate tax, which begins at 37%. (IRC § 2001.) In this situation, it might be better for parent to work at an artificially low rate of pay—or as a volunteer. That way, the business gets the value of the senior's labor, but his or her estate doesn't grow.

C. A Spouse in the Business

When spouses work together in a venture, the tax situation is often the reverse of that involving minor children. Instead of putting your spouse on the payroll, it may save money by keeping her or him off—even though they work for the business. The reason is that *all* employees—except owners and their children under 18—are subject to payroll taxes.

These taxes (Social Security and Medicare) add 15.3% to the cost of wages, up to $62,700, and 2.9% on all pay over that. In addition, federal unemployment taxes add another 6.2% of the first $7,000 of wages paid to every employee.

Finally, if a spouse is on the payroll, other expenses are incurred, such as unemployment and disability taxes, and workers' compensation insurance as well. There are two ways to get around the added expenses of a spouse on the payroll:

1. Let your spouse volunteer, or
2. Share ownership.

Let's take a closer look at both options.

1. Let Your Spouse Volunteer

You won't have the extra expenses discussed above if your spouse works but doesn't get a paycheck. I have never seen any government agency, including the IRS, try to force a working—but unpaid—spouse onto the payroll. However, "volunteers" can't be covered by employee benefit plans—except to the extent the plans cover spouses.

Example: Susie Sanders earns $100,000 in 1994 from her SS Personnel Services business. Susie hires Jocko, her hubby, to help in the office and pays him $20,000 a year. Putting Jocko on the payroll increases the Sanders' joint tax bill by $3,060 (Social Security and Medicare tax of 15.3% x $20,000). By contrast, if Jocko had done the work and not been paid (thereby increasing Susie's income by $20,000), the family would have come out ahead about $2,500 in 1994. ($3,060 minus $580, the amount of Medicare tax of 2.9% that Susie would have had to pay on the extra $20,000 income.)

Payroll tax expense for a working spouse can be partially justified if he or she earns at least $2,000 in wages. He or she is then eligible to contribute up to $2,000 into an Individual Retirement Account. (Chapter 15, Retirement Plans, explains how IRAs save taxes.)

Watch out for Social Security issues. A spouse who is not on the payroll won't get credit in his or her Social Security account. This may not be a real problem if the spouse has already qualified for coverage from a former job. Also, he or she may be eligible for Social Security survivor benefits if the other spouse dies first, as long as the marriage lasted 10 years or more. However, survivor benefits are lower than those paid on primary accounts.

2. Share Ownership

Of course, a husband and wife who join in a family business can be co-owners. The majority of spouses tax-report as co-sole proprietors. In this case, the IRS considers them both owners, not employees. The husband and wife just split the profits or, more commonly, put all income into the family pot.

Because neither spouse is legally an employee, neither has to pay unemployment tax or other expenses of employees. (See Chapter 5, Tax Concerns of Employers.) Co-owners are subject to self-employment taxes (Social Security and Medicare) on all compensation from the business, so both spouses build up their Social Security accounts.

All it takes for a married couple to be treated by the IRS as co-owners of a sole proprietorship is listing it this way at the top of Schedule C of their joint tax return each year.

An alternative is for two spouses to form a partnership. This doesn't normally change the overall income tax consequences for either partner, but in some cases it may be done for income splitting and estate tax reasons. (See Section D, below, and Chapter 9, Partnerships.) Couples who form a partnership must file a partnership tax return in addition to their own individual tax return. If you are considering a formal partnership with a spouse, see a tax pro first to determine if the extra expenses and effort are worth what you are trying to accomplish.

Co-owning spouses can write off business travel. One potential tax advantage of spouses co-owning an enterprise involves out-of-town travel. If they travel together—to conventions or on other business—the expenses of both are tax-deductible. By contrast, if one works for the business as an off-the-books volunteer, her or his travel costs aren't deductible. (See Chapter 14, Fringe Benefits.)

D. Preserving a Family Business

This book deals with the day-to-day tax issues of a small business. We don't cover in depth the vital topic called "estate planning"—how you want to leave your property, including your business, after death, with an eye to minimizing or avoiding probate fees and taxes. However, everyone who owns a business should be concerned about two aspects of estate planning:

- Keeping the operation going after the owner dies, and
- Preventing estate taxes from taking a huge chunk of money from surviving family members or from forcing the liquidation of the business.

CHOOSING AN ESTATE TAX STRATEGY

Lawyers and financial planners can often find ways to squeeze through loopholes in the tax code and avoid or greatly reduce estate taxes. This may involve different kinds of trusts, such as marital bypass trusts and charitable trusts (GRITS, GRATS, QTIPS, etc.). This section discusses two popular strategies for small business owners to reduce estate taxes. But it's a complicated area of the law, and the best strategy for you will depend on the details of your personal and financial situation.

---

1. Death and Taxes

A successful small family enterprise often becomes very valuable over time, sometimes to the point that small-time operators who struggled for years find themselves unexpectedly affluent. The flip side is that significant federal estate taxes will be due after the death of the owners, because the business pushes up the value of their estate. (Roughly speaking, your estate is everything you own at your death.) Estate taxes can be murderously high and may mean selling the business or its assets instead of passing it on to other family members.

Example: When Stella, a single woman, dies, her business, Stella's Diner, is the biggest asset in her estate. The estate has a net value, after debts, of $900,000. Since the first $600,000 of any estate can be passed tax-free, Stella's estate is taxed on the balance ($300,000). Stella's estate will owe a federal tax bill in excess of $120,000, and may owe estate taxes to her state.

There is no federal inheritance tax. Beneficiaries of an estate do not owe tax on anything they inherit. Instead, the estate is liable for the federal and state estate tax. If the event the estate tax isn't paid, the IRS can come after the beneficiaries.

The tax code provides one break that may let families avoid forced liquidations of enterprises on death: an IRS estate tax installment payment plan at a 4% interest rate. An estate with a small business that is worth at least 35% of the estate's total value can pay estate taxes in installments over 14 years. For the first five years, the estate is allowed to pay interest only. (IRC § 6166.)

Example: When Jorge suddenly dies without having done any estate planning, Jorge's Plumbing Supplies is worth several million dollars. Jorge leaves the business to his two sons, but there isn't enough money in his estate to pay the estate taxes. Under the installment payment provision, Jorge's sons can keep the business and pay the estate tax out of future profits over 14 years at a very favorable interest rate of 4%.

While this tax code provision can help business owners' families, the best way to take care of your family is by prior estate planning. With a good estate plan, you might be able to eliminate estate taxes altogether.

ESTATE TAX RELIEF ON THE WAY?

Major estate tax changes are now being considered in Congress. One is to raise the $600,000 estate tax exemption to $750,000 and index this limit for inflation in future years. Another proposal excludes up to $1.5 million of small business assets of family businesses from estate taxes. Stay tuned; changes may be enacted by the time you read this.

Don't overlook state death taxes. Some states also impose death taxes in the form of "estate" or "inheritance" tax. Partial tax relief is granted by the IRC, which provides a federal tax credit for state death taxes paid. (IRC § 2011.) Often this means the combined federal and state death taxes don't exceed the federal tax alone. A few states impose estate taxes higher than the federal credit—but the amount of extra taxes is insignificant in all but multi-million-dollar estates. If this sounds like it might affect you, check with your state's taxing agency, and maybe an estate planning tax pro.

2. Keeping the Business Going With Minimal or No Estate Taxes

Now that you see how the estate tax trap is set, you should be thinking about ways to step around it. The two most popular strategies to keep a family business intact are by holding the business in a corporate form or as a family limited partnership. Both can do the job, but each requires planning long before the business's owner dies.

a. A Family Business Corporation

Incorporating a business makes it easier to pass it on to the next generation or other family members on your death. And incorporating also provides a way to beat—or at least minimize—estate tax that is not available to partners or sole proprietors.

You can give your kids part ownership of your business by transferring stock in a series of annual gifts as discussed in Section B, above. (IRC § 2503.) As long as the value of the stock given to each recipient each year is no more than $10,000, the annual exclusion rule makes the gift nontaxable. It makes no difference whether the business is an S or C corporation. For a very valuable business, this is obviously a long-term planning device, due to the annual $10,000 limitation.

Giving corporate stock is more complicated than giving cash, however, because the stock's fair market value must be determined at the time each gift is made. Valuing a private company's stock is tricky, and ordinarily requires the help of a CPA or other business appraisal specialist.

⚠️

Joint tenancy ownership doesn't avoid estate taxes.
There is a widespread misconception that joint ownership of property with a family member, or anyone else, somehow avoids estate and gift taxes. Sorry, it doesn't. Adding a child's name to a deed or stock certificate as a "joint tenant" may avoid probate proceedings but doesn't remove an asset from the reach of the federal estate tax.

Giving away small business corporation stock does not mean you must relinquish control of the business. You can, for example, transfer stock but keep the voting rights of the shares. One way to do this is by putting the children's stock in a trust and reserving the right to vote the shares held in the trust. Again, call on a good business attorney to help you do this correctly.

If you are transferring a business to family members over time, get an accountant or business appraisal expert to make annual written valuations of your business.

Example: Juan, a widower, owns 70% of the stock of Star-Tar, Inc., which manufactures Spanish guitars. Juan's five children, all active in the business, own the other 30%. A business valuation expert values Juan's corporation at $2.3 million. If Juan gives each of the children $10,000 worth of stock every year, after 12 years he will have probably given away a majority interest in the corporation. Because of the discount allowance for family corporate stock, the value of Juan's minority stock interest could be discounted. Depending on the value of his other assets, Juan's estate may not be liable for any estate taxes. (The same analysis holds true if Juan forms a family limited partnership instead of a corporation, as discussed below.)

TAX DISCOUNTING THE VALUE OF A FAMILY BUSINESS

The tax law—as interpreted by various federal courts—allows "discounts" of the value of small business interests when transferred by gift or on death. This can produce tremendous gift and estate tax savings, or eliminate these taxes altogether. This is particularly true when businesses are passed from one generation to the other. The reduction is called a "marketability" or "minority" discount. It applies to family corporation stock, family limited partnership or limited liability company shares.

In the world of finance, small businesses are difficult to value with precision. If the business is incorporated, chances are its stock is not sold on any exchange and seldom changes hands at all. As a practical matter, outsiders are not eager to get part ownership of any small business; they want to be in control. But since anything will sell if the price is right, 25% to 40% off might entice someone to take a chance on part ownership. So the law recognizes the legitimacy of marketability discounts for small business interests for any seller or transferor. Large discounts (as high as 50%) have been upheld where the interest is a minority or is corporate stock without voting rights, or is a limited partnership.

The marketability discount a transferor of a business interest can claim is determined by ten factors, not all of which will apply to your situation. These factors were laid down in a 1995 Tax Court case (*Bernard Mendelbaum v. Commissioner*, TC Memo 1995-255), which involved a family-owned S corporation. My comments follow each factor as to how important it is in justifying a large discount:

1. Whether or not the stock has also been traded publicly (insignificant: hardly ever the case in a small business).

2. Financial statement analysis (fairly important: best done by an experienced tax pro, mainly to see how profitable the business is; if it is only average or marginal, a larger discount can apply).

3. Dividend policy of the business (usually insignificant; most small businesses don't pay dividends).

4. Nature, history and industry position of the business (not too significant: how the business is positioned in the community from the standpoint of competition and like factors).

5. Strength of company management (important: the success of most small businesses depends primarily on the personalities of the owners).

6. Degree of control inherent in transferred shares (very important: if the transferor still maintains control of the business after the transfer—most often the case with small businesses—large discounts can be justified).

7. Stock transfer restrictions (very important if the stock is very difficult for an owner to transfer, perhaps because it cannot be transferred to a third party without first offering it to a family members on favorable terms and conditions).

8. Required holding period of stock (important: a stock transfer restriction; see comments on # 7 above).

9. Stock redemption policy of the company (important: if the business has not historically redeemed stock of shareholders, this factor allows larger minority discounts).

10. Public offering costs (insignificant: few small businesses with valuations under $10 million would ever justify a public offering).

b. Family Limited Partnerships (FLPs)

Instead of incorporating your family business, you may want to form a family limited partnership (FLP). An FLP is owned by family members and operates under the rules of a limited partnership. Typically, parents form an FLP and transfer their assets, such as an existing business, to this entity. A venture can, however, be formed as an FLP right from the start. (See Chapter 9, Partnerships, for a discussion of limited partnerships.)

An FLP is primarily used to minimize or avoid future estate taxes, but it can also shift present business income to lower bracket family members. (Section B, above, discusses splitting income among family members.)

In a family limited partnership, the parents are usually the "general" partners. Their children are "limited" partners, meaning they are treated like investors who have an ownership interest in—but no right to manage—the operation. As with corporation stock, each child can receive a limited partnership interest worth $20,000 per year (from a set of two parents) as a gift, without tax consequences to anyone. (See "Estate and Gift Tax Basis," above, about the annual exclusion rule for gift taxes.) In addition, limited partners can work in the business and be compensated for their services.

As an estate planning strategy, an FLP allows ownership of a business to be removed from the parents' estates, usually over a period of years. This can be particularly beneficial if the business is appreciating in value, as do most successful enterprises. Given enough time, legally as much as 99% of the parents' ownership can be transferred to the children tax-free, leaving little subject to estate tax on their deaths. All the while, as general partners, Mom and Pop may remain in full control of management; they decide how annual profits are to be split among themselves and the children. It can really be a win-win tax deal for the family.

ESTATE AND GIFT TAX BASICS

Federal estate tax rates are "graduated," meaning the bigger the estate, the higher the tax rate—just like income taxes. The tax bite begins at a steep 37% and ascends to a positively outrageous 55% in fairly short order. However, the first $600,000 in everybody's estate is not taxed at all. Also, with married couples, when the first spouse dies, all property left to the survivor (if the survivor is a U.S. citizen) escapes the estate tax. This is referred to as the unlimited marital deduction. Of course, when the survivor dies, his or her estate is taxed if it exceeds $600,000.

Gifts you make during your life are taxed at the same rate as property remaining in your estate, with one major exception. Under the "annual exclusion" rule, you may make gifts of up to $10,000 in cash or property per recipient, per year, tax-free to as many people as you like. Moreover, these gifts are not taxable income to the donees either. It makes no difference whether the recipients are related to you or not. You may give away property, such as stock in your incorporated business, instead of cash, subject to the same restrictions.

Example: John and Julie Johansen have a combined estate worth $1.5 million, so naturally they are interested in ways to transfer it free of estate and gift tax. One way is by annual gift-giving. They decide to give money annually to their two children, two parents, one grandchild and one old friend. The Johansens can give $120,000 to the six people each year without tax consequences (6 x $10,000 for John, and the same amount for Julie). Their annual gifts do not decrease their lifetime estate tax exclusion of $600,000 each.

If you give more than $10,000 to any one person in one year, the excess gift is subtracted from your lifetime $600,000 tax exemption. You must file a federal gift tax return for that year, but no gift tax is due—unless and until you give more than $600,000, in total, before your death.

You can't use a family limited partnership solely as a device to beat the estate tax. An FLP must have a "business purpose." It must carry on an active for-profit venture. For example, an FLP formed to own a family used vacation home would not meet the business purpose test. An FLP that holds an investment portfolio of marketable securities, while certainly held for the expectation of gain, is not an active business either.

Example: Wally and his wife Wanda, who are in the highest income tax bracket, form an FLP to own their North Oxon Pottery Co. Each of their three children—who are all in the lowest income tax bracket—is given a percentage interest in the business as a limited partner annually over a number of years. (If the interest given to each child is worth under $20,000 each year, there is no gift tax liability.) The children, as limited partners, have no say in the day-to-day affairs of the business. Over time, Wally and Wanda pass most of their business ownership to their children, while controlling the business until they are ready to step down. When Wally and Wanda have both died, the value of their remaining partnership interest is so low that no estate tax is due.

FLPs also have the non-tax feature of protecting the personal assets of the limited partners from business creditors. Limited partners can lose only the value of their partnership interest to creditors and not have their home or bank accounts at risk. Every limited partnership, by law, must have at least one general partner, however, whose liability to creditors is unlimited.

See a tax pro. If you are considering forming an FLP, get all the details from a tax pro or a business attorney. As a general rule, unless your assets are worth at least $1,000,000, an FLP may not justify the expense of legal and accounting fees and any state-imposed costs.

RESOURCES

IRS Publication 950, *Introduction to Estate and Gift Taxes*

IRS Publication 448, *Estate and Gift Taxes*

Plan Your Estate, by Denis Clifford and Cora Jordan (Nolo Press). This book provides a thorough overview of estate planning options and strategies, and discusses federal and state estate tax in detail.

Make Your Own Living Trust, by Denis Clifford (Nolo Press). This book contains forms and instructions for creating two kinds of trusts: simple living trusts that will avoid probate and more complicated trusts to reduce estate taxes.

Social Security, Medicare and Pensions, by Joseph Matthews (Nolo Press). This book explains, among other things, the rules that govern taxation of Social Security benefits. ■

Microbusinesses and Home-Based Businesses

"Of course there's a different law for the rich and the poor; otherwise who would go into business?"

— E. Ralph Stewart

Millions of Americans operate very small businesses, many of them home-based. Many of these ventures supplement a regular job or another business. Most tax rules are the same whether your business has 50 employees and operates from its own building or you, alone, work from your home.

But some special tax code provisions apply to home-based businesses or to enterprises that look like hobbies to the IRS.

This chapter focuses on sole proprietorships, but the principles are applicable to any type of unincorporated business. If your home-based business is incorporated, however, different rules for reporting income and deducting expenses may apply. (See Chapter 7, C Corporations, and Chapter 8, S Corporations.)

MICROBUSINESSES & HOME-BASED BUSINESSES IN A NUTSHELL

1. Business expenses are deductible no matter where they are incurred, but to deduct part of your home rent or depreciation of a home office, you must meet strict tax rules.

2. Losses from home-based and sideline businesses can be claimed against your other income to reduce your tax bill.

3. If you claim losses from your small business, an IRS auditor may challenge you, saying your business was really a hobby. Defend your business loss by showing a "profit motive."

4. Unless you run the very smallest of businesses, you are responsible for making estimated tax payments and paying self-employment taxes.

A. Business Expenses Incurred at Home

Most expenses related to your business are tax-deductible, no matter where they are incurred—at your home, on the road or in a traditional office or shop. Examples of tax-deductible home office expenses: Office supplies, materials, professional and trade memberships and dues, travel, business use of your auto, meal and entertainment expenses, insurance premiums for business assets, local and long-distance telephone calls on the home phone (but not the cost of the basic monthly service), maintenance and repair of office computers and other equipment, depreciation (or IRC § 179 write-off) of furniture and other business assets, interest on business debts, employee wages and benefits, publications and software, advertising. (See IRC § 162, Reg. 1.162 and Chapter 1, Tax-Deductible Expenses, for details).

Claiming home-based business expenses but not a home-based office. Contrary to what some folks think, you may claim all of the above kinds of home-based business expenses *regardless* of whether or not you qualify for the "home office" deduction discussed next below. And deducting expenses for a legitimate home-based business will not increase your audit chances, as will claiming the home office deduction.

B. Deducting the Cost of Your Home

If you operate out of your home, you may (or may not) also be able to tax-deduct part of your rent or take a depreciation deduction based on how your home is used in your business. This is commonly called the "home office" deduction. Regardless of what you might have heard, the home office deduction is alive and well. About 1.6 million folks claim a home office deduction each year, according to the IRS.

A house, apartment, condominium, mobile home, motor home, boat or just about anywhere else with sleeping and cooking facilities can qualify for the home office deduction.

Calculating the amount of rent or depreciation is discussed in Section C below, but first you need to know whether or not you can qualify to take the deduction under the tax code rules. (IRC § 280A.) If you do not, your housing costs are nondeductible personal living expenses (except for home mortgage interest and real estate taxes).

To claim a home office deduction, your home office must be:

- The principal place of your business
- A separately identifiable space in your home, and
- Regularly and exclusively used for business.

All three of the rules must be satisfied, and are discussed in detail in the following sections.

1. Principal Place of Business

Determining whether or not your home qualifies as the "principal place" of your business is not as simple as it sounds. And if it doesn't qualify, you can't claim a tax deduction for depreciation or rent.

If your *only* jobsite is at home, and you spend most of your working hours there, it should qualify as your principal place of business. However, as discussed below, anyone who has a home office but spends a significant amount of time working outside of it may have a problem.

In 1993, the U.S. Supreme Court interpreted the principal place of business rule very narrowly in the highly publicized *Soliman* case. (*Soliman v. Commissioner of Internal Revenue*, 113 S. Ct. 701 (1993).) The decision eliminated the home office deduction for *some* people who were able to claim it in the past. The *Soliman* case concerned a physician who did most of his work at a hospital and only used his home office for paperwork—not what most people think of as a home-based business.

At issue was whether Dr. Soliman had properly taken a tax deduction for depreciation for the office portion of his home. He was an anesthesiologist who performed services mostly in hospital operating rooms. But the doctor had many other work responsibilities—like writing reports, filling out insurance forms and reading medical journals—and since he had no office at the hospital, he did these tasks at home, in a space set aside exclusively as an office. Unfortunately, the IRS audited him and the case ended up in the Supreme Court, which ruled that Dr. Soliman was not entitled to a tax deduction for depreciation of the home office because it was not his "principal place of business."

The Court laid down two tests for determining whether a home office is the principal place of business, when work is performed outside of the home:

- The relative importance of the activities at each business location, and
- The amount of time spent at each location.

Dr. Soliman flunked both of these tests. The hospital was clearly the more important workplace, and he spent only 20% of his time working at his home office. Dr. Soliman's other expenses, such as supplies used at his home office, were still deductible; he just couldn't deduct depreciation for the office space.

In 1994, the IRS issued a set of rules with four examples of how the IRS will apply the "principal place of business" rule in future audits. (Revenue Ruling 94-24.) Here they are, in a somewhat simplified form.

Example 1: A schoolteacher spends 25 hours per week at school, but 30 hours at home grading papers and preparing for class. Even though she spends more time working at home than at school, the IRS denies a home office deduction, because the essence of her business is teaching students.

The above example illustrates that *both* of the *Soliman* tests must be met before the IRS will let you deduct a home office.

Example 2: A plumber works out of his home office. He keeps a full-time employee there to answer phones and do bookkeeping. The plumber is at his home office 10 hours a week and in the field 40 hours a week. The IRS says that he is not entitled to a deduction for rent or depreciation, although he could still deduct all other ordinary business expenses, such as salary of the employee.

PART **3**

Thinking Small

This restrictive reading of *Soliman* is sure to be challenged by a taxpayer in a future court case, who may have a good chance of success.

Example 3: A self-employed writer spends 15 hours a week doing research away from her home office and 30 hours writing there. The IRS says she is entitled to the home office deduction.

If the ratio of time in the office and away from it were reversed, the IRS probably would deny the deduction. This seems to encourage taxpayers to lie about how much time they actually spend at home in order to justify a deduction—and in most cases, I can't see how the IRS could disprove their claims.

Example 4: A home-based jewelry business person who sells goods by mail and at craft shows spends 25 hours a week working at home and 15 hours working outside of the office. A home office deduction is allowed.

Like Example 3, this example is an invitation to fabricate extra hours in your home office and minimize time claimed spent at outside locations.

Keep up to date on home office rules. If you think the IRS interpretations of *Soliman*—or the *Soliman* decision itself—aren't fair, you are not alone. Bills have been introduced in Congress that would nullify this case. The specific tax code section to keep your eye on is IRC § 280A. Stay tuned.

2. Separately Identifiable Space

Assuming your home is the principal place of your business, move on to the second rule. The space in which you work must be separate from the rest of your home to qualify for the home office deduction. A completely separate structure works best as proof of a legitimate home office to the IRS—for example, a detached garage converted to an office. But many self-employed people convert a spare bedroom to a

legitimate home office by removing the bed and personal items. To pass IRS muster, if your home office is not physically divided by walls, some kind of demarcation should be evident.

3. Regular and Exclusive Use

If you still qualify, then let's go to the last rule. It isn't enough to use the home office space occasionally—one or two days a month—for business. The tax code requires "regular" business use, which isn't exactly a precise restriction. If you meet your business customers or clients at your home office, it should satisfy the regular use test. Protect yourself by keeping a record showing appointments, in case you're ever questioned by an IRS auditor.

"Exclusive use" is more straightforward. It means you can't use the space for any other reason than business. This eliminates the possibility of claiming the kitchen table, or the room in which you watch TV in with the kids as your home office. This rule is akin to the "separately identifiable space" rule above.

Don't be afraid of a legitimate home office deduction. Undoubtedly, claiming a home office depreciation or rent expense on your tax return increases your audit risk. As described below, a home office deduction must be shown on IRS Form 8829, Expenses for Business Use of Your Home, and attached to your tax return, so it is easy to spot.

However, even if it doubled your chances of audit, statistically, there's a less than a one in twenty chance of an IRS confrontation. And then, you would lose only if you failed to meet the qualification discussed above. In any event, you will have plenty of time to prepare for an IRS inspection of your home office, to be sure it appears "office-like." If you're audited, take some photographs of the home office to show the auditor unless, of course, the auditor makes a personal visit.

C. Calculating Your Home Office Deduction

If your home office qualifies, you must calculate the amounts you are entitled to deduct on IRS Form 8829, Expenses for Business Use of Your Home. This form is filed with your individual income tax return. (See sample below.)

There is one important limitation on your overall home office deduction: The amount of the deduction cannot be greater than the profit generated by your home-based business. For instance, if your business made a profit of $2,700 before taking a home office deduction, the deduction can't be larger than $2,700 that year.

I surmise that not everyone entitled to a home office deduction is using Form 8829 to claim it. Maybe it is just that this form is too darned intimidating, taking considerable time and patience to complete. If you don't use the form, and claim the deduction, however, you will probably hear from the IRS sooner or later.

Your first task in calculating your home office deduction is to divide the number of square feet used for your home business by its total square footage. The resulting percentage of business use determines how much of your rent, depreciation, insurance, utilities and other directly-related expenses are deductible.

1. Renters

If you rent, figuring up your home office deduction is pretty simple; calculate the percentage of the total space occupied by the office and multiply it by your annual rent payment.

Example: Lois, who makes and paints ceramic frogs at home, rents a 900-square-foot apartment. The room that contains a kiln and working tables is 200 square feet. She pays $8,000 rent per year. Lois is entitled to deduct 22% of her yearly rent—$1,778—as a home office expense. In addition, 22% of her utility and renter's insurance expenses are deductible business expenses.

2. Owners

If you own your home, you still calculate the percentage of your home's square footage used for business. Then some further math is necessary: you need to determine the relative values of the building and the land it rests upon. If your tax assessor doesn't give you this breakdown, you can make a guess; allocating 80% of your property's value to structure and 20% to land is common in most parts of the country. This step is necessary because you cannot deduct any part attributable to the land. (Land never depreciates in the eyes of the tax code.)

Next, you must find the tax code depreciation rules in effect in the year you bought your home. For instance, after 1987, you must use straight-line depreciation. And up until 1994, the period for taking this deduction was 27.5 years; it is now 39 years. (See Chapter 2, Writing Off Long-Term Business Assets, for an explanation of depreciation methods.)

Example 1: Katie uses 400 of her home's 1,800 square feet (22%) for her business. Katie bought her home for $100,000 in 1987 and started her business in 1992. She hasn't modified it. The local property tax assessor says the lot her home is on is worth $20,000 and the structure $80,000. (The $20,000 land portion can't be depreciated.)

Katie calculates her depreciation deduction by first dividing 27.5 years into $80,000 = $2,909 per year. This sum is then multiplied by the business usage fraction, 22%, which gives the figure of $646. That's how much Katie can take as a deduction each year she is in business.

Example 2: Since she bought her home, Katie has made improvements costing $10,000, so her basis for depreciation is $90,000. (How to figure the basis of business property is discussed in Chapter 2, Writing Off Long-Term Business Assets.)

3. Other Home-Related Expenses

Form 8829 requires you to separate all of your home-related business expenses into two categories, called "direct" and "indirect" expenses. The area of your home that is used for an office is a direct home office expense. All other costs, such as your light bill, are indirect expenses. (Instructions for Form 8829 are included in the Appendix.)

Direct Expenses. You get a full tax deduction for anything spent directly for home office expenses, such as insurance on equipment, decorating, modifying, furnishing or for maid service if it's exclusively for your office portion.

Indirect Expenses. You can deduct a prorata share of the utilities, repairs, taxes and insurance expenses for your home as indirect home office expenses. Basic telephone service to your home is not deductible, but any business long distance charges or a second phone line for business are.
(IRC § 262(b).)

To calculate these indirect expense deductions, use the same percentage of your home occupied by the business that you calculated earlier.

Example: Katie, from the previous example, spent a total of $2,110 for gas, electricity and homeowner's insurance in 1995. She also doled out $820 to modify and repaint the office space. Tax result: Katie can write off 22% of the $2,110 ($469) for the indirect overall home expenses and all of the $820 in direct home office expenses. With Katie's depreciation deduction of $646 (Section 2, above), her total home office deduction is $469 + $820 + $646= $1,935. The only limitation on this deduction is that her home-based business must have made a profit of at least this amount.

D. Potential Tax Trap When Selling Your Home

Most homeowners know that the tax code allows you to defer tax on the gain on the sale of your home as long as you acquire another primary residence within 24 months. (IRC § 1034.)

A home office creates a potential tax problem, however. If you take depreciation deductions for a home office, when you sell your home, the total of all of the deductions you have taken in the past are potentially subject to income tax. Don't panic—there is a fairly easy way to avoid this. But first let's see how it works.

Example 1: Thelma operated a management consulting business out of her home for seven years. She claimed a total of $22,000 in depreciation deductions for a home office during this time. Thelma sells her home for $198,000 and buys another home for $210,000 three months later. She must report income of $22,000 in the year of the sale. But Thelma probably can avoid this result. Read on.

The tax code strictly says that home office depreciation deductions are taxed if the home is still regularly and exclusively being used for business at the time of the sale. However, there is a well-recognized loophole: If the home office use is discontinued prior to the sale, the home office is no longer being "regularly and exclusively used" for business. No other tax code provision requires you to pay tax on the deductions previously taken. The tax basis in your home is reduced by the amount of the previous deductions. However, you can postpone paying taxes on the profit by buying and occupying another primary residence within 24 months.
(IRC § 1034.)

Don't claim depreciation in year of sale. Discontinue use of the office for a respectable period of time prior to the sale. Six months is a good general rule. In any event, no tax deduction should be taken for depreciation on the home office in the year of the sale.

Example 2: Thelma sells her home in June 1995, moves into her new home in September and immediately begins using a home office there. She does not claim any depreciation deduction for the old residence for 1995, so she does not have to report the previous deductions as income in that year. She can start claiming the home office deduction for her new home in 1995.

CAN YOU DEDUCT EXPENSES FOR BUSINESS USE OF THE HOME?

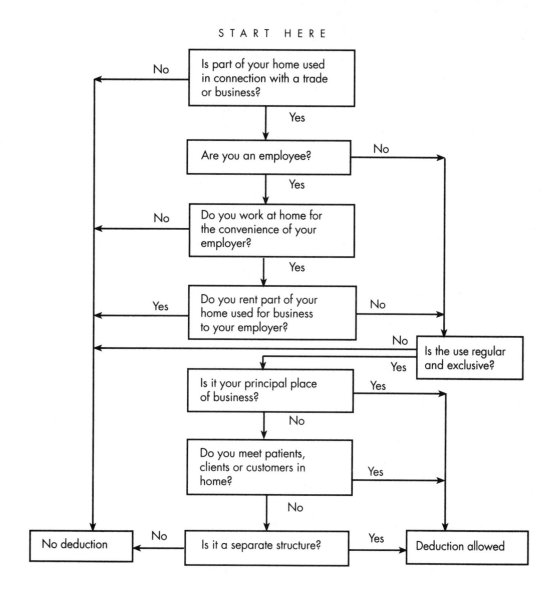

PART 3

Thinking Small

Form **8829**	**Expenses for Business Use of Your Home**	OMB No. 1545-1266
Form **8829**	▶ File only with Schedule C (Form 1040). Use a separate Form 8829 for each home you used for business during the year.	19**94**
Department of the Treasury Internal Revenue Service (T)	▶ **See separate instructions.**	Attachment Sequence No. **66**

Name(s) of proprietor(s)
DAN STEPHENS

Your social security number
465 : 00 : 0001

Part I   Part of Your Home Used for Business

1	Area used regularly and exclusively for business, regularly for day care, or for inventory storage. See instructions	**1**	**200**
2	Total area of home	**2**	**2,000**
3	Divide line 1 by line 2. Enter the result as a percentage	**3**	**10** %

● **For day-care facilities not used exclusively for business, also complete lines 4–6.**
● **All others, skip lines 4–6 and enter the amount from line 3 on line 7.**

4	Multiply days used for day care during year by hours used per day .	**4**	hr.
5	Total hours available for use during the year (365 days × 24 hours). See instructions	**5**	8,760 hr.
6	Divide line 4 by line 5. Enter the result as a decimal amount	**6**	.
7	Business percentage. For day-care facilities not used exclusively for business, multiply line 6 by line 3 (enter the result as a percentage). All others, enter the amount from line 3 . . . . ▶	**7**	**10** %

Part II   Figure Your Allowable Deduction

		(a) Direct expenses	(b) Indirect expenses		
8	Enter the amount from Schedule C, line 29, **plus** any net gain or (loss) derived from the business use of your home and shown on Schedule D or Form 4797. If more than one place of business, see instructions			**8**	**28,845**
	See instructions for columns (a) and (b) before completing lines 9–20.				
9	Casualty losses. See instructions	**9**			
10	Deductible mortgage interest. See instructions .	**10**		**4,500**	
11	Real estate taxes. See instructions	**11**		**1,000**	
12	Add lines 9, 10, and 11.	**12**		**5,500**	
13	Multiply line 12, column (b) by line 7	**13**		**550**	
14	Add line 12, column (a) and line 13.			**14**	**550**
15	Subtract line 14 from line 8. If zero or less, enter -0- .			**15**	**28,295**
16	Excess mortgage interest. See instructions . .	**16**			
17	Insurance	**17**		**400**	
18	Repairs and maintenance	**18**	**300**	**1,400**	
19	Utilities	**19**		**1,800**	
20	Other expenses. See instructions	**20**			
21	Add lines 16 through 20	**21**	**300**	**3,600**	
22	Multiply line 21, column (b) by line 7	**22**		**360**	
23	Carryover of operating expenses from 1993 Form 8829, line 41 . .	**23**			
24	Add line 21 in column (a), line 22, and line 23			**24**	**660**
25	Allowable operating expenses. Enter the **smaller** of line 15 or line 24			**25**	**660**
26	Limit on excess casualty losses and depreciation. Subtract line 25 from line 15			**26**	**27,635**
27	Excess casualty losses. See instructions	**27**			
28	Depreciation of your home from Part III below	**28**		**270**	
29	Carryover of excess casualty losses and depreciation from 1993 Form 8829, line 42	**29**			
30	Add lines 27 through 29			**30**	**270**
31	Allowable excess casualty losses and depreciation. Enter the **smaller** of line 26 or line 30 . .			**31**	**270**
32	Add lines 14, 25, and 31			**32**	**1,480**
33	Casualty loss portion, if any, from lines 14 and 31. Carry amount to **Form 4684**, Section B .			**33**	
34	Allowable expenses for business use of your home. Subtract line 33 from line 32. Enter here and on Schedule C, line 30. If your home was used for more than one business, see instructions ▶			**34**	**1,480**

Part III   Depreciation of Your Home

35	Enter the **smaller** of your home's adjusted basis or its fair market value. See instructions . .	**35**	**75,000**
36	Value of land included on line 35	**36**	**15,000**
37	Basis of building. Subtract line 36 from line 35	**37**	**60,000**
38	Business basis of building. Multiply line 37 by line 7	**38**	**6,000**
39	Depreciation percentage. See instructions	**39**	**4.5** %
40	Depreciation allowable. Multiply line 38 by line 39. Enter here and on line 28 above. See instructions	**40**	**270**

Part IV   Carryover of Unallowed Expenses to 1995

41	Operating expenses. Subtract line 25 from line 24. If less than zero, enter -0-	**41**	
42	Excess casualty losses and depreciation. Subtract line 31 from line 30. If less than zero, enter -0- .	**42**	

For Paperwork Reduction Act Notice, see page 1 of separate instructions.   *Printed on recycled paper* Cat. No. 13232M   Form **8829** (1994)

E. A Microbusiness as a Tax Shelter

The vast majority of home-based businesses are sole proprietorships; if you are operating in one of the other forms, then you also need to look at the specific chapter dealing with that entity.

Hopefully, your home business will be a money maker. However, even if it doesn't pan out, it has the potential to be a "tax shelter." This tantalizing term doesn't refer just to gold mining schemes, ostrich farms or oil wells. A venture becomes a tax shelter by simply using its expenses to offset your taxable income from other sources, such as a regular job. There is no minimum amount of time or money you must invest in the business to qualify for this benefit.

IRS AUDITS OF MICRO BUSINESSES

Rumors to the contrary, home-based businesses are not guaranteed IRS audit bait. In fact, the odds against a small business being audited are about 30 to one in any year. However, tax returns that show business losses—home-based or not—are audited more often; the more years you report losses, the more likely you'll be audited. The size of the loss is probably the biggest factor; a $50,000 loss is more likely to show up on IRS radar than a $5,000 one. (See Chapter 19, Audits.)

---

1. How Business Losses Can Cut Income Taxes

Start by understanding that a tax loss is not necessarily a cash loss. For instance, depreciation deductions for equipment, cars and home offices are not out-of-pocket expenses, but are often referred to as "paper losses." A "loss" in tax code terms may feel like a gain to you personally, or even put money in your pocket. This is the best of both worlds: more cash to spend and a lower tax bill. Here are some examples:

- Assets purchased wholly on credit can still be written off at tax time, as long as they are used for business. Home computers, furniture, VCRs, camcorders, TVs and stereos all qualify. (See Chapter 2, Writing Off Long-Term Business Assets.)

- If you meet the qualifications for a home office deduction, you can deduct some of your rent or depreciation, utilities and home upkeep expenses. These expenses would otherwise not be deductible.

Example: Carol, a clothing store manager who enjoys cooking, forms Carol's Catering as a sideline business. Carol's big job for the year declares bankruptcy before paying, and Carol's Catering ends up with a loss. Carol throws in the towel, having spent $2,500 for food, supplies and equipment.

On her tax return, Carol claims a cash loss of $2,500 plus $2,200 for depreciation and operating costs for using her car for the business. Carol's total business loss of $4,700 is used to offset wages from her regular job, trimming about $1,500 off her income taxes. So, Carol's $2,500 operating paper loss becomes only a $1,000 out-of-pocket loss.

2. The Profit Motive Requirement

To use your business as a tax shelter, your enterprise must be a real one in the eyes of the IRS. The tax law roughly defines a business as "any activity engaged in to make a profit." The important thing to note here is that you don't actually have to make a profit—you must just make an honest effort to do so. This invites imaginative people to claim tax losses for hobbies and other money-losing activities which were really for pleasure. As you may expect, the tax man is lying in wait.

To discourage folks from claiming business losses from pleasurable things like speedboat racing or stamp collecting, the law prohibits tax deductions for activities not engaged in for profit. (IRC § 183.) Expenses from activities carried on

PART **3**

Thinking Small

without a realistic profit motive can be deducted only to the extent that income is produced from these activities. In other words, no loss can be claimed against your income from other sources. (This is called the "hobby loss" provision but a truer description would be the "no hobby loss" rule.)

Example: Carol, of Carol's Catering, is audited. The IRS auditor claims she was only indulging her cooking hobby, not running a business with a profit motive. Her $4,700 cash and paper losses are disallowed, which means they can't be used to offset Carol's income from her regular job. Carol can appeal this decision.

Whether Carol ultimately wins or loses will probably depend on whether or not she can defend her business motive. Put another way, can Carol show that she engaged in business with the clear purpose of making a profit? Below, I discuss the criteria used for determining whether or not a business's purpose is to make a profit.

a. The "3 of 5" Test

To determine whether a particular enterprise has a profit motive, a mechanical tax code test is applied: If a venture makes money in three out of five consecutive years, it is legally presumed to possess a profit motive. (IRC § 183(d).) The IRS relies heavily on this test when auditing unprofitable small businesses.

With proper planning, the 3 of 5 test is not difficult to pass, even for businesses that lose money for long periods. The tax code doesn't say *how much profit* must be made in those profitable years, so a struggling business can forgo taking deductions and, therefore, show a profit in any given year. For example, a business that loses $10,000 in years 1 and 5 and reports a profit of $5 in years 2, 3 and 4, technically satisfies this test.

But even if you flunk the 3 of 5 test, you are not necessarily disqualified from claiming business losses—it may just be a little harder to justify if you are audited. Courts have held that even an activity

that never makes a profit may still qualify. The Tax Court upheld one long-suffering taxpayer who claimed small business losses for 12 straight years! (Lawrence Appley, TC Memo 1979-433.) So don't give up taking losses on your tax return if your business doesn't pass the three of five test. As we shall see in subsection b, below, it is only one factor and not the last word on profit motive—no matter what an IRS auditor may tell you.

Example: Let's return to Carol and her struggling catering business. This time, assume she keeps her business going, but at the end of her second year, she is still losing money. Carol is weighing the tax implications of several options:

1. She can throw in the towel, close her business, take tax losses in both years and hope she isn't audited.

2. She can continue to run her business and take any future losses on her return. If she does this, her likelihood of an audit goes up with every year that she reports a loss.

3. She can close her catering business and start a new sideline venture, which starts the "3 of 5" rule period over again.

4. If the prospect of an audit keeps her awake at night, Carol can continue her catering business but stop claiming losses on future tax returns.

Filing IRS Form 5213, Election to Postpone Determination That Activity Is For Profit, gives you an extra year to show a profit under the "3 of 5" test. For instance, if you lost money in the first three years of operation, but believe that you can turn the corner soon, filing this form gives you an extra year to overcome the presumption your business is a hobby. Few people ever file this form. The reason? It draws the IRS's attention to you and may prompt an audit.

Appeals of unfavorable audit findings on a profit motive issue are frequently successful. If you really tried to make a profit, but can't convince an auditor, you can usually appeal or go to Tax Court. You have a good chance to get at least part of your claimed loss deduction restored. Courts have allowed gentlemen farmers, stamp collectors and garage-based inventors to claim business loss deductions over IRS objections. (See Chapter 20, Appealing IRS Audits.)

Example: In a real case, Gloria, an amateur artist, painted at home in her spare time and tried, mostly in vain, to sell her paintings. She lost money every year, for many years, and was audited. Her business losses were disallowed by the IRS for lack of a profit motive. The Tax Court heard Gloria's story and, finding that she had made a serious effort to sell her art, overruled the IRS. (Gloria Churchman, 68 TC 696.)

b. Other Ways to Show Profit Motive

Another way to show a profit motive—and withstand an audit challenging a business operating loss—is by demonstrating that you ran your venture in a businesslike manner. So be prepared to show an auditor:

- *Business records.* Preferably, have a separate bank account and receipts that back up your expenses.

- *Advertising.* Flyers, business cards, copies of ads, and listings on computer bulletin boards to promote your business are helpful.

- *Your business diary or calendar.* This should show the names of people contacted for business and any business use of your car or home. For example, an entry might look like this:

  "3/1/95 12:30 p.m. Meet Don Skinner, buyer for Bargain Basements at Fabio's Restaurant, Kalamazoo. Discussed sale of 10,000 Tonya Harding T-shirts. Lunch: $27.42 with tip. Cab fare $12 round trip." (See Chapter 3, Recordkeeping and Accounting.)

- *Licenses and permits.* Follow your state and local licensing laws, such as fictitious business name registration, getting an occupational license and, if you sell goods, a sales tax permit.

Example: Carol had flyers advertising her catering service printed and mailed to 2,000 local businesses. She passed out business cards at social events as well. She kept track of her marketing efforts and business expenses rather informally, using a spiral notebook. She kept the majority of her receipts for expenses, but never got around to getting a business license. Even though Carol did not do everything perfectly, these records should go a long way in establishing a profit motive to an auditor.

Try to look like a business. Even if you are just fooling around at something you enjoy—woodworking, bird breeding or sewing—you may reap a tax benefit by taking a few simple steps. Inexpensive indicia of business status, such as business cards, stationery and classified ads in local "shoppers" frequently sway auditors away from concluding that you're not just indulging in a hobby.

F. Estimated Taxes

No matter how small your business, if it makes a profit of at least $400 per year, you must make quarterly estimated income tax payments to the IRS, using IRS Form 1040-ES. (See IRS Publication 505, *Withholding and Estimated Taxes.*) If you don't make estimated tax payments, the IRS will hit you with an "underpayment of estimated taxes" penalty—currently a 8% annual charge.

It's often difficult to figure estimated tax payments because you won't know your profit (or loss) until the year is over. However, as long as at least 90% of your tax liability is paid in four equal installments during the year, you won't incur a penalty.

G. Self-Employment (SE) Tax

All of your business's net profits (of $433 or more) are subject to "self-employment tax," which is for Social Security and Medicare. This is equivalent to the payroll tax for employees of a business. (See Chapter 5, Tax Concerns of Employers.) The tax is 15.3% on all net self-employment income (after deducting business expenses). You are still liable for the SE tax on income even if you are retired and drawing Social Security or Medicare benefits.

Under current law, your obligation for the Social Security tax stops when your total *earned* (1995) income (from all sources) reaches $62,700. (IRC § 1401.) (This amount is subject to annual cost of living adjustment.) You are subject to tax only on the Medicare portion of the SE tax (2.9%) on all further earned income.

Example 1: In her department store job, Alicia is barely aware of employment taxes withheld by her employer, which shrink each paycheck by 7.65%. (Her employer is required to match another 7.65% of her pay, for a total of 15.3%.) If Alicia makes $20,000 at her job, she would have $1,530 (7.65% x $20,000) deducted from her pay and paid as her FICA contribu-

tion. Her employer would contribute an additional $1,530. If instead, she were self-employed, Alicia would have to pony up the whole 15.3%—a total of $3,060 out of her pocket.

Example 2: Wing, who is self-employed, makes $75,000 total this year. The first $62,700 is taxed at the rate of 15.3% ($9,593) and the next $12,300 at 2.9% ($357), for a total SE tax of $9,950.

Payment of self-employment taxes also qualifies for a tax break, in the sense that one-half of the SE taxes you pay are tax-deductible. (IRC § 164.) This is not an expense that can be claimed on the business portion of your tax return. Instead, it is deducted on the first page of your tax return from your total adjusted gross income.

Example: Carol quits her job and operates Carol's Catering as a full-time business. During her first year she makes a profit, and pays self-employment taxes of $1,102. She is in the 28% bracket. Carol can deduct one-half of her SE taxes, $556. This shaves $154 (28% x $1,102 x 50%) off her income tax bill.

A one-time job is not subject to SE tax. For example, John, a retired mechanic, took a short-term job— less than a month—installing windows in an office building. The Tax Court held that this did not establish John in a "trade or business," so he wasn't liable for the self-employment tax. Of course, the income was subject to income tax, though. (*John A. Batok,* TC Memo 1992-727.)

RESOURCES

IRS Publication 587, *Business Use of Your Home*

IRS Publication 334, *Tax Guide for Small Business*

Being Self-Employed, by Holmes Crouch (Allyear Tax Guides). This little book contains some practical tips from a self-educated small businessman.

Small-Time Operator, by Bernard Kamoroff (Bell Springs). This CPA-authored book contains a wealth of information for very small businesses.

The Home Business Bible, by David R. Eyler (John Wiley & Sons). This book has answers to common tax—and non-tax—questions, and also comes with a disk with small business accounting software. ■

PART **3**

Thinking Small

CHAPTER 14

Fringe Benefits

PART **4**

Fringe Benefits

"When I hear artists and authors making fun of businessmen I think of a regiment in which the band makes fun of the cooks."

— **H. L. Mencken**

Everyone has heard of "fringe benefits," "fringes" or "perks," but exactly what are they? The term fringe benefit is mentioned—but not actually defined—in the tax code. Fringes are things of value a business gives owners and employees over and above their regular pay.

A fringe either isn't taxable to the recipient, or is tax-deferred, or is taxable but at an advantageous rate. And from the business owner's point of view, fringe benefit expenses are tax-deductible expenses of doing business. (See Chapter 1, Business Income and Tax-Deductible Expenses.) As with most things that sound too good to be true, Congress has set rules to make sure businesses are not overly generous when providing fringes.

The tax code starts by saying that fringe benefits are taxable. A fringe benefit is tax-free or tax-advantaged only if Congress has granted a specific exemption somewhere in the IRC. This chapter discusses popular fringe benefits favored by the tax code. Most of the specific "exclusions from income" covering fringes are found in IRC § 101 to 137, and are discussed in this chapter.

Just like the old gray mare, tax-free fringe benefits "ain't what they used to be." The current direction of the law is toward making employee benefits taxable. Nevertheless, there are still enough tax-advantaged fringes left to make it worthwhile for small businesses to know the rules.

FRINGE BENEFITS IN A NUTSHELL

1. A business can offer its owners and workers a variety of fringe benefits, which may be wholly or partially tax-free or tax-deferred.

2. The widest selection of fringe benefits can be offered by a regular C corporation business, but this is rarely a good enough reason by itself to incorporate.

3. Retirement plan benefits offer the greatest potential tax savings of any fringe benefit that a business can offer.

A. How Fringe Benefits Save Taxes

The reason fringe benefits are popular is simple. When you take cash profits out of your business, you receive taxable income. If, instead of taking cash, your business provides a nontaxable benefit such as medical insurance, you and your employees get something of value without paying any tax on it.

The tax code has different treatments for different benefits, sometimes without much logical consistency. A fringe benefit may be:

- **Totally tax-free to the employee recipient.** For example, if an employer provides medical insurance, employees pay no tax on the value of the coverage.

- **Partly tax-free to the recipient.** For example, a company car that is also used for personal purposes gives the employee a tax benefit, even though the whole cost of operating the car can't be written off.

- **Tax-deferred—that is, not taxed until a later date.** For example, if an employee receives an option to buy company stock at a below-market price, no tax is due until the stock or option is sold.

- **Fully taxable to the recipient in the year provided.** Such benefits may nevertheless be desirable if an owner or employee can get something cheaper than if they had to buy it on their own—for example, a group insurance policy.

PART **4**

Fringe Benefits

CORPORATIONS AND FRINGES

It may not seem fair, but tax breaks for some types of fringes are available *only* to C corporations. Sole proprietors, limited liability company members, S corporations and partners don't get them. When folks first hear that corporations enjoy advantageous tax treatment, they naturally think about incorporating.

However, the decision to incorporate should rarely be made based on the availability of fringe benefits alone. In reality, very few businesses are profitable enough to afford the full range of fringe benefits in the first place, so how these benefits are treated for tax purposes isn't a big deal. And, if you could afford to take advantage of fringe benefits, one of your first choices would probably be to establish a retirement plan, which is available to all business owners, incorporated or not.

Follow the rules on employee benefit plans or risk the consequences. The IRS audits benefit plans separately or as part of an ordinary audit. If plans are not in compliance with the tax law, then previous tax deductions or contributions to the plan can be thrown out. The business loses the deductions, and the benefit recipients will have to pay taxes on the benefits, so everyone will have a bigger tax bill.

BENEFITS OR CASH

A business may offer an option of taking cash instead of fringe benefits through a "cafeteria" or flexible benefit plan. However, if you choose cash, it is taxable income when received. Qualifying benefits under a cafeteria plan include group term life insurance, health, accident and disability insurance, dependent care assistance and certain 401(k) plans. See a tax pro for help in setting up a cafeteria plan.

TAX-FREE BENEFIT REQUIREMENTS

For a fringe benefit to be totally tax-free, *all* of the following requirements must be met:

- **The tax code must specifically allow it.** Unless a fringe benefit is excluded from income by a special provision of the tax code, its value is taxable income to the recipient.

- **It may have to be in writing.** Certain types of fringes—such as retirement benefits—must be set out in a document that conforms with tax law rules, usually called an employee benefit plan. An unwritten policy probably won't satisfy the tax law.

- **It must have an indefinite life.** The benefit plan must have an indefinite life; in other words, the plan can't expire next year, or when an employee reaches a certain age, or for most any other reason.

B. Retirement Benefits

Dollarwise, the most valuable tax-deductible fringe benefit is—by far—a retirement plan. Business owners and employees can put away money tax-free in retirement funds until it is withdrawn in later years. In the meantime, the fund is invested and any income it produces is also not taxed until it is withdrawn. Retirement plans are available to corporations, partners, limited liability company members and sole proprietors under a variety of names. Because there are many, often complicated, retirement plan rules—mostly directed toward making benefits widely available to a business's employees—Chapter 15 is devoted entirely to retirement plans.

C. Motor Vehicles

Cars are a necessity for most of us. They are most Americans' third largest expenditure, after housing and food. Happily, Uncle Sam is willing to help share the cost of car expenses for business owners and employees. Autos are a prime benefit, if, like most small business owners, you use the same car for both business and personal transportation.

There are several tax-approved methods of providing autos as benefits; some depend on whether or not the business is incorporated. Claiming auto expenses and writing off cars used for business is covered in Chapter 1, Business Income and Tax-Deductible Expenses, and Chapter 2, Writing Off Long-Term Business Assets.

D. Meals

If a business pays for meals of owners and employees, the cost is at least partly tax-deductible and tax-free to the recipient if the meals serve a "business purpose" and are provided in the "course of employment." (IRC § 119.) Rules vary, depending on where and when the meal takes place. Here are the basics:

- Free meals are 100% deductible to the business and tax-free to the employee if given "for the convenience of the employer." This covers people working late or attending

company meetings through the meal hour, but few other situations.

Example: Reggie, the owner of a small incorporated wholesale drapery business, orders food from local restaurants for employees working late. This expense is "for the convenience of the employer," and is deductible and tax-free to the employees, including Reggie.

- Inexpensive meals can be provided to employees from a company facility. As long as prices employees pay cover at least the company's direct costs, the benefit of subsidized meals is tax-free to the employees and the cost is tax-deductible to the company.

- Off-the-premises meals and cocktails for employees are deductible to the business and nontaxable to the employee only if business is discussed and such events are occasional rather than every day. (See Chapter 1, Business Income and Tax-Deductible Expenses.)

Example: Reggie takes her sales manager and a few other employees out to a nice dinner once a month, at which they discuss problems in the business operation and plans for future promotions. Reggie usually spends about $100 for drinks, meals and tips. There should be no problem claiming this as a business expense, and the employees don't have to report the value of the meals as income.

E. Travel, Conventions and Lodging

Most of us like to go out of town occasionally, even if it's for business reasons. If the business pays and we can sightsee or visit friends along the way, all the better. When you travel on business, the enterprise can deduct all of your lodging costs only if you go far enough from home to require rest. Only 50% of your meal costs are deductible, however, because you would have eaten if you had stayed home (and home-cooked dinners aren't deductible). (IRC § 132.)

1. Mixing Business and Pleasure

If your business pays for a vacation—as opposed to a business trip—it must add the cost to your income reported to the IRS. The company deducts the cost of your vacation as additional compensation for your services. That said, let's see how a business can pay—and tax deduct—at least some of your vacation expenses *without* it being income to you.

Have you noticed that more trade shows and conventions are held in resorts and destinations like San Francisco than in cities like Des Moines? Convention planners, aware of this fringe benefit opportunity, know they can attract more people with meetings in desirable locations. The tax code permits a certain amount of pleasure mixed in for business travelers.

To be tax-deductible—and not count as income—the trip's *primary* purpose must be business. Travel for political, investment or social conventions cannot be tax deducted as a business expense. The law doesn't require commerce to be the *sole* purpose—if you have some fun on the side, it's okay with those junketeers in Congress who write the tax laws.

How do you prove your trip had a clear business purpose? Obvious cases—say you are a car dealer and go to Detroit to meet with factory representatives, or you own a bookstore and travel to a booksellers' trade show—shouldn't be questioned by an IRS auditor. On the other hand, if you're a plumber and go to Hawaii to see how they insulate pipes, or own a water-ski shop in Florida and travel to Aspen to check out whether snow skis might be adaptable to your business, expect to be quizzed if you are audited. There are few hard and fast rules, so use your common sense and don't go too far.

The following tax code rules must be followed for business meetings, trade shows and conventions:

- *In the United States.* If you go to a trade show in the U.S., it is tax-free to you, and your expenses are deductible to the business. No problem as long as you go straight there and come back as soon as the show is over.

- *In the Rest of North America.* If you go to Canada, Mexico, Puerto Rico or most of the Caribbean states, travel is tax-free and expenses may be deducted *only* if you stay away no longer than a week and spend at least 75% of your time on business. If not, you must allocate the expenses between business and pleasure, so keep records of how your time is spent.

- *Outside North America.* Travel outside North America is deductible only if you can show a valid business reason for the trip—something you could not accomplish in the U.S. Researching tropical fruit processing in Paraguay may sound okay, but studying high technology there doesn't.

- *Cruise Ships.* Several years ago, I attended a tax seminar on a Hawaiian cruise ship and got a nice business deduction for it. The whole trip is tax-free and deductible in full as long as:

  (a) there is a bona fide program related to your business

  (b) the majority of the days are spent in attendance and the following three requirements are all met

PART 4

Fringe Benefits

(c) The ship is registered in the U.S.

(d) It stops only at U.S. ports (or U.S. possessions), and

(e) The trip costs less than $2,000.

However, most cruises don't qualify because few ships are of U.S. registry. Generally, only companies operating in Hawaii and on the Mississippi River qualify.

TEMPORARY ASSIGNMENT TRAVEL

Your business may send you away from home for up to one year, with company-paid (or reimbursed) travel and living expenses. There is no limit on how much a business can pay and deduct, as long as it is reasonable under the circumstances. A multi-million-dollar business can put you up at the Ritz-Carlton for six months, but if you are a struggling consultant, the Motel 6 would be easier to pass by an IRS auditor. After the first year, living expenses paid by your company are income to you—but are still tax-deductible, as compensation, by the business. (IRC § 162, Rev. Rule. 93-86.)

---

2. Family Travel

Taking the family along brings in more tax rules to make sure you don't try to deduct their expenses. Basically, if you take others with you, you must deduct business expenses no greater than if you were traveling alone. However, your entire car expense for a business trip can be deducted if family members ride along (even though the additional weight probably cuts your gas mileage). The same principle applies to hotels; if your family stays in one standard room, the entire cost is tax-deductible. You can also take advantage of two-for-one or "bring along the family" hotel and airline fare discounts without passing the cost break along to the IRS.

Example 1: Sam (computer retailer), his wife Jeannie, Sam Jr., and daughter Sandra fly to Anaheim, California, so Sam can attend the Worldwide Computer Show. He finds out about the latest technology during the day while Jeannie and the kids go to Disneyland. Expenses for only Sam's portion of the trip are fully deductible.

Example 2: Sam and his family drive to Anaheim instead of fly. Now, the entire car expense can be deducted by the business, even if the back seat is wall-to-wall kids. Once in California, Sam squeezes everyone into a regular room at the Holiday Inn, so the hotel cost is all deductible. But obviously, Sam can't deduct the expense of family meals or anyone's ticket for Disneyland. And if the family stays over for more sightseeing, none of the after-convention expenses are deductible.

The law formerly allowed a spouse's travel expenses to be deducted if his or her presence served a business purpose; now, only a spouse who is a bona fide employee of the business can have expenses deducted.

Keep a copy of programs and workbooks from trade shows along with all receipts for your expenses in case the IRS ever audits. (See Chapter 3, Recordkeeping and Accounting, for the kinds of records to keep.)

3. Lodging at Your Workplace

Owners and employees of a few types of businesses (such as motels and funeral homes) where someone should be present 24 hours a day, can live there tax-free. The business can also deduct costs of the owners' or employees' meals. To qualify, three conditions must be met:

1. Living on the premises must be a condition of employment

2. It must be primarily for the convenience of the employer, and

3. There must be a legitimate need for someone to be at the business around the clock. (IRC § 119.)

WHAT ABOUT FREQUENT FLYER MILES?

If you are like me, you love to get those free vacation trips from airline and credit card company frequent flyer miles. My MasterCard gives me one frequent flyer mile for every dollar I charge, in addition to what the airline gives me for miles flown. The IRS has threatened to tax the receipt of these freebies if the miles resulted from deductible business travel and credit card charges. In effect, the IRS reasons that this is a rebate that should be either taxed or should lower the amount of the original business deduction. If you think about it, there is some logic to this argument. Luckily for us, the IRS hasn't yet figured out how to tax this unofficial fringe benefit, and Congress hasn't pressed the issue by revising the tax code.

F. Clubs and Athletic Facilities

Socializing can yield tax breaks to all business owners and employees. Expenses for entertaining at private clubs or athletic facilities can qualify for tax deductions, as long as a *business purpose* is served. However, membership fees for these facilities may not be deductible. The tax code has become more restrictive in recent years, and you should be aware of some special rules. (IRC § 132, 274, Reg. 1.132, 1.274.)

- *Clubs and Associations:* Dues for *some* private clubs are no longer deductible business expenses or tax-free benefits—even if the membership is used primarily for business.

(Reg. 1.274-2.) Associations where a business purpose is obvious—chamber of commerce, real estate board, business leagues, and public service clubs like Rotary and Lions qualify. The dues of purely social organizations—country clubs, athletic clubs and the like—can no longer be deducted. But 50% of business entertainment expenses that take place at a nondeductible club—such as greens fees and 19th hole libations—are deductible.

- *Athletic Facilities:* A business can deduct the cost of athletic facilities on the business's premises if they are open to all employees. This could be as simple as buying a Nordic Track for an unused storeroom, or as lavish as a company gym and swimming pool. However, memberships in outside athletic clubs don't qualify as tax-free fringe benefits.

G. Association Dues and Subscriptions

Owners and employees of any kind of business can get tax-free trade association memberships and subscriptions to business publications. These are deductible as long as the organizations are not primarily social in nature. (IRC § 162, Reg. 1.162-6, 1.162-15.)

Example: Jessica, owner of a motorcycle parts business, pays $200 per year for membership for her and her employee, Joy, in the Motorcycle Parts Retailers Association. This is a deductible business expense and is a tax-free benefit to both Jessica and Joy.

H. Health Benefits

Given the high cost of health care, medical benefits are an exceedingly important fringe benefit. It makes tax sense for a profitable business—sole

PART 4

Fringe Benefits

proprietorship, limited liability company, partnership or corporation—to provide group hospitalization and medical insurance. Tax rules for health benefits vary, depending upon whether or not your business is incorporated. C corporations get a better shake.

1. Unincorporated Businesses

The rules on deductibility of business-paid health benefits are different for owners than for their employees.

a. Owners

Sole proprietors, partners, limited liability company members and S corporation shareholders active in a business can deduct 30% of the health insurance premiums they pay for themselves and their families. (IRC § 162(L).) The deduction is claimed on a special line for "medical insurance premiums" on the front page of your individual tax return, not as a business expense per se.

Example: Jack, a sole proprietor, pays $3,200 for an annual health insurance policy for himself and his family. Jack can deduct 30% of the premium ($800). Depending on Jack's tax bracket, his tax savings will range from $120 to about $310.

The 1996 limit of 30% on deducting the cost of health insurance premiums for self-employed individuals is slated to be increased annually in stages: 40% in 1997; 45% in 1998 and through 2002; 50% in 2003; 60% in 2004; 70% in 2005, and 80% in 2006.

MEDICAL SAVINGS ACCOUNT

Beginning in 1997, business owners and employees of businesses may qualify for a new tax break called the Medical Savings Account (MSA). What started through the Congressional meat grinder as a plan to make the cost of health care more bearable for many working Americans ended up as an overly complicated and relatively small tax benefit for a few. What follows is a bare bones explanation; be warned that there are many more rules and qualifications for MSAs.

To qualify for an MSA, you or your business (of no more than 50 employees) must have a medical insurance plan. The insurance must have an annual deductible of at least $1,500 (for an individual) or $3,000 (for a family). Then you can establish and make tax-deductible contributions to an MSA, similar to contributions to an IRA retirement account. Money put into an MSA by a business or employee builds up tax-free in the plan, which must be managed by an insurance company or financial institution, similar to an IRA. MSA contributions produce an immediate tax deduction—up to 65% of the insurance plan's deductible portion for individuals or 75% for families. The MSA deduction is taken on the first page of your tax return, close to where IRA contributions are claimed.

Alternatively, employers can contribute to their employees' MSAs, and the contributions will not be included in the income of the employees. Once the funds are in the MSA, they can be distributed for payment of the medical expenses that were not covered by insurance. Similar to the health insurance premium deduction discussed above, this is not technically a business deduction, but is taken by the individual business owner or employee on the personal part of his or her tax return.

b. Employees

In a sole proprietorship, limited liability company, partnership or S corporation, health benefits for non-owner employees are tax-free to them and deductible to the business. As discussed above, owners can deduct only 30% of their health insurance premiums.

Example: Rosemary, a sole proprietor, provides a group health plan to her workers as a tax-free benefit. The $3,000 annual insurance premiums are deductible to the business in full. The portion paid for Rosemary, however, is taxable income to her—but she can deduct 30% of that amount.

Hire your spouse and get fully deductible health benefits for yourself. A loophole in the law allows any small business to fully tax deduct health insurance and doctor's bills if a spouse is working as an employee. This coverage can be provided as a fringe benefit under IRC § 105. The other spouse (owner of the business) can then be provided fully deductible medical benefits not as an owner, but as a spouse of an employee! The business deduction is 100%—not the 30% for self-employed folks. There are several hitches: (1) any other employees of the business have to be given the same health benefits, and (2) there are tax costs (Social Security, Medicare and Unemployment taxes) of putting a spouse on the payroll. He or she must do real work in your business in order to qualify, but doesn't have to be a full-time employee. This is tricky and requires a "medical reimbursement plan" that strictly complies with IRC § 105. Before trying it, see a tax pro.

2. C Corporations

For C corporations, a health plan is a great fringe for everyone. Medical insurance premiums paid for owners and employees are entirely tax-deductible to the corporation and tax-free to the recipients. This beats the stingy 30% insurance premium deductibility limit for owners of unincorporated businesses and the restrictions on individual deductions for medical expenses. (You can deduct medical expenses only to the extent that they exceed $7^1/2\%$ of your adjusted gross income. This limitation takes away the medical deduction for most high-income individuals.)

Example: If Lois's Pets 'R Us, Inc., is a C corporation, the whole amount for her health insurance ($3,000) is tax-deductible to the business and tax-free to Lois, even if Lois were the only person eligible for the plan. Depending on Lois's tax bracket, this could produce a federal tax saving of as much as $1,200.

Health benefits don't have to be from a group plan. Instead, an owner/employee of a C corporation can pick a health policy and be reimbursed by the business, without it counting as income.

And a C corporation could establish a "medical reimbursement plan" which pays for—and deducts—medical costs not covered by insurance for employees, their spouses and dependents. To qualify, a reimbursement plan must cover 70% or more of the employees and all must benefit equally. However, employees who are under age 25, part-time or seasonal, or on the job for less than three years, can be excluded. (IRC § 105(h).)

Example: Fred and Ethel's incorporated business, Sitcom Writers, Inc., uses part-time workers, none of whom must be covered under tax code rules for the business's medical reimbursement plan. Ethel has a frontal lobotomy that costs $25,000; their insurance policy covers $20,000. If the corporation can pay for the additional $5,000, it can deduct it whether paid directly to the medical provider or to Ethel. The payment is tax-free to Ethel either way.

PART 4

Fringe Benefits

Even if your corporation doesn't have a health plan, the cost of physical checkups by an employee's doctor can be deductible by the business. To qualify, there should be a written employment contract between the corporation and employee stating that annual checkups are a condition of employment. (IRC § 162.)

I. Dependent Care Assistance

Any business can have a dependent or day-care assistance plan for its employees' children under age 13. Payments up to $5,000 per worker annually are tax-free to the employee. (If the employee is married but files taxes separately, the maximum is $2,500.) The business can deduct all payments, even if over $5,000, as compensation to the employee. (IRC § 129.)

Alternatively, an incorporated business can add up to $5,000 to an employee/parent's salary for this purpose tax-free. This benefit must be given to every parent, with a few exceptions. You don't have to give it to employees under age 21, or those with less than one year of service, or leased employees or those covered by a collective bargaining agreement. (IRC § 129.)

Even businesses without a dependent care plan (perhaps because it would be too expensive to cover all employees) may still qualify for the "dependent care income tax credit." This tax break is designed to help working parents, and its mechanics are rather complex. (For details, see IRC § 21.)

J. Education Benefits

Any business can pay, and deduct, an owner or employee's education expenses if they are *directly related* to her job. Deductible costs include tuition, fees, books, course supplies, lodging and similar education expenses. There is no dollar limitation,

but the expenses must be reasonable, taking into account the financial circumstances of the business.

A business can also pay up to $5,250 per year for each employee for education expenses even if not directly related to the job. However, this provision is limited to traditional education—hobby-type courses don't qualify. (See IRC § 127, Reg. 1.127, for details.) To qualify, the business must have a written Educational Assistance Plan (EAP). Payments or reimbursements are tax-free to the employee, and an EAP can cover tuition, books and supplies.

The fringe benefit for Educational Assistance Plans (discussed below) expired at the end of 1994, but was reinstated retroactively by Congress in 1996. However, this tax code provision (IRC § 127) is set to expire on June 1, 1997. If you read this after that date and want to use this benefit, check with your tax advisor to see if it has been extended again. Those folks in Washington sure like to keep us guessing.

K. Gifts, Rewards, Discounts and Free Services

A number of relatively small tax-free benefits can be given to employees of any business.

1. Gifts

Small gifts to employees—totaling under $25 per year per recipient—are nontaxable. In tax lingo, such gifts are "de minimus fringe"—so small as to make accounting for the expense unreasonable or impractical. (See IRC § 132, Reg. 1.132.) So, the proverbial Thanksgiving turkey for employees is probably tax-free to them and deductible to the business, but not the more expensive honey-baked ham. This $25 rule applies to all business entities.

2. Achievement Awards

With a "qualified award plan," a business can give gifts valued up to $1,600—gift certificates, watches, TVs, and the like—tax-free to the employees, and deduct the cost each year. These awards must be for special achievement, length of service or safety efforts. They can't be in cash, given to more than 10% of all employees or favor just highly compensated employees. (See IRC §§ 74 and 274 for more details.)

If your business doesn't have a qualified award plan, you still may give special employees these "good habit" awards, but you are limited to a value of $400 per employee in any year. Again, cash cannot be awarded.

3. Free Services

Certain types of businesses—such as hotels, airlines and cruise lines—can provide their services or facilities tax-free to employees and their families. To qualify, the provided benefit must be an "excess capacity" service—something that would remain unused if not given to the employee. It's easy to see how this applies to empty airplane seats and hotel rooms, but I can't think of many other things that would qualify. (IRC § 132, Reg. 1.132.)

4. Employee Discounts

Discounts on goods or services may be given by a business to employees and families tax-free. You can provide anything your business makes or sells at a discount, but never below cost. Discounts must be given across the board to employees and families (or even retired employees), not just to higher-paid

people. Some things, however, can't be discounted without being taxed as income to employees—primarily real estate and investment property. (IRC § 132, Reg. 1.132.)

5. Miscellaneous Minor Benefits

Some fringe benefits are so small that even the IRS doesn't require a business to separately keep track of them, or an employee to report them as income. Examples include infrequent use of the company copy machine, having a personal letter typed by a secretary, coffee and donuts, local telephone calls and even an occasional theater or sporting event ticket. In general, cash can't be given tax-free, but it's okay if used for occasional meals for employees working late, or for their local transportation expenses (under $1.50).

Look out for taxable fringes. As previously discussed, some kinds of items, such as season tickets to sporting events, the use of an employer owned or leased vacation facility, or a company car used for commuting are income to the recipient. The fair market value of these items should be shown on an employee's W-2 form along with wages. While some of these items are not likely to be caught by an auditor, you should be aware of the letter of the law here. (IRC § 132(d), Reg. 1.132.)

L. Special Rules for C Corporations

The tax rules governing fringe benefits discussed so far in this chapter generally apply to C corporations as well as other kinds of business entities. But C corporations also qualify for special tax breaks for certain kinds of fringe benefits.

1. Financial and Tax Planning for Employees

Only a C corporation can provide tax-free financial planning and income tax preparation help to employees. To be tax-free, such benefits must be part of a "qualified" employee benefit plan and widely available to all employees, not just the owners. (See IRC § 127, Reg. 1.127-2 for details.)

If your corporation doesn't have a qualified plan, there's a way to provide this benefit indirectly: The corporation adds the cost of financial or tax counseling (say $500) to an employee's taxable pay. Then the employee claims $500 on his or her tax return on Schedule A as a "miscellaneous" deduction. (Rev. Rul. 73-13.) The downside is that the employee cannot get a full tax deduction benefit, but only a "miscellaneous" deduction.

2. Disability Benefits

C corporations can deduct insurance premiums for disability, wage continuation, sickness and accident policies for employees, including owners. Premium payments are not considered income to employees. However, any payouts for disability are taxable income to the recipients—with a few exceptions involving permanent or total disability. (IRC § 104, Reg. 1.104 and IRC § 105, Reg. 1.105.)

3. Group Life Insurance

If they meet certain conditions, C corporations can provide employees with life insurance and deduct the premiums. (IRC § 79.) Sorry, sole proprietors, partners, limited liability companies and S corporations can't qualify.

Group term life insurance can qualify as a tax-free benefit. Individual policies, or those that accumulate cash reserves—called whole life or universal life—are not eligible.

Death proceeds are limited to $50,000 for each employee. If greater coverage is provided, the cost is still deductible, but the excess cost is taxable to employees. IRS tables show just how much the taxable portion of the premium is for excess coverage, depending on the recipient's age and amount of coverage. The IRS income "inclusions" are below the actual costs, so even if some of the premium is taxable, there is a savings to the employee.

To qualify, C corporations must cover all full-time workers, and can't require physical exams. You don't have to give the same coverage to everyone; the death payoff can be greater for owners.

4. Loans to Shareholders

A shareholder of a C corporation can borrow up to $10,000 from the corporation, interest-free. Anyone borrowing more must either pay interest or pay tax on the amount of interest he should have paid. The interest rate is determined by IRS tables. (IRC § 7872.) (This tax-free loan benefit is not available to sole proprietors, partners, limited liability company members or S corporation shareholders.)

Loan formalities. Chapter 7, C Corporations, covers loan formalities. For example, your corporate minutes must approve the loan and you must execute a promissory note between a borrower and the corporation. By failing to do it right, you risk an IRS auditor concluding a loan is really a disguised dividend, making it taxable income to the borrower.

5. Entertainment Facilities

Corporations and other businesses can't deduct the cost of acquiring and maintaining facilities used *purely* for the entertainment of owners and employees—ski cabins, yachts, hunting lodges and so forth. (IRC § 274(a).) They can be claimed as business expenses when they are actually used for business purposes.

Vacation stays are taxable income to business owners and employees unless they pay the corporation for the lodging. The best you can do is to provide very favorable rental rates to yourself and your employees.

Arguably, a lodge used primarily for business and incidentally for pleasure is not a prohibited entertainment facility. But before you designate that cabin a corporate sub-office, keep in mind that someday you might have to defend it before a skeptical IRS auditor.

Another way to qualify for a benefit here might be for a shareholder who owns an entertainment facility to rent it to the corporation to wine and dine customers or for company meetings. This is okay as long as rent is reasonable and the facility is available for rental for others besides the corporation. The corporation may even lend the shareholder funds to acquire the facility. You are entitled to tax write-offs for interest paid on the loan, depreciation and for other expenses of ownership on investment property such as an entertainment facility.

6. Corporation Job Placement Assistance

Helping former employees find new jobs when a company downsizes is a tax-free benefit and deductible for C corporations. Outplacement job assistance must be related to the employee's previous occupation, trade or business. This benefit must be provided to everyone and the former employees can't be offered the choice of job placement services or cash. (IRC § 132 (d), Rev. Rul. 92-69.)

RESOURCES

The McGraw-Hill Small Business Tax Advisor, by Cliff Roberson (McGraw-Hill). This book explains most of the fringe benefits described in this chapter, in greater detail.

IRS Publication 334, *Tax Guide for Small Business.* If you have only one IRS publication, this should be it. Also, all of the following IRS publications discuss fringe benefits:

- 560, *Retirement Plans for the Self-Employed*
- 502, *Medical and Dental Expenses*
- 503, *Child and Dependent Care Credit.*

Business Entity Analysis (Troutdale, Oregon). This software program compares the tax benefits of fringe benefits—including retirement plans—for the different business entities chosen, and is primarily intended for accountants. ■

PART **4**

Fringe Benefits

Retirement Plans

PART **4**

Fringe Benefits

"No man who knows what the law is today can guess what it will be tomorrow."

— Alexander Hamilton

Only the most wide-eyed optimist believes that our Social Security system will provide enough money for your golden years. And it is unrealistic to think that Social Security benefits will become more generous in the future. Indeed, as the ratio of workers to retirees shrinks, the trend is to effectively reduce Social Security by taxing many benefit recipients who have additional income. This means you should create your own retirement plan to close the gap.

Fortunately, our tax laws help business owners of any size save for a secure retirement. *Any* kind of business, whether corporation, partnership, sole proprietorship or limited liability company, can set up a retirement plan complete with tax breaks. If you don't have a retirement plan, you are missing one of the greatest tax benefits of being in business.

Unfortunately, tax rules on contributions and withdrawals from retirement plans are very complicated. These complexities help explain why only a third of small businesses (fewer than 100 employees) have retirement plans, compared to five-sixths of larger employers. The big companies set up the plans and make it easy for their employees to participate.

This chapter presents a broad outline of retirement plan options available to all business entities. You will need more, so find an expert in helping business owners cope with retirement planning and administration. Stock brokerages, banks and insurance companies offer retirement plan advice, mostly as a means to sell their investment products. Take the time to understand the retirement plan basics, and use these resources to establish a good plan or group of plans.

RETIREMENT PLANS IN A NUTSHELL

1. One of the best reasons for being in business is to have a tax-advantaged retirement plan.

2. Plans allow businesses to tax-deduct contributions to funds that accumulate tax-deferred until they are finally distributed.

3. Businesses with full-time employees usually must include them in their retirement plans, which can be expensive.

4. All small businesses can take advantage of retirement plans, but some plans are available only to incorporated businesses.

5. Federal law heavily regulates the retirement plan area, and professional guidance for setting up and maintaining plans is advisable.

A. Tax-Advantaged Retirement Plans

If your enterprise's retirement plan qualifies for favorable treatment under the Internal Revenue Code, there are four main tax consequences:

1. Up to certain dollar limits, your contributions as an owner or employee are tax-deductible from current income, thus reducing your present income taxes. A contribution to a tax-advantaged retirement plan must be earned income, meaning it must be compensation for work. So, for instance, an investor in a business who isn't active in it can't deduct contributions to a retirement plan.

2. Income generated by investments in your retirement plan accumulates without being taxed until it is withdrawn.

3. The IRS generally imposes penalties for taking money out of a plan before retirement, but there are some exceptions allowed under the tax code.

4. Depending on how much income you have after you retire, withdrawals from your plan usually will be taxed at a lower rate than would apply to the same income taxed when you were working.

Clearly, our government offers business people a deal that is hard to refuse. Not only can you put aside money before it's taxed, but as long as you keep your hands off it, it will grow tax-free as well. A typical retirement plan participant who contributes an average of $5,000 to $8,000 a year can build up $150,000 to $400,000 over a 10-to-20-year period, depending on how his investments perform. If you contribute for 20 to 40 years, or own a very successful business and make maximum contributions, you might be able to accumulate several million dollars. The keys are to start early, make the largest contributions you can, and take full advantage of all that the law allows.

B. Types of Retirement Plans

Tax-favored retirement plans are also referred to as "qualified plans." There are a host of rules for plan eligibility and contributions—who can get into which kinds of plans and how much money can be put into them.

This can get confusing fast, so I'll do my best to guide you through the process. In addition, IRS Publication 560, *Retirement Plans for the Self-Employed*, is one of the better-written IRS publications, and it's free.

Let's start with a chart (below) showing the common types of retirement plans available to different kinds of business entities. In some cases, you may be able to adopt multiple plans. You're not confined to one retirement plan—there is no limit to how many plans you can accumulate over your working life. For instance, I have a client who has established Individual Retirement Accounts, a Keogh plan, Simplified Employee Pensions, deferred-compensation 401(k) plans and a corporate pension and profit-sharing plan!

RETIREMENT PLANS FOR SMALL BUSINESS OWNERS				
	IRA	SEP	KEOGH	401(K)
Sole Proprietorship	Y	Y	Y	N
(with employees other than owner)	Y	Y	Y	Y
Partnership	Y	Y	Y	N
(with employees other than owners)	Y	Y	Y	Y
Limited Liability Company	Y	Y	Y	N
(with employees other than owners)	Y	Y	Y	Y
S corporation	Y	Y	N	N
(with employees other than owners)	Y	Y	Y	Y
C corporation	N	Y	N	Y

PART 4

Fringe Benefits

WHERE TO GO FOR A PENSION PLAN

Picking the right retirement plan is one of the most important financial decisions you are ever likely to make. You need the help of a reputable financial services institution, or perhaps a pension consultant for more complex circumstances. Start by asking your banker, accountant or attorney for their recommendations of where to go. Seek advice from an astute friend or business associate. Then meet the representatives of at least three of these outfits and compare what they have to offer.

For most folks, a "ready-made" prototype plan offered by a mutual fund company, bank and brokerage will fit the bill. These plans are relatively cheap to set up and maintain. They will give you a statement of their fees and a track record of their investment vehicles, which will allow you to evaluate and compare them. Fidelity Investments and Charles Schwab are two of my favorite companies that offer this service.

If you hire a pension consultant, naturally it will cost more for personalized attention. This might make sense if your company is well-established and has a dozen or so employees. Expect to pay $100 or more per hour for a professional's assistance in customizing a pension plan, or several plans, to fit your needs. Or the pro may quote a flat fee. In any event, the bill should not run more than $1,500. Ask the pension pro up front about fees and just how they are calculated. One caution: many

pension pros push plan investments that carry high commission expenses. On the other hand, many brokers and mutual fund companies offer no-load products that may perform as well as the pension pro's picks.

Once you have set up the plan or plans, you must decide who will administer it—that is, take care of the annual paperwork and investment decisions. With off-the-rack plans, it will be Fidelity, Schwab or whatever company you go with. For custom plans, you should not necessarily go with the pension pro, but seek bids from professional plan administrators and money managers. Ask to see how plans they run have performed, and ask for references. Check if their clients are pleased with the administrator serves its clients, such as communicating with plan participants, meeting deadlines and answering questions.

Last, but hardly least, keep an eye on your retirement plan's performance. Most plan managers issue quarterly reports. Take the time to see how well the investments in the plan are performing. Check out the business section of your newspaper to get quotes on holdings, or call your stockbroker for an opinion of the plan investments. Don't be afraid to move the management of the plan to a new administrator if you aren't happy. There is no tax penalty, and this shouldn't be very costly.

Contribute to retirement plans as early in the year as you can. Most self-employed folks contribute to their retirement plans at the last minute—just before they file their tax returns. This is more than a year beyond when you were first able to contribute—that is, on January 1. This not only causes you to miss a full year of tax-free compounding, but it might cause additional taxes if you earned interest or dividends on that money in your non-retirement accounts.

C. Options for Sole Proprietors, Partners and Limited Liability Company Members

Most small business owners are sole proprietors or partners, although an increasing number are members of limited liability companies (LLCs). Generally speaking, these types of businesses can't contribute quite as much to retirement plans as corporations. But for most small business folks who make under $100,000 per year, this is not a drawback, and many excellent tax-advantaged plan opportunities are available to them. On the other hand, owners of fast-growing small businesses, weighing the advantages of incorporating, should consider the greater retirement plan benefits that C corporations can offer.

Unincorporated businesses can choose from three types of plans: Individual Retirement Accounts (IRAs), Simplified Employee Pension plans (SEPs) and Keoghs. A sole proprietorship, partnership or LLC *with employees* can add the increasingly popular deferred-compensation plan, commonly called a 401(k) or salary-reduction plan, to its options.

IRAs, because of the meager contribution limit of $2,000 per year per participant and the other restrictions on who may contribute, are not a sufficient retirement plan for most small business owners.

If your business makes enough to fund a retirement plan, you should go for either a Keogh or SEP plan. It's not unusual to combine the two, or start with a SEP and later switch to a Keogh. SEPs and Keoghs offer the major benefits of other tax-favored retirement plans: you can deduct earnings contributed to the plan, and income earned on funds in the plan accumulates tax-free until withdrawn. But there's one big catch: to take advantage of one of these plans yourself, you may also have to include your employees. (The rules for both Keoghs and SEPs are explained below.)

1. Keogh Plans

The Keogh, named after the New York Congressman who proposed it, is the oldest retirement savings plan for the self-employed. A Keogh can be set up by a sole proprietor, partner or limited liability company member.

A corporation shareholder may not establish a Keogh. Likewise, neither may an employee of someone else's business have his or her own Keogh plan; they must work for a business with an established Keogh and participate through that owner's plan.

Keogh contributions are normally made by an owner for herself and participating employees and put into the plan, where the money is invested. Because Keoghs allow larger annual contributions ($75,000 or even more) than other retirement plans for self-employeds, they are most popular with the ultra-high earners.

Keoghs can be set up by folks with either profitable full-time or sideline businesses. You can have one even if you are covered by a corporate plan from a present or past job. And you can take from other plans and roll them into a Keogh if you leave a job (voluntarily or involuntarily) and go into business for yourself.

There are two varieties of Keoghs:
- defined-contribution Keogh plans
- defined-benefit Keogh plans

An individual may have one or both of these plans.

PART **4**

Fringe Benefits

a. Defined Contribution Keogh Plans

The defined contribution plan (DCP) is the most common Keogh plan. How much you will get back from a defined contribution plan in benefits will depend on the total amount put into the plan and the earnings on the investments. If retirement is quite a few years away, you can make only a rough estimate of how much will be in your pot on retirement. Many computer software retirement planning programs, such as Quicken's Financial Planner, will help you with this calculation. But life and future business income are really too uncertain for most of us to know how much we will be able to really put into a DCP or how our plan investments will perform.

Keogh DCPs can further be subdivided into two types: profit-sharing plans (PSPs) and money purchase plans (MPPs).

Profit-Sharing Defined Contribution Plans. For a business owner, PSP contributions are, as the name implies, normally made from the business's profits. A PSP (unlike an MPP) doesn't require any annual contribution; it is entirely voluntary. The owner of the business decides whether or not to make a contribution both for herself and for her employees.

Example: Bartoleme's Bakery, a sole proprietorship, has a Keogh PSP. Ludwig is the owner. Lisa, his only employee, is paid $25,000 per year. In 1995, the business has a net profit of $150,000. Ludwig chooses to contribute to the plan for himself and Lisa. In 1996, the business loses $20,000, so no contribution is made to the PSP. Technically, a contribution still could be made for Lisa if Ludwig can come up with the money, but as a practical matter it is doubtful that he will.

Keogh Money Purchase Plans (MPPs). MPPs differ from PSPs in that annual contributions are required, whether the business makes a profit or not. Once you set up an MPP, a fixed percentage of everyone's pay (up to 20% for an owner or 25% for an employee) must be put into the retirement plan every year. For this reason, MPPs are found only in older businesses with reliable cash flows. If you are a business owner in an MPP and don't have the

funds to contribute one year, you must notify the IRS for permission to postpone it and catch up later. But for an owner to get permission, she must make an MPP contribution for all employees of the business who are eligible to participate in the plan.

The reason why someone would choose an MPP, with its drawback of requiring annual contributions come hell or high water, is that it allows larger tax deductible contributions than PSPs. (The limits and rules are provided in Section D, below.)

Example: Drake's Poultry Brokers, a sole proprietorship, adopts a Keogh MPP with the maximum annual contribution rate allowed by law. Drake, the owner, and Lark, an employee, are the only workers in the business. Lark makes $28,000 per year. In 1996, the business has a net profit of $100,000, so $7,000 (25% of Lark's pay) must be contributed for her. Drake must contribute $20,000 for himself. In 1997, the business loses $50,000, but still must contribute $7,000 for Lark to the MPP, even if permission is granted by the IRS to Drake to postpone making his contribution.

b. Keogh Defined Benefit Plans

The defined-benefit plan (DBP) usually provides a specific monthly amount on retirement for life, usually based on a formula such as "40% of average compensation based on the highest three years of salary." DBPs are rare, however, because they are the most costly and complex of the Keoghs. Help from a pension professional is needed to help you project a realistic benefit "target" at your anticipated retirement and then see that you contribute enough money each year to reach that target.

The amount of annual DBP contributions necessarily depends on each participant's age, length of employment and compensation. The goal is to have enough money in the plan to provide a fixed sum (such as $1,200 per month) to the participant on retirement. The DBP allows business owners who start late on retirement planning to catch up by making annual contributions larger than the normal Keogh percentage and dollar contribution limits.

Example: Julia, Atmose Company's owner, is 49 and Bert, Atmose's office manager, is 30 when the company adopts a DBP Keogh. They each make contributions sufficient to provide a $3,000 monthly retirement check beginning at age 65. A pension plan professional determines that this will require an annual contribution of $9,800 for Julia, but only $2,900 for the younger Bert. (These figures are hypothetical, and are used for purposes of illustration only.)

c. Participation Rules

Generally, all of a business's employees must be included in its Keogh plan—*if* they meet tax code requirements. Usually, full-time employees age 21 or older who were with the business for one year must be covered.

Part-timers may be excluded if they don't work at least 1,000 hours during the year (about 20 hours a week). (By contrast, SEPs, which are discussed in Section 3, below, require many part-time employees to be covered.)

A Keogh participant who leaves the business can either leave his Keogh account balance in the plan (and wait for retirement to take whatever benefit he is entitled to), or immediately withdraw the funds. If he takes the money before retirement age, he will be subject to early withdrawal penalties and income taxes. (See Section H, below, for retirement plan withdrawal rules.)

d. Keogh Contribution Rules

There is both a dollar limit and a percentage of income limit on how much you can put into a Keogh plan every year. This is not as straightforward a calculation as it might seem, so pay close attention to the specifics here. And the limits apply differently to employees than to owners. To get the maximum allowable Keogh contribution, most folks establish both a Keogh money purchase plan and a profit-sharing plan, called a "paired plan" (both

discussed above). Recall that there are two types of defined-contribution plans:

- *Keogh profit-sharing plan (PSP).* If you are a business *owner,* you may contribute and deduct up to 13.04% of your profits, or $22,500, whichever is less, to a PSP. (Note that this is the same limit as with a SEP.) This works out so that your business must earn $172,500 in profits for you to take the full deduction. The maximum contribution rate for an *employee* to a PSP is 15%, up to $30,000 per year.

- *Keogh money purchase plan (MPP).* The tax code seems to say that a business *owner* can contribute 20% of a business's profits, up to $30,000. However, because the law also says that your net earnings from self-employment must be reduced by one-half of the self-employment tax you paid, so the real limit is closer to 18% or 19%, depending on the amount of earnings. *Employees,* on the other hand, are not subject to the self-employment tax and may contribute up to 25% of their compensation, with a maximum of $30,000 in one year.

When you establish both types of Keogh defined-contribution plans, as many people do, the overall limits are the same as with just the MPP. In effect, by having both plans (or just the MPP), you can contribute 5% to 6% more per year to a retirement plan than with a SEP. There is a hidden price to pay for being able to contribute more to a Keogh than to a SEP, however. Keep in mind that once you establish an MPP, annual contributions are required if you have net earnings from your business. With a PSP, on the other hand, it is always discretionary whether or not you want to make an annual contribution. If you have both plans, you still have an obligation to fund the MPP every year, but most people make the mandatory contribution amount the smaller of the two Keogh accounts by designating the percentages when the accounts are established. For example, a "paired plan" may provide for a 5% MPP and a 15% PSP contribution.

PART 4

Fringe Benefits

Good tax preparation software, such as Turbotax for Business (Intuit), will compute small business retirement plan contribution limits, so you don't have to worry about these overly complex calculations. This is how I do it. (Thank goodness for computers!)

e. Setting up and Administering a Keogh Plan

Establishing a Keogh involves either adopting a "custodial" (also called an account type Keogh plan) or a "self-trusteed" (also called an individually designed or prototype Keogh plan).

The custodial or account type plans are those offered by investment companies such as banks, brokerages, mutual fund and insurance companies, and are by far the most popular choice. These plans conform to IRS requirements, which are typically set forth in one- or two-page documents prepared by the investment company. Sometimes called "safe harbor" plans, they paint with a wide brush through the use of broadly applicable provisions. Account type plans are fine for most small business owners, but individually designed plans may offer more opportunities to larger businesses with highly compensated owners and multiple employees. Account plan fees payable to administrators of your plan range from zero to about $100 per year. Many investment companies build their fees into the investments they sell you to place in your Keogh.

Individually designed or self-trusteed plans can be written to fit special needs and allow you more flexibility in choosing and managing your investments. As with a tailor-made garment, this is a more expensive way to go than off-the-rack wear. Call on a pension consultant for price quotes and details on setting up a self-trusteed plan if you think this might be for you.

FORMALITIES AND RULE CHANGES

A Keogh plan must have either an IRS Letter of Determination or Letter of Notification showing that it is qualified under IRC § 401. A pension professional or investment company usually takes care of this detail. Also, these folks can make sure that your Keogh plan is amended as the law changes, which it does frequently. You must have an Employer Identification Number to report your Keogh plan contributions; you can't use a Social Security Number.

f. Taking Money out of a Keogh

Tax rules for Keogh distributions are in Section H, below. Note that you are not allowed to ever borrow from your Keogh plan, unlike participants in corporate pension plans. Don't ask why—it's the law.

2. Individual Retirement Accounts (IRAs)

Anyone in business or working for someone else can create an Individual Retirement Account, commonly called an IRA. (IRC § 408.) Yes, anyone—even if you have other tax code retirement plans—as long as you are working. And unlike other retirement savings plans, a business owner can establish an IRA without having one for her employees.

IRAs were highly touted back when they started in the early 1970s, but the $2,000 annual contribution limit has caused the IRA to lose much of its original luster. (Bills have been introduced into Congress to increase this limit, but it hasn't happened yet.) The only way you could fully retire on an IRA is if you start contributing as a youth, you make excellent investment choices, inflation remains low, and tax laws don't change. Since the chances of all four happening are probably less than the Tampa Bay Buccaneers winning the Super Bowl, don't hitch your star to this wagon.

However, don't overlook the IRA completely; it can be a useful part of your overall retirement plan. Thanks to tax-free compounding, a fully funded IRA ($2,000 per year) invested at a 6% return grows to $77,985 in 20 years; at 10%, $126,005. A married couple with two IRAs and who contribute over 30 years could amass more than $1 million with moderately successful investments.

a. IRA Eligibility and Contribution Rules

Anyone earning income from her labor (not just collecting interest or dividends from investments) may set aside up to $2,000 annually in an IRA account. However, your IRA contribution is tax-deductible *only if*:

- you are not covered by another tax-favored retirement plan of any kind, or
- you are covered by another plan, but your annual adjusted gross income is less than $25,000 (single) or $40,000 (married filing jointly).

If you make between $25,000 and $35,000 (single), or between $40,000 and $50,000 (jointly with your spouse), your IRA contributions are only partially deductible. If you earn more than the limits, none of the contributions are deductible.

Beginning in 1997, IRA contributions may also be made for non-working spouses. The only rule to meet is that the working spouse must earn at least $4,000 for the couple to get the maximum $4,000 tax deduction.

Make an IRA contribution even if it is not tax-deductible. Many folks earning more than the limits discussed above overlook IRAs nowadays because they can't deduct their IRA contributions. This may be a mistake, because all funds in an IRA—whether tax-deductible or not—still compound tax-deferred until withdrawn. This is a significant long-term tax benefit, particularly for anyone in a tax bracket of 28% or higher. For instance, if your IRA account earns $1,000 one year, you might pay as much as $396 in taxes on this income if it were in a taxable investment. Instead, that $396 stays in the IRA account and builds tax-deferred until it is withdrawn. This can make a huge difference in your investment return over time.

b. Opening an IRA

An individual retirement account must be established at a financial institution using special IRA forms. You can't just open an investment account and call it your IRA. Most banks, mutual fund companies and stockbrokers set up IRAs. These accounts are usually self-directed—meaning you control investment choices such as stocks, certificates of deposit or mutual funds. The IRA investments may be changed at your direction; however, the financial institution may place some restrictions on changes.

c. IRA Withdrawals

See Section H, below, for the rules. You can't borrow money from an IRA, but Congress is considering relaxing this rule.

3. Simplified Employee Pensions (SEPs)

For those who qualify, the Simplified Employee Pension plan (SEP) is the top choice to put aside money for retirement. (IRC § 408(k).) Since SEPs are covered by most of the same tax code provisions as IRAs, they are often called SEP-IRAs. A SEP is only a little more complicated to set and maintain than an IRA. For once, the term "simplified" in the tax code is well used. The newest tax-advantaged retirement plan, the SEP was created because of complaints that Keoghs and corporate-type plans were too rule-heavy, and that IRAs were inadequate.

PART 4

Fringe Benefits

A Simplified Employee Pension account can be either a primary or a supplemental retirement plan. It can cover self-employed people and their employees who work full- or part-time. A SEP is the first plan I established for my law practice. (I have since gone to a Keogh plan for its higher contribution limits, but my earlier SEP is still in place.) The fact that my wife, Brenda, works for a mega-corporation and is in its pension, profit-sharing and 401(k) plans doesn't affect my SEP (or Keogh) plans at all. And if Brenda had time for a sideline business, she could set up her own SEP and keep her company plans too.

How good a deal are SEPs? Let me answer you this way. If you socked away only $5,000 annually in a SEP earning 8%, tax-deferred, your nest egg would reach $247,115 in 20 years. By the way, this is about $150,000 more than going with $2,000 IRA contributions in an account with the same rate of earning. If you put in more, contribute over a longer period, or your investments do better, your SEP could top $1 million.

A separate SEP account is opened for each business owner or employee—unlike a Keogh, where everyone is in the same plan. In a regular SEP, the owner contributes for herself and the employees.

a. SEP Contribution Limits and Deductibility Rules

How much can be tax-deducted and put into a SEP each year? For one thing, this depends on whether you are an owner or employee of a business. For reasons known only to the gnomes in Washington, the contribution limits are lower for owners than for employees. And not all of a SEP contribution may be tax-deductible. The rules are tricky, so pay close attention. I promise you it will be well worth the effort when it comes to writing out those tax bill checks every year, and when retirement time finally rolls around.

i. Business Owner

If you own a business, you may contribute up to $22,500 or 13.04% of your share of the business's net income per year, whichever is less.

These figures are the maximum amounts—you can contribute less in any year. Also, if you contribute more than the maximum, within limits, it won't be tax deductible but will still give you a long-term benefit from tax-free compounding. This is important to keep in mind when you want to build up your retirement account fast—particularly if you are within five or ten years of retirement and you will be short of your financial targets.

Example: Manfred, owner of Pillpushers Pharmacy, puts $5,216 (13.04% of his business's net income of $40,000) into his SEP in 1995.

Generally, SEP contributions for a business *owner* can be made by any profitable business. Profitability is determined by the tax reporting of the sole proprietorship, partnership or limited liability company.

ii. Employee (Non-Owner)

An employee or business owner (or a combination of both) may contribute up to $30,000 or 25% of the worker's compensation, whichever is less. However, the employee can tax deduct as a SEP contribution *only* up to $30,000 or 15% of his compensation, whichever is less. The requirement of business profitability doesn't apply to a non-owner employee.

The same rules apply as with an owner's contributions; just the limits are higher for employees.

iii. Other Points

Only business-earned income of an owner or employee counts for purposes of determining SEP contributions. Capital gains, interest, dividends, royalties and other ways to come into money are not considered "earned." This is not necessarily logical or fair, but nevertheless the tax code imposes this restriction.

Example: Manfred, in the example above, got $32,000 from the sale of property and $3,400 in interest in 1995. Neither amount is within the tax code definition of "earned" income and so doesn't increase the amount Manfred can put in his SEP.

Excessive SEP contributions (those over both the deductible and nondeductible limitations of the tax code) must be withdrawn by the due date of the tax return for that year, including any extensions, or else applied to the next years' contribution. This is not an uncommon problem, particularly if you make your SEP contribution before you have completed your tax return, and didn't earn quite as much income as you had anticipated. Most folks simply instruct their SEP account manager to credit the excess to the next year's contribution.

Example: Manfred in the two examples above, mistakenly contributes $10,000 to his SEP, $4,784 more than is allowed. The excess must be either removed from the SEP account by the due date of the tax return, or credited to Manfred's 1996 SEP by the administrator of the plan.

b. SEP Participation Requirements

With a regular SEP, what is good for the goose is good for the gander. If a business owner makes a SEP contribution for herself, generally, contributions in an amount proportionate to income must be made to the SEP accounts of all *eligible* employees. Everyone over 20 years old, who has been with the company for three of the last five years, and who makes at least $400 per year is eligible. If these folks' SEPs aren't funded, the owner can't contribute to her account.

Example: Melissa, owner of Superfast Delivery Service, has three long-time regular employees. She contributes 5% of her $50,000 business profit, $2,500,

to a SEP. Melissa must also contribute 5% of the wages of each eligible employee to their SEP accounts.

SAVINGS INCENTIVE MATCH PLAN

Beginning in 1997, employers who have no other company retirement plans in operation may establish a Savings Incentive Match Plan (SIMPLE). As you might expect, the rules laid down by Congress are anything but simple. Basically, workers may direct that up to $6,000 of compensation be put into a SIMPLE plan by their employer. The business owner then must match the employee's contributions dollar-for-dollar (up to 3% of the employee's wages). Money put into the plan is fully deductible to the employer (as compensation paid) and is not taxable (until withdrawn) for the employee. Once money is put into the SIMPLE plan, it is pretty much like an IRA account—accumulating earnings tax-deferred on its investments, with penalties for early withdrawals, and fully taxable when taken out for retirement.

As of this writing, the IRS has not yet published a model SIMPLE plan as it has done with SEPs. This should happen by early 1997, and then these new plans should be promoted by banks, brokerages and other financial service companies, so contact these folks for details on implementing a SIMPLE plan.

c. SEP Tax Reporting

You have up to the date you file your tax return to establish and contribute to a SEP. Normally this means your deadline is April 15 of the following year. If you get an extension to file, you have until the last date of the extension to make a SEP contribution—either August 15 or October 15. You may have one SEP account, or several with different sponsors.

You decide every year whether or not to put anything into a SEP, up to the maximum allowed—but you can't make up for any past years in which you didn't contribute.

Even though your SEP contributions are not taxed as income in the year contributed, they are still treated as wages for employment tax purposes that year. This means that Social Security and Medicare taxes (ranging from 2.9% to 15.3%, as discussed in Chapter 5, Employer Tax Concerns) must be paid on earnings put into a SEP. (In contrast, contributions to corporate plans, discussed in Section E below, are not subject to these payroll taxes. Not fair, but it's the law nonetheless.)

d. How to Establish a Simplified Employee Pension Plan

The usual way to set up a SEP is through a bank, insurance company, brokerage house or mutual fund company. They handle the paperwork for a small fee, or may even do it for free if you make your investments through them. Many folks make SEP contributions to "families" of mutual funds. Fidelity Investments and Charles Schwab are two discount brokerage firms that offer hundreds of no-load mutual funds for SEPs as well as individual stocks and other types of investments.

You may change investments within the SEP as you feel necessary. Often, transaction fees are waived if you keep your retirement plans with these companies. Some institutions charge annual SEP account maintenance fees of $10 to $100 per year, while others don't charge anything if your account is a certain minimum size.

You may have an unlimited number of SEP accounts, as long as your total contributions don't exceed the annual limits. I have six different SEP accounts established over the years, all with different brokers or mutual fund families.

e. SEP Withdrawal Rules

See Section H1, below.

D. 401(k) Deferred-Compensation Plans for Businesses With Employees

IRC § 401(k) provides that any business with employees can have a deferred-compensation plan. This is commonly called a "401(k) plan," and sometimes a "salary reduction plan." A partnership or limited liability company without employees can also establish a 401(k), along with a corporation in which only the owner is an employee. Only a one-person sole proprietor (or husband and wife team) is prohibited by law from establishing a 401(k) plan.

"Deferred compensation," like it sounds, means not taking income you earn now, and instead planning to receive it at some time in the future. Why you would want to do that is simple. If you take it now, it is fully taxed. If instead, you put it into a tax-advantaged retirement plan, it not only reduces your tax bite now, it will accumulate earnings tax-free. A typical deferred-compensation, more commonly called a 401(k) plan, provides that an employee, the employer, or some combination of both, make contributions.

Example: Dennis, owner of a management consulting firm, DenCo, is in the 36% tax bracket. His corporation puts $9,000 into his deferred compensation plan in early 1995. The $9,000 is immediately tax-deductible to DenCo, but is not income to Dennis in 1995. If the $9,000 earns $1,000 during 1995, Dennis' total income tax savings are $3,600 (36% tax savings on the $9,000 deferred compensation, and 36% of the $1,000 the investment earned).

A big reason for the popularity of 401(k) plans is that the law allows participants to decide each year whether, and how much, they want to contribute (within tax code limits). Another incentive for employees making contributions is the fact that many plans provide for the company to match, or partially match, the contribution made to the plan by the employee.

1. 401(k) Contribution Limits and Drawbacks

The tax code never allows too much of a good thing. There are overall dollar and percentage of income limits on how much can be contributed to your retirement plans, including 401(k) plans. In 1996, the maximum that can be contributed to a 401(k) was the lesser of 25% of earnings or $9,500. (IRC 402(g).) You don't have to contribute anything if you don't want to, and can contribute far less than the maximum. Typically, contributions range from 2% to 10% of earnings. The ceiling is indexed annually for inflation.

One tax drawback is that Social Security and Medicare taxes aren't deferred, but are imposed on the 401(k) contributions in the year made. This means you pay anywhere from 2.9% to 15.3% of taxes on income that you don't get until some years later. For some folks, this extra reduction in take-home pay is the reason not to contribute the maximum to a deferred-compensation plan.

2. 401(k) Participation Rules

A deferred-compensation plan can't be just for the business owners alone. It must be open to any full-time employee who is 21 or older and has worked at least one year in the business.

The tax code dictates that the ratio of participation of "highly compensated" employees must be close to that of lower rung workers (though it may be slightly higher). For instance, for a business owner to contribute 6% of his salary, his employees must kick in at least 4% of their wages to the 401(k) plan. If the top brass violate this rule by putting in too much in relation to everyone else, the excess must be returned to them (and taxed). Because owners can't force their employees (who tend to be younger and less concerned with saving for retirement) to contribute to a 401(k) plan, this can be major problem. To give an incentive for the little guys, some businesses offer to match contributions of all participants in the plan—although matching is not required by the tax code. More common is for businesses to make a partial match, such as 3% if an employee contributes 6%.

3. Getting Into a 401(k) Plan and Investment Limitations

Like all tax code retirement plans, a 401(k) is established by either a pension pro or a financial institution. The IRS requires more paperwork and imposes more regulatory controls over 401(k) deferred compensation plans than with most other retirement plans. This means a 401(k) plan may be too expensive to set up and run for small businesses with just an owner and a few employees. So, before getting carried away with the notion of a 401(k) for your business, check with experts on the cost.

Another potential drawback is that 401(k) plans offered by institutions typically limit your investment choices within the plan. Your control over 401(k) plan investments is limited because of Department of Labor regulations that don't apply to Keoghs, SEPs or IRAs. For instance, you may be able to invest in only in the plan's established bond, stock, mutuals or money market funds. While you are allowed to allocate between choices, there are usually restrictions in changing from one type of investment to another—such as how many times in a year you can switch your plan money around.

Restrictions on investments has loosened up some recently, so that some 401(k) plans now permit participants to freely select their investments, including playing the stock market. Whether or not this is wise in a retirement savings plan is another question. Mutual funds have become the usual vehicle of choice for most small business 401(k) plans.

PART 4

Fringe Benefits

KEY SELF-EMPLOYMENT RETIREMENT PLAN RULES (NON-CORPORATE)

Type of Plan	Last Date for Contribution	Maximum Contribution	Time Limit to Begin Distributions
IRA	Due date of income tax return (NOT including extensions)	Smaller of $2,000 or taxable compensation	April 1 of year after year you reach age 70½
SEP-IRA	Due date of employer's return (plus extensions)	**Employer** Smaller of $30,000 or 15% of participant's taxable compensation **Self-Employed Individual** Smaller of $22,500 or 13.0435% of taxable compensation	April 1 of year after year you reach age 70½
Keogh	Due date of employer's return (plus extensions) (To make contributions to a new plan in a given year, the plan must be set up by the last day of the employer's tax year.)	**Defined Contribution Plans** **Employer** *Money Purchase.* Smaller of $30,000 or 25% of taxable compensation *Profit Sharing.* Smaller of $30,000 or 15% of employee's taxable compensation **Self-Employed Individual** *Money Purchase* Smaller of $30,000 or 20% of taxable compensation *Profit Sharing* Smaller of $30,000 or 13.0435% of self-employed participant's taxable compensation **Defined Benefit Plans** Amount needed to provide an annual retirement benefit no larger than the smaller of $118,000 or 100% of the participant's average taxable compensation for his or her highest three consecutive years	April 1 of year after year you reach age 70½

4. Taking Money out of a 401(k)

One important advantage that 401(k) plans have over SEPs, Keoghs and IRAs is that you can borrow from your 401(k), and can't from the others. Section H below explains the rules for loans and for withdrawals from all types of retirement savings plans.

E. C Corporation Retirement Plans

If your business is a sole proprietorship, partnership, limited liability company or S corporation, this material will be of interest only if you are considering becoming a C corporation.

At one time, so-called "corporate retirement plans" offered significant advantages over those available to all other business entities. While the gap has narrowed today, a wider range of options and larger contribution limits make corporate plans attractive for very cash-rich small businesses. For one thing, you can borrow from a corporate savings plan, which you can't do from other plans without paying a significant tax penalty. I don't recommend borrowing lightly, but if you have a good reason—a medical emergency or a down payment for a home, for example—it is comforting to know the otherwise untouchable asset of a retirement plan is there for you.

Keep in mind as you are reading this section that if your business is incorporated, then you are one of its employees—perhaps the only one. So whenever you see the word "employee" here, it means you, the owner, as well as anyone else working in your business.

1. What Is ERISA?

The Employee's Retirement Security Act (ERISA) is a complex set of federal laws governing tax-advantaged retirement plans for employees of businesses. I won't bore you with more than the basics, but ERISA has been around since 1974 and has been revised by Congress more times than I can count. The laws are enforced by the Department of Labor and the IRS. Whenever you see the term "qualified plan," it means that it is an employee benefit plan governed by ERISA rules. ERISA retirement plans provide tax advantages very much like all other retirement plans discussed in this chapter.

The Pension Benefit Guarantee Corporation, a federal agency, also gets into the act in the case of corporate defined-benefit plans only. This agency basically protects plan participants from fraud or theft of plan assets. Practically speaking, most smaller businesses don't benefit from this arm of the government because they usually don't have defined-benefit plans.

ERISA rules prohibit corporate plans from discriminating among employees. By this I mean that, generally speaking, plans can't favor business owners and officers of a corporation over other employees in granting tax-advantaged benefits. These prohibitions often make ERISA plans too expensive for typical small businesses. A common dilemma is often that a business can't afford to cover all of its employees in its plans, but wants the benefits for the owners. The law grants some leeway to owners—for instance, employees can be kept out of a corporate retirement plan until after they have stuck around long enough to be valuable to the business. (See Section 2, below.)

PART **4**

Fringe Benefits

PENALTIES FOR ERISA VIOLATIONS

The IRS can audit retirement plans to see if they are complying with ERISA rules. If a violation is found, the plan can be terminated and/or heavy penalties assessed. Penalties could even wipe out all money in the plan—a financial disaster. If you suspect your ERISA plan is not in compliance with the law, and don't want to risk the IRS finding out in an audit, you can come clean without worry. You can report and correct defects in a pension plan and pay only relatively small IRS compliance fees. (Rev. Proc. 92-89.)

TAKING CASH INSTEAD OF A RETIREMENT PLAN

A "cafeteria" or "flexible benefit" plan gives employees a choice between taking cash or selecting among fringe benefits, including retirement plans that are contributed to by the business. If the employee takes cash, it is fully taxed. Whatever the employee chooses, it is deductible for the business. Like most ERISA plans, a flexible benefit plan must be in writing and can't discriminate in favor of highly paid employees.

2. Types of Corporate Retirement Plans

ERISA covers several types of retirement savings plans. The most useful of these for small business are discussed in the following sections. Depending on the type of plan, contributions can be made by the business, the employee or both. The tax advantages of having an ERISA plan are:

- Contributions to an employee's retirement plan are tax-deductible expenses to the corporation, thus reducing its taxable income.

- Contributions to a retirement plan are made with "pre-tax dollars." This reduces a participant's taxable income while increasing the amount he or she can save in a plan.

- Money in retirement plans earns income without being taxed as long as it remains in the plan.

- Withdrawals from a corporate plan can begin as early as age 55, but can be delayed until up to age 70½. Withdrawals are taxed at the participant's then current tax bracket, which is likely to be lower than when she was working.

Participants in corporate retirement plans don't have to stay with the company until retirement age to get their benefits. Whether they leave voluntarily or not, they have a "vested" right to whatever they contributed to the plan the date they leave. They might not be entitled to money contributed by their employer, however, unless they have worked a minimum number of years, often around four or five. And of course, they will have to reach retirement age before the right to collect the benefits kicks in.

Corporate retirement plans are of two types, called defined-contribution and defined-benefit plans. (IRC §§ 414, 415.) Let's look at each one in more detail.

a. Defined-Contribution Plans

The defined-contribution plan (DCP) is the most popular type of corporate retirement plan, because it is usually funded by the employee, not the business. Here, part of an employee's pay is deducted and put into an investment account. The limit is 25% of compensation, if you adopt both a DCP money purchase and profit-sharing plans (discussed below). If the corporation chooses only a profit-sharing plan, the limit drops to 15%. With larger, multi-employee businesses, 5% to 8% is a typical contribution for an employee.

In most DCPs, the employer decides the contribution percentage for everyone. The corporation contributes a lump sum to the DCP, which allocates to each employee's account balance in proportion to his or her compensation. If you are the sole eligible employee, then go for as much as you can afford, all the way up to the 25% limit, giving you the maximum tax deduction bang for your buck.

Example: Sierra Corporation contributes $10,000 to its DCP. Margaret, the owner (sole shareholder and a corporate employee), has an annual salary of $50,000. Her two eligible employees, Jason and Felice, are paid $25,000 each. The contribution is thus allocated $5,000 to Margaret and $2,500 each to Jason and Felice.

DCP contributions can be allocated disproportionately to slightly favor owners over employees. This involves using the "permitted disparity" rules allowing an employee's Social Security benefits to be taken into account in calculating benefits. (IRC § 401(k).) This is technical stuff best left to a pension pro to calculate.

As with most retirement plans, the account balance in a DCP on retirement will depend on how much has been contributed and how fund investments have performed. No fixed lump sum or monthly payments are promised to a DCP participant, as with a defined benefit plan.

Example: Jobe contributes an average of $3,000 per year to Jobe, Inc.'s defined contribution plan for 30 years. The plan investments perform well, and it builds up to $350,000. Josephine puts the same amount into Josephine Inc.'s DCP, but her investments go sour and there is only $125,000 in it when she retires.

We've just described how a typical corporate DCP profit-sharing retirement savings plan works. Since the tax code limits profit-sharing plans to contributions of 15% of compensation, some companies add another type of DCP corporate pension plan, called a money purchase (MP) plan. When an MP plan is adopted alongside a profit-sharing (PS) plan, this allows a total contribution limit of 25%, up to $30,000 per year. This makes sense for mature, very cash-rich corporations, which can afford the maximum contributions every year. Unlike a PS plan, an MP plan creates a long-term obligation on the business, so it shouldn't be adopted without discussing the pros and cons with a pension expert.

b. Defined-Benefit Plan

The traditional corporate retirement plan is called a defined-benefit plan (DBP). It has lost out to the less expensive defined-contribution and 401(k) plans in all but the largest corporations, and so will only be briefly mentioned here. A DBP promises a specific monthly benefit for life on retirement. Or a lump sum can be taken with some DBPs, if the plan allows it and there is spousal consent.

With a DBP, each participant knows how much he or she will get every month. In general, the longer an employee is with the company, the larger the monthly benefit. Typically, a DBP is based on a percentage of the average of the highest three years of pay multiplied by the number of years of service with the company.

Example: Julian's corporation adopted a benefits percentage of 1.5% in its Defined Benefit Plan. Contributions were made over the life of the plan to assure that this amount would be paid. This was all figured out by an insurance company which administered the DCP and directed how much should be contributed to the plan every year to achieve its goal. Julian worked for the company 20 years, and in his three highest salary years, he earned an average of $100,000 per year. His benefit is computed as follows:

> 1.5% x 20   *(years of service) = 30%*
> x <u>$100,000</u>   *(highest average 3 years of pay)*
> = $30,000   *per year, or $2,500 per month*

While knowing how much you will get every month may be comforting, it is not necessary to have a DBP to get this security. Generally, you can achieve the same result by using a lump sum withdrawal from any type of retirement plan to purchase an annuity.

3. Corporate Plan Distributions

For a discussion of corporate plan distributions, please see Section H3 below.

F. Setting up and Administering Corporate Retirement Plans

A huge industry has sprung up over the last 20 years to help businesses set up and service benefit plans. If you are with me so far, you may have some inkling of just how complicated all of the rules are; this is definitely not amateur stuff. In addition to pension consultants, life insurance companies, banks and mutual funds all establish and administer retirement plans. They do the paperwork and make annual tax reports for you, so you don't have to learn more than the basics. Some institutions work with independent pension consultants, but most "bundle" these services. Unfortunately, this may leave you to your own devices and an 800 number. The typical outfit is more qualified in explaining its range of in-house investment products than fitting a retirement plan or plans to your needs.

G. IRS Problems With Retirement Plans

Most retirement plans are overseen by professional administrators, so there are rarely any IRS difficulties. When problems do arise, they usually are uncovered in IRS audits of the business, or its owners. Here are some things to watch out for.

1. Technical Violations

Since the IRS knows better than anyone how complex the retirement plan law is, audits are conducted by specially trained agents. Targets are selected from an IRS review of Forms 5500, which plan administrators must file annually.

A technical violation occurs when, for example, an eligible employee was not covered by the retirement plan, or an investment was made in a prohibited asset, like a sugar futures contract. Under the IRS's Voluntary Compliance program, a business can report any defects before the IRS initiates contact and hence avoid penalties. The IRS will respond by issuing a "compliance statement" showing what is necessary to fix things, such as putting the eligible employee in the plan or selling the improper investment.

2. Over-Funded Retirement Plans

Corporate plan investment accounts (defined-benefit plans only) sometimes become "too fat" under

ERISA rules. This means that the account balances are too high relative to projected pay-outs. Perhaps the plan investments produced a compounded return of 12%, where the projections only called for 9%. In this case, the company can't make any further contributions to the plan until things balance out. Complex IRS formulas determine when a plan is overfunded. Since most of you won't have a defined-benefit plan, I won't go into more details. If your company does have such a plan, you should be working with a pension professional, who will see that overfunding doesn't occur.

3. Excess Contributions

The most common problem with retirement plans is that excess contributions are inadvertently made. As discussed, there are strict percentage-of-compensation and absolute dollar limits on contributions for each year the plan is in effect. If contributions are made throughout the year for employees (as is often the case), they may not match up with the business' profits, which can't really be determined until the end of the year. If there is a contribution shortage, there is no problem (unless it is a defined-benefit plan). However, if there is an overage, the funds must be returned to the plan participants and, in turn, become taxable income to each individual. If excess contributions aren't removed from the plan and the IRS discovers it, stiff tax penalties are assessed against the retirement plan.

H. Taking Money out of Retirement Plans

This is the part we all wait for, the retirement plan payoff. Here is how it plays out, tax-wise. Money taken out of any retirement plan becomes taxable income (except in the case of loans, which are possible only from certain types of plans, as discussed

later in this section.) Withdrawals are taxed at your income tax bracket in the year you take out the money. Hopefully, when you retire, your income tax bracket will be lower than when you were working, which could mean a drop from as much as 39.6% to as low as 15%. But this really depends on your total financial circumstances at the time and any further tax law tinkering by Congress. If you don't meet all of the tax code rules at the time you pull money out of your retirement account, you will be subject not only to income tax on the withdrawals but to a special penalty tax as well.

There is a 20% IRS withholding tax on retirement plan withdrawals. This withholding tax can be avoided if you directly transfer or roll over the funds to another retirement savings plan. This doesn't necessarily mean that you owe 20% in taxes on the distribution. Depending on your other income, exemptions and deductions—you may owe nothing, or you may owe more than 20%. The withholding tax requirement thus works as an incentive for you to keep filing tax returns after retiring (sorry)—especially if you are due a tax refund.

Sometimes your pension account will consist of both taxable and nontaxable contributions. This would be the case if you had a nondeductible IRA or had both deductible and nondeductible contributions in the same account. (See Section C2, above.) Or you may have made contributions to your SEP that were over the deductibility limit but within the maximum overall limits. These "after-tax" contributions have already been taxed once, so you are just getting a return of your investment. But you do have to pay tax on the earnings that accumulated over the years. For instance, say you made deductible IRA contributions of $40,000 and nondeductible contributions of $15,000, and the IRA is worth $90,000 at your retirement. Only $75,000 would be taxable when you started taking distributions.

All this means you must be careful to identify distributions so that you don't pay tax on the same income twice. Unfortunately, the IRS doesn't make this process as easy as it might appear if, as most folks do, you take the distributions over a number of years instead of all at once. In this case, you must prorate each distribution payment between taxable and nontaxable each year, which will require additional account earnings to be prorated as well. IRS Publication 575, *Pension and Annuity Income*, gives a formula for doing this. Another alternative to this headache is to ask the IRS to do the calculation for you. There is a $50 fee for this service; IRS Publication 939, *Pension General Rule*, explains how to apply for it.

There are proposals before Congress to liberalize the rules on borrowing and withdrawing money from retirement funds. Stay tuned.

Don't get the idea that the withdrawal rules are any easier than the rest of the overly complicated tax law on retirement plans; they are not. The rules are different for just about every type of plan withdrawal. For example, some plans allow you to take a lump sum distribution on retirement and defer taxes on it for five or ten years, depending on the year you were born. It might pay to check with a tax or pension pro before taking any money out of a retirement plan.

1. IRA, SEP and Keogh Plan Withdrawals

There are five basic rules you should be aware of before taking any money out of your IRA, SEP or Keogh retirement plan:

a. Generally, if you take a distribution before turning age 59½, you will be liable for a premature withdrawal penalty of 10%. There are several exceptions to this rule:

- If you become permanently disabled at any age, there is no withdrawal penalty.

- You may make withdrawals without penalty if they are part of a series of withdrawals over at least five years, or until age 59½, whichever is longer. (However, there may be an early withdrawal penalty by the investment sponsor.)

- Loans may be taken from 401(k) and corporate plans (if the plans allow it) subject to tax code rules, but never from SEP, IRA or Keogh plans.

b. A withdrawal is reported on your next filed tax return, and is subject to income tax at your tax bracket rate. The balance in your account continues to accumulate tax-deferred.

c. You must start withdrawing money by age 70½ at the latest, or face a penalty tax similar to early withdrawals. The IRS publishes tables showing the minimum annual withdrawals required, which are based on your life expectancy.

d. You can "income average" withdrawals (spread the tax liability out over a period of five or ten years) with a lump sum withdrawal from a corporate plan, 401(k) or Keogh, but you can't do this with a SEP or IRA.

e. On your death, any funds still in your SEP, Keogh or IRA will go to your named beneficiary or to your estate. The plan will terminate unless your spouse is the beneficiary. In this case, the spouse may elect to allow the plan to remain active and accumulate earnings tax-deferred. Alternatively, the widow or widower can roll the plan into a new SEP or IRA and name younger family members as beneficiaries, stretching the tax deferral benefits even further.

2. 401(k) Plan Withdrawals

There are a number of ways of getting your money out of a 401(k) plan. To do so without being penalized, you must be:

a. Retired and at least 59½ years old, or

b. Have left the business and be at least 55 years old, or

c. Have died (meaning your heirs or named beneficiaries take it), or

d. Be disabled, or

e. Take a loan from the plan, if specifically allowed under the plan documents. You must provide collateral (which can be done by pledging the balance of your 401(k) account), and you may borrow not more than 50% of your plan balance, or $50,000, whichever is less. You must repay the loan, with interest, at commercial loan rates, generally within five years. Some folks borrow for children's college expenses or to buy a home. For home purchases or improvements, you may extend the repayment schedule for up to 30 years.

You may also take money out if you have a qualifying "hardship," but you will be charged a premature withdrawal penalty. For this reason, you are better off taking a loan, not a withdrawal. Hardship reasons include medical expenses, school tuition for a family member or buying a home. See Reg. 1.401(k)-1(d)(2) or check with a tax or pension pro before withdrawing for a hardship.

If your withdrawal doesn't meet the above rules, you will be assessed a penalty tax of 10% plus income tax at your tax bracket rate, reportable on your next filed tax return.

Example: Jocko takes a $10,000 withdrawal from his 401(k) which doesn't qualify under tax code rules. This will cost him $1,000, plus income tax at his tax bracket (which will range from 15% to 39.6%), meaning a total tax cost of $2,500 to $4,960.

3. Corporate Plan Withdrawals

Corporate plan distribution rules are more liberal than with other plans, in that you can start taking out money without penalty as early as age 55. Before that age, the 10% premature penalty tax kicks in.

Like all other retirement savings plans, you must start withdrawing funds by age 70^1/$_2$. There is an exception to this rule for those who continue to work past age 70^1/$_2$. These hearty folks can put off withdrawals as long as they don't own more than 5% of the stock of the corporation. A minimum amount must be withdrawn each year after attaining 70^1/$_2$, based on your life expectancy under IRS tables. The intent of the law is that you will have

cleaned out your account on the day you die—even though this is hardly likely for anyone except the Amazing Kreskin.

Example: Wally, who is retired, takes $210,000 out of his corporate plan in 1996 to help his son, Wally, Jr. go into business. Wally will be liable for a penalty tax of $8,250 (15% of $55,000), in addition to income tax on the $210,000 at his tax bracket rate. Wally would be better off splitting this withdrawal up, say by taking out $155,000 in 1996 and the balance after January 1, 1997.

Rolling over retirement plan funds. Generally, you don't have to leave your retirement funds in a corporate account when you leave a company and are eligible to start taking distributions. (Or, you can switch your account balance to a new employer's plan if you keep on working.) Many folks roll over (transfer) their retirement funds into an IRA. This allows you to keep accumulating earnings tax-deferred and to freely select and manage your investments, which you can't do in a corporate plan. However, be careful when rolling a pension plan into an IRA if some of your plan account balance was from nondeductible contributions. For instance, if your pension account has $120,000 in it, with $18,000 from your after-tax contributions, you can roll over only $102,000. If you don't pay attention and you transfer the whole amount, you will not only incur a penalty tax, but you will pay tax twice on the $18,000.

RESOURCES

IRS Publication 590, *Individual Retirement Arrangements* (SEPs & IRAs)

IRS Publication 560, *Retirement Plans for the Self-Employed*

Social Security, Medicare and Pensions, Joseph Matthews (Nolo Press). As the title indicates, this book covers the whole realm of retirement income, not just retirement plans, from a recipient's point of view.

Everyone's Money Book, Jordan E. Goodman and Sonny Bloch (Dearborn Financial Publishing). This encyclopedic book includes a worthwhile retirement plan chapter discussing some tax-wise options in taking money from different kinds of retirement plans.

How to Pay Zero Taxes, Jeff Schnepper (Addison-Wesley). Although the title overpromises, the book includes some innovative tax twists on using retirement plans.

Retirement Savings Plans, David A. Littell (John Wiley & Sons). This is a fairly technical book written for tax professionals. It contains a number of forms, examples and sample plans.

Gerald K. Shaver, E.A., California Benefit Services, 1259 16th Ave., San Francisco, CA 94122. Mr. Shaver is a very knowledgeable pension consultant and was instrumental in putting this chapter together. ■

Buying a Business

"The rule of my life is to make business a pleasure, and pleasure my business."

— Aaron Burr

Instead of starting from scratch, you can usually find someone with a business who wants to sell. Buying an established enterprise may be more costly—but less risky—than starting a new one.

There's a lot to be said for taking over a proven bussiness with an existing customer base and location.

No federal tax is due when you buy a business, but buyers do have tax concerns, including some you won't face if you start from the ground up. I am talking about:

- outstanding tax liabilities that you may acquire along with the business, and

- potential tax audits and bills for years before you took over the business.

This chapter covers the tax concerns in buying a business. The flip side, selling a business, is covered in Chapter 17. Take a look at both chapters, no matter which side of the fence you are on, to get a rounded tax picture.

Whether you want to acquire a service, retail, wholesale or manufacturing business, tax issues are remarkably similar. Once you understand them, you must ferret out any undisclosed problems. Since some tax problems may not be discoverable until it is too late, you'll need to take steps to protect yourself.

Get professional advice. Among things to worry about when buying an existing business: undisclosed debts, overstated earnings, poor employee relations, overvalued inventory and pending lawsuits, to name a few. Hidden liabilities can exist in all sorts of areas—from land contaminated with toxic chemicals, to accounts receivable that look solid but prove to be uncollectible, to inventory that's defective or dated. Apart from the tax considerations, check for these potential time bombs.

A business-savvy attorney should be on your team for all but the smallest business acquisitions. A lawyer can represent you or just act as your coach. She can act as an escrow agent or recommend a company to handle the exchange of money for the enterprise you're acquiring. Some attorneys are not as familiar with the tax aspects of business transfers as they should be, so it may wise to run the deal by a tax pro, too. (See Chapter 22, Help Beyond the Book.) And you should keep in mind, if a professional advisor screws up and misses something, they may be liable for any losses you suffer as a result of the bad advice.

If you are buying more than the value of a business's "hard" assets, consult with a business appraiser. It is preferable to find someone with experience in valuing businesses in the same industry.

BUYING A BUSINESS IN A NUTSHELL

1. You and the seller must assign a value to all business assets transferred and report it to the IRS.

2. You can write off goodwill and other intangible business assets you purchase, over 15 years.

3. Beware of outstanding tax liabilities; always check for tax liens, and require the seller to agree to indemnify you for any tax debts attaching to assets you're buying.

4. There is no federal tax on the purchase of a business, but states and localities may impose transfer taxes.

A. Buying the Assets of a Business

A business is simply a collection of assets. Someone who offers a business for sale is trying to sell all these assets together, from the IRS point of view. A buyer may not want all of a business's assets. You want to buy Sal's Pizza Parlor for its location, but you don't want to use Sal's business name or the old pizza ovens and furniture. If you make Sal a good enough offer, he may sell just the building to you and not the rest of the assets. However, the tax consequences of this arrangement may be different than if you had purchased all of the assets. How the business is legally structured—sole proprietorship, partnership, limited liability company or corporation—also has important tax consequences to both the buyer and seller.

1. Unincorporated Businesses

If you buy a partnership, limited liability company or sole proprietorship, you are just getting its *assets*—a store lease, inventory, customer list and so on. Normally, you don't take over business-related *liabilities*—including tax debts. Your contract should require the seller to pay all debts before closing or out of escrow. If not, then the business's debts remain the seller's personal responsibility after the transfer.

Tax debts. The IRS never releases the seller from unpaid taxes when a business is transferred. But you normally don't have to worry about the seller's tax debts *unless* the IRS or state taxing agency has filed a tax lien against the business or the owner. See Section B1 below for how to find out whether tax liens have been filed.

Example: Angelo, a sole proprietor, sells his profitable business, Korner Mart, to Luigi. Angelo has not filed or paid income taxes for the past three years. The IRS hasn't caught on to Angelo—yet. Luigi takes the business assets free of any tax liability of Angelo, who remains personally liable for taxes he should have paid on the business income before the sale.

You are not required to notify the IRS prior to purchasing or selling a business.

2. Corporations

The tax situation is more complex when you buy an incorporated business. Whether you buy corporate shares or its assets instead is a crucial choice, because:

- If you buy only a corporation's *assets*, you don't assume its liabilities, including taxes.

- If you buy a corporation's shares of *stock*, however, you end up with both its assets and liabilities—including known and unknown taxes. An example of an unknown tax debt would be one that resulted from an IRS audit that has not yet begun. The seller of the corporate shares is released from all corporate debts unless he personally guarantees them or agrees to be liable for them after the transfer.

Why should you ever consider buying a corporation's stock, given the potential for legal trouble? Because some owners will sell only if a buyer takes corporation stock. There are several

reasons why a seller may insist. One, as mentioned, is to rid himself of any potential tax liabilities, since the buyer assumes these along with the stock. But even a perfectly honest seller may have a tax reason for selling stock instead of assets. (See Chapter 17, Selling a Business or Its Assets.)

B. Buying Shares of Stock

If you buy the stock of a corporation, you implicitly take over any tax debts of the business—disclosed or not—along with its assets. For instance, a potentially devastating tax problem can be inherited from a corporation that misclassified its employees as independent contractors and so did not file payroll tax returns.

Example: Renate buys all of the stock of XTC corporation. Unbeknownst to Renate, XTC's employment tax returns were not filed or taxes paid for a period three years ago. But when she bought the stock, no tax liens had been filed. When the IRS catches on, the corporation will be held liable for the taxes—whether Renate knew about them or not. She may have a claim against the seller for not disclosing the tax delinquency, but this is no concern of the IRS.

Generally, business sale contracts include a guarantee from the sellers that the enterprise doesn't owe taxes, and that the sellers will be liable to the buyer if this turns out not to be true. (And if past employment taxes aren't paid, the IRS may go after the former owners, too. See Chapter 5, Tax Concerns of Employers.)

If you buy corporate shares (perhaps the seller adjusts the price, or installment terms, so it's hard to resist), protect yourself against hidden tax liabilities. But even with the best investigation of a business and its owners, it's impossible to predict whether or not tax problems will crop up. For example, no one knows whether the IRS (or any state taxing agency) will audit tax returns the corporation filed for several years before you bought its shares.

PART 5

Buying or Selling a Business

1. Investigation

Get a business attorney or tax pro to help you check out a seller's tax situation before purchasing stock. Require copies of all business income and employment tax returns of the business for the last three years. Demand proof from a seller that taxes have been paid. Copies of filed tax forms along with cancelled checks should be forthcoming.

Your expert should look for unreported income, unfiled tax returns and unpaid taxes, as well as anything that doesn't jibe with what corporation records should show. If a red (or at least a pink) flag is raised, probe further. What to look for depends on the type of business or owner you are investigating. For instance, if independent contractors are used in the business, check to see whether IRS reporting rules were met. (See Chapter 5, Tax Concerns of Employers.) If a business's tax returns look strange to a tax pro, ask why. If items catch your attention, they might interest an IRS auditor as well.

Your stock purchase agreement should provide for an inspection of the business books, and the right to back out if irregularities are found. Require the selling shareholder(s) to furnish a current credit report; be suspicious if he or she won't. Tax liens against the shareholders will show up on their personal credit reports; tax liens against their corporation, however, will not.

Put seller disclosure requirements in your purchase contract. It's too late after the agreement is signed. Use a clause something like this one: "Seller agrees to furnish copies of all business income and employment tax returns for the past three years within ten days of acceptance of this offer. Seller will give full access to all business records to buyer or his representative, for the purposes of verifying that there are no present or potential tax liabilities. Seller will provide a copy of a current credit report on all of the majority shareholders of the corporation."

IRS Information. Sellers are not always honest about business income and expenses; they sometimes dummy up tax returns. Without obtaining confirmation from the IRS, you can't be sure that the returns or business schedules in returns the seller shows you were the ones actually filed. So, provide in your purchase agreement that the seller will give you a signed IRS Disclosure (Form 2848D) for the individual shareholders and the business. This allows you, or your attorney or tax pro, to get access to their IRS tax records. Allow several weeks for the IRS to send this information. These computer printouts are furnished without charge and show a business owner's (or corporation's) tax filing and payment history, and if any taxes are owing. Pay particular attention to whether employment tax returns were filed, and compare the disclosures the seller provided against the IRS records.

These printouts are in IRS code and sometimes are difficult to decipher. Enlist the help of an experienced tax pro to help you. Or, call the IRS and ask them to explain the code references to you.

Public Records. Your county records office has books or computer files showing any recorded federal and state tax liens against a business or its owners. If taxes are owed, the IRS may have recorded a "Notice of Federal Tax Lien" under the name and tax ID number (either the Social Security or employer identification number) of the business or its owners. The IRS doesn't always file lien notices on tax debtors, but it is always worth checking.

Look up the names of the owners and also the business's name in your local public records office, often called the County Recorder's Office or Land Registry Office. In many counties you can now search records by computer; other offices still use microfiche readers or handwritten record books. Ask a clerk for help, or hire a credit bureau, title company or attorney to search the records for you.

Example: Harold wants to know if Alco Motors, Inc., a business he is considering buying, has any past tax liabilities. He goes to the county records office and searches the name index for "Alco Motors, Inc." He looks back ten years, because this is how long a tax lien is normally valid. No liens appear. This is a positive sign, but not a guarantee that Alco Motors has no past federal tax liabilities. It only demonstrates that none appear on the records.

State Records. Check corporations for liens with your state's Secretary of State or Department of Corporations (the official titles may vary from state to state). As with searching local records, you can do it yourself or pay someone to do it, as mentioned above.

Send Form UCC-3 to your Secretary of State's office. ("UCC" means Uniform Commercial Code, a set of laws that has been adopted in most states.) Forms are usually available from your Secretary of State's office or from stationery stores, reference libraries, business attorneys or accountants. For a small fee you will receive a UCC filing report showing state tax liens, judgment liens and financing liens on business equipment. States do not always file tax liens with the IRS, so not finding one doesn't guarantee that taxes aren't owing.

2. Indemnification

In the purchase agreement, the seller of stock should promise to pay any taxes and other corporation liabilities discovered after the closing. While this "indemnification clause" obligates the seller to pay any hidden tax liabilities, you are still not out of the tax woods. If the seller disappears or can't pay, the pledge will be worthless and the corporation will be stuck with any tax liabilities.

3. Holdbacks and Offsets

Your best protection from unknown tax liabilities when buying stock is to require the seller to put part of what you pay (perhaps 5% to 30%) in an account with an escrow company, attorney or bank after closing. This "holdback" money is used to pay any corporate liabilities, including taxes discovered after the sale. The longer money is held back for

contingencies, the better—but many sellers won't agree to holdbacks for longer than a few months. Many sellers will go along with your request as long as the holdback account pays interest to them.

If you aren't paying for the stock in full (you pay some cash up front and sign an installment note for the balance) when you take over, include an "offset" provision in your agreement. This will let you offset future payments on the note against any undisclosed taxes or other debts discovered after closing.

C. Assigning a Price to Business Assets

As you negotiate the purchase of a business or its assets, you will be evaluating each of the major assets. That's good, because the tax code requires you and the seller to jointly agree on allocations of the purchase price to each asset or group of assets. These amounts allocated must be at the "fair market value" and be reported to the IRS by each side.

You will also use these values to calculate your depreciation deduction for each asset, and to figure the taxable gain or loss when you sell or dispose of it.

It is not always easy to precisely value business assets; you may need to bring in a professional

PART 5

Buying or Selling a Business

appraiser for real estate or other assets. There is usually room for flexibility in valuing assets. The overall price paid for a business or its assets usually reflects how eager the parties are to make a deal, not how much each item is really worth. These allocations have tax significance to both parties—but especially to a buyer.

Example: Tony buys Ace Tool & Die from Jim for $95,000. After hiring a business appraisal expert to determine the fair market value of the assets, they agree to allocate the purchase price as follows: $65,000 for machinery, $10,000 for goodwill and $20,000 for a patent right. This is reported to the IRS by both parties when they file their tax returns. In the event either Tony or Jim is audited, they can produce a report from the appraiser backing up their allocations.

Back up major asset valuations with appraisals. Professional appraisals, though not strictly required by the IRS, are a good idea—especially if the price of the business purchased is over $100,000. If you are ever audited, the IRS may question the asset valuations and allocations. If the numbers are not supportable as being in line with fair market values, the IRS can refigure them. This usually results in your having to take longer depreciation periods assigned to the assets, which decreases your annual depreciation deductions. You will no doubt get an audit bill for the IRS's efforts.

The allocation of the purchase price is reported to the IRS on Form 8594, Asset Acquisition Statement. Both buyer and seller file this form with their individual income tax returns for the year of the sale.

The IRS allocation process has two parts. First, you must classify the assets into three categories, discussed below. Then you must assign dollar values to each category according to tax code rules.

1. Classifying Assets for the IRS

The cost allocation rules create three distinct categories of business assets. (IRC § 1060(a).) Both buyer and seller must put each asset transferred into one of three categories:

- Cash and cash-like assets
- Tangible property, and
- Intangible property.

If you don't quite understand what this means—which is probably the case—don't worry, and read on.

a. Cash and Cash-Like Assets

Cash and cash-like assets include:
- Money, such as petty cash on hand (if any)
- Bank and money market accounts (usually the seller cleans these accounts out)
- Notes and accounts receivable (money owed the business when it's sold, which are taken over by the new owner). These may be subject to a discounted value if their collectibility is in doubt. Often, buyers do not take over a business's accounts receivable; and
- Marketable securities (stocks of other companies that are readily salable), which is rarely the case in business transfers).

This is the easiest category as valuations are usually obvious, with the possible exception of notes and accounts receivable.

b. Tangible Property

Generally, "tangible" means anything you can touch. When it is applied to business assets, this category includes:
- *Merchandise inventories.* You'll need to determine whether all the goods are salable. If some are out-of-date, the value may be lowered (discounted) or the goods listed at no value.

- *Land and leaseholds, buildings.* Get the written opinion of a real estate agent or appraiser as to the value of land, leases and buildings.
- *Machinery.* For expensive equipment, get a written appraisal or estimate by a dealer in this type of machinery.
- *Office furniture and fixtures.* This includes computers and other electronic gear. Unless the items have trivial value, get written estimates from a used computer or furniture dealer or professional appraiser.

c. Intangible Property

In general, an "intangible" asset can't be touched or physically possessed. It is usually a *right* to something, which is recognized in a document. Typical examples: patents, copyrights, trademarks, client or customer lists, trade secrets and covenants not to compete (promises from the seller that he won't go into a similar business for some time in the future). The most common intangible asset is "goodwill" (defined and explained below).

Intangible assets are difficult to value. Significant intangibles should be valued by accountants or other experts. But even among experts, opinions of value may vary widely.

The tax code allows a buyer to tax deduct the cost of any intangibles over a period of 15 years. So the price of goodwill, along with customer lists and covenants not to compete, can be written off (amortized) at the rate of 1/15 per year. (IRC § 197.) Accelerated depreciation is not allowed for intangible property.

WHAT IS GOODWILL?

Goodwill comprises the reputation and customer relationships of an existing business. If the price you pay for a going concern exceeds the fair market value of all the rest of the assets of the business, the IRS considers the excess the price of the goodwill.

Example: Sam pays $100,000 for Honest John's Network Communications Emporium. The cash and tangible assets of the business add up to $69,000: $1,000 in the cash drawer, $15,000 in inventory on hand, $3,000 worth of machinery and a building worth $50,000. Why is Sam willing to pay $31,000 above the value of all of its identifiable assets? Because Honest John's has a good location and has made a decent profit for several years, and Sam thinks that a lot of John's customers will stick with the business. He pays this premium for the business's goodwill.

---

2. Assigning Dollar Values

After you and the seller have divided assets into the three categories, you must jointly assign specific dollar values to each group. Keep in mind that these valuations will be used to figure your tax basis for depreciation—how much tax write-off you get—and to determine your gain or loss when you later dispose of these assets. (See Chapter 2, Writing Off Long-Term Business Assets, for details.) If you haven't already done so, this is a good time to bring in a tax pro.

You and the seller must go through a four-step allocation process in order to correctly fill out IRS Form 8594, Asset Acquisition Statement:

1. Subtract the total value of *cash and cash-like* items received (category one, above) from the purchase price.

2. Subtract the fair market values of the *tangible* assets you're buying.

PART 5

Buying or Selling a Business

3. Allocate any amount of the purchase price remaining to *specifically identifiable intangibles* such as patents, franchises, agreements not to compete and trademarks, at their fair market values.

4. If there's any amount still not allocated, label it *goodwill,* the final kind of intangible asset.

Example: Gunter, a sole proprietor, owns a geothermal energy consulting firm. Kinte agrees to buy his business for $100,000. They make the following asset allocations:

$1,000 in the business's bank account at the time of the transfer is allocated to cash.

$14,500, the fair market value of office equipment included in the deal, goes in the second category, tangible assets.

$42,000 is assigned to a patent on a small geothermal measurement instrument, which has been appraised at this figure, and is ascribed to the third category, specifically identifiable intangible assets.

$42,500, the remaining sum not accounted for, is attributed to the only category left, goodwill.

Making favorable asset allocations. A buyer and seller should agree on the allocation of purchase price of assets as part of negotiating the agreement to purchase the business. Because there is almost always flexibility in valuing assets, the buyer should propose the allocation of purchase price in a way that provides the most tax benefit. A tax pro can help you make the analysis.

Typically, you'll want to allocate as much of the purchase price of an established business as possible to assets with the fastest tax write-offs—that is, those with the shortest depreciation periods. If it's at all realistic, attribute the lion's share of the price to business equipment. Usually equipment and fixtures can be depreciated over three, five, seven or ten years.

Conversely, assign smaller values to intangible assets, because they have a long tax write-off period, 15 years. Commercial real estate, with a depreciation period of 39 years, also means a long time to write off your costs.

If the business has been a loser, you are likely buying its tangible assets only; there won't be any goodwill or an intangible asset allocation to worry about. (See Chapter 2, Writing Off Long-Term Business Assets.)

D. State and Local Taxes

The state, county or city where the business or its assets are located may impose a transfer tax on either the buyer or the seller. This is common whenever real estate changes owners. If the tax is on the seller, then your agreement should provide that it be paid out of escrow at closing. Be aware that if the seller doesn't pay, the taxing agency can usually come after you or the business assets.

Also, some states or localities impose taxes, such as annual personal property taxes, on business fixtures and equipment or on the business's inventory. Make sure that these types of taxes are not delinquent, or are paid at the time of closing; if they are not, you may inherit them.

RESOURCES

IRS Form 8594, *Asset Acquisition Statement and Instructions.* The instructions provide more details than are given here.

The Legal Guide for Starting and Running a Small Business, by Fred Steingold (Nolo Press). This self-help book has a lot of non-tax pointers on buying a business.

Tax Guide for Buying and Selling a Business, by Stanley Hagendorf & Wayne A. Hagendorf (Knowles Publishing, 800-299-0202). This is a fairly sophisticated manual intended for tax professionals. ∎

CHAPTER 17

Selling a Sole Proprietorship Business

"The business of America is business."
— **Calvin Coolidge**

This chapter focuses on the consequences of selling the assets of a sole proprietorship business. The flip side, buying a business, is covered in Chapter 16. If you haven't already, take a look at that chapter as well, to get a rounded tax picture, since 85% of all businesses are sole proprietorships. However, if you are not a solo, go to these other chapters:

- The tax aspects of transferring a partnership (or limited liability company interest) are covered in Chapter 9, Partnerships.
- Selling a corporation's shares is covered in Chapter 8, S Corporations, and Chapter 7, C Corporations.

Congress, realizing that there are opportunities for people to play tax games on business transfers, has enacted laws to ensure that Uncle Sam gets his cut. An IRS auditor who later smells a rat can spring a nasty tax trap.

PART **5**

Buying or Selling a Business

To pass IRS muster, the sale of a business must be bona fide—that is, the price and terms must be realistic in the business world. If you sell to a stranger, chances are the deal is fair and the IRS won't bother you as long as you report it and pay any taxes due. But if you deal with a relative, an IRS auditor may find the sale wasn't made on realistic terms and hit you with a tax bill.

SELLING A BUSINESS IN A NUTSHELL

1. Selling a business or its assets is a taxable event, meaning that it usually produces a gain or loss to the seller.

2. Tax rules for gains or losses on sales of a business interest depend on the form of the business—sole proprietorship, partnership, limited liability company, or S or C corporation.

3. A business is a collection of assets. The IRS requires the buyer and seller to allocate the purchase price to specific assets.

4. Transfers of businesses between related parties are suspect by the IRS.

A. Selling Assets of a Sole Proprietorship

From the IRS's point of view, a business is just a collection of assets from equipment and inventory to goodwill and patent rights. If you sell your business the tax code requires that you and the buyer assign a specific value to each asset and report this to the IRS. Whenever you sell a business asset, you might have a taxable gain on the sale, and Uncle Sam wants his share of your gain. On the other hand, if you have a loss from the sale, the result may produce a tax savings for you. (The process and rules for allocating the purchase price of a business to specific assets are covered in Chapter 16, Buying a Business.)

Example: Harry sells his business, Bagel World, to Sally for $45,000. They agree that the kitchen equipment and ovens are worth $30,000, the furniture $2,000, computers and cash registers $3,000, the store lease $9,000, and the goodwill of the business $1,000. Harry's taxable gain or loss must be figured on each of these items.

You must report the sale of your business by attaching Form 8594, Asset Acquisition Statement, to your personal income tax return. While there is no way of knowing whether or not the IRS will ever review the sale, filing Form 8594 does increase your audit chances. Be prepared for a later visit from the IRS, just in case.

1. Figuring Gain or Loss

Whenever a sole proprietorship business is sold, each asset transferred must be analyzed separately for tax consequences.

Example 1: Don, who owns Don's Trucking, sells a diesel engine rebuilding machine to Bruce for $15,000. Don paid $30,000 for it and had taken depreciation deductions totaling $20,000 in past years. These deductions reduced Don's tax basis in the machinery to $10,000. (See Chapter 2, Writing Off Long-Term Business Assets, for an explanation of how basis is determined.) Since Don sells the machine for $5,000 more than his tax basis, he has a taxable gain of $5,000— even though he sold it for less than he originally paid for it.

Example 2: Now assume Don's machinery is in bad shape and he gets only $8,000 from Bruce—$2,000 less than his tax basis. Don has a loss of $2,000 for tax purposes.

Example 3: Don's machinery became worthless due to technological advances, continuing malfunctions and the unavailability of parts. Don's tax basis is $10,000 when he sells the machinery to Guiseppe, a scrap metal dealer, for $1, so Don has a tax loss of $9,999. Don could instead junk the equipment himself and take a $10,000 tax write-off, but a documented sale is a better way to show the IRS how the equipment was disposed of.

2. How Gain or Loss Is Taxed

When a sole proprietor sells or exchanges business assets, the resulting gain or loss is usually treated like ordinary income or loss like any other operating business profit or loss. The tax code's special capital gain and loss rules don't apply when the operating assets of a business are sold. Any gain is taxed at your personal tax rate and, in general, any loss reduces your total income for tax purposes.

Save taxes by using an installment sale. If you are facing a large taxable gain on the sale of your business that would otherwise hit you all in one year, consider selling on the installment plan. For example, if you sell it with 20% down and the balance over five years (with interest, of course), you will pay tax on the gain spread out over five years. This is a way to, in effect, "income average." You will likely be in a lower tax bracket for each year by doing it this way. Of course, there is the risk that extending credit to the buyer increases your chances of not getting paid. See IRC § 453 for other rules on installment sales, or see a tax pro for analysis before agreeing to an installment sale.

B. The Importance of an Arms-Length Deal

If a business or its assets change hands for an artificially low price, the IRS loses out. But it sometimes can be difficult to show the true sales price to the IRS, because business transfers may involve exchanges, complex promissory notes and unusual terms dreamt up by attorneys and accountants. Even if the sale price looks fair, the terms may not be commercially reasonable, which is the tax law's requisite. For instance, a business sold for no money down, with the purchase price payable over 50 years at an interest rate of 3%, is not a deal any seller would make without an ulterior motive—most likely, tax avoidance. And such deals often mean a relative is the buyer.

The IRS is empowered to look past the stated terms of the deal and rewrite it to reflect its true "economic substance," to produce more tax revenue.

If you make an "arms-length" deal with an unrelated party, the IRS normally accepts the price as fair. After all, why would you help a stranger? If, however, you sell your business to a family member, or a concern owned partly by one, at a low price, you could face an IRS audit. While the IRS doesn't routinely monitor sales of businesses, if an auditor questions a sale, it's up to you to show you made a bona fide business transaction. The IRS can disregard your figures and terms if the auditor is not convinced, and if it would result in an increased tax bill.

Example: Bill, a sole proprietor nearing 70 and in poor health, sells his highly successful coffee shop chain, Moonbucks, to his son Junior for $100,000. This sales price equals Bill's basis in the business assets of Moonbucks, but doesn't include any value for the tremendous amount of goodwill the business has built up. Any other buyer would be glad to pay $1 million for

Moonbucks. So by selling to Junior at the bargain price, Bill is avoiding income taxes. If Bill were audited, the IRS would most likely assess Bill taxes on an additional $900,000 of income, because this was not an arms-length deal.

THE ESTATE TAX ANGLE

Income taxes aren't the IRS's only concern when family members are involved. The IRS is also looking ahead to collecting federal estate taxes someday. As discussed in Chapter 12, Family Businesses, everyone may leave a $600,000 estate tax-free, but anything over that is taxed starting at 37% and going as high as 55%. To avoid estate tax, older business owners often sell property to relatives for bargain prices, or on special terms.

Example: After he sells Moonbucks (truly valued at $1 million) to his son for $100,000, Bill's estate is valued at $500,000—well within the amount that can be passed at his death tax-free. However, if Bill owned Moonbucks at his death, his estate would be worth $1,400,000, and federal estate tax would be over $300,000. So, besides beating the income tax by selling Moonbucks to Bill Junior for $100,000, his estate escapes tax as well. (See Chapter 12, Family Businesses, for some tax advantageous but legal ways to minimize estate taxes when transferring businesses to family members.)

C. How to Protect Yourself From IRS Challenges

There is no way to "IRS-proof" the sale of your enterprise, but you can do several things to reduce the odds of an IRS attack.

1. Set a Reasonable Price and Terms

Unless a relative is involved, you will be selling your business for the best deal you can make, so your price and terms will be realistic. Except in small deals, have your business assets evaluated by someone experienced in the field. There are many business valuation specialists, including accountants and business brokers. A seller of new or used equipment or a dealer in the same type of merchandise as you are offering can evaluate your assets or make offers for them. Keep the written opinion or offer of one or more of these experts in case the IRS auditor comes calling.

If you are making a special deal to family or friends, you can take some legitimate steps that will save you a bundle in taxes. This involves transferring your business over several years instead of all at once. This tax planning opportunity (or loophole if you like) is called the "minority interest" discount. It works likes this: Whenever you sell less than all of your business—for instance, a one-third interest to your brother-in-law—you may discount the value of the minority interest in the business for tax purposes. The larger the discount, the less taxable profit results to you from the sale. Reductions of 40% off the value of a minority interest in a business have been upheld in the courts against IRS attacks. (See Chapter 12, Family Businesses, and run this by a tax pro before trying it.)

2. Observe the Formalities

From a tax standpoint, selling an enterprise doesn't require any special formalities. The terms of the sale can be written on the back of a napkin, for all the IRS cares. Keep in mind that the IRS's only interest is whether it is losing any taxes that should have been paid as a result of the transaction.

Just the same, the more "legal" a deal appears to be, the less likely the IRS is to challenge its tax implications at an audit. I'm not saying that you can make anything fly with a lot of legal boilerplate and neat typing, but you are ahead of the game if you can show you follow normal business formalities.

IRS auditors are fairly unsophisticated about business, but some develop a keen sense of when something isn't quite right. Using an attorney to handle the sale and producing a raft of supporting documents lends an air of legitimacy to the deal. For all but the smallest deals, have a business attorney do the paperwork. If the sale is big enough, a tax pro should be consulted as well.

3. Allocate Asset Values Fairly

When a business—or substantially all of its assets—is sold, both the buyer and seller must assign values in writing to assets being transferred. A report is then made on Form 8594 and with the IRS (along with the parties' individual tax returns). (See Chapter 16, Section C, for details on allocating values to business assets.) Usually the IRS accepts the valuations, but an auditor may question whether the overall price is fair and if the parties are related.

You and the buyer must attach an identical Form 8594, Asset Acquisition Statement, to your tax returns. If the forms aren't identical, an IRS computer cross-check might discover the discrepancy, and lead to an audit of either the buyer or the seller or both.

4. Keep Your Records After the Sale

Good records will help you sell your enterprise, but don't turn them over to the buyer along with the business. If you are required to show your business records to the buyer under the sale contract, give copies but don't release originals. You remain responsible for an IRS audit bill for the period up until the business was sold, and will need these records. Normally you have three tax years after the year the business is sold to worry about an audit, but to be on the safe side, keep the records six years. (See Chapter 19, Audits.)

RESOURCES

IRS Publication 544, *Sales & Other Dispositions of Assets.*

IRS Form 8594, Asset Acquisition Statement and Instructions. The instructions provide more details than are given here.

The Legal Guide for Starting and Running a Small Business, by Fred Steingold (Nolo Press). This self-help book has a lot of non-tax pointers for sellers of a business.

Tax Guide for Buying and Selling a Business, by Stanley Hagendorf & Wayne A. Hagendorf (Knowles Publishing, 800-299-0202). This is a fairly sophisticated manual intended for tax professionals. ■

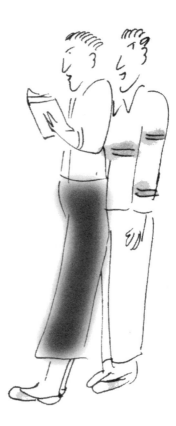

PART 5

Buying or Selling a Business

CHAPTER 18

When You Can't Pay Your Taxes

PART 6

Dealing With the IRS

"Creditors have better memories than debtors."

— Benjamin Franklin

The IRS has enormous legal powers to collect past due taxes—they are tougher than any other bill collector you're ever likely to face, with the possible exception of the Mafia. The IRS can seize just about anything that you own, including your bank account, home and wages, to satisfy a tax debt. It doesn't need a court order or judgment before closing your business and grabbing your property. In most cases, the IRS only has to send you a "demand letter" before it acts—and in some circumstances, it doesn't have to give you any warning at all. The IRS can close your business down by seizing your assets or even padlocking your doors.

As awesome as the IRS collection machine is, it won't crush you if you know how it works and your legal options. For instance, you can bargain for more time to pay or for a reduction of the amount owed. If your financial situation is truly dire, you may be put "on hold" while the IRS bothers other poor souls.

If you're behind on taxes and want to stay in business, keep in touch with the IRS. A business is a sitting target; it can't run. The worst thing you can do when you get behind in your taxes is to bury your head in the sand. The IRS might leave you alone for a while, but usually not for long enough.

Father Time is especially cruel to tax debts—they grow larger every day with the addition of interest and penalties. Unless you are out of business, flat broke, unemployed and likely to remain that way, IRS tax collectors will hound you relentlessly.

On the plus side, the IRS collection machine is slow to start and react, which gives you time to negotiate or plan your next move. You'll get a raft of computerized tax bills and maybe telephone calls. It

might be several years before you have to confront the IRS face-to-face. It's not that the IRS doesn't care; it's just that with limited personnel they try everything else before assigning a real person to your case. Don't get too comfortable, though, just because no one knocks on your door. Every year the computerized IRS collection system gets bigger, faster and meaner. Computer-generated tax liens and levies can make your life every bit as miserable as human collectors can.

IRS COLLECTIONS IN A NUTSHELL

1. The IRS has legal powers that no other debt collector has; it can seize bank accounts and just about anything else that you own, sometimes without warning.

2. You don't have to disclose financial information to an IRS collector unless you are formally served with a summons.

3. The IRS can, but rarely does, shut businesses down. In these cases, it is usually for unpaid payroll taxes.

4. Business owners are usually allowed to pay off old tax bills in monthly installments, but interest—and maybe penalties too—is always running.

5. Some folks can make a deal with the IRS to settle a tax bill for pennies on the dollar through the Offer in Compromise process.

6. If you file for bankruptcy, you may be able to hold off the IRS and wipe out some tax debts.

A. If You Owe Less Than $10,000

If you owe less than $10,000, chances are your account is a fairly low IRS priority. It may be a lot of money to you, but it's small potatoes to the IRS. Typically, the IRS won't assign a case to a collector if the balance due is less than $10,000—but will hound you by mail and telephone.

If you owe business payroll taxes, however, there is no minimum threshold to vigorous collection efforts. (Chapter 5, Tax Concerns of Employers, explains how the IRS pursues business owners who fall behind on payroll taxes.)

B. Getting More Time to Pay

Generally, if you can't pay a tax bill you have received, call or write the IRS at the number or address on the bill and request more time. A request for a 30- to 60-day delay is usually honored if you haven't called more than once or twice before. If asked, explain why you need the extra time—for example, because you are applying for a loan or looking for a new job.

Request more time to pay even if you won't be able to meet the new deadline. It is easier to get several short extensions—a month or two—than one long one. This is the way the IRS operates, presumably to keep the pressure on you.

If you are granted a reprieve by phone, chances are you won't receive anything in writing from the IRS to confirm your deal. A new due date will be entered into the computer, but don't expect a reminder from the IRS when the time is up. Note the new deadline on your calendar; then contact the IRS before it is up if you still need more time.

C. Paying in Installments

Another way to get more time is to ask the IRS for an installment payment agreement. If it's granted, you pay the IRS monthly, like a credit card balance. And, as with your VISA or MasterCard, an interest charge is added. The IRS also imposes a $43 "user fee" for setting up an installment plan. A monthly payment plan relieves you of the worry that the IRS will seize your wages or assets—as long as you make payments.

You have no legal right to pay overdue taxes in installments, but the IRS usually agrees to monthly payments. The hitch is that you must show you can't pay your bill in full from your present resources. Indeed, the *Taxpayer Bill of Rights* (IRS Publication One) says that you have the right to *propose* an installment agreement, and that the IRS must fairly consider it.

To request to pay in installments, call or write to the IRS. If writing, send a copy of the tax bill or, even better, file IRS Form 9465, Request for Installment Payments. If you have already been in contact with a name at the IRS, direct your request directly to her. If the IRS agrees, you'll get written confirmation and monthly payment vouchers. For more information, see *Stand Up to the IRS*, by Frederick W. Daily (Nolo Press).

TIME LIMIT ON IRS TO COLLECT TAX DEBTS

There is some justice, even in the tax world. The law limits the IRS to ten years from the date a tax is assessed to collect it. (IRC § 6402(a).) After that, you are home free! However, taking certain actions—filing for bankruptcy, making an Offer in Compromise or signing an IRS waiver form—can extend the time to collect beyond ten years. Nevertheless, since a business failure or other catastrophe can put you into a very deep tax hole, it is comforting to know that there is some light at the end of the tunnel.

1. Interest and Penalties

There is no free lunch with the IRS. A major downside to paying the IRS on the installment plan is that interest and late-payment penalties keep adding up. Currently, interest and penalties run at a combined rate of 15% total per year. If your install-ment payments are low and the unpaid balance chunky, you may find the total amount you owe the IRS is increasing every month while you are making payments.

Example: Brenda is audited and is found to owe the IRS $40,000 for back payroll taxes from her failed graphic design studio. The IRS determines Brenda can pay a maximum of $400 per month. She is also charged 15% interest and penalties, adding $5,600 per year to her bill. One year later, after paying $400 per month, Brenda owes $40,800, which is $800 more than her original bill! (Brenda has some other alternatives in dealing with the IRS, discussed below.)

2. Under $10,000 Payment Plans

If you owe less than $10,000 and send in Form 9465, chances are that you will get an installment payment plan. Generally, your proposed payments must be sufficient to pay the bill in full within 36 months. Monthly payments must be equal. Interest, currently 9%, and late payment penalties of 1/2% per month, will be running. You can make larger payments than called for in the plan.

The IRS is tougher on payroll taxes. If you owe back payroll taxes—even if it's less than $10,000—the IRS may not allow you to use the IRS Form 9465 procedure. It may require detailed financial infor-mation and faster payoffs.

3. Over $10,000 Payment Plans

If you owe over $10,000, your monthly payment amount is whatever the IRS perceives as your "maximum ability" to pay. This is determined by the IRS's evaluation of the financial information on

its "collection information statements" of what you have told them. (These forms are discussed in Sec-tion D, below.)

The IRS rarely accepts less than $50 per month, and I have seen payment plans requiring $5,000 per month—it all depends on your financial cir-cumstances. The IRS welcomes any payments over the agreed-upon amount. Prepaying cuts down the interest and penalty charges that always continue to run during the installment plan.

If the IRS asks for more in monthly payments than you can afford—as is frequently the case—you can always attempt to negotiate a lower amount. How successful you are may depend on your pow-ers of persuasion.

Make sure your requests get to the right IRS department. When writing about a bill, always send the IRS a copy of the notice, using the bar-coded IRS return envelope that came with it. This ensures that your request for more time or an installment agreement gets to the right department in time to keep things from getting out of hand.

4. If You Fall Behind on Your Payments

If you get into an installment plan, make the pay-ments faithfully each month. If you don't, the IRS can void the agreement and start seizing your bank accounts and other property without further notice.

If you flat can't make a payment, call and write the IRS and explain your circumstances. Ask that the agreement not be defaulted. If it is reinstated, you may be charged an additional fee of $24 for this privilege. Promise to catch up in the next month or request that the monthly amount be low-ered because of an unexpected reversal of fortune. The IRS may be sympathetic and go along with you as long as you stay in touch.

D. What to Expect When the IRS Gets Serious

To protect yourself if you get behind on taxes, you should know how the IRS is likely to proceed. A raft of threatening past due notices and a year or more may pass before the IRS gets real serious. If you owe more than $10,000 in income taxes, or payroll taxes in any amount, you may be called or visited by an IRS Revenue Officer—the elite collectors of the IRS who are both feared and respected for their powers.

1. The Sneak Attack

Revenue Officers usually show up at your business or home unannounced, often before 9 or after 5. The collector will start asking questions right then and there. She may want to talk to your employees if the business's payroll tax returns filings and payments are an issue.

Keep calm and resist the urge to curse your luck or the IRS. Instead of talking to the IRS Officer on the spot, tell her that you need time to get financial information together. Emphasize that you want to deal with your tax problems and will meet her at the IRS office in a week or two. Most Revenue Officers will go along if you seem sincere. Avoid making any financial commitments to pay at this time.

2. Meeting With the Collector

At the interview, the IRS will ask for information about your business and personal finances. This data is usually recorded on IRS Collection Information Statement forms. Form 433-A is used for your personal finances, and Form 433-B for your business's assets, liabilities, income and expenses. After these forms are filled in, you will be asked to read, verify and sign them.

It is a good idea to know what information the IRS wants before the meeting with the Revenue Officer. You can obtain copies of Forms 433-A and 433-B from IRS offices or by calling 800-829-1040. They are also reprinted in *Stand Up to the IRS*, by Frederick W. Daily (Nolo Press).

Don't be rushed into signing a 433 form. Data on these forms is the *key* to further IRS collection efforts, so the importance of accurate information on them can't be overemphasized. If you make a misstatement on these forms—intentional or not—you'll lose vital credibility with the tax collector. Keep in mind that she has a great deal of discretion whether to hammer you or cut you some slack.

Avoid having a Revenue Officer complete the financial forms for you during an interview. Ask to take them home and send or bring them back to her later. Expect her to resist, but hold your ground! Tell her you want to be sure everything is correct and your memory is not good enough to do it right then and there; you need to check your records before you would feel comfortable signing them.

Beware of the "necessary living expenses" trap. When filling out IRS Form 433-A, pay strict attention to the "necessary living expenses" questions. This is the crucial area in the IRS determination of how big your payments must be (or what kind of Offer in Compromise it will accept, as discussed in Section E, below). The IRS expects you to sacrifice by keeping a minimal lifestyle until the tax debt is paid off, so showing expenses for private schools, trips to Hawaii or champagne-and-caviar grocery bills won't be tolerated.

Don't underestimate your family's living expenses—list where every penny goes every month. Include in the "comments" section on the IRS form when and how your expenses may increase in the near future (a baby is on the way, your car needs a new transmission and so on). If your income is likely to decrease, your spouse is about to be laid off, or one of your major customers declared bankruptcy, mention that as well.

ARE YOUR PERSONAL ASSETS AT RISK?

Whether or not the IRS can come after your personal assets for business-related taxes—or for your business assets when you owe personal taxes—depends on the form of your business entity and the type of taxes owed.

If you operate as a sole proprietorship, there is no legal distinction between your business and you. Accordingly, the IRS can grab just about anything you own for any kind of tax.

If you are in a partnership or limited liability company, the IRS can go after your share in property owned by the partnership. The IRS can also go after any general partner for 100% of a tax debt of the partnership.

If your business is incorporated as a C or S corporation, on the other hand, your personal assets may be shielded. Conversely, because a corporation is a separate tax entity from its owners, the IRS can't seize corporation assets for bills owed by its shareholders unless they are fraudulently using the corporation to keep assets away from the IRS. If, however, a corporation owes payroll taxes, the IRS can go directly after personal assets of all responsible shareholders (as discussed in Chapter 5, Tax Concerns of Employers).

On the other side of the coin, while the IRS can't take corporate assets to satisfy your personal tax debts, it can seize your shares of stock in a corporation. But since stock of a small business corporation is difficult to sell, the IRS rarely bothers to take it.

3. Actions the Tax Collector Can Take

Entrepreneurs are natural-born optimists. Typically, when small business people get behind on their bills—including taxes—they believe that things will "turn around" any day and they'll pay back every-

one. Maybe so; after all, America was built by folks who have made dreams come true.

IRS collectors, however, aren't an optimistic lot. They want their money now, not pie in the sky. If you don't pay, the IRS will ask for a list of everyone who owes you money (your business's accounts receivable), and the name of your bank. This gives the IRS a road map for places to go to seize assets—which can force you out of business real fast.

After analyzing your finances, a Revenue Officer can proceed in one or more of the following ways:

- Demand immediate payment of the full amount if she believes you can pay.

- Ask you to apply for a loan from at least two financial institutions.

- Tell you to sell any assets not currently used in your business, or personal items she considers extravagant—for example, a second home or a pleasure boat.

- Propose an installment agreement allowing monthly payments. (See Section C, above.)

- Suggest you submit an Offer in Compromise (see Section E, below) to settle the tax bill for less than the balance due.

- Begin "enforced collection" against your business—and maybe personal—assets as well. This means seizing bank accounts, accounts receivable, equipment and other things you own. (See Section F, below.)

- Report your file as "currently uncollectible," if you don't have enough assets or income to make even a minimal payment. Fortunately, even the IRS has heard about getting blood from turnips. In IRS lingo, this is called "53-ing" a case. If you are in desperate straits and don't have significant income or assets that could be seized, a collector can submit Form 53 to her superiors. If approved, IRS collection efforts are put on hold, but interest and penalties continue to mount.

Being currently uncollectible doesn't last forever—every six to 18 months, the IRS computer will bring up your account, and you may be asked to update your financial statement. If you rejoin the ranks of the employed, the IRS expects you to notify them—but they won't find out automatically.

Regardless of which course the IRS collector pursues, she will demand that—if your business is still operating—you make all required tax filings. These include personal income tax returns and business payroll tax returns (if you have employees). If you are taking income from your sole proprietorship, limited liability company or partnership, you will be required to make quarterly estimated tax payments as well. She will want to see evidence that these filings are current.

If you don't pay payroll taxes, your business is in jeopardy. The IRS will aggressively move to shut a business down if it is operating without making payroll tax deposits. You may be allowed to stay in business if you owe payroll taxes for past periods, but only if you keep current on new taxes and agree to a payment plan for old ones. Otherwise the IRS will shut you down to stop the losses to the government from growing.

WILL THE IRS CLOSE DOWN YOUR BUSINESS?

Revenue Officers will do whatever it takes to scare you into coming up with money to pay your back taxes. But their bark is worse than their bite. In fact, at the IRS, padlocking the doors of a delinquent taxpayer's business is considered an admission of failure, not a badge of honor. It doesn't usually result in revenue for the government, because auction sales of business equipment typically don't bring much in—often not enough to cover the costs of seizing, storing, advertising and selling the items. A more practical reason a shutdown is not likely to happen is that it is simply too much trouble and paperwork, and keeps the collectors from working on more potentially productive cases.

With that said, you should also know that the IRS will aggressively move to close down a business that is behind in its payroll tax filings and payments. You may be allowed to stay in operation, but only if you get current for the quarter and agree to a payment plan for past quarters. Otherwise, expect the IRS to put you out of business in order to stop the losses to the government from growing.

4. Cooperating With the Collector

As mentioned, IRS collectors typically ask where you bank and for a list of the business's accounts receivable. Obviously, the IRS can use this information to start seizing your money. While lying to any IRS employee is a crime, not answering questions is legal. If you don't provide financial data, the IRS won't beat you with rubber hoses or throw you in jail. Instead, an IRS collector may issue a summons—a legally enforceable order that requires you to appear and provide data or information under oath. If a collector issues a summons, it usually means she suspects you of hiding assets. However, the IRS doesn't use its power to issue summonses very often.

PART 6

Dealing With the IRS

If you do receive a summons, don't ignore it. This could get you hauled in front of a federal judge, who can throw you in jail. If you have few assets, or the IRS already knows about them, you probably have little to lose by disclosing them. If you are still in business and trying to preserve your assets from seizure, seek out a tax pro—preferably an attorney—before answering a summons.

E. Dealing With a Monster Tax Bill

I see people all the time who have amassed huge tax bills with virtually no assets and no hope of ever being able to pay.

Example: The Smiths' computer store was faced with a new deep-discounting competitor down the street. Trying to keep their business afloat, the Smiths ran up $800,000 in bills—including $300,000 to the IRS for payroll taxes—by the time they called it quits. After closing down, Sam Smith goes to work as a salesperson, earning $25,000 per year, and Jeannie Smith earns $15,000 a year as a part-time bank teller. The Smiths' combined earnings are less than the annual IRS interest and penalties on their taxes. Even if they cut expenses to the bone, they will never be able to pay off their tax bill. What should they do?

Fortunately, there are ways to reduce or even eliminate gargantuan tax bills. One is the Offer in Compromise. Another, despite what you may have heard, is bankruptcy. Let's look at both possibilities.

1. The Offer in Compromise

Under its Offer in Compromise program, the IRS sometimes accepts a few cents on the dollar and calls things square. (IRC § 57(10)1, 7122.) For example, in 1994, after hounding country singer Willie Nelson since 1980, the IRS accepted a final compromise settlement of $9 million on a $32 million tax bill. The IRS claims to now accept almost half of the Offers in Compromise that are properly submitted.

Don't think that the IRS takes the forgiving of any tax debt lightly. It will accept less only if it is doubtful more will be collected later. To get the IRS to accept an Offer in Compromise, you must demonstrate to the IRS that it's in their best interests.

An Offer in Compromise *must* be made on IRS Form 656. It must be accompanied by a completed IRS Form 433-A (individual) and, if you are still in business, Form 433-B (business) financial statements. (These are the forms used in all IRS collection situations, discussed in Section D, above.)

Later, you'll be asked to provide verification—such as bank statements for the past three to 12 months, expense receipts, vehicle titles, mortgage notes, rental and lease agreements and a list of outstanding debts. A collector may want to see your home or business, so she can observe your assets and lifestyle firsthand.

Example: The Smiths, whose failed computer business left them with $300,000 in tax debts, make an Offer in Compromise. They give a Form 433-A and documentation to verify their poor financial state. Form 433-B is not necessary, because the Smiths are no longer in business. After losing most of their assets in bankruptcy, the Smiths' financial form is relatively simple. They offer the IRS $25,000, to be provided by a relative. Will the IRS accept this? I think the Smiths have a good shot.

For details on how to present an offer to the IRS, see Chapter 6 of *Stand Up to the IRS,* by Frederick W. Daily (Nolo Press).

2. Bankruptcy

Bankruptcy offers small business taxpayers who have impossibly large bills another way out. Despite IRS misinformation to the contrary, it is possible to wipe out *certain* business and personal federal tax debts—but not all kinds of taxes—through the federal bankruptcy courts. Although details of bankruptcy are beyond the scope of this book, let's briefly review the tax basics.

AUTOMATIC STAY

One of the most alluring features of filing for bankruptcy is the "automatic stay." It works like this: The moment you file a bankruptcy petition, all creditors—including the IRS—are stopped cold. No further seizures, or even threats, can be made by the IRS as long as your case is pending. Some folks file bankruptcy just to buy time, without intending to follow through—simply to stop the IRS from seizing property or putting them out of business.

A variety of bankruptcy options are available to small business people. These are usually referred to by the place they are found in the federal bankruptcy code: Chapter 7, Chapter 11, Chapter 12 and Chapter 13. As you will see, each chapter allows you to get a different kind of "relief" from your tax problems.

a. Chapter 7

Straight liquidation bankruptcy, called Chapter 7, allows anyone to wipe out unsecured debts—including older income taxes. However, payroll taxes or Trust Fund Recovery Penalty taxes can never be wiped out in bankruptcy.

The rules get complicated fast, but bankruptcy may be the answer to your prayers if you qualify.

Income taxes due more than three years ago can be wiped out in a Chapter 7 bankruptcy, *if*:

- tax returns for these debts were filed at least two years ago, *and*
- the tax bill has been on the IRS's books (assessed) for at least 240 days.

Example: As a result of the failure of their business in 1991, Tom and Barbara Keene owe $500,000 to general creditors and $300,000 in payroll taxes to the IRS. They owe another $20,000 for their jointly filed individual income taxes for 1991, which they weren't able to pay when the return was filed on April 15, *1992. This is added to the $70,000 they owe the IRS from an audit of the 1991 tax return, completed January 15, 1995.*

If the Keenes file a Chapter 7 bankruptcy in 1995, the general creditor bills of $500,000 can be wiped out. The $300,000 in payroll taxes are not dischargeable. The $20,000 of 1991 individual taxes are dischargeable after April 15, 1995 (three years after they were due). The added $70,000 audit debt would qualify for discharge only if the bankruptcy were filed more than 240 days after January 15, 1995.

Obviously, bankruptcy is not for everyone. See *How to File for Bankruptcy* by Stephen Elias, Albin Renauer and Robin Leonard (Nolo Press) for more information.

b. Chapter 13

Bankruptcy repayment plans for individuals and small business people are known as Chapter 13 plans. This provision permits any debtor except a corporation to repay their debts monthly, including any kind of taxes. There are some restrictions on who can use Chapter 13. (A special provision, Chapter 12 of the Bankruptcy Act, gives farmers a repayment option similar to Chapter 13.)

When you file for Chapter 13 bankruptcy, you must propose a plan revealing how much disposable income you have to pay creditors on a monthly basis. Repayment plans usually last three years, but the bankruptcy judge may allow five years. A plan must provide for full payment of some types of debts, but others can be reduced or even wiped out by the court. Tax bills for periods within the past three years must be paid in full—but interest and penalties stop accruing after the petition is filed. If the income tax bill is over three years old, it may be reduced by the judge.

A Chapter 13 bankruptcy can cover up to $250,000 of unsecured debts (this includes tax debts) and $750,000 of secured debts (such as a mortgage).

PART **6**

Dealing With the IRS

Example: Jim and Jackie Jones owe creditors a total of $90,000, including $40,000 in income taxes which are more than three years old. The Joneses file for Chapter 13 bankruptcy and propose a debt repayment plan of $500 per month to the court. If the bankruptcy judge approves the plan, they will be ordered to make monthly payments to a bankruptcy trustee for a period of 36 to 60 months. After that time, the balance of the debts, including those owed to the IRS, can be discharged by the court.

c. Chapter 11

Chapter 11, termed a bankruptcy "reorganization," is similar to Chapter 13 in that it requires some repayment of debts. It is useful for those with debts in excess of Chapter 13 limits. This option, while open to individuals or any type of business, is too complicated for most small businesses, and requires expensive legal assistance. A "fast-track" Chapter 11 procedure for small businesses with debts up to $2 million was created in 1994; it simplifies the procedures somewhat, but you still will need a good attorney by your side.

F. When the IRS Can Take Your Assets

If you and the IRS don't agree on payment of back taxes, or you don't file for bankruptcy, you face what the IRS calls "enforced collection." This usually means a tax lien and levy, which though closely related, are not the same thing, as we shall see.

1. Federal Tax Liens

The IRS may record a "notice of federal tax lien" in the public records in your county or state. (IRC § 6323(F).) This shows the world, or at least anyone that wants to look, that you have a federal tax debt and the amount you owe. Lien notices are often listed in local newspapers and business publications. Credit bureaus collect and report tax lien information.

The legal effect of a lien is that it becomes a charge against your property, much like a mortgage or deed of trust on real estate. A tax lien is usually the kiss of death to an individual or a business's credit rating. It means the IRS has the right to take just about any property that you own to satisfy a tax debt. Lenders will shun you, and others may not do business with you, fearing that the IRS might grab their money or goods in your possession.

Ordinarily, the IRS records a tax lien if you owe more than $10,000 and you don't agree to pay it off within a year. The IRS doesn't always file a tax lien notice, so you might escape this black mark. Whenever you are dealing with a collector, always ask the IRS not to file a lien. Once on your records, it is difficult to get a tax lien removed without making full payment to the IRS.

2. Federal Tax Levies: Seizing Property

A tax lien notice doesn't take any of your property—a tax levy does. A levy occurs when the IRS physically seizes property to satisfy a tax debt. The IRS may grab something directly from you (for example, your office equipment), or it may make a written demand to someone holding your property (your bank, for example). A levy may follow a tax lien notice, or happen without a tax lien being filed, or it may never happen at all.

Property seizures are most likely when you refuse to deal with the problem or can't be located. When you hear about the IRS padlocking a business or taking someone's home, you can bet it didn't come out of the blue. The IRS first warns the individual or business owner several times.

Once the IRS has your property, it is not easy to get it back. You'll need to show the IRS it's in its best interest to release it. For instance, you might get back an essential business asset if losing it means you will have to close your doors, and be deprived of any means to pay your tax debt.

Example: Harry, owner of Pavco, a road contracting business, owes $75,000 in back payroll taxes. The IRS seizes his paving trucks, effectively putting Harry out of business. He might offer to pay $10,000 per month for the next five months if the IRS will release the trucks. With his trucks back, Harry can stay in business.

a. What the IRS Can and Cannot Take

The IRS usually seizes bank accounts first, because it can be done by the push of a button. A computer-generated levy form is sent to any financial institution that the IRS suspects holds money for you. The next most popular target is your wages—even if due from your own corporation. And if you have received payments from other sources in the past that show up on their computer (Form 1099), the IRS might send levy notices to them as well. The IRS can intercept any money owed you for goods or services. Any tax refunds coming from the IRS or states are taken automatically. An officer can grab money or property held for you by any other third parties—such as relatives or friends.

Most anything you own is subject to IRS levy, including your residence—*no matter what your state homestead laws provide*—and your pension plan. However, the IRS does not aggressively go after homes and retirement plans because of the political heat and bad publicity generated. The IRS wants to be perceived as a tough, but fair, agency. Before taking levy measures, the IRS will have usually tried, and failed, to get your cooperation in entering into a payment plan, selling your assets or otherwise taking steps to deal with your tax debt.

It can make sense to stonewall an IRS request for information, at least in the short term. Never lie to an IRS collector about anything. Instead, say something like, "I intend to pay the money I owe as soon as possible. I take my debt seriously and am sincerely trying to make the necessary money. I'm sorry, but for my own peace of mind, I can't divulge private information about my bank accounts or other assets." The collector won't be overjoyed, but she won't throw you in chains either.

b. What the IRS Can't Take

Some of your assets are exempt from IRS seizure by law. The IRS won't take the shirt off of your back or the clothes in your closet. Unfortunately, the assets that are exempt from IRS levy have very low dollar limits. The IRS can't touch your family's wardrobe, personal effects (under $1,650 in value), tools of your trade (up to $1,100 in value), or a portion of your wages as determined by IRS tables. (IRC § 6334(a)(a).)

Example: Brian and Wynona, a married couple with two small children, had a retail seafood business that failed. They are now working for Wal-Mart. If they don't negotiate a deal and the IRS levies their wages, they'll be allowed to keep only about $250 per week, total, with the rest going to the IRS. Unless they own expensive and unnecessary assets (a race car, vacation home, boats and so forth), the IRS is highly unlikely to seize any of their personal property.

Before seizing assets from your business premises, the IRS must ask for your permission. If you refuse, the IRS can take property from the public areas of the business, such as cash in the drawer, furniture and equipment, but needs a court order to seize anything in non-public areas. The IRS cannot come into your home to seize assets, unless you agree or the officer has a court order.

Example: The IRS levies on Yick Wo's Chinese restaurant's assets. It can empty out the cash register, but can't remove the woks from the kitchen—unless Yick Wo agrees or the IRS has a court order.

3. Getting Liens and Levies Released

It is possible to get a tax lien removed from your property, but the IRS will insist on full or at least partial payment in return. A typical scenario for small business folks is when they find a buyer for their business assets, but the IRS has recorded a tax lien. In general, the IRS will approve the transfer free of the tax lien if it receives virtually all of the proceeds of the sale and is convinced that the assets are being sold for their market value.

Example: Valjean, who owns a motorcycle repair shop he operates as a sole proprietorship, owes a $40,000 tax audit bill. The IRS collector threatens to shut the operation down and sell off the contents of the shop. Booger, Valjean's mechanic, offers to buy the business for $20,000—the value of the shop's tools and equipment. To get the IRS to go along with the sale and grant a partial release of the tax lien in return for the $20,000, Valjean must convince the IRS that $20,000 is as much or more than they could get at an auction. Valjean won't get any money from the sale, but will get a reduction of his tax bill.

RESOURCES

IRS Publication 594, *Understanding the Collection Process*. This is a short, relatively clearly written pamphlet.

Stand Up to the IRS, by Frederick W. Daily (Nolo Press). This book discusses solving IRS collection problems in greater detail than is given in this chapter. It also contains many useful forms for dealing with the IRS.

How to File for Bankruptcy, by Stephen Elias, Albin Renauer and Robin Leonard (Nolo Press). This book explains bankruptcy alternatives and how to handle your own Chapter 7 bankruptcy case.

Chapter 13 Bankruptcy: Repay Your Debts, by Robin Leonard (Nolo Press). This book explains how to use Chapter 13 of the bankruptcy code to pay off your tax debts. ∎

CHAPTER 19

Audits

"It is not the thief who is hanged, but one who was caught stealing."

— H. L. Mencken

An audit is an IRS examination of you and your tax return. The IRS's goal is to verify that your tax return accurately reflects your income and tax deductible expenses. Besides looking at your records, auditors make subjective decisions about your honesty during an audit.

As a small business owner, you are four times more likely to be audited than other folks. Although odds are low in any one year (about one in 35), if you stay in business very long, chances are you'll be audited at least once. And, if irregularities are found, audit lightning is likely to strike again. Indeed, a few business owners with a record of being fast and loose are audited every year or two.

How to prepare for, avoid and defend yourself in an audit is covered in detail in my companion book, *Stand Up to the IRS* (Nolo Press). The fraud and criminal chapters there may be of interest as well, so check it out if you're facing an audit. It's in most public libraries as well as all major bookstores.

AUDITS IN A NUTSHELL

1. In a small business audit, you must convince the IRS that your business reported all of its receipts and was entitled to all deductions that are questioned.

2. Delaying an audit usually works to your advantage, as the IRS is under deadlines to finish its cases.

3. You may keep the IRS from holding an audit at your place of business.

4. You may hire a tax pro to handle an audit for you. If you do, you won't have to meet the IRS face-to-face.

5. Don't expect to come out of an audit without owing something—the odds are against you.

6. Talk to the auditor's manager if you are being treated unfairly or the auditor is being unreasonable.

7. If you are missing receipts or records, try to reconstruct them by other means.

8. If you are worried about tax fraud, bring in a tax pro to handle the audit.

A. Who Gets Audited?

Audit victims are seldom selected randomly. Small businesses and their owners are pulled from the IRS audit hopper in several very deliberate ways:

1. Computer Picks

At least 80% of small businesses are sole proprietorships. Their owners report their business income on "Schedule C" of their Form 1040 individual tax returns. An IRS computer program, known as the DIF scoring process, scans every Form 1040 and assigns it a numerical grade. The highest scores, roughly 10% of these returns, are human-reviewed for "audit potential."

Business partnerships, limited liability companies and small corporations all file separate returns too, and are computer scored. However, the audit rate of these business entities is less than half that of individual income tax returns with sole proprietorship income.

How the DIF program works is a highly guarded IRS secret, but I can make some educated guesses based on what former IRS employees have told me. The most important factor is the *ratios* of a business's income to various types of its expenses. For instance, if the IRS computer data shows restaurants in your area report food costs as 32% of gross sales on average, and yours claims 55%, you will get a higher DIF score. However, it may take more than one item, such as one ratio variance, to be enough of a "red flag" to get you audited. Computer scoring is by far the most likely way a small business becomes an audit candidate.

2. Special Projects and Market Segment Specialization Program

Every year the IRS targets certain businesses, professions and industries for audit. These campaigns are called "industry specialization" or "market seg-

ment specialization programs." Recent victims range from funeral home operators, car dealers, attorneys and airline pilots to plastic surgeons.

The IRS zeroes in on certain businesses because experience has shown a high degree of noncompliance with the tax laws. The IRS further breaks down these market segments into subcategories. For instance, in 1993 the IRS completed a study of attorneys. It found that lawyers practicing criminal and immigration law were less likely to report all of their income than other kinds of attorneys. Another study found that airline pilots, as a group, invested in questionable "tax shelters" more often than people in other occupations. Also, the IRS reasons that these high-earning professionals and business people are the ones most likely to be able to pay additional tax assessments.

3. Informants' Tips

Tips to the IRS—usually from disgruntled former business associates, employees or ex-spouses—can trigger an audit. But don't be overly concerned about someone on your enemies' list—the IRS knows that many tips result from spite or jealousy, so only 2% of all audits are picked this way. Anonymous tips are usually ignored altogether.

However, if other people know things—you're keeping two sets of books or paying your house painter with a business check, or you skim cash from the till—be at least a little worried. I do not recommend tax cheating, but if you try it, at least don't brag about it. Today's bookkeeper can easily become tomorrow's disgruntled former employee and cause you trouble if he or she can document your tax-cheating to the IRS.

4. Follow-Up Audits

Audits of other individuals or businesses can lead to you being audited. For instance, if one of your partners gets audited, you may be the next one in line. If you are in more than one business, you may be hit with a "package audit" of all your enterprises—corporations, investment groups, trusts or whatever you have your finger in. The IRS is suspicious of folks who operate in a myriad of business forms, as this presents opportunities for shifting or hiding income between the entities.

5. Prior Audits

If you were audited once and flunked, your odds of a return visit go up greatly. The IRS knows that people who were once overly aggressive—claiming phony tax deductions or not reporting income—are likely to try it again.

This doesn't mean you will be audited just because your returns were once found in error. I have seen business people lose audits badly, yet never hear from the IRS again. The IRS audit machine operates in hit-or-miss fashion, so don't assume the worst.

6. Governmental Investigations

Law enforcement and IRS criminal investigations can lead to an audit. For instance, when a police agency finds a lot of cash in someone's possession, they may contact the IRS. Similarly, if you are charged with embezzlement or drug dealing, it may be brought to the IRS's attention. However, the information flows between law enforcement agencies is often poor, so trouble with one agency doesn't mean you will be bothered by another.

7. Amended Returns and Refund Claims

You are allowed to file amended tax returns—for example, if you discover an overlooked deduction. Generally, you have 36 months after the original due date of the return to amend it to lower your tax liability. (Form 1040X is used for this purpose.)

While the IRS has discretion to reject any amended tax return, it usually will accept it.

Most people file amended returns to get a refund. And, as you most surely know, the IRS is not in business to give money back. So, not surprisingly, the audit likelihood for amended returns is rather high—about one in three in my experience. If an amended return is audited, the original tax return—not just the items amended—is subject to examination.

8. Chance Selection

The IRS selects a relatively small sampling of individual and business taxpayers (about 50,000) at random per year for a Taxpayer Compliance Measurement Program (TCMP) audit. While this may sound like a large number, TCMP audits are less than 5% of all audits the IRS conducts in any one year. TCMP results are used to build the IRS statistical base for computerized audit scoring of future year's tax returns of all individuals and businesses. Congress has been highly critical of these very intrusive audits and they may be discontinued in the future.

IRS COMPUTER-GENERATED BILLS AND NOTICES

The IRS often sends computerized notices about some suspected problem with your individual or business tax filings. The notice may look like a bill at first glance. For instance, the IRS claims you forgot to report $400 in interest from your savings account. The notice says that you did not report it, and may state how much additional tax you owe—on the assumption that they are right.

This notice is not an audit; instead you have just been hit by an IRS "automated adjustment," usually designated as a CP-2000 letter. If the IRS is right—you did forget the $400 interest—then consider it a bill.

But, what if the IRS computer is wrong—you really did report the $400 on your return, but mistakenly listed it under "dividends" instead of interest? In this case, handle it by calling, writing or mailing documentation to the IRS showing that they are wrong. Send a copy of the notice to the IRS office address on the notice. Don't go to your local IRS office; since they didn't send the notice, they can't help.

B. How Long Do You Have to Worry About an Audit?

The general rule is that a tax return can't be audited after 36 months from the date it was filed. Note that the time limit (called a statute of limitations) starts to run only if and when you actually file a tax return. Years in which you never file a tax return are open to IRS scrutiny forever.

Audit notices are usually sent out between 12 and 18 months after you file your tax return. Generally speaking, if you haven't heard from the IRS within 18 months, you won't be audited.

However, there are some circumstances that give the IRS more time to audit:

- If you understate your income by at least 25% on a tax return, the audit deadline is extended to six years.
- If you file a fraudulent tax return, there is no time limit. Tax fraud, as explained below, is more than just a little fudging. Luckily the IRS rarely tries to audit anyone after six years, even if fraud is suspected.

Once an audit is started, the Internal Revenue Manual directs it to be wrapped up within 28 months—beginning on the date you filed your tax return. Legally, although the IRS has 36 months, the 28-month cutoff is imposed to give the IRS time for potential appeals processing. (See Chapter 20, Appealing IRS Audits.)

Bottom line. These statutory and internal IRS audit time limits mean that the auditor is under pressure to close out your audit file. This can work in your favor, since the older an audit case gets, the more anxious the IRS is to bring it to a conclusion. The auditor can do this more easily if you agree with the audit report, and her performance is partially judged on getting you to sign it. This opens up the possibility of negotiating, as will be explained in Section J, below.

Don't try to disguise personal expenses as business. With small businesses, the IRS auditor is ever on the lookout for people who bury personal expenses in their business. Cars, travel and entertainment are often targets. In these areas, particularly, it pays to keep good records.

C. How the IRS Audits Small Businesses

The IRS conducts two kinds of audits of small businesses and their owners: "office audits" and "field audits." The difference is not only where the audit is held, but the intensity of the process.

1. Office Audits

If your operation is a sole proprietorship grossing less than $100,000 per year, and you are audited, the IRS is likely to request you come in to their office. Usually, just one year's tax return is selected for an office audit. Just as it sounds, you go to the IRS offices with your box of records (see below for what you must bring). A business office audit with a tax examiner usually lasts two to four hours. IRS statistics show a typical business taxpayer emerges owing additional taxes averaging about $4,000, but I have seen far larger bills.

2. Field Audits

If your enterprise is a partnership, corporation or a sole proprietorship with gross annual receipts over $100,000 per year, the audit is usually held outside the IRS office. Called a "field audit," this process is much more intensive than an office audit. Field auditors are called Revenue Agents, and are much better trained in accounting than are IRS office tax auditors. The average field audit "adjustments"—meaning additional tax, penalty and interest assessed—totals over $17,000. The IRS may devote as much as 40 hours (including time to write a report) to a field audit of a small business.

Conduct your audit off the premises. One of the most important rights of a small business person is to keep an IRS field auditor away from the business premises—even though the IRS usually wants to do it there. If your premises are tight, you can keep the auditor away by stating it would interfere with your operation. Demand that the audit be held elsewhere—at the IRS office, or if you have a tax pro represent you, at her office.

The audit should be conducted away from your business, even if it is not an inconvenience to your operation. Indeed, it might be easier for you to have it held at your place. But you should know why the IRS wants to come to you. The auditor wants to observe your operation to form an opinion as to whether it is more successful than your tax return indicates. For instance, while there, the auditor might question your employees and get the wrong idea about something.

Example: An IRS auditor sees a picture of a vacation house or race car on the desk of Benny, owner of Benny's Burgers. Since he reported only $15,000 to $20,000 in income for the past six years, the auditor asks how he can afford this luxury item. If Benny can't come up with a satisfactory answer, the auditor will look hard for evidence of unreported income.

Another reason to have the audit off your premises is to better control records that are available. The auditor may ask for additional records that are back at the business. Since this delays things, and the auditor is often in a hurry, she may not bother. And even if she does ask for more documents, you'll have a chance to review them first.

YOUR AUDIT RIGHTS—THE TAXPAYER BILL OF RIGHTS

To stem IRS taxpayer abuses, Congress passed the *Taxpayer Bill of Rights* in 1988. This law is explained in IRS Publication 1, *Your Rights as a Taxpayer*. This pamphlet is available by calling 1-800-829-1040 or at most IRS offices. It sets forth your rights during any IRS (noncriminal) process, including audits, appeals and collections. Your rights include:

- having a say in the time and place of the audit
- hiring a representative to meet with the auditor instead of going yourself
- audio recording IRS meetings, and
- speaking with an IRS employee's manager if you are being treated unfairly.

Should you hire a tax pro? It is more economical to go it alone if yours is an office audit and you have nothing to hide. Field audits, which tend to turn up much more expensive tax problems, are another matter. Here, you should involve a tax pro. If you are worried about a serious violation of the law that could result in criminal charges, always bring in a professional, preferably a tax attorney. (See Chapter 22, Help Beyond the Book.) Your representative must be an attorney, Certified Public Accountant or Enrolled Agent, and must have your written Power of Attorney (IRS Form 2848). Tax attorneys are the most expensive way to go (expect $125 to $400 per hour for our time), and CPA's may charge about the same or slightly less. The lowest rates are charged by Enrolled Agents (more like $50 to $150 per hour). The typical amount of professional time for a field audit ranges from 10 to 50 hours. You do the math.

D. The Auditor's Powers

Forget what you have heard about being innocent until proven guilty in America. When dealing with an IRS auditor, the law specifically places the burden of proof on you to back up what is in your tax return. Proving the correctness of the return to an auditor is not all that easy—the IRS wins over 80% of all audits, mostly because people can't verify data on their returns. Recordkeeping, not outright cheating, is the downfall of most audit victims.

Congress gives the IRS broad powers in auditing businesses. While IRS powers are not unlimited, it is allowed to do the following in the course of an audit:

- inspect your business premises
- view your home office
- scrutinize your records; and
- summon records held by others.

Let's look more closely at each of these.

1. Inspect Business Premises

Even though you may be able to have an audit conducted away from your business (see above), an auditor nevertheless may enter your premises if it is open to the public. This is common with a field audit. However, an auditor cannot go into your business's private area—such as a storeroom or your office—unless you consent. But just because you can keep the IRS out of portions of your premises doesn't necessarily mean that you should. If you have nothing to hide, then don't just be obstinate—it may make them suspicious. But give the agent a guided tour rather than let them wander around alone.

2. View Home Offices

If you claimed a home office expense on your tax return, the IRS auditor may want to see it. Most of the time, photographs and diagrams of the business space will be enough to satisfy the auditor. Occasionally, auditors request to see your home office. Legally, you don't have to let an auditor into your home unless she has a court order. If you don't, she will probably disallow your home office depreciation or rental expense—on the basis that you haven't proven you had a home office. Remember, in an audit, the burden of proving deductions on a tax return is always on you.

3. Scrutinize Your Records

Whether the audit is at the IRS office, your business or at your tax pro's, the auditor will expect to see the business's records. If they are on a computer, she may ask you to show them to her on the screen or print them. She has the right to see check registers, bank statements, canceled checks, receipts and invoices. If you keep a formal set of books you must show those as well. If you don't present all these items, the auditor may give you a written "document request" with a date to produce them. If she still doesn't get what she wants, she can issue a summons to you (just like the "third party summons" discussed below).

In the end, if you never come up with acceptable records, the auditor is legally authorized to create her own figures—meaning that deductions will be disallowed and income may be added. In most circumstances, you don't want this to happen.

Do your records contain a smoking gun? If there is something that is possibly incriminating in your records, you may withhold them by claiming your Constitutional right against "self-incrimination." Whether or not this makes sense is a judgment call that should be discussed with an attorney. Keep in mind that there is no "attorney-client" privilege with your accountant.

4. Summon Records Held by Others

To get financial information about you and your operation, an auditor can require records from your tax preparer, banks, suppliers, customers and other third parties. This is done by the IRS issuing a written order, called a "third-party" summons. Usually an auditor won't issue a summons without first attempting to get this information informally from you. Typically, she'll first ask you for bank statements and canceled checks, invoices or any other records used to prepare your returns. In most circumstances you should be cooperative, as these are things an auditor can get with a third-party summons anyway.

E. Should You Get Audit Help?

Many small business owners can handle an IRS office audit without professional representation. However, if you fear that some serious irregularity may come to light, at least consult with a tax pro before the audit. For the typical office audit, hiring a tax pro to represent you isn't likely to be cost-effective. But when it comes to the more serious field audit, think hard about bringing in a tax pro from the get-go, for several reasons:

- Field audits produce much larger tax bills (on average four times greater) than do office audits. So it's a lot easier to justify the expense of a tax pro in a field audit. Her fees are a tax-deductible business expense to boot.

- The IRS uses its most experienced personnel for field audits. So, it's more likely that you will be overmatched if questions come up about documents or tax law.

- If you hire a representative, the field audit can be conducted at her office—not yours.

By law, you may take anyone with you to an audit that you like. Typically this would be your tax preparer or bookkeeper to explain the business receipts and records, or possibly a more sophisticated tax pro, such as a CPA or tax attorney. Or, you can bring along a friend to lend moral support.

You do not have to personally attend an audit, in most cases. Small businesses often send bookkeepers, managers or any other employee with knowledge of the business' tax affairs to the audit instead of the owner. But if for any reason you don't want to show your face, it may be preferable to have a tax pro show up for you. There is no legal requirement that you ever have to meet the auditor—unless they issue a summons to you. Keeping out of the picture means that there is no possibility of you giving any damaging answers to the auditor's questions. A tax pro speaks the same language as the auditor and may have dealt with her before, so has an idea of what makes her tick. If tough questions are raised, a tax pro can say "I don't know, let me check with my client." This may cause the auditor to adjourn the audit so you and the pro can talk things over.

Perhaps most important of all, a tax pro is more likely than you to spot an auditor going into problem areas. For example, you claimed deductions for expenses on which you didn't keep good records, or they look more like personal, than business, expenses.

Never forget that it's your job to prove to the IRS auditor the accuracy of your tax return, what lawyers call the "burden of proof." It is not up to the IRS to disprove anything. Typically this means verifying an expense deduction on your tax return. For instance, can you produce an invoice showing that you incurred the expense? Can you prove that you paid it, with a cash receipt, check or credit card statement? Can you show it was business-related?

Example: An auditor challenges a deduction that Ethan, owner of Ethan's Travel Service, took as a business entertainment expense of $300. Ethan's first job is to prove he incurred the expense—he didn't just make it up. So, Ethan comes up with a VISA receipt, and his monthly VISA bill and his check showing it was paid. Next, Ethan shows notations on the charge slip and in his business diary that the expense was for taking Harry, a longtime customer, and his fiancee out to dinner at the Ritz-Carlton. They discussed a worldwide cruise for their honeymoon. This should be enough to satisfy the auditor that Ethan was entitled to claim this expense as a business deduction.

TAX FRAUD AND HOW TO AVOID IT

Careless mistakes, or even overstating a deduction, on a tax return is not tax fraud, which is roughly defined as a deliberate attempt to evade taxes. To put your mind at rest, tax fraud is charged in less than 5% of all audits. However, when it happens, a fraud penalty of 75% can be tacked on to any tax found owing as a result. And in very serious cases, where the fraud covers three or more years (found in less than 1% of all audits), the IRS may call in its Criminal Investigation Division.

If you believe you have major skeletons in your tax closet—income you didn't report or phony business deductions—see a tax pro before the audit starts. A professional can better help before fraud has been discovered or you have tried to explain your way out of it to anyone at the IRS. Never discuss fraud with anyone from the IRS until you have seen a good tax pro, preferably an attorney.

F. Preparing for Your Audit

Before meeting the auditor, thoroughly review the tax returns being audited. Make sure you can explain how you—or a tax return preparer—came up with the figures. If you can't, then consult the preparer or another tax pro. Identify any problems with items of income or expense deductions. Research tax law, if necessary. Be ready to be able to legally back up your right to take tax deductions or other tax benefits claimed on your return.

Find all records to substantiate the tax return and organize them logically and clearly. As discussed above, generally the IRS has a right to look at any records relating to your tax return. Organize what the IRS auditor will insist on seeing; don't expect them to wade through a mess in a shoebox.

PART 6

Dealing With the IRS

Neatness counts. Forget about dumping a pile of receipts before an auditor and telling her to go at it. A disorganized set of records means more time spent digging, and the greater reward the IRS expects. On the other hand, auditors frequently reward those with good, orderly records by giving these folks the benefit of the doubt and by making smaller adjustments. Neatness builds your credibility with the auditor—even if you are not really all that honest. It has something to do with the accountant's mentality, I guess. Also, pre-audit organization of receipts, checks and other items refreshes your recollection for the audit meeting.

G. What to Bring to an Audit of Your Small Business

Be prepared to show your return was based on good business records. Audit success usually turns on documenting of expenses. Proof should be in writing (but auditors have discretion to accept oral explanations). A list of items the auditor wants to see usually accompanies your audit notice. At a minimum, the IRS will expect you to produce the following documents:

a. Bank Statements, Canceled Checks and Receipts

The auditor will want to see records—both personal and business—from all your bank accounts. As a rule, keep business-related canceled checks as well as any invoices or sales slips. If you paid some expenses with cash, keep the paperwork (handwritten notes, receipts or petty cash vouchers) showing the payments.

b. Electronic Records

Most banks don't return canceled checks anymore, and many business expenses are charged on credit or debit cards. So, bank and charge card (VISA, MasterCard, American Express) statements are now accepted by the IRS as proof of payment. They must show the name, date, amount and address of the payee. Of course, the statements don't show the business nature of the expense, so you can't rely on these to be your only record of expenses.

c. Books and Records

The auditor will ask to see your books. As explained in detail in Chapter 3, Recordkeeping and Accounting, the tax code doesn't require small businesses to keep a formal set of books, so don't let an auditor tell you otherwise. If you keep records using only a check book and cash register tapes, simply bring those. If you maintain more formal records—such as ledgers and journals—the auditor is entitled to see them. If your data is on a computer the auditor will want to see a printout.

If you don't produce adequate records, the auditor is legally permitted to estimate your income and expenses—plus impose a separate penalty for your failure to keep records.

d. Appointment Books, Logs and Diaries

Many businesses, especially those offering services, track activities and expenses using calendars, business diaries, appointment books and logs. An entry in a business diary helps justify an expense to an auditor—as long as it appears to be reasonable.

You must keep specific records of your use of certain equipment, called "listed property."

(IRC § 280F.) (See Chapter 3, Recordkeeping and Accounting.) Computers at home used for business, cellular phones, and vehicles used for both business and personal purposes are all listed property. Most purely business equipment is not in this category—mechanic's tools, a lathe or a carpet loom and so forth—so it is not necessary to keep records of usage. But when assets are put to both business and personal use, the auditor will expect records of usage. For example, if you use a computer for both business and pleasure, you should keep track of the business portion. One way is with a note pad next to the computer. If using a computer, remove non-business software from the hard disk (those video games and recipe programs) before powering up the computer for an auditor.

If you haven't kept usage records, reconstruct them by memory or reference to projects that you worked on during the year.

e. Auto Records

Business use of your personal auto requires detailed records showing the work portion. A log is the best way to keep track, but is not required by the tax code. Otherwise, keep all gas and repair receipts and present them in an orderly fashion with notations of trips showing how the car was used for business. Another way to do this is to add up the gas bills and divide by the number of miles per gallon that your car averages. Show the auditor your auto trip receipts and link them up to sales trips in your business diary or calendar.

f. Travel and Entertainment Records

By law, out-of-town business travel and entertainment expenses (T & E, in auditor lingo), require more careful recordkeeping than other expenses. You *must* have a written record of the specific business purpose for the travel or entertainment expense, as well as a receipt for it. (IRC § 267.)

The best way to keep a record is by an appointment book or log, noting each time you incur a business expense. Typically, most folks aren't disciplined enough to document all expenses as they are happening. It is okay to put together a log or diary after you have received an audit notice. But be upfront about it—don't insult the auditor's intelligence by trying to pass off wet-inked documents as old records. Remember, it's key to develop and maintain credibility with the auditor.

Example 1: Bianca, a self-employed designer, reconstructs a calendar book with a notation for June 18, 1995, as follows, "Round-trip cab fare to office of John Johnson, prospective client. $14.00 (no receipt). Lunch at Circle Restaurant. Discuss proposal to decorate new offices at 333 Pine St. $32.00 (VISA charge) plus cash tip of $6.00 (no receipt)." Bianca supplements her book with an explanation of details, if asked. The auditor is usually satisfied with this approach if it appears reasonable.

Example 2: Sam (the owner of the computer store, remember) went to an out-of-town computer retailers' convention. He spent $1,800 and claimed it as business travel expenses on his tax return. On audit, Sam produces charge card statements to prove the $1,800 was spent for hotels, meals and convention registration. The auditor wants more and asks Sam to justify the business purpose of this trip. Sam produces an ad for the convention, an agenda of events and notes he took at programs. It looks legitimate, and Sam's explanation of why it was important for him to be there is convincing, so the auditor allows the deduction in full.

g. Expenses for Renting or Buying Property

If you are claiming business rental expenses, bring in a copy of your lease, or if you own the property or equipment, bring in the purchase contract. This establishes your right to claim these expenses as well as a beginning tax basis of the property, if depreciation expenses are taken.

ELEMENTS TO PROVE CERTAIN BUSINESS EXPENSES

	Expense			
	Travel	**Entertainment**	**Gift**	**Transportation (Car)**
Amount	Amount of each separate expense for travel, lodging and meals. Incidental expenses may be totaled in reasonable categories, such as taxis, daily meals for traveler, etc.	Amount of each separate expense. Incidental expenses such as taxis, telephones, etc., may be totaled on a daily basis.	Cost of gift.	Amount of each separate expense, including (1) Cost the car (2) Mileage for each business use of the car, and (3) Total miles for the tax year.
Time	Date you left and returned for each trip, and number of days for business.	Date of entertainment. For meals or entertainment directly before or after a business discussion, the date and duration of the business discussion.	Date of gift.	Date of the expense or use.
Place	Name of city or other destination.	Name and address or location of place of entertainment. Type of entertainment if not otherwise apparent. Place where business discussion was held if entertainment is directly before or after a business discussion.	N/A	Name of city or other designation if applicable.
Description	N/A	N/A	Description of gift.	N/A
Business Purpose	Business reason for travel or the business benefit gained or expected to be gained.	Business reason or the business benefit gained or expected to be gained. Nature of business discussion or activity.	Business reason for giving the gift or the business benefit gained or expected to be gained.	Business reason for the expense or use of the car.
Business Relationship	N/A	Occupations or other information—such as names or other designations—about persons entertained that shows their business relationship to you. If all people entertained did not take part in business discussion, identify those who did. You must also prove that you or your employee was present if entertainment was a business meal.	Occupation or other information—such as name or other designation—about recipient that shows his or her business relationship to you.	N/A

WHAT TO DO ABOUT MISSING DOCUMENTS

Myth: Every deduction must be proven or it won't be allowed.

Fact: Courts say that taxpayers can't be expected to keep perfect records. If your tax documentation is incomplete (which is often the case with small business people), don't despair. You are only required to demonstrate to the IRS you are in "substantial compliance" with the tax laws. The substantial compliance rule has been interpreted to mean you may do any of the following when you don't have original documentation in an audit:

- offer oral explanations to auditors in place of missing records
- reconstruct records
- approximate expenses

For example, Elijah produced a small music festival and rented tents from a traveling carnival company, which insisted on payment in cash. Elijah forgot to get a receipt for the payment of $800, and the carnies moved on to parts unknown. Elijah can reconstruct this expense with his oral explanation, a picture of the tents that appeared in the local paper and a letter from a ticket taker who saw him make the payment. The auditor also asked to see Elijah's office utility bills for the year under audit. He could only come up with nine months of bills and the utility company could not provide

duplicates because they only kept bills for the past 12 months. Elijah can approximate the missing expense data by averaging out the other nine months of bills.

Even if you can't figure out a way to document an expense, you can simply create the paperwork (as long as you tell the auditor this is what you have done). For instance, write a repair receipt with the name and address of the person who did the work, the date and amount paid.

Also, you may be able to rely on the *Cohan* rule for expenses—other than travel and entertainment. This rule comes from a court case (*Cohan v. Commissioner of the Internal Revenue,* 349 F.2d 540, 2nd Cir. 1930) allowing George M. ("Give my regards to Broadway") Cohan to approximate business expenses in an IRS audit. The case stands for the proposition that some approximations of business expenses are acceptable—as long as it was reasonable to believe that some amount was spent, and you explain why records are not available. Acceptable excuses include that they were lost, destroyed or the transactions were not the type that receipts are normally given for, such as cab fares or tips.

If less than $75 each, business-related travel and entertainment expenses don't require substantiation.

H. Don't Rush a Field Audit

Most people want to get an audit over as quickly as possible. With an office audit this may not be a bad idea, but with a field audit faster isn't always better.

Slowing down an audit often works to your advantage. Needing time to get records together or asking the IRS for a delay for any other plausible reason is both permissible and wise. The older an audit file gets, the more anxious the IRS is to close it out, for several reasons. Most important is the statute of limitations, discussed above, which normally gives the IRS only three years from the time you file to audit. In addition, the IRS has internal rules requiring its auditors to complete their work within 26 to 28 months after a return is filed. After an auditor is finished, her report must still be processed, reviewed and approved, which all lengthen the process. This means an auditor is under considerable pressure to close your case well short of these deadlines.

Improving your bargaining position isn't the only reason to ask for a delay. Since you never can be too well prepared for an audit, usually it makes sense to ask for one or two delays as a matter of course. If you are like most people, it takes time to dig out papers from the recesses of your garage or storeroom and put them into some semblance of order. You may have to contact your bank to get copies of checks or other items. After getting it all together, you may decide to see a tax pro or research the tax law on your own. Assuming you work for a living, this project takes a lot of time to do right.

You may have your annual family reunion at the time the audit is scheduled, or become ill, or be just too busy at work or have some other good excuse for a delay. If you need a postponement, call the IRS office and tell them. In most cases, your wish will be granted and the audit reset for a month or two.

CASH TRANSACTIONS CATCH THE IRS'S ATTENTION

The IRS is suspicious of all businesses that are inherently "cash intensive." Bars, game arcades, restaurants, waiters, car dealers, cab drivers, minimarts, gambling industry workers, bellhops, immigration lawyers, pawnshops and laundromats are frequent targets of specialized IRS audits. The IRS knows what kind of business you are in because you tell them on your tax return. Occupations must be stated both in plain English and by listing a four-digit code on 1040 forms. It is a crime to misstate the nature of your business on a tax return—a prostitute was once convicted of tax fraud for telling the IRS she was in "public relations."

If yours is a predominantly cash operation, an IRS auditor will be particularly interested in your lifestyle. Sports cars, rental property, vacation homes, boats and a lot of assets in general could mean an intense audit or, at worst, an IRS criminal investigation.

The tax code requires all businesses—including financial institutions—to report transactions of cash over $10,000. Not just greenbacks, but also "cash equivalents"—traveler's checks, money orders and bank drafts—must be listed on IRS Form 8300. While aimed at money launderers and drug dealers, this form applies to legitimate business persons as well.

Structuring a transaction to avoid this law—say, making three cash deposits of $4,000 on three different days—is also required to be reported on Form 8300. Penalties for not following cash reporting rules range from fines to audits and even jail. (See IRS Publication 1544, *Reporting Cash Payments of Over $10,000*, for details and a copy of Form 8300.) This law doesn't apply to non-business cash transactions. So, for instance, a parent giving a child more than $10,000 in cash doesn't have to file Form 8300. (But there will be a federal gift tax filing requirement if this happens.) Personal checks of any amount are not within the cash reporting requirement.

I. What Auditors Look for When Examining a Business

First, the IRS training manual tells its auditors that they are examining *you*, not just your tax return. The auditor wants to see how you match up with the income reported on your return—"economic reality" in IRS speak. If your business is audited, the IRS will likely investigate these issues:

- *Did you report all of your business sales or receipts?* If you "forgot" to report a significant amount of business receipts—$10,000 or more—then strongly consider hiring a tax pro to handle the audit and remove yourself from the process altogether. If the auditor finds evidence of large amounts of unreported income, and it looks intentional on your part, they may call in the IRS criminal investigation team. However, if there is any kind of halfway plausible explanation ("someone must have forgotten to record September's sales"), then don't worry about jail. The auditor will probably just assess the additional tax you should have paid in the first place, plus interest and most likely a 20% penalty on the tax for the error.

- *Did you write off personal living costs as business expenses?* Let's face it, every small-time operator has claimed a personal expense as a business one. If it is relatively small—a few personal long-distance calls on the business telephone line—the IRS won't get too excited. But, if you deducted $2,000 in repairs on your motorhome during a trip to Yellowstone, an auditor may figure this out by looking at your receipts—and disallow it, with penalty added.

- *Does your lifestyle square with your reported income?* An auditor sizes you up for dress style, jewelry, your car and the furnishings in your home or office—if they have a chance to make these observations. Someone who looks like a Vegas high roller, with a tax return stating they are a missionary, will cause any auditor to dig deeper.

- *Did you take cash or otherwise divert money into your own pocket without declaring it?* Expect the auditor to suspect skimming if yours is the type of business that handles a lot of cash. (See, "Cash Transactions Catch the IRS's Attention," on the previous page.)

- *Did you write off personal auto expenses as business?* Claiming costs for personal use of your set of wheels for business is so common that the IRS seems to expect to find it. That doesn't mean they will accept it, however. Don't count on an auditor believing you use your one-and-only auto 100% for business and never to run to the grocery store or the dentist. If you operate your car for both business and pleasure and claim a high percentage of business usage, keep good records—preferably a log.

- *Did you claim personal entertainment, meals or vacation costs as business expenses?* Travel and entertainment expenses are another area where the IRS knows it can strike gold. Be ready with documentation of all travel and entertainment deductions. Taking buddies to the ball game and calling it business won't work unless you can explain the business relationship in a credible fashion.

- *If you have employees, are you filing payroll tax returns and making tax deposits?* Employment taxes are a routine part of every audit of a small enterprise. See "Employment Classification Is a Hot Issue," below, and Chapter 5, Tax Concerns of Employers.

- *And last but not least, if you hire people you call "independent contractors," are they legally employees?* (Again, see "Employment Classification Is a Hot Issue," below, and Chapter 5.)

This list is by no means complete—these are just the most likely things an IRS auditor looks for.

EMPLOYMENT CLASSIFICATION IS A HOT ISSUE

In almost every small business examination, auditors search for employees misclassified as independent contractors. These enterprises are improperly avoiding payroll taxes. Once the IRS raises this issue, it's up to you to prove that the workers were truly independent contractors. The IRS auditor may talk to the people in question, or she can take other steps to find out if workers have been properly classified. You can't stop her from contacting anyone, nor should you try. It is okay to give workers the afternoon off when the IRS comes calling.

So far, you know that unreported income, poor business recordkeeping and mixing business and personal use of property are obvious IRS audit targets. You'll also want to think about areas in which your tax return(s) are most vulnerable, and try to determine the auditor's concerns in advance. Here are some things you should be aware of.

1. The Income Probe

The number one issue auditors are trained to look for in business audits is unreported receipts. Particularly if your operation is cash-intensive (see "Cash Transactions Catch the IRS's Attention," above), expect the auditor to start with the "income probe." Anticipate a series of questions. A very disarming favorite is, "Did you report all of your income?" Another is "Do you keep a lot of cash around?" Don't be rattled or conclude that big brother IRS has secret knowledge here. Auditors ask everyone questions like these to put you on the defensive early in the game.

Next in the income probe is the "bank deposit analysis." Office auditors do not always take the time to do this, but field auditors routinely add up all your business bank deposits to see if the total is more than your reported income. The auditor will

also ask to see *all* of your personal account records to check that the deposits are consistent with your business receipts. If you don't produce bank records voluntarily, the auditor, her suspicions redoubled, will likely summons them. If you cover up the existence of bank accounts, or otherwise lie to the auditor, you risk being investigated for tax evasion.

Audit your bank accounts in advance. You or your tax pro should do your own bank deposit analysis before meeting with a field auditor. If bank deposits exceed the income reported, you need to come up with explanations. This doesn't mean you have to make up anything. Common bank deposits that aren't taxable income: loans, sales of assets (only the gain, if any, is taxed), transfers from other financial accounts, inheritances and money held for relatives are a few legitimate explanations.

2. Is It a Legitimate Business Expense?

After the income probe, the auditor moves on to verifying business expenses. Remember, the tax code makes you prove that deductions were for profit-making purposes; it's not up to the IRS to disprove them. Any expense may be questioned, but certain ones are zeroed in on to see if they are nondeductible personal expenses in whole or part:

- Travel and entertainment (see Chapter 1 and discussion above)
- Home office (see Chapter 13)
- Asset purchases (see Chapter 2), and
- Auto expenses (see Chapter 1).

Review these chapters for the rules on deductibility on all items that affect your business to make sure you are on firm ground before the audit begins.

J. How to Behave at an Audit

Auditors know very little about you before the meeting. Your auditor won't have other years' tax returns. She will have the tax return under audit and a printout of all W-2s and 1099s from outfits that paid you money that year. A field auditor may also have a credit report and a listing of real estate and vehicles in your name. Try to keep it this way—the less she knows about you, the better.

The Internal Revenue Manual says the first taxpayer interview is the most important phase of an audit. As I have said, whether you handle this interview yourself or have a tax pro go for you, remember that both you and your business are under the microscope. Take a tip from Shakespeare and be true to thine own self. If you lay bricks for a living, don't try to look like a lawyer, and vice versa. Here are some other words to live by.

1. Keep Chit-Chat to a Minimum

Talking about the weather or football is okay, but mum is the word about your business and personal affairs. Because audits are so stressful, many of us cover our nervousness by talking. IRS auditors rely on this natural tendency and listen for clues or admissions. For instance, if you fill in a silence by remarking how jet-lagged you are from a trip to Bora Bora, the auditor may wonder how you can afford it. After all, she may earn about what you say you do, but can't swing the bus fare to Omaha. Don't be surprised if she asks point-blank how you did it. Similarly, idle talk about your kids' private school or an expensive hobby may raise suspicions, if you own a fingernail salon. If you feel like talking, ask the auditor questions about herself—anything to take the focus off you.

2. Answer Questions Concisely

When the auditor asks a direct question, the best comeback is usually "yes" or "no." Resist the temptation to overexplain, ramble on, or answer questions that weren't asked. If you are in doubt about how best to reply, say, "I don't know" or "I'll get back to you on that" or "I'll have to check my records," or "Ask my accountant." Often the auditor will let it go. If she doesn't, at least you slowed the process down, which is to your advantage.

Example: The auditor asks Sue what percentage of sales in her Clothes Horse boutique were for cash. In fact, Sue doesn't keep separate figures for cash sales apart from credit card and check sales. Sue might make a fairly accurate guess, or she could go into a long explanation of how most customers pay for clothes with credit cards or checks. But, why should Sue risk giving an answer that may be misinterpreted by an auditor who doesn't know much about small business practices? It would be better to simply say, "I have no idea because I don't keep those kinds of records." Or, if the auditor pushes it, Sue could say, "If you give me time, I can review my records, come up with an accurate answer and get back to you."

IT'S OKAY TO ASK FOR TIME OUT

You can stop or recess an audit for just about any good reason—to go to the bathroom or eat lunch, or for the day if you feel ill or need to confer with a tax pro. *Your Rights as a Taxpayer* (IRS Publication 1) states you may get tax advice or bring in a representative at any time during the audit process. If you find you are in over your head, confused or can't answer a question, politely tell the auditor that you need a recess. Usually the auditor is tightly scheduled and may not have time to meet again for at least a few weeks. This gives you an opportunity to regroup and consider your next step rather than do something you might regret.

PART **6**

Dealing With the IRS

3. Don't Be Hostile or Phony

What about trying to charm the auditor with your wonderful personality or good looks? Up to a point, this is fine. All rumors to the contrary notwithstanding, auditors are human. The IRS also gives its employees wide latitude in the audit process. This means that a lot of judgment calls are made. If you are pleasant and run an honest-looking business, you may get the benefit of the doubt if the audit turns up problems. Conversely, if you come in radiating hostility, you are daring the auditor to reciprocate. Nevertheless, don't try too hard to ingratiate yourself. Auditors regularly cope with people who think sucking-up is a way to get ahead. If you come across as phony, you will turn the auditor off.

4. Complain if the Auditor is Abusive

Most auditors are straightforward and professional, but a few seem intent on giving taxpayers a hard time, whether they deserve it or not. You may run into an auditor who is impolite, hostile or downright nasty. Perhaps you upset her or she is just having a bad day.

Under the Taxpayer Bill of Rights, you are entitled to courteous treatment from the IRS. If necessary, remind her of this and ask her politely to lighten up. If she doesn't, tell her you are too upset to continue, and want to call off the audit for the day. Or say that you want to consult a tax pro before going further. This is another privilege guaranteed by the Taxpayer Bill of Rights. Threatening this can reform an auditor's attitude because she is always under time pressure to wind up audits. If she balks, demand to speak with her manager and describe the unfair treatment you are receiving. If all else fails, walk out. You can then send a tax pro to the next appointment in your place, or appeal the audit result. (See Chapter 20, Appealing IRS Audits.)

Never offer favors to an auditor. If an audit takes place at your office—or your tax pro's—it's fine to give an agent a cup of coffee. Don't go beyond that, whether it is lunch or a small discount at your store. Studies show IRS agents have an excellent record for honesty. Any perceived bribery attempts (or threats, for that matter) are reported by the auditor to his superiors. This can result in an especially thorough audit, if not a criminal investigation.

K. How to Negotiate With an Auditor

Despite the IRS claim that auditor's can't negotiate, give-and-take is common during the audit process. You do not need to meekly sit back and swallow whatever the auditor dishes out. Negotiating is possible because the IRS wants to wrap up your case by getting you to sign off on an auditor's report. To facilitate this, indirect deal-making is common. Here are some strategies to try with an auditor over these issues.

1. Don't Just Sit There

One of my favorite tactics is to keep asking the auditor about disallowances she is considering as the audit progresses. If you don't ask, she won't usually volunteer this information, so you will be in the dark until you get her Examination Report. Don't let an auditor take the easy way out—make her face you and justify her decisions. You can argue your position right then and there. Or if she is making an adjustment because you didn't produce records, you can ask for time to come up with the documents or reconstruct them.

Example 1: The auditor tells Sue, owner of the Clothes Horse boutique in the example above, that she is disallowing a $400 expense paid to Helena, a fashion consultant. Sue showed a canceled check but hasn't produced anything showing the nature of the services Helena provided. Sue could ask for time to get a statement from the consultant describing the work, and bring it to another audit meeting or mail it to the auditor.

Example 2: The auditor isn't convinced that it was necessary for Paul to buy a $40,000 airplane for his plumbing subcontracting business. Paul could then get a letter from Morgan, the general contractor who hired him, saying that he needed Paul to visit a project in a remote area to supervise the job.

Example 3: The auditor tells Barbara, a direct mail consultant, that she is disallowing her deduction for the theft of a computer because there is no documentation of the loss. Barbara could get a copy of the police report showing that she reported this theft and send it to the auditor.

2. Talk Percentages, Not Dollars

Auditors don't talk about the dollars, but will discuss "adjustments." For instance, your auditor wants to disallow a $500 deduction. Don't reply, "Would you take $300?" Instead, talk in terms of percentages, based on your disagreement about whether the adjustment should be made in the first place. Although this amounts to the same thing, percentages, not dollars, is the only basis IRS auditors can negotiate on. I'll illustrate what I mean below.

Keep in mind the difference between arguing and negotiating. When you argue, you are usually disputing an auditor's conclusion ("It was really a business trip and my receipts and other documents prove it"). By contrast, negotiating is the art of

reaching an accommodation you can both live with. ("Perhaps the trip can be viewed as both for business and pleasure, so how about agreeing that 70% of expenses were for business and 30% for pleasure?")

Let's say you lost all paperwork for an $820 office supply deduction. The auditor wants to disallow 100% of your deduction. You could counter by suggesting 50% along these lines: "Since I made a decent profit and obviously worked hard to earn it, you know that I must have had some expenses for office supplies. I lost these records, but my reconstruction of expenses is reasonable. I should be allowed at least half of these expenses."

Example: Bertha is a part-time wedding consultant with a small shared downtown office. At an audit, Bertha was asked to produce paperwork showing she paid $932 in cash for parking at a nearby garage. Bertha didn't bother to keep the cash receipts. The auditor says she is going to disallow 100% of this deduction. Bertha could counter by saying, "You know that I live 12 miles away and there is no public transportation coming near my office, so I must have driven and there is no street parking here. I am right, but I will agree to your disallowing 25% of parking expenses just to get it over with."

YOUR ACE IN THE HOLE

An auditor's job performance is judged largely based on how many cases she closes marked "agreed." This means she wants you to consent to her findings and not appeal or go to Tax Court. It is time-consuming for the government, so the auditor is told to get your consent. This gives you negotiating power. It doesn't mean an auditor wants your signature so badly she will allow totally bogus business expenses or overlook unreported income. But it does give the auditor incentive to negotiate with you.

3. Arguing Issues

Most audit issues fall into two broad categories: verification and justification. So far we have focused on verification problems. For instance, lost paperwork is a common verification issue. In the previous example, the auditor didn't question Bertha's legal right to claim a parking expense, but whether it was verifiable.

A justification issue, on the other hand, arises if the auditor questions whether Bertha's wedding consulting really was a profit-seeking, legitimate business—or really just a pastime engaged in for family and friends. If primarily for pleasure, Bertha wasn't entitled to claim *any* parking expense—whether she paid it or not. (See Chapter 13 for a discussion of why a hobby is not a business for tax purposes.) Unlike verification issues, justification or legal issues (such as whether or not your corporation is valid), may require the help of a tax pro. If a legal justification issue comes up, ask for a recess to do some research or confer with a tax pro.

4. Adjustments in Your Favor— Taking the Offensive

An audit is not a one-way street. The Internal Revenue Manual says auditors must make adjustments in your favor whenever found. Even the most hard-nosed auditor knows that you occasionally make mistakes in the IRS's favor or overlook claiming tax benefits on your returns. This is another good reason to go over your return with a fine-toothed comb before the audit. If you find any missed deductions or if you were too conservative—for instance, you didn't take a business expense deduction for entertainment because you were afraid of raising an audit flag—then bring it up now. You no longer have anything to lose, and everything to gain.

Bring up items in your favor after the auditor has completed her review. Psychologically, it's better not to raise anything in your favor until after the audi-

tor has decided on all adjustments against you. If you bring them up earlier, the auditor may look harder for offsetting items. By contrast, if you wait until after she is locked in, things can only get better if she accepts any of your positive change items.

5. Don't Try to Negotiate Based on Inability to Pay

The worst way to negotiate is by saying to an auditor you can't afford the extra taxes. Once you concede an adjustment, attempts to throw yourself on the auditor's mercy effectively end the audit. *Whether you ever pay the tax bill from the audit is not the auditor's concern. Their job is to audit you.*

It is illegal for an auditor to hold an unfavorable report over your head unless you agree to a payment plan. If they try it, ask to see their manager pronto. They will back down, I promise.

After the audit is finished, your case goes to the IRS Collection Division, a completely separate department.

Take heart—it may be possible to negotiate an audit bill down by using the IRS Offer in Compromise procedure. Alternatively, your debt may qualify under one of the provisions in the bankruptcy law. Or, if all else fails you can usually get an installment payment plan. (See Chapter 18, When You Can't Pay Your Taxes, for details.)

L. Your Options After Getting an Audit Report

After the auditor is finished, you will be handed or, more likely, mailed an IRS Examination Report. This signals that the IRS considers the audit completed—but the report may still be changed if you act quickly enough. You have three choices after getting the report:

1. Agree

You may be ready to throw in the towel by signing and sending the report back to the auditor. If you do this, it's all over; you can't change your mind. If tax is due, you will get a bill with interest and penalty (if any), included. The audit report is not officially a tax bill. The final bill is issued by the IRS Service Center.

Check your bill. Sometimes statements from the IRS Service Centers differ from those given by auditors. Don't ask me why, it just happens. If the bill is for more than the auditor's report, complain to the Service Center. If less, then you may have lucked out and decide not to bring it up.

GETTING AN AUDIT PAYMENT PLAN

The audit is over and you (reluctantly) agree with the IRS that you owe some money. Naturally, your thoughts turn to how you are going to pay. The auditor may ask if you can pay on the spot. If you can't, she won't push it and may offer to help you set up a payment plan. If she doesn't bring up a payment plan, you may raise the subject. This is one of several alternatives open for handling an IRS debt. You don't have to discuss payment at all with an auditor; it's optional. You can wait until you are contacted by the IRS collection division, with no harm done except that the IRS interest meter is running. If you want to pay the IRS in installments, the auditor can process a payment plan request and it will be granted, if:

- the total owed is under $10,000, and
- all of your tax returns due have been filed, and
- all current tax payments are made (such as quarterly estimated taxes for self-employed people).

If you owe more than $10,000, the auditor may process the forms to request an installment agreement, but it is out of her hands as to whether you will be granted a payment plan.

Even if you know you owe, you may not be ready to commit to pay on any particular schedule. You may want to think it over, or ask a relative for a loan, or simply not deal with it for the moment. Fine; just say "no." Your case will simply be shipped off to your IRS Service Center, which will send out a bill in month or two.

2. Argue

Examination Reports aren't chiseled in stone. If you don't think an audit report is fair, call the auditor and tell her why. If she can't be persuaded and you feel your argument is a good one, ask to speak to her manager. Don't be shy—*Your Rights as a Tax-*

payer over the auditor's head. The manager does not have to meet with you, but she should at least give you a chance to make your key points on the phone. Tell her just where you think the auditor missed the boat. Be sure to let her know you will continue to fight (see next chapter on how to do this), if you can't reach a compromise. This call may not be productive, but you don't have anything to lose by trying.

Example: Phil, a full-time college professor and part-time jazz musician playing at small clubs on weekends, was audited. The IRS disallowed expenses in Phil's music business for piano lessons of $675 and opera singing lessons of $290. The auditor did not believe that these lessons were business-related, since Phil was a drum player. Phil called her manager and explained that both types of lessons enhanced his musical abilities, but he would accept disallowance of the opera lessons ($290) if the IRS allowed the piano lesson ($675) deduction. The manager agreed.

3. Do Nothing

Eventually, IRS audit reports become final—with or without your signature. The IRS may sit on your case for weeks or months after sending you the report before taking any action, however. If you really have no points to negotiate or money to pay, you may want to take this "do nothing" option. It will greatly delay your final audit bill, but interest is mounting.

M. When Your Audit Is Final

Whether you argue with or don't respond to the IRS, you will eventually be notified in writing that the audit report is final. If you don't the report, the IRS will either:

- Inform you that you can appeal within 30 days (see the next chapter on how to appeal an audit), or
- Inform you of your right to go to the U.S. Tax Court. You must act within 90 days of the date of the letter if you want to stop the audit from being finalized. (See the next chapter, "Appealing IRS Audits.")

RESOURCES

Stand Up to the IRS, by Frederick W. Daily (Nolo Press). This self-help book discusses IRS audit, appeal and Tax Court strategies in more detail than covered here.

Representing the Audited Taxpayer Before the IRS, by Robert McKenzie (Clark Boardman Callaghan). As the title suggests, this book is written for tax professionals, but much of it is understandable to laypeople as well.

IRS Publication 1, *Your Rights as a Taxpayer.* This pamphlet is clearly written and is a must-read for all taxpayers. ■

CHAPTER 20

Appealing IRS Audits

"Nor shall any person...be deprived of life,
liberty, or property, without due process of law."
— Fifth Amendment,
Constitution of the United States

You don't have to accept an IRS audit report. In most instances, you can appeal it within the IRS. If you are not given this opportunity, you can always go to federal Tax Court. (IRC §§ 9011, 9041.) An audit appeal is simple to initiate, and for small cases—under $10,000—you can do it yourself with a little help.

IRS statistics reveal that 85% of taxpayers who appeal are able to reduce their audit bill. The average appeals settlement produces a 40% reduction of the tax bill from the auditor's Examination Report. Many folks do even better. And even if you don't win your appeal, you will have delayed the final tax bill for many months.

APPEALING IRS AUDITS IN A NUTSHELL

1. If you can't live with an audit result, you can usually appeal within the IRS—and you always have the right to go to court.

2. The majority of audit appeals are successful in reducing tax bills.

3. Collection of your tax bill is greatly delayed if you appeal, but interest and penalties still keep accumulating.

4. Prepare for an appeal hearing by carefully organizing your records, researching basic tax law and, perhaps, getting advice from a tax pro.

5. Filing in Tax Court is simple; most folks do it without a lawyer when contesting $10,000 or less in taxes and penalties for any one tax year.

A. IRS Appeals

If you don't sign off on an auditor's Examination Report, in most cases the IRS mails you a "30-Day Letter." This gives you the right to appeal to the IRS Appeals Office, which is completely separate from the audit division. Until and unless this letter is issued, however, you cannot appeal.

The IRS is not required by law to let you appeal an audit, and sometimes it doesn't. But don't worry—the IRS still must notify you in writing of your right to contest the audit in the U.S. Tax Court. In this case, turn to Section B, below.

1. Writing an Appeal Letter

To appeal, write a "protest" letter to the IRS. (If you owe less than $2,500 in additional taxes, interest and penalties, you can simply tell the auditor that you want to appeal; but play it safe and put it in writing.) A sample protest letter is shown below. It should include:

- Your name (or name of your business, depending on which one the audit report specifies), and your taxpayer identification number (either your Social Security number, if you are a sole proprietor, or federal Employer Identification Number for other kinds of entities).

- A statement that you are appealing an Examination Report.

- The specific findings in the report that you dispute—something like this: "I disagree with the auditor's disallowance of business expense for travel in the amount of $797," or "I disagree with the finding by the auditor that my dog obedience business was not carried on for profit."

- A brief explanation of why the report is wrong. For example, "The trip in question was necessary to see a potential customer who lived in South Dakota," or "I operated in a businesslike manner and trained many dogs to be responsible members of the community."

- Your signature, date and these magic words: "Under penalty of perjury, I declare that the facts presented in this protest and in any accompanying documents are, to the best of my knowledge and belief, true, correct and complete."

Attach a copy of the Examination Report and the 30-Day Letter from the IRS. Send the letter to the IRS office that audited you, addressed to the "District Director." Your letter will be forwarded to the IRS Appeals Office.

SAMPLE PROTEST LETTER

October 1, 19xx

District Director
Internal Revenue Service
Your town, Your state 99999

Protest of Sam Smith
SSN 666-66-6666

Dear Sir/Madam:

I wish to appeal from the Examination Report of 9/5/xx, a copy of which is attached. I request a hearing. The tax year protested is 19xx.

I disagree with the disallowance of business expense deductions shown on Schedule C of $13,937 and penalties and interest in the amount of $2,817.

The adjustments were incorrect because the deductions were for legitimate expenses of advertising, promotion, travel and entertainment and were reasonable and necessary for my business.

Under penalty of perjury, I declare that the facts presented in this protest and in any accompanying documents are, to the best of my knowledge and belief, true, correct and complete.

Sincerely,

s/_____

Sam Smith
cc: IRS auditor
enclosed: copy of IRS 30-Day Letter and examination report

2. Settling Without a Hearing

Within a few months after you request an appeal, you should get a call or letter from the IRS Appeals Office asking you to come for a hearing. Or an Appeals Officer may offer to handle the case by phone or correspondence. This is worth a try. Send in explanations, copies of documents, citations to legal authority, affidavits of witnesses or whatever else you believe supports your position. A tax pro can help with this part if you feel that you need it.

If the Appeals Officer wants to discuss your case by phone and you are ready, go ahead; otherwise, request a later time when you can be fully prepared. (See Section 3, below, on how to present a case to an Appeals Officer.) But if you feel that you could do a better job in person, then insist on a meeting. I think you most always get a better shake by dealing face-to-face.

It's time to consult a tax pro. Even if you decide to handle your appeal yourself, it makes sense to consult a tax pro. He or she should have some insights on why you lost with the auditor and ideas on how to best organize your records and present your case. Appeals Officers appreciate a well-prepared presentation and are more likely to settle when they see their opponent is not a fool.

3. The Appeals Hearing

If you don't get anywhere by phone or mail, ask for a face-to-face meeting. Since most IRS offices don't have Appeals Officers, you may have to travel to another city. Your hearing will probably be just you and the Appeals Officer, meeting one-on-one in a private room. Auditors or other IRS personnel seldom attend. No formal or electronic recordings of Appeals Hearings are made, so take notes.

Most folks find Appeals Officers much more open and easier to deal with than auditors. Even though Appeals Officers work for the IRS, they are not supposed to just rubber-stamp auditors' decisions. Their aim is to mediate a settlement to keep your case from ending up in court. Your aim is to use this second chance to sell your position and convince the officer that you have already paid all or most of the taxes you rightly owe.

Expect an appeal hearing to last an hour or two. Start with a brief explanation of why you think the Examination Report is wrong. Next, show any documents supporting your position. Emphasize any material you now have but didn't show at the audit, such as new documents or a reconstruction of expenses. If you can't produce any missing documents, explain why.

IRS rules require an Appeals Officer to believe that you have some chance—no matter how small—of winning if you were to go to court. This means that Appeals Officers can't make a "nuisance" settlement—that is, give in just so you will go away. You'll need some evidence, even if it consists of records put together after the fact to replace ones that were missing, to provide the Appeals Officer with a hook on which to hang a compromise settlement. (Chapter 19, Audits, explains how reconstructed records can be used.)

Almost any kind of auditor's adjustment—other than one resulting from a plain error on your part—is subject to negotiation. The most common small business appeal issues include your entitlement to a home office, travel and entertainment expenses, advertising and business car write-offs. Making a deal on appeal is often done by "trading" issues. If you get the Appeals Officer to see that you have an arguable point on at least one issue, you are on your way to a compromise.

Don't expect total victory in an appeal, although it is certainly possible. Better is to stay flexible; give-and-take is the proper attitude.

Example: Rusty is an independent building materials sales rep. He regularly calls on customers using his car, and wines and dines his larger accounts. But an IRS auditor disallowed Rusty's auto expenses of $1,740 as well as his business entertainment expenses of $820, due to his poor recordkeeping and inability to produce paperwork. Rusty can argue to the Appeals Officer that he needs his car to make calls and that it is customary for salespersons in his business to buy customers lunch

or take them to baseball games. Rusty can back up his claims with signed statements from customers saying that he has bought them a meal or entertained them while on business. To settle, Rusty might offer to accept the disallowance of the entertainment expenses if the Appeals Officer allows his automobile expense deduction, or offer to accept a 50% disallowance of each.

Mention your Tax Court option. If the Appeals Officer is not amenable to any kind of settlement, tell him you are sorry because this means you will have to go on to Tax Court. If he thinks you are serious, he may make a last-ditch effort to work things out.

4. Payment After an Appeals Settlement

If and when you reach a settlement, Appeals Officers can request—but cannot insist on—immediate payment of any tax due. They can also process a monthly payment plan request. Legally, however, the amount you owe must be treated as a separate issue from how you are going to pay. So an Appeals Officer can't make any settlement conditioned on your immediate payment or acceptance of a payment plan. Most Appeals Officers are rather elitist—they don't like the tax collection business, and feel that it is beneath their status to even ask for payment.

B. Contesting an Audit in Court

There is no legal requirement to go through the IRS appeals process before you can contest an audit in court. If you don't appeal—or do but aren't happy with the way it comes out—you can go further. There are now three legal forums open to you: United States Tax Court, United States District Court, and the Court of Federal Claims.

Almost everyone chooses Tax Court, for two good reasons: First, the District and Claims courts require you to first pay the tax the IRS claims is due and then sue for a refund. Second, few people succeed in these courts without lawyers, which guarantees large legal fees.

Tax Court, on the other hand, allows you to contest an audit for an audit filing fee at $60, and offers a reasonable chance of success without a lawyer. About 15% of taxpayers who lose their audits file in Tax Court. Most of these souls come out ahead, too.

1. About Tax Court

The U.S. Tax Court is an independent federal court, *not* part of the IRS. (IRC 7441-46.) Contesting an audit in Tax Court requires filing a "petition," which is simple if yours qualifies as a small case. (See Section 2, below.)

The chances of at least partial victory are good: over half of those filing in Tax Court either settle with the IRS lawyers before trial, or get at least some reduction in their audit bill. For instance, the judge may uphold the IRS on a tax adjustment, but drop a penalty, saving you hundreds or maybe thousands of dollars. In cases under $10,000, 47% of taxpayers win at least partial victories over the IRS auditor. In larger cases, 60% of all petitioners come out ahead. However, less than 10% win a total victory in Tax Court.

2. Can You Do It Yourself in Tax Court?

Whether or not you want to go it alone in Tax Court may depend on how much money is at stake. Most Tax Court disputes involve *factual* issues—not complex tax law points. So, many people without law degrees come out just fine representing themselves in Tax Court and save on tax pro costs.

To go to Tax Court, you must have received an IRS "Statutory Notice of Deficiency," also called a "90-Day Letter." Expect this letter within one to six months after your audit has been completed if you did not sign the Examination Report. It is sent by certified or registered mail. If you move during this time, make sure the auditor has your new address.

a. Under $10,000: Informal "S" Cases

The Tax Court allows cases disputing less than $10,000 (per tax year audited) to be treated under rules much like your local Small Claims Court. These are referred to as "S," or small cases. Procedures are informal, and you present your case to one judge in your own words, without using legal jargon.

b. Over $10,000: Regular Cases

If yours is a regular case (more than $10,000 per year is in dispute), you may need a lawyer. (A small number of CPAs and Enrolled Agents are also allowed to practice in Tax Court.) If you proceed without a lawyer, you will be held to the same standard of knowledge of tax law and court procedures as an attorney. A compromise solution may be to use a tax lawyer as a legal coach, who gives advice but doesn't appear in court.

Filing a petition is a wise move. Often, just filing a Tax Court case produces a settlement offer from the IRS. If not, you can always chicken out before going into court, and all you will be out is the $60 filing fee. Alternatively, you can try to settle it yourself, and bring in a lawyer only if you fail. At least you delay the final tax bill for many months (although the interest continues to run).

3. Filing Your Petition in Tax Court

It is easy to get a small (under $10,000 per year) case before the Tax Court. First, call or write to the Clerk of the U.S. Tax Court, 400 Second Street, NW, Washington, DC 20217, (202) 606-8754. Request a petition form and pamphlet explaining the court's rules. The staff of the Tax Court is very helpful and will get these items to you within a few days.

Carefully follow the instructions for filling in the forms and filing your case. Mail the petition (via U.S. Postal Service, certified mail, Return Receipt Requested) and other required papers. Be sure to enclose your check or money order for the filing fee. You should receive an acknowledgment letter and case number from the clerk within a week or two. The Tax Court will send the IRS attorneys a copy of your petition.

4. Tax Court Pre-Trial Procedure

Within a few months after filing your case, you should hear from someone at the IRS, usually either an Appeals Officer or lawyer. This is an important contact; the majority of cases are settled by these folks. You might even settle your case by phone or through the mail without ever meeting these people or having to go before a judge. (The discussion in Section A, above, on how to negotiate a settlement on an appeal, is applicable here as well.)

If you reach a settlement, a Stipulated Tax Court "Decision" will be prepared for your signature. It goes back to the IRS and then to a judge for approval, and the case is over. It might take a few months to complete the paperwork, so don't be concerned if you don't get the final decision right away. (The only thing to worry about now is paying the bill.)

If no compromise is reached, you'll get a notice of a trial date. Expect it to be in six to 12 months. Trials are held in about 100 of the largest cities, so you may have to travel several hundred miles for yours—another reason to try to settle before trial.

5. Settling Before Trial

Frequently, IRS lawyers agree to a last-minute deal—sometimes in the hallway outside the courtroom—just before your trial is to begin. If they don't bring up the possibility, you can. Try offering something new—such as agreeing to some part of an adjustment that you previously did not accept. Less than 10% of all folks get a total victory in a Tax Court trial, so be realistic.

Example: Karen's auto parts business was audited, and additional taxes of $5,100 were found, including $1,300 for disallowed business expenses. Karen could offer to accept the $1,300 tax if the IRS will concede the balance of $3,800. A proposal like this might tip the scales with the IRS attorney, or he might come back with a compromise. It may not work, but it doesn't cost anything to try.

6. Your Tax Court Trial

How your trial will be conducted depends on whether or not it qualifies for the simplified procedures for small cases (less than $10,000 contested per tax year).

a. All Cases

On the date you are scheduled for trial, show up on time. Typically, many other IRS victims will be there, and the clerk will start things off by calling roll. Chances are your case won't be heard on that day; you will probably be assigned a time and date later in that week (or the next one) to come back for trial.

The judge sits on a wooden throne (like on TV), or at the end of a conference table (if there is no formal courtroom). Once your case is called, come forward and sit at a separate table facing the judge. The IRS attorney will be at another table. Bring your notes and all papers you want the judge to see with you. If you have witnesses, bring them to the table or have them sitting nearby. Address the judge as "your honor."

The judge will not be familiar with your case. He or she has only the Tax Court file, including only your petition, the IRS's response (called an "answer") and a copy of the Examination Report. The judge does not have the IRS's file or any of the documents that you submitted to the auditor or Appeals Officer.

You and your witnesses will be sworn to tell the truth. You may sit or stand, according to the preference of the judge, as you present your case. A table will be provided for you to lay out your documents and sit at when the IRS attorney is presenting the IRS's case.

Start by asking the judge if you can give a brief sketch of why you disagree with the IRS, don't go into the details just yet. Then, either ask permission to start calling your witnesses, or begin by presenting your documents (whatever you want the judge to consider). Bring an extra copy of everything you give the judge for the IRS's attorney—and don't forget a copy for yourself. Briefly explain each document by saying something like, "Your honor, this a bill from the plumber who fixed the pipes, which the IRS auditor would not allow me to claim as a business expense deduction." Expect the judge and the IRS attorney to ask you questions. Questioning is relatively informal, especially if yours is an "S" case; just explain and show things as if you were trying to convince a friend about your case.

Example: Thom's hardware store was damaged by a flood. He immediately hired Jim to make emergency repairs. Jim insisted on payment of $3,800 in cash and Thom agreed. Thom got a receipt from Jim for payment but lost it in the confusion. Jim has since moved to parts unknown after his ex-wife came after him for unpaid child support. An IRS auditor disallowed the $3,800 deduction—not because this type of expense was not legally allowed, but because Thom couldn't prove that he paid it. So Thom's dispute with the IRS is over the question of whether he paid this amount—not whether it's a legitimate business expense.

PART 6

Dealing With the IRS

At the Tax Court hearing, Thom starts by explaining what happened in his own words. Since he has the right to present a witness to back up his story, Thom presents Deena, an employee, who observed the damage and saw Jim do the work. Even though Deena didn't see Thom pay Jim, she nevertheless can testify that this seemed to be a normal business relationship, and that the amount of damage was consistent with the amount Thom claims he paid. This testimony should help the judge infer that Jim didn't work without pay.

Thom also shows the judge anything supporting his case, for example a news clipping or photo of the damage. Then it is up to the judge to determine if Thom, Deena and the documentation are believable enough to overturn all or some of the auditor's findings.

b. Cases Over $10,000 Only

If your case involves over $10,000 per tax year and goes before a judge, you should know something about Tax Court procedures if you hope to win. Start by consulting the books in the "Resources" list at the end of this chapter.

On the day of your trial, there may be other cases heard before yours. You may find it enlightening (or stupefying) to spend a few hours watching and learning about the judge's habits and courtroom procedures firsthand.

7. Tax Court Decisions

Unlike Judge Wapner, who wraps it all up in 15 minutes and makes his decision on the spot, Tax Court judges usually mail out their decisions a few weeks or months after a trial.

Small case (under $10,000) Tax Court decisions are final; they cannot be appealed by you or by the IRS. Regular tax court decisions (over $10,000 cases), may be appealed to a higher court—the U.S. Court of Appeals. Appealing a Tax Court decision definitely requires an attorney, but consider this before you hire one: less than 15% of all Tax Court decisions are reversed.

If you don't win outright, it will be several more months after receiving the judge's decision before you actually get a tax bill. Interest is added to the bill starting from the time the original tax return was filed—or the date it should have been filed, if later.

RESOURCES

IRS Publication 1, Your Rights as a Taxpayer

IRS Publication 5, Appeal Rights and Preparation of Unagreed Cases

IRS Publication 556, Examination of Returns, Appeal Rights and Claims for Refund

Stand Up to the IRS, by Frederick W. Daily (Nolo Press). This companion book has detailed information and tips on handling appeals and Tax Court cases.

Represent Yourself in Court, by Paul Bergman and Sara Berman-Barrett (Nolo Press). This book is full of practical tips on how to present documents to a court and what to say (and not to say) to a judge.

Rules of Practice & Procedure, United States Tax Court. If you are handling a regular Tax Court case (over $10,000 contested per tax year) on your own, you need to familiarize yourself with the rules of court. This book is available through the Tax Court Clerk, 400 Second St., N.W., Washington, DC, 202-606-8754. Call to find out the current price. You can also find it in most federal court buildings and law school libraries. ■

CHAPTER 21

Penalties and Interest

"Laws and institutions require to be adapted, not to good men, but to bad."

— **John Stuart Mill**

When the IRS hits your business with a tax bill, it usually adds penalties and interest. These extra charges can be shocking—I once saw a $7,000 tax bill with $15,000 in penalties and interest tacked on to it. Some penalties are added automatically by IRS computers. IRS personnel may also impose

PART **6**

Dealing With the IRS

penalties if they find that you violated a tax code provision—for example, you paid taxes or filed a return late, or you owe more taxes from an audit. The IRS doesn't just dream up these penalties—each penalty has been authorized by our elected representatives in Washington.

Once penalties are decreed, if you don't take steps to get them off your bill, the IRS assumes you accept them. Happily, the IRS can remove a penalty from your bill just as easily as they added it. The key to the kingdom of tax penalty relief is showing a "reasonable cause" for your failure to comply with the tax law.

And by the way, tax penalties are not tax-deductible when you pay them.

PENALTIES AND INTEREST IN A NUTSHELL

1. Whenever the IRS finds a business was late in filing a return or making a payment or otherwise breached the tax laws, it is likely to impose a penalty.

2. If your business is hit with a penalty, it may be canceled if you can show "reasonable cause."

3. You are entitled to a full explanation from the IRS of any penalty imposed and how it was calculated.

4. It is difficult, but not impossible, to get the IRS to drop interest charges on tax bills.

A. Common Reasons for Penalties

The number of penalties available to the IRS to punish wrongdoers is staggering. This section covers the ones that are most likely to be imposed on a small business person.

1. Inaccuracies

The IRS can hit you with a 20% penalty if it finds you were negligent (unreasonably careless) or substantially understated your taxes. You typically incur this "accuracy-related" penalty when you can't prove a deduction on an audit, or you forgot to report all of your income and the IRS discovers it.

2. Civil Fraud

If the IRS finds that you underreported your income with a fraudulent intent (it doesn't look like a mistake to the IRS), you can be fined 75% of the amount of the resulting tax deficiency. (IRC § 6651(f).) Don't worry too much about this civil (noncriminal) tax fraud penalty—it's imposed in less than 2% of all audits. (You may also be charged with the crime of tax fraud, which is even rarer (IRC § 7201).)

3. Failure to Pay on Time

The IRS usually adds a penalty of $1/2$% to 1% per month to an income tax bill that's not paid on time. This penalty is automatically tacked on by the IRS computer whenever you file a return but don't pay the full amount owed, or pay it late. (IRC § 665(a).)

Late payment penalties for failing to make payroll tax deposits on time are much higher.

4. Filing Late

If you're late in filing certain income tax returns or other forms, the IRS can penalize you an additional 5% per month on any balance due. However, this penalty can be applied only for the first five months following the return's due date, up to a 25% maximum charge.

5. Filing and Paying Late

A special rule applies if you both file late and underpay. The IRS can (and probably will) impose a "combined penalty" of 25% of the amount owed if you don't pay in the first five months after the return and tax are due. After five months, the "failure to pay" penalty continues at 1/2% per month until the two penalties reach a combined maximum of 47 1/2%. This is a slightly lower (2 1/2% less overall) penalty than if the two penalties were applied separately. Wow, those IRS folks sure can be generous. (IRC § 665(c).)

Example: Mortimer the mortician lets April 15 pass without filing his tax return or making any payment. He finally gets around to filing on September 16 and owes $4,000. The IRS will tack on a 25% penalty ($1,000). Interest will be charged as well.

IRS penalties are "stackable." Late filing and paying penalties can be imposed by the IRS in addition to any other penalties, such as for fraud and filing an inaccurate return. Congress and the IRS believes the more the merrier when it comes to penalizing taxpayers.

6. Underpaying Estimated Taxes

Undoubtedly, many of you will get hit with the estimated tax penalty. I know I have been, for whatever that is worth to you. All self-employed individuals must estimate their income tax for the year and pay it in quarterly installments throughout the year. You must come pretty close to paying everything you will owe, although you don't have to guess the amount precisely. Here are the rules:

- If you earn less than $150,000, your quarterly tax payments must equal at least 90% of your final income tax bill, or at least 100% of your last year's tax bill.

- If you earn more than $150,000, you must pay at least 110% of your last year's tax bill in estimated payments or risk the underpayment penalty on whatever amount you come up short.

The penalty for not complying is currently calculated at a 9% annual rate on the amount that was underpaid for each quarter. Quarterly payments should be equal—you can't play catch-up with larger payments later in the year and still avoid this penalty.

B. Interest on Tax Bills

Congress requires the IRS to charge interest on tax bills, and has given the IRS very limited discretion in canceling interest charges. The interest rate is set by Congress, adjusted every quarter and compounded daily—currently it's 9% annually. It is charged on a monthly basis. If payment is received after the 15th day of any month, you are charged another full month's interest at the current rate. If you are audited and end up owing more tax, interest is charged starting on the original date the tax return was due.

C. Understanding Penalty and Interest Notices

If you receive a tax bill with a penalty and interest amount attached, you probably won't understand how these charges were computed, and the notice won't explain it very well, if at all. Calling or visiting your local IRS office to ask for an explanation of any notice is not always fruitful, because many IRS staffers don't understand these computer-generated and heavily coded notices. A better way is to call the IRS taxpayer assistance line (800/829-1040) and request a Penalty and Interest Explanation Notice (PINEX).

PART 6

Dealing With the IRS

A PINEX is a multi-paged computer printout that is fairly easy to understand. It includes:

- A listing of your business (or personal) tax accounts for the years you request, showing all tax penalty and interest computations.

- Dates, interest rates, penalties assessed and any credits to your account, such as your quarterly payments, abatements (reductions) by the IRS or any refunds applied.

- Explanations of why particular penalties were charged with tax code citations authorizing each penalty.

- A summary of your account with balance due, including up-to-date penalty and interest amounts.

D. How to Get Penalties Reduced or Eliminated

Once you understand why and how the IRS hit you with penalties, you are in a better position to request that these charges be reduced or eliminated. The IRS term for this process is "abatement." About one-third of all penalties are eventually abated, according to IRS statistics. I suspect, however, that even more penalties would be canceled if people contested them vigorously.

Just telling the IRS that you don't like a penalty, or can't afford to pay it, won't work. You must show "reasonable cause," meaning a good excuse. The IRS handbook, The Internal Revenue Manual (IRM), directs that, "Any sound reason advanced by a taxpayer as the cause for delay in filing a return, making deposits...or paying tax when due will be carefully analyzed."

The manual lists seven categories of excuses for abating a tax penalty (except fraud):

1. Death or serious illness of the taxpayer or immediate family

2. Unavoidable absence

3. Destruction by fire or other casualty of the business or records

4. Inability to determine the tax because of reasons beyond the taxpayer's control

5. Civil disturbances

6. Lack of funds, but only when the taxpayer can demonstrate the exercise of ordinary business care and prudence, and

7. Other reasons establishing that the taxpayer exercised ordinary business care but couldn't comply within the time limits.

When requesting an abatement, try to fit your excuse into categories 1 to 6 first. If you honestly can't, try the catch-all number 7. This category covers mistaken reliance on bad advice from a tax pro or from the IRS, or just about any other excuse you can come up with.

If in doubt, try for an abatement. It is always worth a try to get a penalty abated. I have seen people with all sorts of excuses—some a tad farfetched—succeed. And one thing is for certain: if you don't ask, you have no chance.

1. How to Request a Penalty Abatement

As soon as you receive a tax notice with penalties, request an abatement in writing, following the form letter below. Be straightforward. State that you are requesting an abatement of penalties, identify the tax bill, and tell the IRS what your reasonable cause is. Attach a photocopy of the IRS notice with the penalty you want to removed shown on it, along with any documentation supporting your request. Keep several copies of your letters and attachments.

Most penalties are imposed by the IRS Service Center that sent the tax bill, so mail your abatement request there. The IRS is notorious for ignoring, losing or taking seemingly forever to answer correspondence, so you may need to send additional copies later. Wait about 45 days before sending your follow-up request. Photocopies of your first request and documents should be sufficient—just change the date of the request.

Stress your clean IRS record. If you can do so honestly, emphasize that you have never before had a penalty assessed against you, been behind in paying taxes, or asked for an abatement of penalties. Even if such claims are not true, the IRS penalty examiner may not bother to check it out, so let your conscience be your guide.

2. If Your Abatement Request Is Rejected

If the IRS Service Center officially rejects your request, you should get a written notice denying abatement. If you want to go further, take one or more of these actions:

1. Write to the Service Center and ask for penalty appeals consideration. There is no IRS form for appeals—just write a clear letter headed "Penalty Appeal" and explain your "reasonable cause." Attach the tax bill in question and any documentation supporting your case.

2. Call or visit your local IRS office and speak with a Taxpayer Service Representative or a Collection employee. They also can consider "reasonable cause" applications and cancel penalties. Don't mention that a service center turned you down. If you're turned down, request in writing that they forward your case for appeals consideration.

3. File an Offer in Compromise on IRS Form 656 based on doubt as to your liability for the penalty. This is a formal procedure for contesting or negotiating any unpaid IRS bill, including a penalty charge. Don't offer any money when contesting a

penalty because you are claiming that you aren't liable for it, no matter the amount. Follow the directions accompanying Form 656 precisely. Attach your explanation and documents supporting your position, if any. (Offers in Compromise are discussed in Chapter 18, When You Can't Pay Your Taxes.)

4. If none of the above suggestions work, pay the penalty and then file IRS Form 843, Claim for Refund and Request of Abatement. Attach a letter and substantiating documents (as you did to your abatement request letter), or write your explanation in the space provided on the form. If your claim is refused, you can sue in U.S. District Court or the Court of Federal Claims for a refund. Seldom are tax penalties large enough to justify the expense of a lawsuit, however.

SAMPLE LETTER REQUESTING ABATEMENT OF PENALTIES

To: Adjustments/Correspondence Branch
IRS Service Center
P.O. Box 9941
Ogden, UT 84409

Re: Request for Penalty Abatement

From: Sanford Majors
43 Valley Road
Salt Lake City, UT 84000

SSN: 555-55-5555

November 3, 199x

To Whom It May Concern:

I am requesting an abatement of penalties asserted in the IRS notice enclosed dated 5/5/9x of $2,312.10.

The reason I [select one]: filed late, paid late, didn't report some income was that [fill in your reason, such as]:

- I was suffering from a nervous breakdown

- My wife had just passed away

- My house burned down on April 14 with all of my tax records

- I was a hostage in Lebanon

- any other excuse

Enclosed is a [describe your documents, such as]:

- Letter from Dr. Freud explaining my condition which prevented me from filing my tax return on time

- Death certificate confirming my wife's passing

- Report from the fire department

- Letter from the U.S. State Department confirming my status as a hostage

- any other documentation

I have also enclosed payment that covers the amount of the underlying taxes I owe. [Optional, but a good idea if you can afford to make the payment.]

Please abate these penalties for "reasonable cause." I can be reached at 801-555-3444 during daytime hours.

Thank you,

Sanford Majors

Sanford Majors

Enclosed: IRS Tax Notice; Doctor's letter, death certificate, fire report, letter from State Department [or whatever]

E. How to Get Interest Charges Removed

It is not easy to get interest removed from a tax bill, unless it was charged due to a clear IRS error. In four instances, however, you might have a chance.

1. Logically enough, if a tax or penalty is abated, interest on that amount should be canceled too. The IRS computer should do this automatically, but always check a tax bill to verify that the excess interest was removed. If you suspect a mistake, call the IRS at the number on the notice or at 800-829-1040. Ask them to explain on the phone or send you a PINEX. (See Section C, above.) If you continue to get incorrect bills, complain to the IRS office that sent the bill.

2. You may be able to cancel interest charges that result from delays by the IRS. For instance, if you settled an audit agreeing to pay more tax, and the IRS didn't send a bill until a year later, the year's interest should be canceled, since it accrued because the IRS didn't promptly bill you. However, you can't get interest abated if it accumulated while you were (unsuccessfully) challenging an IRS bill in an audit appeal or in court.

3. If the IRS concludes that you will never be able to pay the bill, it may accept less by way of an Offer in Compromise. (See Chapter 18, When You Can't Pay Your Taxes.)

4. Interest, along with the tax and penalties, may be reduced or eliminated through bankruptcy. (See Chapter 18, When You Can't Pay Your Taxes.)

F. Designating Payments on Delinquent Tax Bills

If you make payments on tax bills that include both penalties and interest, you are usually allowed to tell the IRS where to apply the payments. Does it make a difference? Yes, it might. If the bill is for a business-related tax, you should designate that the payment be first applied to interest. The reason is that the interest is a deductible business expense.

(Tax penalties, however, are never deductible, and neither is interest on a personal (nonbusiness) tax bill.)

On exception to the "first to interest" designation is for past due payroll taxes. If your bill includes payroll taxes, payments should be designated to be first applied to "the trust fund portion" of the delinquent payroll tax. (See Chapter 5, Tax Concerns of Employers.)

You can also direct the IRS to apply payments to specific tax periods for which you are delinquent. Generally, you want payments first applied to the most recent—not the oldest—tax period, for several reasons:

- The heaviest penalties are charged in the first few months after a tax return is due.
- The older a tax bill gets, the more likely the IRS is to compromise it, lose it in the shuffle, or let the ten-year statute of limitations on collection run out.
- Tax bills even three years old may qualify for discharge in bankruptcy.

If you don't tell the IRS which tax period to apply the payment, it will automatically apply it to the oldest tax period.

To designate payments, write the tax period on the face of the payment check, along with your taxpayer identification number (your Social Security or the Employer Identification Number of your business). Also, send a letter with the check stating specifically which tax period you want the payment applied to.

RESOURCES

Stand Up to the IRS, by Frederick W. Daily (Nolo Press). This book discusses penalties, interest and how to deal with them in greater detail than we go into in this chapter.

IRS Notice 746, *Information About Your Notice, Penalty and Interest.* This notice is usually sent with your first tax bill that contains a penalty or interest charge. If you need a copy, call 800-829-1040 or go to your local IRS office. ■

CHAPTER 22

Help Beyond the Book

"The avoidance of taxes is the only
intellectual pursuit that still carries any reward."
— **John Maynard Keynes**

If you follow the news, you realize that tax laws are always being reworked by Congress. You need to keep up with changes that affect you, your business or industry.

PART 6

Dealing With the IRS

The average small business person can't afford to call a tax pro with every question. Fortunately, much tax information is available for free (or close to it), if you are willing to look. The IRS provides free publications on basic tax law—at least from the IRS's point of view. Trade associations publish specialized newsletters and magazines that cover tax concerns common to their members. General tax newsletters, books and annual publications are plentiful, and small business tax material is widely available in libraries.

You'll probably need a good tax advisor as well. But you can keep costs under control by learning as much as you can on your own first. The more you know before meeting the tax pro, the better position you will be in to judge his or her capabilities. And, of course, the less tax education you will have to pay for. Throughout this book I alert you to times it makes economic sense to talk to a tax pro.

A tax pro can help you set up your record keeping system and choose an accounting method. And like most small business folks, you may want to use a pro if you don't feel comfortable doing your own tax return. (Who does?) Everyone's business and individual tax situation is unique; like your wardrobe, some custom fitting always works better than off-the-rack. Here are some places to do your shopping.

TAX HELP IN A NUTSHELL

1. There are a lot of good resources for answering tax questions, starting with free IRS publications.

2. Oral advice from the IRS is not legally binding on the IRS and cannot be relied upon.

3. It pays to find and establish a relationship with a tax professional.

A. Finding Answers to Tax Questions

Our income tax law is a product of all three branches of our federal government. The legislative branch, Congress, enacts the provisions that make up the Internal Revenue Code (IRC).

The executive branch, specifically the Treasury Department, of which the Internal Revenue Service is a part, administers the tax law. It also publishes interpretations of many tax code provisions which serve as guides as to how the IRS will apply the law.

The judicial branch, the federal courts, interpret the tax code in light of the Constitution and what they divine as Congress's intent. When the IRS applies the tax code differently than Congress intended, it may be overturned by the federal courts. These court decisions are published ("reported") and serve to guide taxpayers on how to interpret the tax code.

This section discusses many resources that are available to augment and explain the tax information in this book: IRS publications, self-help tax preparation guides, text books, court decisions and periodicals. Some are free, and most others are reasonably priced. Tax publications for professionals are expensive, but are often available at public or law libraries.

1. IRS Booklets and CD-ROM

The IRS publishes over 350 free booklets explaining the tax code, and many are fairly straightforward. But where there is a gray area in the law, you can bet the booklet will present only the IRS's interpretation—even, in a few instances, when courts have made contrary rulings.

These booklets, called IRS Publications ("pubs," for short), range from several pages to several hundred pages in length. They are available in IRS offices, or by calling 800-829-FORM (3676), or by sending in an order form. There is no charge, not even postage. (A list of free IRS tax publications for small businesses is in the Appendix.)

Your best bet is to order a package of IRS forms and publications called *Your Business Tax Kit.* The kit includes Forms SS-4 Application for Employer Identification Number and 1040-ES Estimated Tax For Individuals. And it has a number of publications mentioned throughout this book:

- Pub 334, *Tax Guide for Small Business* (at 325 pages, the largest booklet)
- Pub 583, *Taxpayers Starting a Business*
- Pub 910, *Guide to Free Tax Services*
- Pub 1057, *Small Business Tax Education Program Brochure*
- Pub 1544, *Reporting Cash Payments of Over $10,000* and
- Pub 1779, *Employee or Independent Contractor.*

If you have a computer with a CD-ROM and don't mind spending $46 (it's a deductible business expense), you can get all IRS publications, plus 600 forms, IRS Regulations and back year tax forms (to 1991) on CD-ROM Publication 1796 (Stock Number 648-095-00004-0). Contact the Superintendent of Documents for ordering information, at 202-512-1800.

Don't rely exclusively on the IRS for information. The IRS's free publications run the gamut from good to bad to plain ugly. While some are clearly written and useful, others are misleading, and a few are nearly incomprehensible. I am always amused to see IRS publications with disclaimers warning you against relying on them. The IRS is not legally bound to follow its own writings that explain the tax law. Amazing, isn't it?

2. Free IRS and Social Security Telephone Information

The IRS offers a series of prerecorded tapes on tax topics on its toll-free telephone service (TELETAX) at 800-829-4477. (See IRS Publication 910 for a list of topics.) You can also talk to a live IRS taxpayer service representative at 800-829-1040, but expect difficulty getting through from January to May. Avoid calling on Mondays or during lunchtime.

The Social Security Administration also has an 800 number: 800-772-1213. It is staffed 7 a.m. to 7 p.m., and has prerecorded topics 24 hours a day. Among other things, you or an employee of your business can get a statement of earnings, Form W-2 and Form 1099 income information for past years, an estimate of benefits, and new or replacement Social Security cards.

Be alert for bad advice. The IRS is notorious for giving misleading or outright wrong answers to taxpayers' telephone questions. In the IRS's defense, often taxpayers don't ask the right questions or really understand the answers given. Our overly complex tax code is as much to blame as the IRS. Unfortunately, the IRS does not stand behind oral advice that turns out to be incorrect. If you rely on what someone at the IRS tells you to make an important decision and the IRS is wrong, you'll be liable for any tax that should have been paid, plus interest and penalties. If it's important, always check what the IRS tells you with a tax pro.

3. Free IRS Programs

In larger metropolitan areas, the IRS offers small business seminars on how to comply with the tax law—for example, payroll tax reporting. You can ask questions about tax procedures at these half-day meetings given at schools and federal buildings. Call the IRS at 800/829-1040 to see if there are any programs offered near you and to get on the IRS small business mailing list.

4. IRS Written Opinions

The IRS is legally bound by advice it gives in writing, but written guidance is difficult and expensive to get. You must request an "IRS Letter Ruling" and pay a fee of $3,000. Expect to wait many months for your answer. If you are still interested, see a tax pro for details.

A better (and far cheaper) bet might be to look up the letter rulings that have been issued to other taxpayers with a similar question—if you can find one. Letter rulings are published in the Internal Revenue Cumulative Bulletin, and in private tax service publications found in larger public and law libraries. I won't kid you; it is not easy to research letter rulings and even harder to find one on the point you are interested in. However, if you want to try, you should know how these rulings are identified and indexed. For example, "Ltr. Rul. 892012" refers to a ruling issued in 1989, in the 20th week and which was the 12th letter ruling issued that week. My suggestion is that you ask a tax pro to do this for you instead.

5. Internal Revenue Code

All tax laws are in the Internal Revenue Code (IRC), written by Congress and often referred to as "the code" or the "tax code." It's a thick book with tiny print and is found in the reference section of most libraries, IRS offices, tax pros' offices and larger bookstores. The IRC is revised once or twice a year, mostly minor changes by Congress. On average, major revisions to the tax code are made every three to four years.

The IRC is found in Title 26 of the United States Code (USC for short). The USC encompasses all of our federal laws. "Title" simply refers to the place within the massive USC where the IRC is found. The IRC is divided up into sections, which, in turn, are subdivided into more parts, ad infinitum. The tax code book is a crazy-quilt that contains laws that apply to everyone next to provisions just for left-handed sheep breeders in New Jersey.

Example: "IRC § 179(b)(4)(A)" means that this particular tax law is found in Title 26 of the USC, the Internal Revenue Code, § 179, subsection (b), paragraph 4, subparagraph A.

Most folks don't ever need to look the IRC, and just lifting it is an exercise; it is available at larger bookstores for about $25. (See order information at the back of this book.) The USC (including the IRC) is also available on CD-ROM from the Government Printing Office.

6. IRS Interpretations of the Tax Code

Congress, when enacting a tax law, can't foresee all possible applications. So frequently the Treasury Department is authorized to issue interpretations of broad tax code provisions.

a. Regulations

The most authoritative IRS interpretations are called "Treasury Regulations" or just "Regulations" or "Regs." These show the mechanics of how many (but not all) tax code provisions operate. Regulations often include examples, which can be extremely helpful. Regs are usually found in a four- to six-volume set, called Treasury Regulations, and found in most larger libraries and some bookstores. Regulations are somewhat easier to read and comprehend than the tax code.

Whenever you want to go beyond the IRC for an answer, first check to see if there is a matching regulation for that code section. Start with the number of the IRC section; if there is a corresponding regulation, it will bear the same number, usually preceded by the numeral "1."

Example: "Reg. 1.179" refers to a Treasury regulation interpreting IRC Section 179.

b. Other IRS Pronouncements

The IRS makes other written statements of its position on various tax matters. They do not have the force of law, but guide IRS personnel and taxpayers as to how specific tax laws should be understood and obeyed.

Revenue Rulings (Rev. Rul.) are IRS written statements of how the tax law applies to a specific set of facts. These are published as general guidance to taxpayers. Private companies such as Prentice Hall, Commerce Clearing House and Research Institute of America reprint IRS Revenue Rulings. They are indexed by IRC section and subject matter. A Revenue Ruling usually contains a hypothetical set of facts, followed by an explanation of how the tax code applies to those facts. While looking for a Revenue Ruling might pay off, it is not easy to find one that precisely covers your situation.

Example: "Rev. Rul. 92-41" refers to IRS Revenue Ruling number 41, issued in 1992.

IRS Letter Rulings are IRS answers to specific written questions and hypothetical situations posed by taxpayers. (See Section 4, above.)

IRS Revenue Procedures (Rev. Procs.) are another way the IRS tells taxpayers exactly how to comply with certain tax provisions, though they are primarily written for guidance to tax professionals and preparers. Rev. Procs. often explain when and how to report tax items, such as claiming a net operating loss on a tax return. They are published in the *Internal Revenue Cumulative Bulletin,* found in larger public and law libraries and widely reprinted in professional tax publications.

Example: "Rev. Proc. 91-15" refers to a published Revenue Procedure number 15, issued in 1991.

From time to time, the IRS gives general guidance and statements of policy in official "announcements" and "notices" similar to press releases from other government agencies. They are published in the weekly *Internal Revenue Cumulative Bulletin.* Seldom will it pay you to spend any time searching for an IRS announcement or notice, as these are too broad to answer specific questions.

The Internal Revenue Manual (IRM) is a series of handbooks that serve as internal guides to IRS employees on points of tax law and procedure. The IRM tells IRS employees, such as auditors or collectors, how specific tax code provisions should be enforced. The manual is for IRS internal use, but most of it is public and reprinted by private tax book publishers. It is also available to the public in larger IRS offices that have Freedom of Information Act reading rooms, and in law libraries and some tax pros' offices. The IRM may be helpful in understanding some IRS procedures—for example, it gives the criteria the IRS uses to determine whether "reasonable cause" exists for the abatement of a tax penalty.

IRS Forms are well known to us all, especially Form 1040, your annual personal income tax return. The IRS issues more than 650 other forms, listed in Publication 676, *Catalog of Federal Tax Forms*. Order any of them by calling 800-829-FORM or 800-829-1040. Many of the forms come with instructions, which are sometimes very helpful.

7. Court Cases

Federal courts have interpreted the tax law in thousands of court cases. The most likely place to find a published (reported) Tax Court decision is in a set of books called the *Tax Court Reports*. Other courts, namely the U.S. District Courts, U.S. Courts of Appeal, Court of Federal Claims and U.S. Bankruptcy Courts and of course, the Supreme Court all rule on tax issues as well. Almost all cases decided by these courts are published. Chances are good that at least one of these courts has adjudged the point you are interested in; the trick is finding it.

Researching cases is a topic well beyond this book, but I can make a few suggestions. Begin by finding your nearest law library with public access. Call your local federal court, college library or a lawyer's office to find out where to go. Besides the volumes that simply reprint court decisions, there are books by tax research companies that summarize the cases and put them into a coherent order.

You can access tax case books by starting with the number of an IRC section, a case reference you have run across or a general topic, such as "depreciation." Armed with this information, you have two choices: try to find the material yourself or ask the law library staff for help. If the law librarian has the time (and knows her way around the tax section), she might show you how to use the books. Also look at the legal research books listed at the end of this chapter.

8. Federal Small Business Programs

The Small Business Administration (SBA) guarantees business loans and also puts out some good publications. You might also benefit from personal help offered by the Service Corps of Retired Executives (SCORE) program, under the auspices of the SBA. This is a group of retired business people who volunteer their time to help small-time operators. They are not necessarily tax experts, but if they were successful business people, you can bet they know a thing or two about the tax game. Call the SBA answer desk at 800-827-5722, or visit the SBA office nearest you. Or you can write to the SBA at 1441 L Street, NW, Washington, DC 20461.

Small Business Development Centers (SBDCs) are joint projects with the SBA and state governments. There are several hundred in the U.S. and are usually affiliated with major state universities. SBDCs provide free or low-cost seminars and counseling to small business people. If you can't locate an SBDC in your state, call the SBA.

Other federal agencies also offer publications—some for free and others at reasonable prices—to assist small businesses. For a list of federal publications, write to:

Superintendent of Documents
U.S. Government Printing Office
PO Box 371954
Pittsburgh, PA 15250-7954

9. Private Tax Guides and Software

There are a multitude of commercially published tax guides, including annual tax preparation guidebooks that sell for $20 or less. Most of them are directed at taxes for individuals, but many deal with small business tax issues as well. Some of my favorites are listed at the end of this chapter.

Annual tax professional deskbooks are one-volume guides with more detailed tax information than the preparation guides. They presume some basic tax knowledge on the reader's part.

When you're preparing a return, tax preparation computer programs can supply some basic tax guidance and reduce your chances of making mistakes. If you are computer literate, TurboTax and MacIntax (both published by Intuit) are recommended. But if you do it yourself, I suggest having the tax return reviewed by a tax pro before filing. This is cheaper than having the pro prepare a return from scratch, and lets you know whether or not you really know what you're doing.

10. Trade Association Publications

Every business or trade has its own publications and newsletters that closely track tax issues of common interest. By reading them, you can learn about specific tax issues your tax pro might not know of—or may at least find out before she does if a new case or IRS ruling appears to be significant. Also, programs dealing with tax issues are sometimes offered at conventions and trade shows.

11. Online IRS and Tax Info

The IRS has its own "home page" accessible through the World Wide Web. In the first week of operation, more than a million computer users checked it out. Currently, you can download over 600 forms and publications, and peruse summaries of 150 tax topics and answers to frequently asked questions. This information can be accessed through a "keyword" search. The IRS has promised to greatly expand the contents of the home page over the next year. The IRS' Internet address is: http://www.irs.ustreas.gov. A help desk (703/487-4608) offers advice on using this service. You can find other interesting tax-related web sites by using a "tax" word search through popular search engines such as Yahoo.

All of the major commercial online services—CompuServe, America Online and Prodigy—offer tax information to their subscribers, as well as access to the World Wide Web. You can also post your tax questions on their bulletin boards and forums and maybe even reach tax experts through various chat rooms. Many tax pros will give you online advice—but of course, don't blindly rely on this gratuitous advice from strangers. This is totally free speech, meaning there isn't any control on people expressing their opinions online. I have seen quite a bit of tax protest nonsense and other such stuff there.

B. Finding and Using a Tax Pro

Mastering all the tax information applicable to you is probably impossible, given everything else you have to do in business. Fortunately, it's also unnecessary. Armed with a good basic understanding of how your business is taxed, it makes sense to get to know a tax professional. Ideally, you should form a long-term relationship with a tax pro, calling her when you really need her (and, of course, paying her promptly). Just what are tax pros and how can you find one?

1. Types of Tax Advisors

Not all tax pros are created equal. The industry is lightly regulated, and just about anyone can claim to be a "tax expert." You need someone who is experienced in helping small businesses—not the outfit that advertises "rapid refunds" or a big name national CPA firm. Ideally, you want a professional who understands your particular type of business—whether it be a small manufacturing outfit, a restaurant or retail clothing store. Here are the types of tax professionals who may help you:

- *Tax Return Preparer*. The IRS does not require people who call themselves tax return preparers to be tested or licensed—which in my opinion is a big mistake. While some states license tax preparers, most let just about anybody do it. I am talking about both the mom-and-pop operations as well as the

PART 6

Dealing With the IRS

familiar chains. Unless a tax preparer is a member of one of the three categories of tax pros below, be careful about relying on her for business tax help.

- *Enrolled Agent (EA).* An EA is a tax advisor and preparer who is licensed by the IRS. This professional designation is earned by either passing a difficult IRS test or having at least five years of experience working for the IRS. There are approximately 24,000 EAs in the United States. An Enrolled Agent is generally the least expensive of the tax pros, and is very adequate for most small business tax advice and reporting. Many also offer bookkeeping and accounting assistance.

- *Tax Attorney.* A tax attorney is a lawyer with either a special tax law degree (LL.M. in taxation), or a tax specialization certification from a state Bar Association. If you have a serious tax or IRS problem, require legal representation in court, or need complex tax and estate planning, go to a tax attorney.

- *Certified Public Accountant (CPA) and other accountants.* CPAs are licensed and regulated by each state, like attorneys. They perform sophisticated accounting and business-related tax work and prepare tax returns. CPAs shine in giving business tax advice but generally are not as aggressive as tax lawyers when facing IRS personnel. Some states license accountants other than CPAs, such as Public Accountants. Many of these folks are competent, but are not as highly regarded as CPAs.

Get the right tax pro. Enrolled Agents offer good value and are reliable for straight tax return preparation and routine tax questions. CPAs should be considered only by larger businesses or for complex business tax returns. Tax attorneys should be brought in when you have grave IRS problems.

2. How Tax Pros Can Help

A tax pro can assist you in a number of ways:

Information and Advice. A good tax pro can be a very effective teacher. (If your present advisor told you about this book or gave it to you, hurrah! You can be pretty sure you are working with someone who respects your ability to help yourself.) She can provide advice on making key tax decisions, such as choosing the best entity for your business.

Recordkeeping. Some people would pay half their business profits to avoid doing their own recordkeeping. If that's you, so be it. That's why God created accountants and bookkeepers. For those of you who are not frightened by computers, there is small business software that makes recordkeeping almost fun. See Chapter 3, Recordkeeping and Accounting, to see what this entails before automatically hiring someone to do it. Or you can get help from a pro in setting up a manual or computerized system tailored for your business, which you can run yourself.

Tax Form Preparation. Once you get past the recordkeeping, you'll be facing tax preparation and filing deadlines. The tax code is growing in complexity every year; Congress talks about tax simplification, but don't hold your breath. Until that day, most small business people should consider professional assistance in preparing their tax returns. Or, if you insist on doing your own tax return, you can have it reviewed by a tax pro before filing it. For doing-it-yourselfers, I recommend Turbotax for Business or MacIntax for Business, both published by Intuit. These programs will prepare any type of small business tax return—sole proprietorship, S or C corporation, partnership or limited liability company. I have seen many self-prepared tax returns that cheat their makers; a tax pro can earn his keep by pointing out tax deductions or other benefits that you might miss.

Advice in Dealing With the IRS. If you ever need help in dealing with the IRS, a tax pro can act as your coach. Thorny questions may be answered in a minute or two by a tax pro familiar with your business.

Representation. You don't have to deal with the IRS if you hire a tax pro to do it for you. Only attorneys, CPAs and Enrolled Agents qualify to represent someone before the IRS. Experienced tax pros are costly, but they know IRS procedures and how to handle IRS bureaucracy. A tax pro can neutralize the intimidation factor the IRS knows that it holds over you, and if you have something to hide, they can keep the lid on it better than you can.

3. How to Choose a Tax Pro for Your Business

There are several ways to find a good tax pro; asking the IRS is not one of them. Instead, try the following:

- *Personal referrals.* Ask business associates or even competitors for the names of pros that have helped them. Then interview at least three of them to see how well you relate to each other. This is the top way to find a good pro.

- *Advertising.* Trade journals, directories, phone books and newspapers carry lists of tax pros. Look under "accountants," "tax return preparers," and "attorneys-tax." Some tax pros offer free consultations; the fact that they are advertising indicates they have time for new clients.

- *Professional associations and referral panels.* Most local Bar Associations and CPA Societies can refer you to a local tax pro. They usually give names from a list on a rotation basis, so a referral shouldn't be construed as recommendation or certification of competence. The National Association of Enrolled Agents (800-424-4339) can help you locate an EA in your area.

Once you have the names of tax pros, start weeding through them. A good way to break the ice is to call and tell the pro where you got his name. Then tell him about your small business, and ask if he has clients in similar businesses. If he appears too busy or doesn't have the experience you are looking for, ask him to recommend someone who fits the bill.

If you worked with a tax preparer in the past, maybe this is the person you want to stick with, but maybe not. Ask her how much experience she has with small businesses like yours. Test her attitude toward the IRS and knowledge of small business tax law by pulling out some questions from this book. If she is not the one for the job, ask her to refer you to an expert. Someone with prior IRS work experience may be good, but then again, they may have been permanently brainwashed to the IRS point of view.

Don't be in a hurry to hire a tax pro. It should be more like looking for a mate for life than a casual date. After all, knowing and complying with the tax laws is a key to whether your business lives or dies. You should be asking yourself some questions as well: Does the tax pro give you a feeling of confidence? Does she seem knowledgeable? How long has she been doing tax work? Can you envision her going to bat for you in front of the IRS?

4. Tax Pros' Fees

Tax pros aren't cheap, especially for a start-up business without much cash flow. But never hire a tax pro based on price alone. An expensive expert who saves you from getting in trouble with the IRS is money well spent.

Get a clear understanding of fees at your first meeting. Does the expert charge by the hour or use flat (fixed) fees for bookkeeping, accounting and tax form preparation? Most professionals charge hourly, with fees varying from as low as $25 per hour for some Enrolled Agents up to $250 for top CPAs and tax attorneys.

Ask for a written fee agreement before the work begins, so all parties know where they stand—and so you have a basis for disputing a tax pro bill if necessary.

To some extent, you will be able to control costs here. Tax pros can be consulted on an as-needed basis, or can be hired to take over everything from bookkeeping to IRS representation.

PART 6

Dealing With the IRS

Everything is negotiable. If you like the tax pro, but not her fee, ask if she can do it for less. Phrase your request by saying something like "I am new in business and need to watch my pennies." If she believes you'll be a good client, or you catch her in a slow period, she may discount her normal rates. The best time to find a tax pro and negotiate fees is after the "tax season"—meaning the summer or fall.

RESOURCES

At the end of each chapter is a list of resources related to that topic. Start there first, and then go to the more general list here.

Internal Revenue Code (IRC). This book has more fine print than you ever thought you would find in one place, but it is the starting point for most tax research.

Regulations (Federal Income Tax Regulations). Only slightly more comprehensible than the IRC, these are written by the Treasury Department to elaborate on the tax code.

Legal Research: How to Find and Understand the Law, by Stephen Elias & Susan Levinkind (Nolo Press). This book is not directed toward tax research, but is worth scanning for law library researching.

The Ernst and Young Tax Guide (John Wiley & Sons). This is my favorite annual tax preparation guidebook. It includes tips and explanations of the tax law far superior to the IRS's publications.

Master Tax Guide (Commerce Clearing House), *Master Federal Tax Manual* (Research Institute of America) and *Federal Tax Guide* (Prentice-Hall). Probably your best chance of understanding most tax issues is reading one of these lengthy, privately-published professional tax manuals.

IRS Practice & Policy (Tax Management Inc.) and *IRS Practice & Procedure*, by Michael Saltzman (Warren, Gorham & Lamont). These books and newsletters are written for tax professionals to explain how the IRS handles tax matters. (800-372-1033.)

The Legal Guide for Starting & Running a Small Business, by Fred Steingold (Nolo Press). This is a good companion book to the one in your hand; it covers the non-tax aspects of small business as well as any book I have ever seen.

Stand Up to the IRS, by Frederick W. Daily (Nolo Press). This book contains more detailed information on dealing with the IRS.

The Employer's Legal Handbook, by Fred Steingold (Nolo Press). This book covers all aspects of being an employer, including tax obligations, in greater detail than covered here.

Hiring Independent Contractors, by Stephen Fishman (Nolo Press), explains how to reap the benefits—and avoid the pitfalls—of using independent contractors.

The Home Office and Small Business Answer Book, by Janet Attard (Henry Holt Publishing), lists guilds, associations and societies that might have publications that touch on specialized tax issues.

Representation Before the Collection Division of the IRS, Representing the Audited Taxpayer Before the IRS and *Representation Before the Appeals Division of the IRS* (Clark, Boardman & Callaghan). Tax pros should have these three excellent looseleaf books in their libraries, and they are also written clearly enough to be of use to most anyone else. (212-929-7500.) ∎

Glossary

The terms in this glossary are defined as they are used by the IRS and in this book. Some terms may have different meanings in other contexts.

ABATEMENT. The IRS's partial or complete cancellation of taxes, penalties or interest owed by a taxpayer.

ACCELERATED DEPRECIATION. A method of depreciation that allows a business to deduct the cost of property more rapidly than by using straight-line depreciation.

ACCOUNTANT. Someone who works with financial data. Often denotes a person with special training, such as a Certified Public Accountant.

ACCOUNTING. Process by which financial information about a business is recorded.

ACCOUNTING METHODS. See Cash Method and Accrual Method.

ACCOUNTING PERIOD. See Calendar Year Accounting Period and Fiscal Year Accounting Period.

ACCOUNTS PAYABLE. Money owed by a business to suppliers, vendors and other creditors.

ACCOUNTS RECEIVABLE. Money owed to a business for goods or services rendered. A business asset.

ACCRUAL METHOD (also called Accrual Basis). Accounting for income in the period earned, and for expenses when the liability was incurred. This is not necessarily in the period when it is received or paid. See also Cash Method.

ADJUSTMENT. (1) An IRS change, usually by an auditor, to a tax liability as reported originally on a tax return. (2) Deductions from an individual taxpayer's total income on Form 1040, lines 23 through 30.

ADJUSTED BASIS. See Basis (Tax Basis).

ADJUSTED GROSS INCOME (AGI). On personal income tax returns, this figure is the result of reducing a taxpayer's total income by certain adjustments allowed by the tax code. From this figure, personal deductions are subtracted to arrive at taxable income.

ALTERNATIVE MINIMUM TAX. An alternate flat tax on individuals or corporations that may apply when a taxpayer claims certain tax benefits that reduce tax liabilities below specified levels. Its intent is to prevent higher-income taxpayers from realizing too many tax benefits from accelerated depreciation or investments in nontaxed items such as municipal bonds.

AMORTIZATION. A tax method of recovering costs of certain assets by taking deductions evenly over time. This is similar to straight-line depreciation and unlike an accelerated depreciation method. For example, the Internal Revenue Code directs that computer software and points paid for certain mortgage loans must be amortized.

APPEAL. Administrative process allowing taxpayers to contest certain decisions, typically audits, within the IRS.

ASSESS. The IRS process of recording a tax liability in the account of a taxpayer.

ASSET (BUSINESS). Any property with a useful life of at least one year that is used in a trade or business. Examples: machinery, buildings, vehicles, equipment patents and monies held or owed to a business. See also Accounts Receivable.

AUDIT. A review of business records. An IRS audit is the examination of a taxpayer, his or her tax return and supporting data to determine whether he or she has violated the tax laws.

AUDITOR. An IRS Examination Division employee who reviews the correctness of a tax return. See also Revenue Agent, Tax Auditor (Examiner).

BAD DEBT (BUSINESS). Money owed for a business debt that cannot be collected and can be deducted as an operating expense.

BALANCE SHEET. A statement listing a business's assets (what it owns), liabilities (what it owes) and net worth (the difference between the assets and liabilities). A balance sheet shows the financial position of a business at a given point in time.

BANKRUPTCY. A federal law providing a way for individuals or businesses to wipe out certain debts. There are different kinds of bankruptcy. A defunct business will likely file Chapter 7 bankruptcy, wherein its assets are distributed to creditors and any remaining debts are canceled. Chapters 11 and 13 bankruptcy allow businesses and individuals to repay debts over time while remaining in operation.

BASIS (TAX BASIS). The tax cost of an asset, which may be adjusted upward by improvements or downward by depreciation. Basis is used to calculate depreciation and amortization deductions and to determine gain or loss on the sale or other disposition of an asset.

BOOKS (BUSINESS). The collection of records of financial accounting of business activity kept on paper or in a computer file.

BOOKKEEPER. Someone who records financial data in the accounting records of a business and maintains the accounting system.

BUSINESS. An activity carried on with the intent to make a profit.

BUSINESS LICENSE: A permit issued by a local or state governmental agency for a business to operate. Most enterprises are required to have one or more licenses and must go through an application process and pay a fee for this privilege. A business license is not issued by the IRS or required to qualify as a taxable entity, however.

CALENDAR YEAR ACCOUNTING PERIOD. A 12-month period for tax purposes that ends on December 31. See also Fiscal Year Accounting Period.

CAPITAL. The investment in a business by its owners. See also Equity.

CAPITAL ASSET. Any type of property, either held for investment or used in a business, that has a useful life of more than one year.

CAPITAL EXPENDITURE. Cost for acquisition of, or improvements to, an asset.

CAPITAL GAIN OR LOSS. A gain or loss from the sale or exchange of a capital asset—the difference between the amount realized on the sale or exchange of an asset and the amount of the adjusted basis of the asset.

CAPITALIZED EXPENDITURE. An expenditure for a capital asset that must be tax deducted over more than one year, as opposed to an ordinary expense. For example, repairing a broken window is an ordinary expense, but remodeling a storefront is an expense that must be capitalized.

CARRYOVERS. Tax rules often limit the ability of a taxpayer to use deductions, losses and credits in the year incurred. The excess of a tax deduction, loss or credit over what can be used in a current year is called a carryover, which may be taken in past or future years.

CASH METHOD. Accounting for income by reporting it when actually or constructively received, and reporting expenses when paid. Also called cash basis method. See also Accrual Method, Constructive Receipt of Income.

CERTIFIED PUBLIC ACCOUNTANT (CPA). The most highly qualified of all accounting professionals. CPAs are licensed by the state and must meet rigorous educational and testing requirements.

CHART OF ACCOUNTS. A complete list of a business's expense and income accounts by category. It includes all accounts that appear on the business's balance sheet, as well as the accounts that track particular kinds of expenses or income.

CONSTRUCTIVE RECEIPT OF INCOME. Income not physically received but treated by the tax code as if it had been because it is accessible to the recipient without qualification. See also Cash Method.

CORPORATION. A state-registered business that is owned by shareholders and reports taxes separately from its owners. The tax code considers all corporations to be taxable entities, called C corporations, unless the corporation has properly elected "S" status. See S Corporation.

COHAN RULE. A federal court decision allowing taxpayers to use reasonable approximations of expenses when records are missing. The Cohan rule has its limitations and cannot be used to approximate travel and entertainment business expenses.

COST OF GOODS SOLD (CGS). The amount paid by a business for inventory that is sold during a tax year. The formula for determining the CGS is: the beginning inventory plus the cost of purchases during the period, minus the ending inventory at the end of the period. Also called "cost of sales."

DEATH BENEFIT: A fringe benefit payment that is tax-deductible to a C corporation, within dollar limitations, and not taxable to the recipient.

DEDUCTIBLE BUSINESS EXPENSE: An expenditure by a business that may be deducted from the business's taxable income under the tax code.

DEDUCTION. An expense that the IRC allows an individual or business to subtract from its gross income to determine its taxable income. Example: The cost of this book.

DEFERRED COMPENSATION. Earned income of a taxpayer that is put into a retirement account and not taxable until removed from the account.

DEFICIENCY (TAX). Any difference found by the IRS between a taxpayer's reported tax liability and the amount of tax the IRS says that the taxpayer should have reported.

DEPENDENT CARE PLAN: A fringe benefit that can be given tax-free to eligible employees of a business to care for their dependents and is deductible to the business, within limitations.

DEPRECIABLE ASSET. Property used in a business with a useful life of at least one year and deductible over a period set by the IRC. Includes buildings, vehicles and equipment used in a business, but not land, which is never depreciable.

DEPRECIABLE BASIS. See Basis.

DEPRECIATION. An annual tax deduction allowed for recovering the cost of a tangible asset over a period of years, such as a business auto or real estate improvement. The amount of the deduction each year depends on which of the deprecia-

tion methods allowed in the tax code for the kind of asset is applied.

DISALLOWANCE (AUDIT). An IRS finding at audit that a taxpayer was not entitled to a deduction or other tax benefit claimed on a tax return.

DIVIDEND. Corporation profits distributed to shareholders as a return on their investment in the corporation. Also see Unearned Income.

DOCUMENTATION. Any tangible proof that substantiates an item on a tax return, such as for an expense claimed as a deduction.

DOUBLE-ENTRY SYSTEM. A system of accounting that records each business transaction twice (once as a debit and once as a credit), and is more accurate than single-entry accounting.

EARNED INCOME. Compensation for services rendered. Also see Unearned Income.

EDUCATION BENEFITS. Financial assistance to an employee that is tax-free to the recipient and a tax-deductible expense to the business, within tax code limitations.

EMPLOYEE. A worker under the direction or control of an employer, and subject to payroll tax code rules. See also Independent Contractor.

EMPLOYER IDENTIFICATION NUMBER (EIN). A 13-digit number assigned to a business by the IRS, upon application. See also Taxpayer Identification Number.

EMPLOYMENT TAXES. See Payroll Taxes.

ENROLLED AGENT (EA). A type of tax professional permitted to practice before the IRS along with attorneys and CPAs. An EA must demonstrate competence by passing an IRS test or have at least five years' work experience with the IRS.

ENTRY. A transaction recorded in the accounting records of a business.

EQUITY. The net worth of a business, equal to its assets minus its liabilities. Also refers to an owner's investment in the business.

ERISA (Employees' Retirement Security Act). A federal law that governs employee benefits, such as pension and retirement plans. See also Pension Plan.

ESTIMATED TAXES (ES). Tax payments to the IRS by self-employed individuals, in advance, for their anticipated income tax liability for the year. ES payments are required to be made quarterly.

EXAMINATION. See Audit.

EXAMINATION REPORT. The findings issued by an IRS auditor after an audit is concluded.

EXCISE TAX (FEDERAL). A tax, usually at a flat rate, imposed on some businesses for a certain type of transaction, manufacturing, production or consumption.

EXPENSE. A business cost. See also Deductible Business Expense.

FAIR MARKET VALUE. The price a buyer and seller of any kind of property agree on as just, when neither is under any compulsion to buy or sell.

FAMILY LIMITED PARTNERSHIP. A business that is a limited partnership of only related members. It can be used to shift present business income and to transfer a business to succeeding generations at a tax savings. See also Limited Partnership.

FEDERAL TAX DEPOSITS (FTD). An employer is required to place payroll taxes withheld from employees, as well as employer contributions for Social Security and Medicare taxes, in a federal depository (bank).

FEDERAL INSURANCE CONTRIBUTIONS ACT (FICA). Social Security and Medicare taxes, which are generally applicable to everyone with earned income. Employers and employees split the tax; self-employeds pay the entire tax. Also see Payroll Taxes, Self-Employment Tax.

FISCAL YEAR ACCOUNTING PERIOD. A 12-month period ending on the last day of any month except December. See also Calendar Year Accounting Period.

FIXED ASSET. A business asset with a useful life of greater than one year as determined by the Internal Revenue Code. See also Depreciable Asset.

401(k) PLAN. A tax-advantaged deferred compensation arrangement in which a portion of a worker's pay is withheld by the business and invested in a plan to earn income tax-deferred until withdrawn.

FRAUD. See Tax Fraud.

FRINGE BENEFIT. Any tax-advantaged benefit allowed a business owner or employee. A fringe benefit may be partially or totally tax-free to the recipient and tax-deductible to the business. Prime examples are health and retirement plans.

FUTA (Federal Unemployment Tax Act). An annually paid tax on all employers for unemployment insurance.

GENERAL JOURNAL. A book or computer file where all financial transactions of a business are recorded. Also called General Ledger.

GOODWILL. The excess value of a going business, over and above the worth of all of its other assets.

GROSS INCOME. Income from all sources required to be reported on a tax return, before any adjustments or deductions are taken.

GROUP LIFE INSURANCE BENEFIT. See Fringe Benefit.

HOBBY LOSS PROVISION (IRC § 183). An IRC limitation on tax-deducting losses or expenses of any activity that is not carried on with a profit motive.

HOME OFFICE. That portion of a taxpayer's home in which he or she carries on a business activity. If the home office is used regularly and exclusively for business and meets other tax code tests, then a deduction—up to the amount of business income—may be taken for the business portion of the home, for depreciation on the structure or rent paid.

IMPROVEMENTS. Additions to or alterations of a capital asset, which either increase its value or extend its useful life. See also Capitalized Expenditure.

INCOME. All money and other things of value received, except items specifically exempted by the tax code. See also Gross Income.

INCOME STATEMENT. See Profit & Loss Statement.

INDEPENDENT CONTRACTOR. A self-employed individual whose work hours and methods are not controlled by anyone else, and is not subject to payroll tax rules. See also Employee.

INDIVIDUAL RETIREMENT ACCOUNT (IRA).
A retirement plan established by an individual
allowing up to $2,000 in tax-deductible contribu-
tions of earned income per year, and tax-deferred
accumulation of income in the account.

INFORMATION RETURN (INCOME). A report
filed with the IRS by a business showing amounts
paid to a taxpayer, such as Form W-2 (wages), or
Form 1099 (independent contractor and other
types of income). No tax is due with an information
return, but there are penalties for not filing one or
for filing late.

INSTALLMENT PAYMENT AGREEMENT (IA).
An IRS monthly payment plan for unpaid federal
taxes.

INTANGIBLE PROPERTY. Assets that consist of
rights rather than something material. For example,
the accounts receivable of a business is an intangible asset because it is the right to receive payment
rather than the money itself. The funds, when received, become a tangible asset.

INTENT TO LEVY. A notice to a delinquent
taxpayer that the IRS intends to seize (levy) his or
her property to satisfy a tax obligation. This warning is usually issued at least 30 days prior to any
confiscation. Intent to Levy Notices don't necessarily mean the IRS will actually make any seizures.
See Levy.

INTEREST. Cost of borrowing or owing money,
usually a tax-deductible business expense. The IRS
adds interest to overdue tax bills.

INTERNAL REVENUE CODE (IRC). The tax
laws of the U.S. as enacted by Congress. Also called
the "tax code" or simply the "code."

IRC § 179. A tax rule allowing the deduction of
up to $17,500 for the purchase of certain trade or
business property in the year the property is placed
in service.

IRC § 1244 STOCK. Corporation stock issued
under the rules of IRC § 1244, which allows an
ordinary tax loss to be claimed, within tax code
limitations, by the shareholder.

INTERNAL REVENUE SERVICE (IRS). The
branch of the U.S. Treasury Department that

administers the federal tax law. Also called "the
Service" by tax professionals, and worse by most
other folks.

ITEMIZED DEDUCTIONS. Expenses allowed
by the tax code to be claimed on an individual
income tax return, such as medical expenses, mortgage interest, and charitable expenses.

INVENTORY. Goods a business has on hand for
sale to customers, and raw materials that will become part of merchandise.

INVESTMENT. Money spent to acquire an asset,
such as the purchase of a partnership interest or
stock in a corporation.

JOINT TAX RETURN. A combined income tax
return filed by two spouses.

JOURNAL. See General Journal.

KEOGH PLAN. A type of retirement plan for
self-employed people, allowing part of their earnings to be taken from their income and accumulate
tax-deferred in an investment account until withdrawn.

LEASE. A rental agreement for the use of property, such as buildings or equipment. Lease payments are deductible if the property is used in a
trade or business.

LEVY. An IRS seizure of property or wages from
an individual or business to satisfy a delinquent tax
debt. See Intent to Levy.

LIABILITY (BUSINESS). Money owed by a business to others, such as a mortgage debt, payroll
taxes or an account payable.

LIEN. See Tax Lien.

LIMITED LIABILITY COMPANY (LLC). A relatively new form of business recognized by the IRS
that is taxed much like a partnership, and shields
its owners from liability for business debts, like a
corporation.

LIMITED PARTNERSHIP. A type of partnership
that consists of at least one general partner with
unlimited liability for business debts, and one or
more limited partners whose liability is limited to
their investment in the partnership. Also see Limited Liability Company.

LISTED PROPERTY. Certain types of assets used in a business on which the IRC requires special recordkeeping, such as cellular phones, home-based computers and personal cars used for business.

LOSS (OPERATING). An excess of a business's expenses over its income in a given period of time, usually a tax year.

LOSS CARRYOVER. See Carryovers, Loss (Operating).

MACRS (MODIFIED ACCELERATED COST RECOVERY SYSTEM). An IRC-established method for rapidly claiming depreciation deductions.

MANUAL ACCOUNTING SYSTEM. An accounting system maintained by hand, using paper.

MEDICAL EXPENSE REIMBURSEMENT BENEFIT. See Fringe Benefits.

MEDICARE TAX. A federal tax of 2.9% on all of an individual's earned income. See Self-Employment Tax, Payroll Taxes.

MILEAGE LOG. A record of miles traveled in a vehicle used for business.

NET INCOME. Gross income less expenses; a business's profit for a given tax year.

NET LOSS. See Loss (Operating), Net Operating Loss.

NET OPERATING LOSS (NOL). A net loss from a business operation for a given tax year. For tax-reporting purposes, an NOL may be used to offset income of unincorporated business owners from other sources in the year of the loss. A corporate NOL may only be used by the corporation to offset tax liabilities in other years. An NOL may be carried over to other years to reduce tax liabilities or secure refunds of taxes. See Carryovers.

NET WORTH. See Equity.

NINETY-DAY LETTER. Official notice from the IRS that a taxpayer has ninety days to contest an IRS audit by filing a Petition to the United States Tax Court, or else the decision will become final.

NOTICE OF DEFICIENCY. See Ninety-Day Letter.

NOTICE OF TAX LIEN. See Tax Lien.

OPERATING EXPENSE. A normal out-of-pocket cost incurred in a business operation, not including depreciation or amortization expenses. Examples are rent, wages and supplies.

ORDINARY INCOME. Any earned income, such as from work, and not from the sale of a capital asset or from an investment. See Unearned Income.

OFFER IN COMPROMISE. A formal written proposal to the IRS to settle a tax debt for less than the amount the IRS claims is owed.

PARTNERSHIP. A business of two or more individuals (or other entities), which passes its income or losses to its individual partners. A partnership does not pay taxes but is required to file an annual tax return.

PAYROLL TAXES. The federal income taxes withheld and FICA contributions—including both Social Security and Medicare—that a business must deposit to an IRS account for its employees.

PENALTIES (TAX). Fines imposed by the IRS on taxpayers who disobey tax rules.

PENSION PLAN. A tax-advantaged arrangement under which payments are made to a tax code approved account for an owner's or employee's retirement. Tax on the accumulated funds is deferred until they are withdrawn.

PERSONAL ASSET. Property owned by an individual, which may also be used in a business.

PERSONAL PROPERTY. Any possession that is not real estate—such as cash, equipment or vehicles. See also Real Property.

PERSONAL SERVICE CORPORATION (PSC). A tax code qualified incorporated business composed of one or more members of a specific profession. It must file an annual tax return.

POSTING. The act of entering financial transactions into an accounting record, or transferring data from a book of original entry to a ledger.

PROFIT & LOSS STATEMENT (INCOME STATEMENT). A writing showing a business's gross income, and subtracting from that figure its expenses and the cost of goods sold to reveal a net profit or loss for a specific period.

PROFIT MOTIVE. An intention to make a profit is imposed by the IRC on anyone going into business. See also Hobby Loss Provision.

PROPRIETORSHIP. A business structure owned by an individual (or married couple) that is neither incorporated nor any other type of legal tax entity.

PRORATE. To allocate or split one figure between two items, such as prorating business and personal use of an asset.

PROTEST. A request to appeal a decision within the IRS. See Appeal.

QUALIFIED PENSION PLAN. A tax code–qualified and IRS-approved employee benefit plan, such as a pension or profit-sharing plan. See ERISA.

REAL PROPERTY. Real estate, consisting of land and structures attached to it. See also Personal Property.

RECORDKEEPING. The listing of financial transactions for a business. See also Records.

RECORDS. Tangible evidence, usually in writing, of the income, expenses and financial transactions of a business or individual.

REGULATIONS (Regs). Treasury Department interpretations of selected Internal Revenue Code provisions.

REPRESENTATIVE. A tax professional who is permitted to represent a taxpayer before the IRS. He or she must be a Certified Public Accountant, Tax Attorney or Enrolled Agent.

RESEARCH AND DEVELOPMENT EXPENSES. Certain tax-deductible costs for developing new products or services.

RETAINED EARNINGS. The accumulated and undistributed profits of a corporation. Retained earnings are subject to tax.

RETIREMENT PLAN. See Pension Plan.

REVENUE AGENT. An IRS examiner who performs audits of taxpayers or business entities in the field, meaning outside IRS offices. See Tax Auditor.

REVENUE OFFICER. Certain IRS tax collectors.

S CORPORATION (SUB-CHAPTER S CORPORATION). A state-incorporated business that elects special tax treatment to pass through its income or loss to shareholders, similar to a partnership. See Corporation.

SHAREHOLDER (Stockholder). An investor in a corporation whose ownership is represented by a stock certificate. A shareholder may or may not be an officer or employee of the corporation.

SINGLE-ENTRY ACCOUNTING. A system of tracking business income and expenses that requires only one recording of each financial transaction. See also Double-Entry System.

SERVICE BUSINESS. Any enterprise that derives income primarily from providing services, not goods, to its customers. Examples: restaurants, programs and accountants.

SEIZURE (IRS). See Levy.

SELF-EMPLOYED. A person who works in his or her own business, either full or part-time.

SELF-EMPLOYMENT (SE) TAX. Social Security and Medicare taxes on net self-employment income. The SE tax is reported on the individual's income tax return.

SIDELINE BUSINESS. A for-profit activity carried on in addition to an individual's full-time employment or principal trade or business.

SIMPLIFIED EMPLOYEE PENSION (SEP, SARSEP or SEP-IRA). A pension plan allowing self-employed business owners and their employees to deduct and put part of their earnings into a retirement account to accumulate tax-deferred until withdrawn. See also Individual Retirement Account (IRA), Keogh Plan.

SOLE PROPRIETORSHIP. See Proprietorship.

SOLIMON RULE. A U.S. Supreme Court decision that limits the use of the tax deduction for home offices for some businesses.

STANDARD MILEAGE RATE DEDUCTION. A method for deducting automobile expenses based on the mileage driven for business, used in lieu of claiming actual operating and depreciation expenses.

STATUTES OF LIMITATION (TAX). Varying limits imposed by Congress on assessing and collecting taxes, charging tax crimes, and claiming tax refunds.

STOCK DIVIDEND. See Dividend.

STRAIGHT-LINE DEPRECIATION. A tax code method of depreciating assets of a business by deductions in equal annual amounts. The period of time is specified by the tax code for each category of property.

SUMMONS. A legally enforceable order issued by the IRS compelling an individual taxpayer or business to provide information, usually financial records.

TANGIBLE PERSONAL PROPERTY (ASSET). Anything of value that is physically movable, such as equipment, vehicles, machinery and fixtures not attached to a building or land.

TAX ATTORNEY. A lawyer who specializes in tax-related legal work and has a special degree (LL.M.-tax) or certification from a state bar association.

TAX AUDITOR (EXAMINER). An IRS employee who determines the correctness of tax returns filed by individual taxpayers and business entities at the IRS offices. See also Revenue Agent, Audit.

TAX BASIS. See Basis.

TAX CODE. See Internal Revenue Code (IRC).

TAX COURT (U.S.). A federal court where an individual or business taxpayer can contest an IRS tax assessment without first paying the taxes claimed due.

TAX FRAUD. Conduct meant to deceive the IRS or cheat in the assessment or payment of any tax liability. Tax fraud can be punished by both civil penalties (money) and criminal ones (imprisonment and fines).

TAX LAW. The Internal Revenue Code (IRC) and the decisions of federal courts interpreting it.

TAX LIEN NOTICE (FEDERAL). An IRS announcement of a tax debt placed in the public records where the debtor resides or the business is located.

TAX LOSS CARRYOVER. See Carryovers.

TAX PRO. An expert working privately in the tax field. See Certified Public Accountant, Enrolled Agent, Tax Attorney.

TAXABLE INCOME. An individual's or business's gross income minus all allowable deductions, adjustments and exemptions.

TAXPAYER BILL OF RIGHTS. A 1988 federal law imposing limitations on IRS conduct and establishing taxpayer rights in dealing with the IRS. Highlights of this law are contained in IRS Publication 1.

TAXPAYER IDENTIFICATION NUMBER (TIN). An IRS-assigned number used for computer tracking of tax accounts. For sole proprietors without employees, it is their Social Security number. For other business entities the TIN is a separate 13-digit number called an Employer Identification Number. See EIN.

TAX RATE. A percentage of tax applied to income, which may be fixed or may change at different income levels, and is set by Congress.

THREE-OF-FIVE TEST. A rebuttable IRS presumption that a business venture that doesn't make a profit in three out of five consecutive years of operation is a not a business for tax purposes. See also Profit Motive, Hobby Loss Provision.

TRANSACTION. A financial event in the operation of a business. Examples: paying an expense, making a deposit or receiving payment for selling a service.

TRUST FUND RECOVERY PENALTY. Also known as the 100% Penalty. A tax code procedure for shifting payroll tax obligations from a business (usually a corporation) to individuals associated with the business.

UNEARNED INCOME. Income from investments or other income that isn't compensation for services. See Earned Income, Dividend.

USEFUL LIFE. The period of time the tax code directs to be used to depreciate a business asset.

WRITE-OFF. An expression for a tax-deductible expense, usually referring to depreciating or taking an IRC § 179 expense for an asset used in business. See Depreciation. ■

Appendix

IRS Publications List

Forms Checklist

Business Owner Tax Information

How to Get IRS Forms and Publications

W-9 Request for Taxpayer Identification Number and Certificaton

SS-4 Applicaton for Employer Identification Number

Instructions for Form 8829

IRS PUBLICATIONS LIST

GENERAL GUIDES

1	Your Rights as a Taxpayer
17	Your Federal Income Tax (For Individuals)
225	Farmer's Tax Guide
334	Tax Guide for Small Business
509	Tax Calendars for 1997
595	Tax Guide for Commercial Fishermen
910	Guide to Free Tax Services

EMPLOYER'S GUIDES

15	Employer's Tax Guide (Circular E)
51	Agricultural Employer's Tax Guide (Circular A)
80	Federal Tax Guide for Employers in the Virgin Islands, Guam, American Samoa, and the Commonwealth of the Northern Mariana Islands (Circular SS)

SPECIALIZED PUBLICATIONS

Pub. 55	Recordkeeping for Individuals
349	Federal Highway Use Tax on Heavy Vehicles
378	Fuel Tax Credits and Refunds
463	Travel, Entertainment, and Gift Expenses
505	Tax Withholding and Estimated Tax
510	Excise Taxes for 1996
515	Withholding of Tax on Nonresident Aliens and Foreign Corporations
517	Social Security and Other Information for Members of the Clergy and Religious Workers
521	Moving Expenses
523	Selling Your Home
525	Taxable and Nontaxable Income
526	Charitable Contributions
527	Residential Rental Property
529	Miscellaneous Deductions
533	Self-Employment Tax
534	Depreciation
535	Business Expenses
536	Net Operating Losses
537	Installment Sales
538	Accounting Periods and Methods
541	Tax Information on Partnerships
542	Tax Information on Corporations
544	Sales and Other Dispositions of Assets
550	Investment Income and Expenses
551	Basis of Assets
555	Federal Tax Information on Community Property

556	Examination of Returns, Appeal Rights, and Claims for Refund
557	Tax-Exempt Status for Your Organization
560	Retirement Plans for the Self-Employed
561	Determining the Value of Donated Property
575	Pension and Annuity Income (Including Simplified General Rule)
583	Taxpayers Starting a Business
587	Business Use of Your Home
589	Tax Information on S Corporations
590	Individual Retirement Arrangements (IRAs)
594	Understanding the Collection Process
596	Earned Income Credit
597	Information on the United States–Canada Income Tax Treaty
598	Tax on Unrelated Business Income of Exempt Organizations
901	U.S. Tax Treaties
907	Tax Highlights for Persons with Disabilities
908	Bankruptcy and Other Debt Cancellation
911	Tax Information for Direct Sellers
917	Business Use of a Car
924	Reporting of Real Estate Transactions to IRS
925	Passive Activity and At-Risk Rules
926	Employment Taxes for Household Employers
937	Employment Taxes and Information Returns
939	Pension General Rule
946	How to Depreciate Your Property
947	Practice Before the IRS and Power of Attorney
953	International Tax Information for Business
1045	Information and Order Blanks for Preparers of Federal Income Tax Returns
1542	Per Diem Rates
1544	Reporting Cash Payments of Over $10,000
1546	How to Use the Problem Resolution Program of the IRS

SPANISH LANGUAGE PUBLICATIONS

1SP	Derechos del Contribuyente
556SP	Revisión de las Declaraciones de Impuesto, Derecho de Apelación y Reclamaciones de Reembolsos
579SP	Cómo Preparar la Declaración de Impuesto Federal
594SP	Comprendiendo el Proceso de Cobro
596SP	Crédito por Ingreso del Trabajo
850	English–Spanish Glossary of Words and Phrases Used in Publications Issued by the Internal Revenue Service

FORMS CHECKLIST

Some of the federal taxes for which a sole proprietor, a corporation or a partnership may be liable are listed below. If a due date falls on a Saturday, Sunday or legal holiday, it is postponed until the next day that is not a Saturday, Sunday or legal holiday. A statewide legal holiday delays a due date only if the IRS office where you are required to file is located in that state.

YOU MAY BE LIABLE FOR	IF YOU ARE	USE FORM	DUE ON OR BEFORE
Income tax	Sole proprietor	Schedule C or C–EZ (Form 1040)	Same day as Form 1040
	Individual who is a partner or S corporation shareholder	1040	15th day of 4th month after end of tax year
	Corporation	1120 or 1120–A	15th day of 3rd month after end of tax year
	S corporation	1120S	15th day of 3rd month after end of tax year
Self-employment tax	Sole proprietor, corporation, S corporation, or partnership	Schedule SE (Form 1040)	Same day as Form 1040
Estimated tax	Sole proprietor, or individual who is a partner or S corporation shareholder	1040–ES	15th day of 4th, 6th, and 9th months of tax year, and 15th day of 1st month after the end of tax year
	Corporation	1120–W	15th day of 4th, 6th, 9th and 12th months of tax year
Annual return of income	Partnership	1065	15th day of 4th month after end of tax year
Social security and Medicare taxes (FICA taxes) and the withholding of income tax	Sole proprietor, corporation, S corporation, or partnership	941	4–30, 7–31, 10–31, and 1–31
		8109 (to make deposits)	See IRS Publication 334, Chapter 34
Providing information on social security and Medicare taxes (FICA taxes) and the withholding of income tax	Sole proprietor, corporation S corporation, or partnership	W–2 (to employee)	1–31
		W–2 and W–3 (to the Social Security Administration)	Last day of February
Federal unemployment (FUTA) tax	Sole proprietor, corporation, S corporation, or partnership	940–EZ or 940	1–31
		8109 (to make deposits)	4–30, 7–31, 10–31, and 1–31, but only if the liability for unpaid tax is more than $100
Information returns for payments to non-employees and transaction with other persons	Sole proprietor, corporation, S corporation, or partnership	See IRS Publication 334, Chapter 36	Form 1099—to the recipient by 1–31, and to the IRS by 2–28 See also IRS Publication 334, Chapter 34
Excise taxes		See IRS Publication 334, Chapter 37	See the instructions to the forms ■

Business Owner Tax Information

The IRS has many publications containing information about the federal tax laws that apply to businesses. Publication 334, *Tax Guide for Small Business,* is a good place to start to learn more about sole proprietorships, partnerships, corporations, and S corporations. Look in section **Free Tax Publications** for other materials that can explain your business tax responsibilities.

Employee or Independent Contractor Status

A worker is either an employee or an independent contractor. The classification is determined by the facts and circumstances of his/her work relationship.

Generally, an employee is controlled by an employer in ways that a true independent contractor is not. If the employer sets the work hours, provides the tools needed to do the job, and can hire and fire, the worker is an employee, not an independent contractor.

An independent contractor will usually maintain an office and staff, advertise, and have a financial investment risk. Independent contractors will file a Schedule C and be able to deduct certain expenses that an employee would not.

Those who should be classified as employees, but aren't, may lose out on social security benefits, workers' compensation, unemployment benefits, and, in many cases, group insurance (including life and health), and retirement benefits. For details, get Publication 15-A, *Employer's Supplemental Tax Guide.*

Tax Tips Newsletter

The IRS publishes *Tax Tips,* a monthly newsletter for first-time small business owners. Written in simple terms, the newsletter covers basic business tax law, helpful bookkeeping and recordkeeping hints, explanations of how the IRS works, and where to go for additional help.

The twelve-month subscription is available free by sending a postcard with your name and address to:

Internal Revenue Service
Attn: *Tax Tips* Editor, M:C:DP
1111 Constitution Avenue
   NW
Washington, DC 20224

Tax Tips is also available on IRIS, an electronic bulletin board system located on FedWorld (via the Internet or through direct dial). See section **FedWorld** for dialing instructions.

> ▶ *Did You Know?*
>
> The IRS is responding to tax law, regulation, and policy concerns raised by small businesses through its Small Business Affairs Office. Read below for more information.

Small Business Affairs Office (SBAO)

One of the ways the IRS is listening and responding to concerns regarding tax laws, regulations, and policy raised by small businesses is through its Small Business Affairs Office (SBAO). Established in March 1994, this office is a national contact within IRS for small business owners to voice concerns.

The SBAO recommends changes to the federal tax system, such as recordkeeping requirements, payroll tax reporting, and simplifying tax forms. SBAO works with many other IRS offices and other government agencies (Small Business Administration) helping them understand small business owner needs and

concerns of reducing burden.

This office, however, does not handle small business owners' individual tax problems. If a problem has not been resolved after repeated attempts through normal IRS channels, small business owners should contact their local Problem Resolution Office for assistance. See section on *Problem Resolution Program (PRP)* under **Free Tax Services** for more information.

Write to the IRS Small Business Affairs office if you have questions.

Internal Revenue Service
Small Business Affairs
   Office C:SB
ICC Building, Room 1211
1111 Constitution Avenue NW
Washington, DC, 20224

SSA/IRS (Social Security Administration/Internal Revenue Service) *Reporter* (Newsletter)

If you are an employer and have not been receiving a copy of the *SSA/IRS Reporter,* tell your local IRS Public Affairs Office.

The *SSA/IRS Reporter* is a quarterly newsletter that keeps you up-to-date on changes to taxes and employee wage obligations. This newsletter, produced jointly by the Social Security Administration and the IRS, is mailed to over six million employers along with quarterly Forms 941 and instructions.

22

How to Get IRS Forms and Publications

You can visit your local IRS office or order tax forms and publications from the IRS Forms Distribution Center listed for your state at the address on this page. Or, if you prefer, you can photocopy tax forms from reproducible copies kept at participating public libraries. In addition, many of these libraries have reference sets of IRS publications that you can read or copy.

Where To Mail Your Order Blank for Free Forms and Publications

If you live in:	Mail to:	Other locations:
Alaska, Arizona, California, Colorado, Hawaii, Idaho, Montana, Nevada, New Mexico, Oregon, Utah, Washington, Wyoming, Guam, Northern Marianas, American Samoa	Western Area Distribution Center Rancho Cordova, CA 95743-0001	**Foreign Addresses—** Taxpayers with mailing addresses in foreign countries should mail this order blank to either: Eastern Area Distribution Center, P.O. Box 25866, Richmond, VA 23286-8107; or Western Area Distribution Center, Rancho Cordova, CA 95743-0001, whichever is closer. Mail letter requests for other forms and publications to: Eastern Area Distribution Center, P.O. Box 25866, Richmond, VA 23286-8107.
Alabama, Arkansas, Illinois, Indiana, Iowa, Kansas, Kentucky, Louisiana, Michigan, Minnesota, Mississippi, Missouri, Nebraska, North Dakota, Ohio, Oklahoma, South Dakota, Tennessee, Texas, Wisconsin	Central Area Distribution Center P.O. Box 8903 Bloomington, IL 61702-8903	
Connecticut, Delaware, District of Columbia, Florida, Georgia, Maine, Maryland, Massachusetts, New Hampshire, New Jersey, New York, North Carolina, Pennsylvania, Rhode Island, South Carolina, Vermont, Virginia, West Virginia	Eastern Area Distribution Center P.O. Box 85074 Richmond, VA 23261-5074	**Puerto Rico—**Eastern Area Distribution Center, P.O. Box 25866, Richmond, VA 23286-8107. **Virgin Islands—**V.I. Bureau of Internal Revenue, Lockhart Gardens, No. 1-A Charlotte Amalie, St. Thomas, VI 00802

Detach at This Line

- -

Order Blank

We will send you 2 copies of each form and 1 copy of each publication or set of instructions you circle. Please cut the order blank on the dotted line above and **be sure to print or type your name and address accurately on the bottom portion.**

Enclose this order blank in your own envelope and address your envelope to the IRS address shown above for your state.

To help reduce waste, please order only the forms, instructions, and publications you think you will need to prepare your return.

Use the blank spaces to order items not listed. If you need more space, attach a separate sheet of paper listing the additional forms and publications you may need.

You should either receive your order or notification of the status of your order within 7-15 work days after we receive your request.

1040	Schedule F (1040)	Schedule 3 (1040A) & Instructions	2210 & Instructions	8606 & Instructions	Pub. 502	Pub. 550	Pub. 929
Instructions for 1040 & Schedules	Schedule H (1040)	1040EZ	2441 & Instructions	8822 & Instructions	Pub. 505	Pub. 554	Pub. 936
Schedules A&B (1040)	Schedule R (1040) & instructions	Instructions for 1040EZ	3903 & instructions	8829 & Instructions	Pub. 508	Pub. 575	
Schedule C (1040)	Schedule SE (1040)	1040-ES (1996) & Instructions	4562 & instructions	Pub. 1	Pub. 521	Pub. 590	
Schedule C-EZ (1040)	1040A	1040X & Instructions	4868 & Instructions	Pub. 17	Pub. 523	Pub. 596	
Schedule D (1040)	Instructions for 1040A & Schedules	2106 & Instructions	5329 & Instructions	Pub. 334	Pub. 525	Pub. 910	
Schedule E (1040)	Schedule 1 (1040A)	2106-EZ & Instructions	8283 & Instructions	Pub. 463	Pub. 527	Pub. 917	
Schedule EIC (1040A or 1040)	Schedule 2 (1040A)	2119 & Instructions	8582 & Instructions	Pub. 501	Pub. 529	Pub. 926	

Name
Number and street
City or town   State   ZIP code

★ U.S. GOVERNMENT PRINTING OFFICE: 1995-389-630

Form W-9

Rev. March 1994)

Department of the Treasury
Internal Revenue Service

Request for Taxpayer Identification Number and Certification

Give form to the requester. Do NOT send to the IRS.

Please print or type

Name (If joint names, list first and circle the name of the person or entity whose number you enter in Part I below. **See instructions on page 2 if your name has changed.**)

Business name (Sole proprietors see instructions on page 2.)

Please check appropriate box: ☐ Individual/Sole proprietor ☐ Corporation ☐ Partnership ☐ Other ▶ ....

Address (number, street, and apt. or suite no.)

Requester's name and address (optional)

City, state, and ZIP code

Part I — Taxpayer Identification Number (TIN)

Enter your TIN in the appropriate box. For individuals, this is your social security number (SSN). For sole proprietors, see the instructions on page 2. For other entities, it is your employer identification number (EIN). If you do not have a number, see **How To Get a TIN** below.

Note: *If the account is in more than one name, see the chart on page 2 for guidelines on whose number to enter.*

Social security number

OR

Employer identification number

List account number(s) here (optional)

Part II — For Payees Exempt From Backup Withholding (See Part II instructions on page 2)

▶

Part III — Certification

Under penalties of perjury, I certify that:

1. The number shown on this form is my correct taxpayer identification number (or I am waiting for a number to be issued to me), **and**

2. I am not subject to backup withholding because: **(a)** I am exempt from backup withholding, or **(b)** I have not been notified by the Internal Revenue Service that I am subject to backup withholding as a result of a failure to report all interest or dividends, or **(c)** the IRS has notified me that I am no longer subject to backup withholding.

Certification Instructions.—You must cross out item **2** above if you have been notified by the IRS that you are currently subject to backup withholding because of underreporting interest or dividends on your tax return. For real estate transactions, item **2** does not apply. For mortgage interest paid, the acquisition or abandonment of secured property, cancellation of debt, contributions to an individual retirement arrangement (IRA), and generally payments other than interest and dividends, you are not required to sign the Certification, but you must provide your correct TIN. (Also see **Part III instructions** on page 2.)

Sign Here | Signature ▶   Date ▶

Section references are to the Internal Revenue Code.

Purpose of Form.—A person who is required to file an information return with the IRS must get your correct TIN to report income paid to you, real estate transactions, mortgage interest you paid, the acquisition or abandonment of secured property, cancellation of debt, or contributions you made to an IRA. Use Form W-9 to give your correct TIN to the requester (the person requesting your TIN) and, when applicable, (1) to certify the TIN you are giving is correct (or you are waiting for a number to be issued), (2) to certify you are not subject to backup withholding, or (3) to claim exemption from backup withholding if you are an exempt payee. Giving your correct TIN and making the appropriate certifications will prevent certain payments from being subject to backup withholding.

Note: *If a requester gives you a form other than a W-9 to request your TIN, you must use the requester's form if it is substantially similar to this Form W-9.*

What Is Backup Withholding?—Persons making certain payments to you must withhold and pay to the IRS 31% of such

payments under certain conditions. This is called "backup withholding." Payments that could be subject to backup withholding include interest, dividends, broker and barter exchange transactions, rents, royalties, nonemployee pay, and certain payments from fishing boat operators. Real estate transactions are not subject to backup withholding.

If you give the requester your correct TIN, make the proper certifications, and report all your taxable interest and dividends on your tax return, your payments will not be subject to backup withholding. Payments you receive will be subject to backup withholding if:

1. You do not furnish your TIN to the requester, or

2. The IRS tells the requester that you furnished an incorrect TIN, or

3. The IRS tells you that you are subject to backup withholding because you did not report all your interest and dividends on your tax return (for reportable interest and dividends only), or

4. You do not certify to the requester that you are not subject to backup withholding under 3 above (for reportable

interest and dividend accounts opened after 1983 only), or

5. You do not certify your TIN. See the Part III instructions for exceptions.

Certain payees and payments are exempt from backup withholding and information reporting. See the Part II instructions and the separate **Instructions for the Requester of Form W-9.**

How To Get a TIN.—If you do not have a TIN, apply for one immediately. To apply, get **Form SS-5**, Application for a Social Security Number Card (for individuals), from your local office of the Social Security Administration, or **Form SS-4**, Application for Employer Identification Number (for businesses and all other entities), from your local IRS office.

If you do not have a TIN, write "Applied For" in the space for the TIN in Part I, sign and date the form, and give it to the requester. Generally, you will then have 60 days to get a TIN and give it to the requester. If the requester does not receive your TIN within 60 days, backup withholding, if applicable, will begin and continue until you furnish your TIN.

Note: *Writing "Applied For" on the form means that you have already applied for a TIN OR that you intend to apply for one soon.*

As soon as you receive your TIN, complete another Form W-9, include your TIN, sign and date the form, and give it to the requester.

Penalties

Failure To Furnish TIN.—If you fail to furnish your correct TIN to a requester, you are subject to a penalty of $50 for each such failure unless your failure is due to reasonable cause and not to willful neglect.

Civil Penalty for False Information With Respect to Withholding.—If you make a false statement with no reasonable basis that results in no backup withholding, you are subject to a $500 penalty.

Criminal Penalty for Falsifying Information.— Willfully falsifying certifications or affirmations may subject you to criminal penalties including fines and/or imprisonment.

Misuse of TINs.—If the requester discloses or uses TINs in violation of Federal law, the requester may be subject to civil and criminal penalties.

Specific Instructions

Name.—If you are an individual, you must generally enter the name shown on your social security card. However, if you have changed your last name, for instance, due to marriage, without informing the Social Security Administration of the name change, please enter your first name, the last name shown on your social security card, and your new last name.

Sole Proprietor.—You must enter your **individual** name. (Enter either your SSN or EIN in Part I.) You may also enter your business name or "doing business as" name on the business name line. Enter your name as shown on your social security card and business name as it was used to apply for your EIN on Form SS-4.

Part I—Taxpayer Identification Number (TIN)

You must enter your TIN in the appropriate box. If you are a sole proprietor, you may enter your SSN or EIN. Also see the chart on this page for further clarification of name and TIN combinations. If you do not have a TIN, follow the instructions under **How To Get a TIN** on page 1.

Part II—For Payees Exempt From Backup Withholding

Individuals (including sole proprietors) are **not** exempt from backup withholding. Corporations are exempt from backup withholding for certain payments, such as interest and dividends. For a complete list of exempt payees, see the separate Instructions for the Requester of Form W-9.

If you are exempt from backup withholding, you should still complete this form to avoid possible erroneous backup withholding. Enter your correct TIN in Part I, write "Exempt" in Part II, and sign and date the form. If you are a nonresident alien or a foreign entity not subject to backup withholding, give the requester a completed **Form W-8**, Certificate of Foreign Status.

Part III—Certification

For a joint account, only the person whose TIN is shown in Part I should sign.

1. Interest, Dividend, and Barter Exchange Accounts Opened Before 1984 and Broker Accounts Considered Active During 1983. You must give your correct TIN, but you do not have to sign the certification.

2. Interest, Dividend, Broker, and Barter Exchange Accounts Opened After 1983 and Broker Accounts Considered Inactive During 1983. You must sign the certification or backup withholding will apply. If you are subject to backup withholding and you are merely providing your correct TIN to the requester, you must cross out item **2** in the certification before signing the form.

3. Real Estate Transactions. You must sign the certification. You may cross out item **2** of the certification.

4. Other Payments. You must give your correct TIN, but you do not have to sign the certification unless you have been notified of an incorrect TIN. Other payments include payments made in the course of the requester's trade or business for rents, royalties, goods (other than bills for merchandise), medical and health care services, payments to a nonemployee for services (including attorney and accounting fees), and payments to certain fishing boat crew members.

5. Mortgage Interest Paid by You, Acquisition or Abandonment of Secured Property, Cancellation of Debt, or IRA Contributions. You must give your correct TIN, but you do not have to sign the certification.

Privacy Act Notice

Section 6109 requires you to give your correct TIN to persons who must file information returns with the IRS to report interest, dividends, and certain other income paid to you, mortgage interest you paid, the acquisition or abandonment of secured property, cancellation of debt, or contributions you made to an IRA. The IRS uses the numbers for identification purposes and to help verify the accuracy of your tax return. You must provide your TIN whether or not you are required to file a tax return. Payers must generally withhold 31% of taxable interest, dividend, and certain other payments to a payee who does not give a TIN to a payer. Certain penalties may also apply.

What Name and Number To Give the Requester

For this type of account:	Give name and SSN of:
1. Individual	The individual
2. Two or more individuals (joint account)	The actual owner of the account or, if combined funds, the first individual on the account [1]
3. Custodian account of a minor (Uniform Gift to Minors Act)	The minor [2]
4. a. The usual revocable savings trust (grantor is also trustee)	The grantor-trustee [1]
b. So-called trust account that is not a legal or valid trust under state law	The actual owner [1]
5. Sole proprietorship	The owner [3]

For this type of account:	Give name and EIN of:
6. Sole proprietorship	The owner [3]
7. A valid trust, estate, or pension trust	Legal entity [4]
8. Corporate	The corporation
9. Association, club, religious, charitable, educational, or other tax-exempt organization	The organization
10. Partnership	The partnership
11. A broker or registered nominee	The broker or nominee
12. Account with the Department of Agriculture in the name of a public entity (such as a state or local government, school district, or prison) that receives agricultural program payments	The public entity

[1] List first and circle the name of the person whose number you furnish.

[2] Circle the minor's name and furnish the minor's SSN.

[3] You must show your individual name, but you may also enter your business or "doing business as" name. You may use either your SSN or EIN.

[4] List first and circle the name of the legal trust, estate, or pension trust. (Do not furnish the TIN of the personal representative or trustee unless the legal entity itself is not designated in the account title.)

Note: *If no name is circled when more than one name is listed, the number will be considered to be that of the first name listed.*

Form **SS-4**
(Rev. December 1993)
Department of the Treasury
Internal Revenue Service

Application for Employer Identification Number

(For use by employers, corporations, partnerships, trusts, estates, churches, government agencies, certain individuals, and others. See instructions.)

EIN

OMB No. 1545-0003
Expires 12-31-96

Please type or print clearly.

1 Name of applicant (Legal name) (See instructions.)	

2 Trade name of business, if different from name in line 1	**3** Executor, trustee, "care of" name

4a Mailing address (street address) (room, apt., or suite no.)	**5a** Business address, if different from address in lines 4a and 4b
4b City, state, and ZIP code	**5b** City, state, and ZIP code

6 County and state where principal business is located

7 Name of principal officer, general partner, grantor, owner, or trustor—SSN required (See instructions.) ▶

8a Type of entity (Check only one box.) (See instructions.)

☐ Sole Proprietor (SSN) _____
☐ REMIC
☐ State/local government ☐ National guard
☐ Other nonprofit organization (specify) _____
☐ Other (specify) ▶ _____

☐ Estate (SSN of decedent) _____
☐ Plan administrator-SSN _____
☐ Personal service corp.
☐ Other corporation (specify) _____
☐ Federal government/military ☐ Church or church controlled organization
(enter GEN if applicable) _____

☐ Trust
☐ Partnership
☐ Farmers' cooperative

8b If a corporation, name the state or foreign country (if applicable) where incorporated ▶

State	Foreign country

9 Reason for applying (Check only one box.)

☐ Started new business (specify) ▶ _____
☐ Hired employees
☐ Created a pension plan (specify type) ▶ _____
☐ Banking purpose (specify) ▶

☐ Changed type of organization (specify) ▶ _____
☐ Purchased going business
☐ Created a trust (specify) ▶ _____
☐ Other (specify) ▶

10 Date business started or acquired (Mo., day, year) (See instructions.)

11 Enter closing month of accounting year. (See instructions.)

12 First date wages or annuities were paid or will be paid (Mo., day, year). **Note:** *If applicant is a withholding agent, enter date income will first be paid to nonresident alien. (Mo., day, year)* . . . . ▶

13 Enter highest number of employees expected in the next 12 months. **Note:** *If the applicant does not expect to have any employees during the period, enter "0."* . . . . ▶

Nonagricultural	Agricultural	Household

14 Principal activity (See instructions.) ▶

15 Is the principal business activity manufacturing? . . . . ☐ Yes ☐ No
If "Yes," principal product and raw material used ▶

16 To whom are most of the products or services sold? Please check the appropriate box. ☐ Business (wholesale)
☐ Public (retail) ☐ Other (specify) ▶ ☐ N/A

17a Has the applicant ever applied for an identification number for this or any other business? . . . . ☐ Yes ☐ No
Note: *If "Yes," please complete lines 17b and 17c.*

17b If you checked the "Yes" box in line 17a, give applicant's legal name and trade name, if different than name shown on prior application.

Legal name ▶   Trade name ▶

17c Enter approximate date, city, and state where the application was filed and the previous employer identification number if known.

Approximate date when filed (Mo., day, year)	City and state where filed	Previous EIN

Under penalties of perjury, I declare that I have examined this application, and to the best of my knowledge and belief, it is true, correct, and complete. | Business telephone number (include area code)

Name and title (Please type or print clearly.) ▶

Signature ▶   Date ▶

Note: *Do not write below this line.   For official use only.*

Please leave blank ▶	Geo.	Ind.	Class	Size	Reason for applying

For Paperwork Reduction Act Notice, see attached instructions.   Cat. No. 16055N   Form **SS-4** (Rev. 12-93)

General Instructions

(Section references are to the Internal Revenue Code unless otherwise noted.)

Purpose

Use Form SS-4 to apply for an employer identification number (EIN). An EIN is a nine-digit number (for example, 12-3456789) assigned to sole proprietors, corporations, partnerships, estates, trusts, and other entities for filing and reporting purposes. The information you provide on this form will establish your filing and reporting requirements.

Who Must File

You must file this form if you have not obtained an EIN before and

- You pay wages to one or more employees.
- You are required to have an EIN to use on any return, statement, or other document, even if you are not an employer.
- You are a withholding agent required to withhold taxes on income, other than wages, paid to a nonresident alien (individual, corporation, partnership, etc.). A withholding agent may be an agent, broker, fiduciary, manager, tenant, or spouse, and is required to file Form 1042, Annual Withholding Tax Return for U.S. Source Income of Foreign Persons.
- You file Schedule C, Profit or Loss From Business, or Schedule F, Profit or Loss From Farming, of Form 1040, U.S. Individual Income Tax Return, and have a Keogh plan or are required to file excise, employment, alcohol, tobacco, or firearms returns.

The following must use EINS even if they do not have any employees:

- Trusts, except the following:
  1. Certain grantor-owned revocable trusts (see the instructions for Form 1040).
  2. Individual Retirement Arrangement (IRA) trusts, unless the trust has to file Form 990-T, Exempt Organization Business Income Tax Return (See the Instructions for Form 990-T.)
- Estates
- Partnerships
- REMICS (real estate mortgage investment conduits) (See the instructions for Form 1066, U.S. Real Estate Mortgage Investment Conduit Income Tax Return.)
- Corporations
- Nonprofit organizations (churches, clubs, etc.)
- Farmers' cooperatives
- Plan administrators (A plan administrator is the person or group of persons specified as the administrator by the instrument under which the plan is operated.)

When To Apply for A New EIN

New Business.—If you become the new owner of an existing business, DO NOT use the EIN of the former owner. If you already have an EIN, use that number. If you do not have an EIN, apply for one on this form. If you become the "owner" of a corporation by acquiring its stock, use the corporation's EIN.

Changes in Organization or Ownership.—If you already have an EIN, you may need to get a new one if either the organization or ownership of your business changes. If you incorporate a sole proprietorship or form a partnership, you must get a new EIN. However, DO NOT apply for a new EIN if you change only the name of your business.

File Only One Form SS-4.—File only one Form SS-4, regardless of the number of businesses operated or trade names under which a business operates. However, each corporation in an affiliated group must file a separate application.

EIN Applied For, But Not Received.—If you do not have an EIN by the time a return is due, write "Applied for" and the date you applied in the space shown for the number. DO NOT show your social security number as an EIN on returns.

If you do not have an EIN by the time a tax deposit is due, send your payment to the Internal Revenue service center for your filing area. (See Where To Apply below.) Make your check or money order payable to Internal Revenue Service and show your name (as shown on Form SS-4), address, kind of tax, period covered, and date you applied for an EIN.

For more information about EINS, see Pub. 583, Taxpayers Starting a Business and Pub. 1635, EINS Made Easy.

How To Apply

You can apply for an EIN either by mail or by telephone. You can get an EIN immediately by calling the Tele-TIN phone number for the service center for your state, or you can send the completed Form SS-4 directly to the service center to receive your EIN in the mail.

Application by Tele-TIN.—Under the Tele-TIN program, you can receive your EIN over the telephone and use it immediately to file a return or make a payment. To receive an EIN by phone, complete Form SS-4, then call the Tele-TIN phone number listed for your state under Where To Apply. The person making the call must be authorized to sign the form (see Signature block on page 3).

An IRS representative will use the information from the Form SS-4 to establish your account and assign you an EIN. Write the number you are given on the upper right-hand corner of the form, sign and date it.

You should mail or FAX the signed SS-4 within 24 hours to the Tele-TIN Unit at the service center address for your state. The IRS representative will give you the FAX number. The FAX numbers are also listed in Pub. 1635.

Taxpayer representatives can receive their client's EIN by phone if they first send a facsimile (FAX) of a completed Form 2848, Power of Attorney and Declaration of Representative, or Form 8821, Tax Information Authorization, to the Tele-TIN unit. The Form 2848 or Form 8821 will be used solely to release the EIN to the representative authorized on the form.

Application by Mail.—Complete Form SS-4 at least 4 to 5 weeks before you will need an EIN. Sign and date the application and mail it to the service center address for your state. You will receive your EIN in the mail in approximately 4 weeks.

Where To Apply

The Tele-TIN phone numbers listed below will involve a long-distance charge to callers outside of the local calling area, and should be used only to apply for an EIN. THE NUMBERS MAY CHANGE WITHOUT NOTICE. Use 1-800-829-1040 to verify a number or to ask about an application by mail or other Federal tax matters.

If your principal business, office or agency, or legal residence in the case of an individual, is located in:	Call the Tele-TIN phone number shown or file with the Internal Revenue Service center at:
Florida, Georgia, South Carolina	Attn: Entity Control, Atlanta, GA 39901 (404) 455-2360
New Jersey, New York City and counties of Nassau, Rockland, Suffolk, and Westchester	Attn: Entity Control, Holtsville, NY 00501 (516) 447-4955
New York (all other counties), Connecticut, Maine, Massachusetts, New Hampshire, Rhode Island, Vermont	Attn: Entity Control, Andover, MA 05501 (508) 474-9717
Illinois, Iowa, Minnesota, Missouri, Wisconsin	Attn: Entity Control, Stop 57A, 2306 E. Bannister Rd., Kansas City, MO 64131 (816) 926-5999
Delaware, District of Columbia, Maryland, Pennsylvania, Virginia	Attn: Entity Control, Philadelphia, PA 19255 (215) 574-2400

Note: Household employers are not required to file the Form SS-4 to get an EIN. An EIN may be assigned to you without filing Form SS-4 if your only employees are household employees (domestic workers) in your private home. To have an EIN assigned to you, write "NONE" in the space for the EIN on Form 942, Employer's Quarterly Tax Return for Household Employees, when you file it.

Indiana, Kentucky, Michigan, Ohio, West Virginia	Attn: Entity Control Cincinnati, OH 45999 (606) 292-5467
Kansas, New Mexico, Oklahoma, Texas	Attn: Entity Control Austin, TX 73301 (512) 462-7843
Alaska, Arizona, California (counties of Alpine, Amador, Butte, Calaveras, Colusa, Contra Costa, Del Norte, El Dorado, Glenn, Humboldt, Lake, Lassen, Marin, Mendocino, Modoc, Napa, Nevada, Placer, Plumas, Sacramento, San Joaquin, Shasta, Sierra, Siskiyou, Solano, Sonoma, Sutter, Tehama, Trinity, Yolo, and Yuba), Colorado, Idaho, Montana, Nebraska, Nevada, North Dakota, Oregon, South Dakota, Utah, Washington, Wyoming	Attn: Entity Control Mail Stop 6271-T P.O. Box 9950 Ogden, UT 84409 (801) 620-7645
California (all other counties), Hawaii	Attn: Entity Control Fresno, CA 93888 (209) 452-4010
Alabama, Arkansas, Louisiana, Mississippi, North Carolina, Tennessee	Attn: Entity Control Memphis, TN 37501 (901) 365-5970

If you have no legal residence, principal place of business, or principal office or agency in any state, file your form with the Internal Revenue Service Center, Philadelphia, PA 19255 or call (215) 574-2400.

Specific Instructions

The instructions that follow are for those items that are not self-explanatory. Enter N/A (nonapplicable) on the lines that do not apply.

Line 1.—Enter the legal name of the entity applying for the EIN exactly as it appears on the social security card, charter, or other applicable legal document.

Individuals.—Enter the first name, middle initial, and last name.

Trusts.—Enter the name of the trust.

Estate of a decedent.—Enter the name of the estate.

Partnerships.—Enter the legal name of the partnership as it appears in the partnership agreement.

Corporations.—Enter the corporate name as set forth in the corporation charter or other legal document creating it.

Plan administrators.—Enter the name of the plan administrator. A plan administrator who already has an EIN should use that number.

Line 2.—Enter the trade name of the business if different from the legal name. The trade name is the "doing business as" name.

Note: *Use the full legal name on line 1 on all tax returns filed for the entity. However, if you enter a trade name on line 2 and choose to use the trade name instead of the legal name, enter the trade name on all returns you file. To prevent processing delays and errors, **always** use either the legal name only or the trade name only on all tax returns.*

Line 3.—Trusts enter the name of the trustee. Estates enter the name of the executor, administrator, or other fiduciary. If the entity applying has a designated person to receive tax information, enter that person's name as the "care of" person. Print or type the first name, middle initial, and last name.

Line 7.—Enter the first name, middle initial, last name, and social security number (SSN) of a principal officer if the business is a corporation; of a general partner if a partnership; and of a grantor owner, or trustor if a trust.

Line 8a.—Check the box that best describes the type of entity applying for the EIN. If not specifically mentioned, check the "other" box and enter the type of entity. Do not enter N/A.

Sole proprietor.—Check this box if you file Schedule C or F (Form 1040) and have a Keogh plan, or are required to file excise, employment, or alcohol, tobacco, or firearms returns. Enter your SSN (social security number) in the space provided.

Plan administrator.—If the plan administrator is an individual, enter the plan administrator's SSN in the space provided.

Withholding agent.—If you are a withholding agent required to file Form 1042, check the "other" box and enter "withholding agent."

REMICs.—Check this box if the entity has elected to be treated as a real estate mortgage investment conduit (REMIC). See the Instructions for Form 1066 for more information.

Personal service corporations.—Check this box if the entity is a personal service corporation. An entity is a personal service corporation for a tax year only if:

● The principal activity of the entity during the testing period (prior tax year) for the tax year is the performance of personal services substantially by employee-owners.

● The employee-owners own 10 percent of the fair market value of the outstanding stock in the entity on the last day of the testing period.

Personal services include performance of services in such fields as health, law, accounting, consulting, etc. For more information about personal service corporations, see the instructions to **Form 1120,** U.S. Corporation Income Tax Return, and **Pub. 542,** Tax Information on Corporations.

Other corporations.—This box is for any corporation other than a personal service corporation. If you check this box, enter the type of corporation (such as insurance company) in the space provided.

Other nonprofit organizations.—Check this box if the nonprofit organization is

other than a church or church-controlled organization and specify the type of nonprofit organization (for example, an educational organization.)

If the organization also seeks tax-exempt status, you must file either **Package 1023** or **Package 1024,** Application for Recognition of Exemption. Get **Pub. 557,** Tax-Exempt Status for Your Organization, for more information.

Group exemption number (GEN).—If the organization is covered by a group exemption letter, enter the four-digit GEN. (Do not confuse the GEN with the nine-digit EIN.) If you do not know the GEN, contact the parent organization. Get Pub. 557 for more information about group exemption numbers.

Line 9.—Check only **one** box. Do not enter N/A.

Started new business.—Check this box if you are starting a new business that requires an EIN. If you check this box, enter the type of business being started. **DO NOT** apply if you already have an EIN and are only adding another place of business.

Changed type of organization.—Check this box if the business is changing its type of organization, for example, if the business was a sole proprietorship and has been incorporated or has become a partnership. If you check this box, specify in the space provided the type of change made, for example, "from sole proprietorship to partnership."

Purchased going business.—Check this box if you purchased an existing business. DO NOT use the former owner's EIN. Use your own EIN if you already have one.

Hired employees.—Check this box if the existing business is requesting an EIN because it has hired or is hiring employees and is therefore required to file employment tax returns. **DO NOT** apply if you already have an EIN and are only hiring employees. If you are hiring household employees, see **Note** under **Who Must File** on page 2.

Created a trust.—Check this box if you created a trust, and enter the type of trust created.

Note: *DO NOT file this form if you are the individual-grantor/owner of a revocable trust. You must use your SSN for the trust. See the instructions for Form 1040.*

Created a pension plan.—Check this box if you have created a pension plan and need this number for reporting purposes. Also, enter the type of plan created.

Banking purpose.—Check this box if you are requesting an EIN for banking purposes only and enter the banking purpose (for example, a bowling league for depositing dues, an investment club for dividend and interest reporting, etc.).

Other (specify).—Check this box if you are requesting an EIN for any reason other than those for which there are checkboxes, and enter the reason.

Line 10.—If you are starting a new business, enter the starting date of the business. If the business you acquired is already operating, enter the date you acquired the business. Trusts should enter the date the trust was legally created. Estates should enter the date of death of the decedent whose name appears on line 1 or the date when the estate was legally funded.

Line 11.—Enter the last month of your accounting year or tax year. An accounting year or tax year is usually 12 consecutive months, either a calendar year or a fiscal year (including a period of 52 or 53 weeks). A calendar year is 12 consecutive months ending on December 31. A fiscal year is either 12 consecutive months ending on the last day of any month other than December or a 52-53 week year. For more information on accounting periods, see **Pub. 538,** Accounting Periods and Methods.

Individuals.—Your tax year generally will be a calendar year.

Partnerships.—Partnerships generally must adopt the tax year of either (1) the majority partners; (2) the principal partners; (3) the tax year that results in the least aggregate (total) deferral of income; or (4) some other tax year. (See the instructions for **Form 1065,** U.S. Partnership Return of Income, for more information.)

REMICs.—Remics must have a calendar year as their tax year.

Personal service corporations.—A personal service corporation generally must adopt a calendar year unless:

● It can establish a business purpose for having a different tax year, or

● It elects under section 444 to have a tax year other than a calendar year.

Trusts.—Generally, a trust must adopt a calendar year except for the following:

● Tax-exempt trusts,
● Charitable trusts, and
● Grantor-owned trusts.

Line 12.—If the business has or will have employees, enter the date on which the business began or will begin to pay wages. If the business does not plan to have employees, enter N/A.

Withholding agent.—Enter the date you began or will begin to pay income to a nonresident alien. This also applies to individuals who are required to file Form 1042 to report alimony paid to a nonresident alien.

Line 14.—Generally, enter the exact type of business being operated (for example, advertising agency, farm, food or beverage establishment, labor union, real estate agency, steam laundry, rental of coin-operated vending machine, investment club, etc.). Also state if the business will involve the sale or distribution of alcoholic beverages.

Governmental.—Enter the type of organization (state, county, school district, or municipality, etc.).

Nonprofit organization (other than governmental).—Enter whether organized for religious, educational, or humane purposes, and the principal activity (for example, religious organization—hospital, charitable).

Mining and quarrying.—Specify the process and the principal product (for example, mining bituminous coal, contract drilling for oil, quarrying dimension stone, etc.).

Contract construction.—Specify whether general contracting or special trade contracting. Also, show the type of work normally performed (for example, general contractor for residential buildings, electrical subcontractor, etc.).

Food or beverage establishments.—Specify the type of establishment and state whether you employ workers who receive tips (for example, lounge—yes).

Trade.—Specify the type of sales and the principal line of goods sold (for example, wholesale dairy products, manufacturer's representative for mining machinery, retail hardware, etc.).

Manufacturing.—Specify the type of establishment operated (for example, sawmill, vegetable cannery, etc.).

Signature block.—The application must be signed by: (1) the individual, if the applicant is an individual, (2) the president, vice president, or other principal officer, if the applicant is a corporation, (3) a responsible and duly authorized member or officer having knowledge of its affairs, if the applicant is a partnership or other unincorporated organization, or (4) the fiduciary, if the applicant is a trust or estate.

Some Useful Publications

You may get the following publications for additional information on the subjects covered on this form. To get these and other free forms and publications, call 1-800-TAX-FORM (1-800-829-3676).

Pub. 1635, EINs Made Easy

Pub. 538, Accounting Periods and Methods

Pub. 541, Tax information on Partnerships

Pub. 542, Tax information on Corporations

Pub. 557, Tax-Exempt Status for Your Organization

Pub. 583, Taxpayers Starting A Business

Pub. 937, Employment Taxes and Information Returns

Package 1023, Application for Recognition of Exemption

Package 1024, Application for Recognition of Exemption Under Section 501(a) or for Determination Under Section 120

Paperwork Reduction Act Notice

We ask for the information on this form to carry out the Internal Revenue laws of the United States. You are required to give us the information. We need it to ensure that you are complying with these laws and to allow us to figure and collect the right amount of tax.

The time needed to complete and file this form will vary depending on individual circumstances. The estimated average time is:

Recordkeeping	7 min.
Learning about the law or the form	18 min.
Preparing the form	44 min.
Copying, assembling, and sending the form to the IRS	20 min.

If you have comments concerning the accuracy of these time estimates or suggestions for making this form more simple, we would be happy to hear from you. You can write to both the **Internal Revenue Service,** Attention: Reports Clearance Officer, PC:FP, Washington, DC 20224; and the **Office of Management and Budget,** Paperwork Reduction Project (1545-0003), Washington, DC 20503. **DO NOT** send this form to either of these offices. Instead, see **Where To Apply** on page 2.

Printed on recycled paper

☆ U.S. Government Printing Office: 1993 — 363-331/99125

1995

**Department of the Treasury
Internal Revenue Service**

Instructions for Form 8829

Expenses for Business Use of Your Home

Section references are to the Internal Revenue Code.

Paperwork Reduction Act Notice

We ask for the information on this form to carry out the Internal Revenue laws of the United States. You are required to give us the information. We need it to ensure that you are complying with these laws and to allow us to figure and collect the right amount of tax.

The time needed to complete and file this form will vary depending on individual circumstances. The estimated average time is: **Recordkeeping,** 52 min.; **Learning about the law or the form,** 7 min.; **Preparing the form,** 1 hr., 16 min.; and **Copying, assembling, and sending the form to the IRS,** 20 min.

If you have comments concerning the accuracy of these time estimates or suggestions for making this form simpler, we would be happy to hear from you. You can write or call the IRS. See the Instructions for Form 1040.

General Instructions

Purpose of Form

Use Form 8829 to figure the allowable expenses for business use of your home on **Schedule C** (Form 1040) and any carryover to 1996 of amounts not deductible in 1995.

If all of the expenses for business use of your home are properly allocable to inventory costs, do not complete Form 8829. These expenses are figured in Part III of Schedule C and not on Form 8829.

You must meet specific requirements to deduct expenses for the business use of your home. Even if you meet these requirements, your deductible expenses are limited. For details, get **Pub. 587,** Business Use of Your Home (Including Use by Day-Care Providers).

Note: *If you file* **Schedule F** *(Form 1040) or you are an employee or a partner,* **do not** *use this form. Instead, use the worksheet in Pub. 587.*

Who May Deduct Expenses for Business Use of a Home

Generally, you may deduct business expenses that apply to a part of your home **only** if that part is exclusively used on a regular basis:

1. As your principal place of business for any of your trades or businesses; or

2. As a place of business used by your patients, clients, or customers to meet or deal with you in the normal course of your trade or business; or

3. In connection with your trade or business if it is a separate structure that is not attached to your home.

In determining whether a business location in your home qualifies as your principal place of business, you must consider the following two factors:

1. The relative importance of the activities performed at each business location; and

2. The amount of time spent at each location.

First, compare the relative importance of the activities performed at each location. A comparison of the relative importance of the activities performed at each business location depends on the characteristics of each business. If your business requires that you meet or confer with clients or patients, or that you deliver goods or services to a customer, the place where that contact occurs must be given a greater weight in determining where the most important activities are performed. Performance of necessary or essential activities at the business location in your home (such as planning for services or the delivery of goods, or the accounting or billing for those activities or goods) is not controlling.

If you are unable to clearly identify the location of your principal place of business after comparing the relative importance of the activities, you should compare the amount of time spent on business at each location. This may happen when you perform income-producing activities at both your home and some other location.

You may find, after applying both factors, that you have no principal place of business.

Exception for storage of inventory.—You may also deduct expenses that apply to space within your home if it is the **only** fixed location of your trade or business. The space must be used on a regular basis to store inventory from your trade or business of selling products at retail or wholesale.

Exception for day-care facilities.—If you use space in your home on a regular basis in the trade or business of providing day care, you may be able to deduct the business expenses even though you use the same space for nonbusiness purposes. To qualify for this exception, you must have applied for (and not have been rejected), been granted (and still have in effect), or be exempt from having a license, certification, registration, or approval as a day-care center or as a family or group day-care home under state law.

Specific Instructions

Part I

Lines 1 and 2.—To determine the area on lines 1 and 2, you may use square feet or any other reasonable method if it accurately figures your business percentage on line 7.

Do not include on line 1 the area of your home you used to figure any expenses

allocable to inventory costs. The business percentage of these expenses should have been taken into account in Part III of Schedule C.

Special computation for certain day-care facilities.—If the part of your home used as a day-care facility included areas used exclusively for business as well as other areas used only partly for business, you **cannot** figure your business percentage using Part I. Instead, follow these three steps:

1. Figure the business percentage of the part of your home used exclusively for business by dividing the area used exclusively for business by the total area of the home.

2. Figure the business percentage of the part of your home used only partly for business by following the same method used in Part I of the form, but enter on line 1 of your computation only the area of the home used partly for business.

3. Add the business percentages you figured in the first two steps and enter the result on line 7. Attach your computation and write "See attached computation" directly above the percentage you entered on line 7.

Line 4.—Enter the total number of hours the facility was used for day care during the year.

Example. Your home is used Monday through Friday for 12 hours per day for 250 days during the year. It is also used on 50 Saturdays for 8 hours per day. Enter 3,400 hours on line 4 (3,000 hours for weekdays plus 400 hours for Saturdays).

Line 5.—If you started or stopped using your home for day care in 1995, you must prorate the number of hours based on the number of days the home was available for day care. Cross out the preprinted entry on line 5. Multiply 24 hours by the number of days available and enter the result.

Part II

Line 8.—If all the gross income from your trade or business is from the business use of your home, enter on line 8 the amount from Schedule C, line 29, **plus** any net gain or (loss) derived from the business use of your home and shown on Schedule D or Form 4797. If you file more than one Form 8829, include only the income earned and the deductions attributable to that income during the period you owned the home for which Part I was completed.

If some of the income is from a place of business other than your home, you must first determine the part of your gross income (Schedule C, line 7, and gains from Schedule D and Form 4797) from the business use of your home. In making this determination, consider the amount of time you spend at each location as well as other facts. After determining the part of your gross income from the business use of your home, subtract from that amount the **total expenses** shown on Schedule C, line 28, plus any losses from your business shown on Schedule D or Form 4797. Enter the result on line 8 of Form 8829.

Columns (a) and (b).—Enter as direct or indirect expenses only expenses for the business use of your home (i.e., expenses allowable only because your home is used for business). If you did not operate a business for the entire year, you can only deduct the expenses paid or incurred for the portion of the year you used your home for business. Other expenses not allocable to the business use of your home, such as salaries, supplies, and business telephone expenses, are deductible elsewhere on Schedule C and should not be entered on Form 8829.

Direct expenses benefit only the business part of your home. They include painting or repairs made to the specific area or rooms used for business. Enter 100% of your direct expenses on the appropriate line in column (a).

Indirect expenses are for keeping up and running your entire home. They benefit both the business and personal parts of your home. Generally, enter 100% of your indirect expenses on the appropriate line in column (b).

Exception. If the business percentage of an indirect expense is different from the percentage on line 7, enter only the business part of the expense on the appropriate line in column (a), and leave that line in column (b) blank. For example, your electric bill is $800 for lighting, cooking, laundry, and television. If you reasonably estimate $300 of your electric bill is for lighting and you use 10% of your home for business, enter $30 on line 19 in column (a). **Do not** make an entry on line 19 in column (b) for any part of your electric bill.

Lines 9, 10, and 11.—Enter only the amounts that would be deductible whether or not you used your home for business (i.e., amounts allowable as itemized deductions on **Schedule A** (Form 1040)).

Treat **casualty losses** as personal expenses for this step. Figure the amount to enter on line 9 by completing Form 4684, Section A. When figuring line 17 of Form 4684, enter 10% of your adjusted gross income excluding the gross income from business use of your home and the deductions attributable to that income. Include on line 9 of Form 8829 the amount from Form 4684, line 18. See line 27 below to deduct part of the casualty losses not allowed because of the limits on Form 4684.

Do not file or use that Form 4684 to figure the amount of casualty losses to deduct on Schedule A. Instead, complete a separate Form 4684 to deduct the personal portion of your casualty losses.

On line 10, include only **mortgage interest** that would be deductible on Schedule A and that qualifies as a direct or indirect expense. **Do not** include interest on a mortgage loan that did not benefit your home (e.g., a home

equity loan used to pay off credit card bills, to buy a car, or to pay tuition costs).

If you itemize your deductions, be sure to claim **only** the personal portion of your deductible mortgage interest and real estate taxes on Schedule A. For example, if your business percentage on line 7 is 30%, you can claim 70% of your deductible mortgage interest and real estate taxes on Schedule A.

Line 16.—If the amount of home mortgage interest you deduct on Schedule A is limited, enter the part of the excess mortgage interest that qualifies as a direct or indirect expense. Do not include mortgage interest on a loan that did not benefit your home (explained above).

Line 20.—If you rent rather than own your home, include the rent you paid on line 20, column (b).

Line 27.—Multiply your casualty losses in excess of the amount on line 9 by the business percentage of those losses and enter the result.

Line 34.—If your home was used in more than one business, allocate the amount shown on line 34 to each business using any method that is reasonable under the circumstances. For each business, enter on Schedule C, line 30, only the amount allocated to that business.

Part III

Lines 35 through 37.—Enter on line 35 the cost or other basis of your home, or if less, the fair market value of your home on the date you first used the home for business. **Do not** adjust this amount for depreciation claimed or changes in fair market value after the year you first used your home for business. Allocate this amount between land and building values on lines 36 and 37.

Attach your own schedule showing the cost or other basis of additions and improvements placed in service after you began to use your home for business. Do not include any amounts on lines 35 through 38 for these expenditures. Instead, see the instructions for line 40.

Line 39.—If you first used your home for business in 1995, enter the percentage for the month you first used it for business.

Jan.	2.461%	May	1.605%	Sept.	0.749%
Feb.	2.247%	June	1.391%	Oct.	0.535%
March	2.033%	July	1.177%	Nov.	0.321%
April	1.819%	Aug.	0.963%	Dec.	0.107%

Exception. If the business part of your home is qualified Indian reservation property (as defined in section 168(j)(4)), get **Pub. 946,** How To Depreciate Property, to figure the depreciation.

If you first used your home for business:

• After May 12, 1993, and before 1995, enter 2.564% (except as noted below).

• After 1988, and before May 13, 1993 (or you either started construction or had a binding written contract to buy or build a home used for business before May 13, 1993), enter 3.175% (except as noted below).

• During 1987 or 1988, **OR** you stopped using your home for business before the end of the year and you began using that home for business after 1988, see Pub. 946 for the percentage to enter.

• Before 1987, get **Pub. 534,** Depreciating Property Placed in Service Before 1987, for the percentage to enter.

Line 40.—If no additions and improvements were placed in service after you began using your home for business, multiply line 38 by the percentage on line 39. Enter the result on lines 40 and 28.

If additions and improvements were placed in service:

• During 1995 (but after you began using your home for business), figure the depreciation allowed on these expenditures by multiplying the business part of their cost or other basis by the percentage shown in the line 39 instructions for the month placed in service.

• After May 12, 1993, and before 1995, figure the depreciation by multiplying the business part of their cost or other basis by 2.564% (except as noted below).

• After 1988, and before May 13, 1993 (or you either started construction or had a binding written contract to buy or build the addition or the improvement used for business before May 13, 1993), figure the depreciation by multiplying the business part of their cost or other basis by 3.175% (except as noted below).

• During 1987 or 1988 (but after you began using your home for business), **OR** you stopped using your home for business before the end of the year and you began using that home for business after 1988, see Pub. 946 to figure the depreciation.

• Before 1987 (but after you began using your home for business), see Pub. 534 to figure the depreciation.

Attach a schedule showing your computation and include the amount you figured in the total for line 40. Write "see attached" below the entry space.

Complete and attach **Form 4562,** Depreciation and Amortization, **only** if:

1. You first used your home for business in 1995, or

2. You are depreciating additions and improvements placed in service in 1995.

If you first used your home for business in 1995, enter on Form 4562, in column (c) of line 15h, the amount from line 38 of Form 8829. Then enter on Form 4562, in column (g) of line 15h, the amount from line 40 of Form 8829. But **do not** include this amount on Schedule C, line 13.

*U.S. Government Printing Office: 1995 — 389-489

Printed on recycled paper

Index

A

Accelerated cost recovery system (ACRS) depreciation, 2/13

Accelerated depreciation, 2/12-13

Accountants. *See* CPAs; Tax professionals

Accounting, 3/2-15
    methods, 3/12-14
        changing, 3/14
    resources, 3/15
    time periods, 3/14-15, 11/4

Accounts, defined, 3/3-4

Accrual accounting method, 3/13-14

Accumulated earnings (AE) tax, 7/18

Achievement awards, as fringe benefits, 14/11

ACRS (accelerated cost recovery system) depreciation, 2/13

Actual expense method, for vehicle expenses, 1/10

Advertising and publicity, deductibility, 1/19-20, 1/21

Agricultural producers, and uniform capitalization rules, 1/11

Alternate ACRS depreciation, 2/13

Alternative minimum tax, 7/18-19

Amended tax returns, and audits, 19/4

Amortization expense, 1/7, 3/10. *See also* Depreciation

Appeals
        of audit, 13/11, 20/1-8
        of employee misclassification ruling, 5/14-15
        hearing, 20/3-4
        of Trust Fund Recovery Penalty (TFRP), 5/9

Appointment books, and audits, 19/10-11

Appraisals of business asset value, 16/5-6

Arms-length deals, when selling business, 17/3-4

Asset logs, 3/9

Assets
        allocation, 16/5-8, 17/5
        capitalized, 2/2-6
        classifying for IRS for business sale, 16/6-6

depreciating, 2/11-19

enforced collection, 18/10-12

expensing, 2/6-10

leasing vs. buying, 2/19-21

long-term, 2/2-21

records, 3/9-11

resources, 2/21

tax basis, 2/3-5

writing off, 2/2-21

"Associated" test, for entertainment expenses, 1/14, 1/16

Association memberships, as fringe benefits, 14/7

Athletic facility memberships, as fringe benefits, 14/7

Audits, 19/2-22
        appeals, 13/11, 20/1-8
        and asset purchases, 2/19
        bad debts, 1/14
        behavior at, 19/17-18
        compensation for services, 7/15, 8/8
        fringe benefits, 14/3, 14/5
        home-based/microbusinesses, 13/4, 13/9, 13/11
        incorporation, 7/9
        negotiations, 19/18-20
        partnerships, 9/18
        payment plan, 19/21
        preparation for, 19/9-10
        professional help with, 19/7, 19/8-9
        recordkeeping, 3/8, 19/7, 19/7-8, 19/10, 19/10-13
        reports, 19/21-22
        resources, 19/22, 20/8
        retirement plans, 15/18
        statute of limitations, 6/3, 19/5
        types, 19/5-6

Automated adjustment, 19/5

Automatic stay, in bankruptcy, 18/9

Automobiles. *See* Vehicles

Awards, as fringe benefits, 14/11

I

Improvements, real estate, 1/7
    deductibility, 1/20
Income
    defined, 1/2-3
    foreign, 1/3
    gross,1/3
    records, 3/7-8
Income probe, and audit, 19/16
Income splitting
    and C corporations, 7/6, 7/9
    and family businesses, 12/2-6
    and PSCs, 11/5
Income taxes
    brackets, 1/4, 1/5
    deductibility, 1/19
    See also Estimated tax payments; Payroll taxes; etc.
Incorporating. *See* Corporations
Indemnification, in purchase agreement, 16/5
Independent contractors, 5/9-10, 5/10-11
    and audits, 19/16
    contracts with, 5/11
    misclassification, 5/12-15, 19/16
    tax returns, 1/20
Individual Retirement Accounts. *See* IRAs
Informants, and audits, 19/3
Information returns, 9/4
Inheritances, 1/3, 2/4
Installment payments
    of estate taxes, 12/8
    of income taxes, 18/3-4, 19/21
Installment sale, of business, 17/3
Insurance benefits
    group life insurance, as fringe benefit, 14/12
    and PSCs, 11/4
Intangible property
    as business asset, 16/7
    defined, 2/3
Interest, 21/3
    charges, deductibility, 1/18
    on late tax payments, 18/3-4
    notices, 21/3-4
    removal of charges, 21/7
    resources, 21/7
    See also Penalties and fines
Internal Revenue Code (IRC), 1/2, 1/4, 22/2, 22/4
    Section 162, 1/5-6

    Section 179, 2/6-10, 3/10, 3/10-11
    Section 280A, 13/4
    Section 351, 7/11-13
    Section 1244, 4/3-4, 7/13-14, 11/4
Internal Revenue Cumulative Bulletin, 22/4
Internal Revenue Manual (IRM), 22/5-6
Internal Revenue Service (IRS)
    free tax services, guide, Appendix/4
    Internet site, 22/7
    programs and seminars, 22/3-4
    publications and forms, 22/2-3
        checklist, Appendix/3
        list of titles, Appendix/1-2
        order blank, Appendix/4-5
    telephone information, 22/3
    written opinions, 22/4
    See also Forms and schedules
Internet sites, 22/7
Inventories, 2/5-6
    and taxes, 6/2
Investments, deductibility, 1/12
Investors, losses, 4/3
IRAs (Individual Retirement Accounts), 15/8-9
    ownership by children, 12/4
    and spouse, 12/6
    withdrawals, 15/20
    See also Retirement plans
IRS. *See* Internal Revenue Service
IRS Revenue Procedures (Rev. Procs.), 22/5

J

Job placement assistance, as fringe benefits, 14/13
Joint tenancy ownership, and estate taxes, 12/9
Journals. *See* Logbooks

K

Keogh plans, 15/5-8
    withdrawals, 15/20
    See also Retirement plans
"Kiddie tax," 12/4-5

Tax years, 3/14-15, 11/4
Taxes
    deductibility, 1/19
    installment payments, 18/3-4
    payment problems, 18/2-12
    See also Forms and schedules; *specific taxes or types of taxes*
Taxpayer Bill of Rights, 18/3, 19/6, 19/18
Telephone calls and service, deductibility, 1/17, 1/21, 13/6
TELETAX, 22/3
Temporary assignment travel, 14/6
Third-party summons, 19/8
30-day Letter, 20/2
3 of 5 test, 13/10-11
Time limits. *See* Statutes of limitations
Tips, deductibility, 1/17, 1/21
Tolls, deductibility as travel expense, 1/17
Trade association publications, and tax issues, 22/7
Trade shows, 14/5-6
Traffic tickets, deductibility, 1/11
Transactions, defined, 3/3
Transfer taxes, 16/8
Transit passes, deductibility, 1/11
Transportation, deductibility, 1/11, 1/21
    and entertainment expenses, 1/15
    and travel expenses, 1/17
Travel expenses
    and audits, 19/11, 19/12
    deductibility, 1/17, 12/7
    as fringe benefit, 14/4-7
    records, 3/9
Treasury regulations, and tax law, 1/4, 22/5
Trials. *See* U.S. Tax Court
Trucks. *See* Vehicles
Trust fund concept, for payroll taxes, 5/3
Trust Fund Recovery Penalty (TFRP), 5/3, 5/5
    appeal, 5/9
    indemnification clause, 5/5
TurboTax for Business software, 3/7, 15/8, 22/7

U

U.S. Code, 22/4
U.S. District Court, 20/4-5
U.S. Tax Court, 20/4, 20/4-8
    clerk, address, 20/6
    decisions, 20/8
    trials, 20/7-8
Unemployment taxes (FUTA), 8/8
    and children as employees, 12/3
Uniform capitalization rules, 1/11
Uniform Limited Partnership Act, 9/2
Uniform Partnership Act, 9/2
Unincorporated businesses
    buying, 16/2-3
    losses, 4/2-3
    medical and health benefits, 14/8-9, 14/9
    See also Partnerships; Sole proprietorships; *etc.*
United States Courts. *See* Court of Federal Claims; U.S. District Court; U.S. Tax Court; *etc.*
Unpaid bills, deductibility, 1/13
Unreimbursed business expense rules, 1/20
Useful life concept, 1/7, 2/11

V

Value added tax (VAT), 1/2
Vehicles
    company-owned, 1/10
    deduction rules for expenses, 1/8-11
    depreciation, 2/13, 2/17-18
    employee-owned, 1/10
    as fringe benefit, 14/4
    leasing vs. buying, 2/19-20
    mileage logs, 1/9, 1/9
    personal use, 1/8
    recordkeeping, 1/8, 1/9, 19/11, 19/12
    sports utility vehicles and trucks, 2/18
Voluntary Employees' Beneficiary Association (VEBA), 11/4
Volunteers, 12/6

more books from
NOLO PRESS

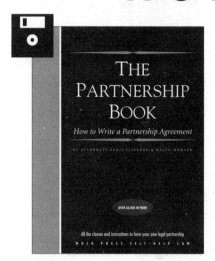

The Partnership Book

How to Write a Partnership Agreement, Book with Disk

Many people dream of going into business with friends. *The Partnership Book* shows how to turn that dream into a sound partnership agreement. It thoroughly explains the legal and practical issues involved in forming a partnership. Sample clauses cover all key issues—from partner's initial contributions to what happens if one leaves.

$34.95/PART

Money Troubles

Legal Strategies to Cope with Your Debts

Feeling overwhelmed by debts? *Money Troubles* is exactly what you need to help you get out from under. From credit card bills to student loans, this book provides legal and practical strategies for getting out of debt and getting a fresh start.

$19.95/MT

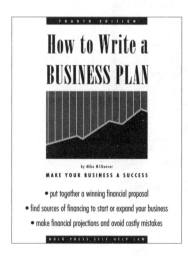

How to Write a Business Plan

If you're thinking of starting a small business or raising money to expand an existing one, this book will show you how to write the business plan and loan package necessary to finance your business and make it work. Includes up-to-date sources of financing.

$21.95/SBS

The Employer's Legal Handbook

The only book that compiles all the basics of employment law in one place. This book covers safe hiring practices, wages, hours, tips and commission, employee benefits, taxes and liability insurance, discrimination, sexual harassment and termination.

$29.95/EMPL

call 800-992-6656 or use the order form in the back of the book • www.nolo.com

more books from
NOLO PRESS

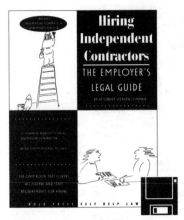

Hiring Independent Contractors

The Employer's Legal Guide, Book with disk

A legal guide for employers, this book clearly lays out; what the risks and benefits are of hiring independent contractors,who qualifies,how to hire independent contractors without risking an audit, how to make good agreements and how to retain ownership of intellectual property.

Includes independent contractor agreements on disk.

$29.95/HICI

Small Business Legal Pro Deluxe CD

This CD contains the complete text of four of Nolo's bestselling books: *The Legal Guide for Starting & Running a Small Business, Tax Savvy for Small Business, The Employer's Legal Handbook* and *Everybody's Guide to Small Claims Court.* Get instant access to information on hiring and firing, leases, deductions, wages, buying or selling a business, audits, preparing a winning small claims case and more.

Windows/Macintosh CD-ROM

SBCD2   ~~$59.95~~   **$35.97**

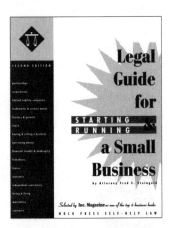

Legal Guide for Starting & Running a Small Business, Vol. 1

Get the information you need to decide whether to form a sole proprietorship, partnership, corporation or limited liability company, hire and fire employees, negotiate a favorable lease, write contracts, resolve business disputes, cope with financial problems and much more.

$24.95 / RUNS

Form Your Own Limited Liability Company

The limited liability company has taken off as the business entity of choice for smaller, privately-held companies. Get the best of both worlds—the informality and tax benefits of a partnership, with the personal protection from business debts and legal liabilities of a corporation. This book provides the step-by-step instructions for forming a limited liability company in all 50 states.

$24.95/LIAB

---

call 800-992-6656 or use the order form in the back of the book • www.nolo.com

CATALOG
...more from Nolo Press

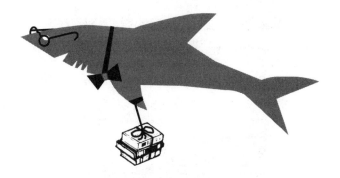

	EDITION	PRICE	CODE
BUSINESS			
Business Plans to Game Plans	1st	$29.95	GAME
The California Nonprofit Corporation Handbook	7th	$29.95	NON
The California Professional Corporation Handbook	5th	$34.95	PROF
The Employer's Legal Handbook	1st	$29.95	EMPL
Form Your Own Limited Liability Company	1st	$24.95	LIAB
Helping Employees Achieve Retirement Security	1st	$16.95	HEAR
Hiring Independent Contractors: The Employer's Legal Guide	1st	$29.95	HICI
How to Finance a Growing Business	4th	$24.95	GROW
How to Form a CA Nonprofit Corp.—w/Corp. Records Binder & PC Disk	1st	$49.95	CNP
How to Form a Nonprofit Corp., Book w/Disk (PC)—National Edition	3rd	$39.95	NNP
How to Form Your Own Calif. Corp.—w/Corp. Records Binder & Disk—PC	1st	$39.95	CACI
How to Form Your Own California Corporation	8th	$29.95	CCOR
How to Form Your Own Florida Corporation, (Book w/Disk—PC)	3rd	$39.95	FLCO
How to Form Your Own New York Corporation, (Book w/Disk—PC)	3rd	$39.95	NYCO
How to Form Your Own Texas Corporation, (Book w/Disk—PC)	4th	$39.95	TCOR
How to Handle Your Workers' Compensation Claim (California Edition)	1st	$29.95	WORK
How to Market a Product for Under $500	1st	$29.95	UN500
How to Mediate Your Dispute	1st	$18.95	MEDI
How to Write a Business Plan	4th	$21.95	SBS
The Independent Paralegal's Handbook	4th	$29.95	PARA
Insuring the Bottom Line	1st	$29.95	BOTT
The Legal Guide for Starting & Running a Small Business	2nd	$24.95	RUNS
Make Up Your Mind: Entrepreneurs Talk About Decision Making	1st	$19.95	MIND

▣ Book with disk

CALL 800-992-6656 OR USE THE ORDER FORM IN THE BACK OF THE BOOK

	EDITION	PRICE	CODE
Managing Generation X: How to Bring Out the Best in Young Talent	1st	$19.95	MANX
Marketing Without Advertising	1st	$14.00	MWAD
Mastering Diversity: Managing for Success Under ADA and Other Anti-Discrimination Laws	1st	$29.95	MAST
▣ OSHA in the Real World: (Book w/Disk—PC)	1st	$29.95	OSHA
Pay For Results	1st	$29.95	PAY
The Partnership Book: How to Write a Partnership Agreement	4th	$24.95	PART
Rightful Termination	1st	$29.95	RITE
Sexual Harassment on the Job	2nd	$18.95	HARS
▣ Taking Care of Your Corporation, Vol. 1, (Book w/Disk—PC)	1st	$26.95	CORK
▣ Taking Care of Your Corporation, Vol. 2, (Book w/Disk—PC)	1st	$39.95	CORK2
Tax Savvy for Small Business	1st	$26.95	SAVVY
Trademark: How to Name Your Business & Product	2nd	$29.95	TRD
Workers' Comp for Employers	2nd	$29.95	CNTRL
Your Rights in the Workplace	3rd	$19.95	YRW

CONSUMER

	EDITION	PRICE	CODE
Fed Up With the Legal System: What's Wrong & How to Fix It	2nd	$9.95	LEG
Glossary of Insurance Terms	6th	$14.95	GLINT
How to Insure Your Car	1st	$12.95	INCAR
How to Insure Your Home	1st	$12.95	INTRO
How to Insure Your Life	1st	$12.95	INLIF
How to Win Your Personal Injury Claim	2nd	$24.95	PICL
Nolo's Everyday Law Book	1st	$21.95	EVL
Nolo's Pocket Guide to California Law	4th	$10.95	CLAW
The Over 50 Insurance Survival Guide	1st	$16.95	OVER50
Trouble-Free Travel...And What to Do When Things Go Wrong	1st	$14.95	TRAV
True Odds: How Risk Affects Your Everyday Life	1st	$19.95	TROD
What Do You Mean It's Not Covered?	1st	$19.95	COVER

ESTATE PLANNING & PROBATE

	EDITION	PRICE	CODE
8 Ways to Avoid Probate	1st	$15.95	PRO8
How to Probate an Estate (California Edition)	8th	$34.95	PAE
Make Your Own Living Trust	2nd	$21.95	LITR
Nolo's Simple Will Book	2nd	$17.95	SWIL
Plan Your Estate	3rd	$24.95	NEST
The Quick and Legal Will Book	1st	$15.95	QUIC
Nolo's Law Form Kit: Wills	1st	$14.95	KWL

▣ Book with disk

CALL 800-992-6656 OR USE THE ORDER FORM IN THE BACK OF THE BOOK

	EDITION	PRICE	CODE

FAMILY MATTERS

	EDITION	PRICE	CODE
A Legal Guide for Lesbian and Gay Couples	9th	$24.95	LG
California Marriage Law	12th	$19.95	MARR
Child Custody: Building Partnership Agreements That Work	2nd	$24.95	CUST
Divorce & Money: How to Make the Best Financial Decisions During Divorce	3rd	$26.95	DIMO
Get A Life: You Don't Need a Million to Retire	1st	$18.95	LIFE
The Guardianship Book (California Edition)	2nd	$24.95	GB
How to Adopt Your Stepchild in California	4th	$22.95	ADOP
How to Do Your Own Divorce in California	21st	$24.95	CDIV
How to Do Your Own Divorce in Texas	6th	$19.95	TDIV
How to Raise or Lower Child Support in California	3rd	$18.95	CHLD
The Living Together Kit	7th	$24.95	LTK
Nolo's Law Form Kit: Hiring Childcare & Household Help	1st	$14.95	KCHD
Nolo's Pocket Guide to Family Law	4th	$14.95	FLD
Practical Divorce Solutions	1st	$14.95	PDS
Smart Ways to Save Money During and After Divorce	1st	$14.95	SAVMO

GOING TO COURT

	EDITION	PRICE	CODE
Collect Your Court Judgment (California Edition)	2nd	$19.95	JUDG
The Criminal Records Book (California Edition)	5th	$21.95	CRIM
How to Sue For Up to 25,000...and Win!	2nd	$29.95	MUNI
Everybody's Guide to Small Claims Court in California	12th	$18.95	CSCC
Everybody's Guide to Small Claims Court (National Edition)	6th	$18.95	NSCC
Fight Your Ticket ... and Win! (California Edition)	6th	$19.95	FYT
How to Change Your Name (California Edition)	6th	$24.95	NAME
Mad at Your Lawyer	1st	$21.95	MAD
Represent Yourself in Court: How to Prepare & Try a Winning Case	1st	$29.95	RYC
Taming the Lawyers	1st	$19.95	TAME

HOMEOWNERS, LANDLORDS & TENANTS

	EDITION	PRICE	CODE
The Deeds Book (California Edition)	3rd	$16.95	DEED
Dog Law	2nd	$12.95	DOG
💾 Every Landlord's Legal Guide (National Edition)	1st	$34.95	ELLI
For Sale by Owner (California Edition)	2nd	$24.95	FSBO
Homestead Your House (California Edition)	8th	$9.95	HOME
How to Buy a House in California	4th	$24.95	BHCA
The Landlord's Law Book, Vol. 1: Rights & Responsibilities (California Edition)	5th	$34.95	LBRT
The Landlord's Law Book, Vol. 2: Evictions (California Edition)	5th	$34.95	LBEV

💾 Book with disk

CALL 800-992-6656 OR USE THE ORDER FORM IN THE BACK OF THE BOOK

	EDITION	PRICE	CODE
Leases & Rental Agreements (National Edition)	1st	$18.95	LEAR
Neighbor Law: Fences, Trees, Boundaries & Noise	2nd	$16.95	NEI
Safe Homes, Safe Neighborhoods: Stopping Crime Where You Live	1st	$14.95	SAFE
Tenants' Rights (California Edition)	12th	$18.95	CTEN

HUMOR

	EDITION	PRICE	CODE
29 Reasons Not to Go to Law School	1st	$9.95	29R
Poetic Justice	1st	$9.95	PJ

IMMIGRATION

	EDITION	PRICE	CODE
How to Become a United States Citizen	5th	$14.95	CIT
How to Get a Green Card: Legal Ways to Stay in the U.S.A.	2nd	$24.95	GRN
U.S. Immigration Made Easy	5th	$39.95	IMEZ

MONEY MATTERS

	EDITION	PRICE	CODE
Building Your Nest Egg With Your 401(k)	1st	$16.95	EGG
Chapter 13 Bankruptcy: Repay Your Debts	2nd	$29.95	CH13
Credit Repair	1st	$15.95	CREP
How to File for Bankruptcy	6th	$26.95	HFB
Money Troubles: Legal Strategies to Cope With Your Debts	4th	$19.95	MT
Nolo's Law Form Kit: Personal Bankruptcy	1st	$14.95	KBNK
Nolo's Law Form Kit: Rebuild Your Credit	1st	$14.95	KCRD
Simple Contracts for Personal Use	2nd	$16.95	CONT
Stand Up to the IRS	3rd	$24.95	SIRS
The Under 40 Financial Planning Guide	1st	$19.95	UN40

PATENTS AND COPYRIGHTS

	EDITION	PRICE	CODE
The Copyright Handbook: How to Protect and Use Written Works	3rd	$24.95	COHA
Copyright Your Software	1st	$39.95	CYS
Patent, Copyright & Trademark: A Desk Reference to Intellectual Property Law	1st	$24.95	PCTM
Patent It Yourself	5th	$44.95	PAT
▣ Software Development: A Legal Guide (Book with disk—PC)	1st	$44.95	SFT
The Inventor's Notebook	2nd	$19.95	INOT

RESEARCH & REFERENCE

	EDITION	PRICE	CODE
Law on the Net	1st	$39.95	LAWN
Legal Research: How to Find & Understand the Law	4th	$19.95	LRES
Legal Research Made Easy (Video)	1st	$89.95	LRME

▣ Book with disk

	EDITION	PRICE	CODE

SENIORS

Beat the Nursing Home Trap: A Consumer's Guide	2nd	$18.95	ELD
Social Security, Medicare & Pensions	6th	$19.95	SOA
The Conservatorship Book (California Edition)	2nd	$29.95	CNSV

SOFTWARE

California Incorporator 2.0—DOS	2.0	$47.97	INCI2
Living Trust Maker 2.0—Macintosh	2.0	$47.97	LTM2
Living Trust Maker 2.0—Windows	2.0	$47.97	LTWI2
Small Business Legal Pro—Macintosh	2.0	$25.97	SBM2
Small Business Legal Pro—Windows	2.0	$25.97	SBW2
Small Business Legal Pro Deluxe CD—Windows/Macintosh CD-ROM	2.0	$35.97	SBCD
Nolo's Partnership Maker 1.0—DOS	1.0	$47.97	PAGI1
Personal RecordKeeper 4.0—Macintosh	4.0	$29.97	RKM4
Personal RecordKeeper 4.0—Windows	4.0	$29.97	RKP4
Patent It Yourself 1.0—Windows	1.0	$149.97	PYW1
WillMaker 6.0—Macintosh	6.0	$29.97	WM6
WillMaker 6.0—Windows	6.0	$29.97	WIW6

SPECIAL UPGRADE OFFER

Get 25% off the latest edition of your Nolo book.

It's important to have the most current legal information. Because laws and legal procedures change often, we update our books regularly. To help keep you up-to-date we are extending this special upgrade offer. Cut out and mail the title portion of the cover of your old Nolo book and we'll give you 25% off the retail price of the NEW EDITION of that book when you purchase directly from us. For more information call us at **1-800-992-6656**. This offer is to individuals only.

◳ Book with disk

CALL 800-992-6656 OR USE THE ORDER FORM IN THE BACK OF THE BOOK

ORDER FORM

Code	Quantity	Title	Unit price	Total
			Subtotal	
		California residents add Sales Tax		
Basic Shipping ($5.50 for 1 item; $6.50 for 2-3 items, $7.50 for 4 or more)				
		UPS RUSH delivery $7.50–any size order*		
			TOTAL	

Name _____

Address _____

_____

(UPS to street address, Priority Mail to P.O. boxes)   * Delivered in 3 business days from receipt of order.
S.F. Bay Area use regular shipping.

FOR FASTER SERVICE, USE YOUR CREDIT CARD AND OUR TOLL-FREE NUMBERS

Order 24 hours a day	1-800-992-6656
Fax your order	1-800-645-0895
e-mail	cs@nolo.com
General Information	1-510-549-1976
Customer Service	1-800-728-3555, Mon.-Fri. 9am-5pm, PST

METHOD OF PAYMENT

☐ Check enclosed
☐ VISA   ☐ MasterCard   ☐ Discover Card   ☐ American Express

Account # _____   Expiration Date _____

Authorizing Signature _____

Daytime Phone _____

PRICES SUBJECT TO CHANGE.

VISIT OUR OUTLET STORES!

You'll find our complete line of books and software, all at a discount.

BERKELEY
950 Parker Street
Berkeley, CA 94710
1-510-704-2248

SAN JOSE
111 N. Market Street, #115
San Jose, CA 95113
1-408-271-7240

VISIT US ONLINE!

on **AOL** — keyword: NOLO   on the **INTERNET** — www.nolo.com

NOLO PRESS 950 PARKER ST., BERKELEY, CA 94710